Junius Brutus Booth

Junius Brutus Booth

Theatrical Prometheus

Stephen M. Archer

Southern Illinois University Press
Carbondale and Edwardsville

Printed in the United States of America
13 12 11 10 4 3 2 1

Library of Congress Cataloging-in-Publication Data

Archer, Stephen M.
Junius Brutus Booth : theatrical Prometheus / Stephen M. Archer.
p. cm.
Includes bibliographical references and index.
1. Booth, Junius Brutus, 1796–1852. 2. Actors—United States—Biography. I. Title.
PN2287.B6A88 1992 91-25752
792'.028'092—dc20 CIP
[B]
ISBN-13: 978-0-8093-3000-3 (pbk.)
ISBN-10: 0-8093-3000-8 (pbk.)
ISBN-13: 978-0-8093-1766-0 (cloth)
ISBN-10 0-8093-1766-4 (cloth)
ISBN-13: 978-0-8093-8592-8 (ebook)
ISBN-10: 0-8093-8592-9 (ebook)

Designed by Kyle Lake

Frontispiece: Photographic portrait of Junius Brutus Booth.
Courtesy of the Hampden-Booth Theatre Library at the Players.

The paper used in this publication meets the minimum requirements of American National Standard for Information Sciences—Permanence of Paper for Printed Library Materials, ANSI Z39.48-1992. ♾

To Mary Ann Holmes—
the Soul of the Maryland Booths

Contents

Illustrations

Illustrations

Acknowledgments

Time and chance have scattered Booth materials across the United States and western Europe. No one could hope to reassemble it without the assistance of dozens of other persons. I have enjoyed the aid and encouragement of gracious and expert friends and colleagues.

Any Booth project begins at the Players, where Louis Rachow and Raymond Wemmlinger freely opened that collection's riches. Materials there established the base for all that followed.

I soon discovered the Preservation Association of Tudor Hall and the Surratt Society and enjoy membership in both. Many of the members shared information and insights in the best traditions of scholarship. Especially helpful have been John Brennan, James O. Hall, Mike Kaufmann, James Wollon, Bob Allen, Jeannine Clarke Dodels, Arthur Loux, Richard Sloan, Father Robert L. Keesler, Gayle Harris, Frank Hebblethwaite, and above all, Howard and Dorothy Fox, who allowed an inquisitive stranger to examine their property and Tudor Hall one Sunday afternoon. I treasure these new friendships.

My professional colleagues, many of them Booth scholars in their own right, lent invaluable advice, information, and perspective to this endeavor. Charles Shattuck's encouragement helped sustain the effort, as did the ongoing support of my good friend Don Wilmeth. My deepest thanks also to Terry Alford, David Anderson, Kathleen Barker, William Fratcher, John Heidger, Tom Hellie, Don Grose, Mary Lago, J. Stanley Longman, L. Terry Oggel, George Speaight, Laurie Stepanian, Nan Stephenson, and Dan Watermeier.

Weldon Durham, Jim Miller, and Carla Waal, friends and colleagues, supported this project, and Jelila Kahlil, Patricia White, and

Susan Burns handled a steady flow of correspondence both domestic and foreign.

Two professors in the Netherlands, Willem Schrickx and Ben Albach, offered their insights and publications, saving me months of research. Wout Spies of the International Theatre Institute in Amsterdam also deserves special mention for his generosity to a stranger in a strange land.

Among the many others who have contributed in various ways I should mention Judith Agrelius, Geoffrey Ashton, Jane Averill, Booth Colman, Franklyn Lenthall, Austin Pendleton, Roberta Rankin, David Reuwer, Bernice Richard, Sama Swaminathan, Louise Taper, Pat Wagner, John M. Whittock, Jr., and Jill Wiegman.

I have listed the archives and collections I visited in the Works Cited, but I would laud the curators, librarians, and staffs for their professionalism and assistance. Jeaneice Brewer, Martha Shirkey, and Josephine Johnson processed my hundreds of interlibrary loan requests at Ellis Library with grace and efficiency. Margaret Howell and her staff supplied microforms from their admirable collection.

In the early stages of this study I wrote inquiries to the libraries in each provincial English city in which Booth appeared. Every one of them replied with relevant material, and several volunteered other sources of information. Their civility and professionalism represent the standard for the world.

I most gratefully received financial assistance as a Weldon Spring grant from the University of Missouri and a summer fellowship from the Folger Shakespeare Library; both facilitated essential archival investigation. A research leave from the University of Missouri enabled me to complete research and a first draft of the manuscript.

Working with editors Kenney Withers, Susan H. Wilson, Natalia Nadraga, and Kathryn Koldehoff partially revealed why Southern Illinois University Press enjoys such a glistening reputation; their skills eliminated many errors in the manuscript and strengthened many weaknesses; those remaining are mine alone.

That my wife, Kelly, would allow an uproarious Shakespearean actor to become so integral a part of our life together impresses even those who know her. She remains as ever the Mary Ann of our household.

Introduction

> a poor player,
> That struts and frets his hour upon the stage,
> And then is heard no more.
> —*Macbeth*, V, v, 24–26

Junius Brutus Booth flourished in America for more than a generation, from 1821 to 1852, as a distinguished Shakespearean tragedian. His public image, that of a drunken, even dangerous lunatic, obscured a private life that, although frequently traumatic, stressed an undeviating respect for all life-forms. An emerging America, not yet shattered by civil war, still defining its own unique characteristics, embraced this eccentric performer. Indeed, theatregoers forgave him his trespasses time and time again. No other expatriate actor won favor so grand or affected the American theatre so deeply as the wandering Londoner, Booth.

Others have told parts of Booth's chronicle. Shortly after he died, two of his children set out to to write a biography of their beloved father. Encouraged by family friends, they hoped to correct the many lies and exaggerations circulating about the actor. As the young John Wilkes Booth complained, "I cannot see why sensible people will trouble themselves to concoct ridiculous stories of their great actors. *We* know that two-thirds of the funny anecdotes about our own father are disgraceful falsehoods."[1]

So John Wilkes and his older sister, Asia Booth, asked their mother for their father's papers. Booth's widow dragged some old trunks to the front room, and, as the children wept and pleaded, burned the contents in the fireplace. Diaries, journals, notebooks, playbills, packets of letters to and from Booth, all she fed into the flames, while her son protested, "Supposing someone should write father's life—you are leaving nothing to refer to—such a lot of incorrect dates and false statements will be made. Give *us* the proofs, and everything that can be of service." Mary Ann Booth kept feeding the flames, pausing occasionally to tear off some celebrity's signature and toss it to her children.

Private people, those Booths. Not without reason.

But the elder Booth, an actor and a star, perforce himself left a few footprints behind. His theatre advertisements, publicity puffs, and reviews lie buried in newspaper and magazine files. Hundreds of playbills, the dead husks of forgotten performances, came to rest in theatrical archives. A few hundred of his letters survive, scattered around the world in public and private collections. Several contemporaries—managers, actors, audience members—recorded their opinions of Booth, although they often fell into prejudice, exaggeration, or misinformation. And some documents lay beyond Mary Ann's hearth: land records, contracts, court transcripts, birth and death records, even a few of Booth's own diaries and journals. From them his story begins to emerge.

Thus the trail, dim and cold, still meanders across the years, full of snares for the unwary. Asia Booth cleared away some of the underbrush in two biographies of her father, but she edited severely, selecting only that which flattered his memory. No one should blame her, any more than they should fault Mary Ann for clinging to her privacy and her dignity. The Booths would later ache for solitude, in 1865 when the family name achieved a fame other than theatrical.

So if Mary Ann frowns down from some other where, her husband, the actor, still speaks to us across the generations. Filled with imperfect virtues, he fought his demons till the end, and like the great actors of every age, he was all of us.

Junius Brutus Booth

1

A Gentleman of the Name of Booth

> will you see the players well bestowed? . . . let them be well us'd, for they are the abstract and brief chronicles of the time.
>
> —*Hamlet,* II, ii, 522-25

They almost always called him "Mr. Booth." Eventually they called him *the* Booth. But Mr. Booth, aspiring tragedian, had not yet reached his twenty-first birthday as he prepared himself to step into the glittering dazzle of Drury Lane Theatre's stage.[1] That unseasonably balmy day, 20 February 1817, Drury Lane playbills throughout London blazoned Mr. Booth's debut there, to perform Iago to Edmund Kean's Othello.

Kean reigned supreme over the London stage, but on that night young Mr. Booth dared to challenge the older star's ascendancy. Professionally, only one of them could survive this encounter unscathed.

The Drury Lane management gleefully realized this bill's wide appeal and correctly expected a distinguished audience to pack the theatre. Patrons besieged the box office, paying the premium price of over a pound each for seats in the pit. Lord Erskine, a former lord chancellor, now a member of the theatre's administrative committee, anticipated an evening of unexcelled high tragedy—and profits. John Howard Payne exclaimed later, "I thought the applause would never stop."[2] William Godwin cried, "This is a night to remember!"[3]

Kean had faced challengers before, and he had inevitably destroyed them. He and his fans had driven earlier rivals off the London stage, often out of the acting profession. Kean's more rabid fans had even organized a club, the Wolves, to crush any pretender to Kean's domination. Composed largely of tavern loafers and idle sycophants, the Wolves met often with the hard-drinking Kean in pubs and barrooms. Some Londoners accused Kean of forming the Wolves himself for his own protection, the members vowing to hound any rival off the stage. And on 20 February 1817, the entire pack, slavering at the prospect of a new victim, had gathered at Drury Lane.

Many theatregoers marveled at the temerity of this Mr. Booth, this upstart, this lad who would cross swords with the mighty Edmund Kean. Some remembered him from the previous year at Covent Garden, Drury Lane's rival theatre. There Booth had played such minor roles as the rustic shepherd, Silvius, in *As You Like It,* but he had stimulated no particular enthusiasm or notice. Other playgoers had seen Booth in the English provinces, starring as the bravura Richard III or the fiendish Sir Giles Overreach, both roles in which Kean had enthralled London audiences. And a few recalled Booth's touring the Continent a few years earlier in similar roles.

But the Drury Lane audience felt no need to travel outside London to see excellent acting. They considered themselves the world's most sophisticated and knowledgeable playgoers, their stage superior to any other, and Kean the best actor alive. Booth's successes elsewhere meant nothing to them; he had yet to prove himself. Provincial stars glutted the market; periodically they came from the country to assail London, seeking adulation, notoriety, and fortune. For the most part they failed miserably and retreated to less sophisticated, more receptive audiences in the hinterlands. Many were called; almost none were chosen.

This new actor, however, this Mr. Booth, seemed made of sterner stuff. Only a week earlier he had arrived in London from Brighton to star as Richard III at Covent Garden. The performers there, secure in their metropolitan contracts, recalled him as the "little Silvius" of the previous season and sneered at his presumptions to stardom. Indeed, one of the actresses, Sally Booth, asked Booth to add the letter *e* to his name, lest audiences think them related. Booth declined, dryly suggesting that Miss Booth had tried for some years to change her own surname through matrimony with a lamentable lack of success.[4]

Thus just as Kean had come from the provinces to Drury Lane in 1814, unheralded, unknown, and facing the hostility of the resident company, so Booth came to Covent Garden three years later. And like Kean, the newcomer quite conquered his audiences; newspaper accounts spoke of the rapturous and unanimous applause as Booth took his bows. Even more telling, when another actor announced the next night's bill as *A Midsummer Night's Dream,* in which Booth would not appear, the audience shouted him down, roaring out "Richard the Third! Booth as Richard!" The actor retreated from the stage, consulted the manager, and returned to placate the audience by informing them Booth would indeed repeat his triumph the next evening. A thunder of applause followed. No new tragedian, fresh from the country, could ask for more.

But the dean of London critics, William Hazlitt, condescended to set the tone of Booth's critical reception the next day in the *London Examiner.*[5] He began, "A Gentleman of the name of Booth . . . came out in Richard . . . on Wednesday," then condemned the new actor as "an exact copy or parody of Mr. Kean." Hazlitt doubted that such a secondhand performance would survive London exposure, adding that the greatest drawback to Booth's acting was "a perpetual strut and an unwieldy swagger." He then added, "though it may pass at Brighton for *grand, gracious, and magnificent,* even the lowest of the mob will laugh at [it] in London."

The other critics, cloaked in anonymity, joined Hazlitt in comparing the newcomer to the established Kean. Both actors were short and dark (Booth stood about five three), with lustrous and commanding eyes, and they both acted in a passionate and detonating style; comparisons inevitably arose, and Kean had risen to stardom first.

Critics then lacked the power the press has today; still, theatregoers read them, and so, as always, did actors. The ever-cautious *London Times* dubbed Booth a "vigorous and spirited actor" with considerable promise, smaller than Kean, with "ill-formed limbs," and added, "His action is often natural and powerful, and would be more so if he were more temperate. He stamps too often."

Most of the critics applauded Booth's tent scene as Richard for the "start of agony and wild alarm with which he rose from feverish slumber" but accused him of aping Kean. The *London Sun,* however, considered Booth's voice superior to the older actor's. The *London Morning Chronicle* agreed to Booth's many merits and bright promise but urged restraint, the critic complaining, Booth "traverses more extent of the stage than any Actor we ever beheld."

Quibbles aside, Booth had succeeded where many had failed. Perhaps London audiences welcomed a change after three years of Kean; perhaps rumors of Kean's dissolute life diluted his appeal. Certainly the Covent Garden audiences found Booth fascinating; after his second performance of Richard, they again rose and demanded a third performance the next night, Friday the fourteenth. This time the management demurred, but they announced their new star would again play Richard on Monday the seventeenth, and the audience happily dispersed. That proposed performance never took place.

Booth's spectacular debut had divided London theatregoers into two distinct camps, literally called *Keanites* and *Boothites*. The Wolves would not swerve from their loyalty to Kean; they attacked Booth as an impudent upstart, a mere imitator of his better. The Boothites, equally passionate, considered their champion unique, even superior, beating Kean at his own game.

For the rest of his life, Booth suffered from comparisons to Kean, even after his rival's death. On 20 February 1817, however, they strode onto the Drury Lane stage as worthy opposites. London buzzed about the coming showdown, and interest mushroomed concerning this Mr. Booth's past.

Many English actors of the time inherited their profession, being children of theatrical parents. Not so Mr. Booth. An untrustworthy family legend suggested that the Booth family had originated in Spain with the surname of either Bethe or Botha.[6] Ricardo Botha, a Spanish Jew and Madrid lawyer, was said to have been exiled from Spain in the seventeenth century for publishing inflammatory pamphlets against the royalist government. The state confiscated his property, and Ricardo supposedly fled with his family to Lisbon, where he continued denouncing the Spanish government. His son, Roberto, presumably moved to London, changed his name to Robert, and became a silversmith in the Clerkenwell section of London. Robert Booth would thus have been a neighbor of John Wilkes, the republican agitator, onetime lord mayor of London, and vehement supporter of the North American colonies.

Whatever the Booths origins, at least two generations of the family lived and worked in Clerkenwell before the actor's birth.[7] Junius Brutus Booth's grandfather, John Booth, was christened in St. James parish in Clerkenwell on 28 December 1723 and married Elizabeth Wilkes on 15 February 1747 at the St. George Chapel, Mayfair. His new wife, born about 1726, claimed relation to John Wilkes.[8] John Booth worked as a silversmith in Clerkenwell; a small silver spoon made by him remained in the family for several generations.[9]

John and Elizabeth Booth produced seven children.[10] Richard Booth, the actor's father, was born last, on 16 November 1759. John Booth championed John Wilkes' political career, and perhaps Wilkes' radical influence inspired the Booths' ardent republicanism. Richard so much espoused the American colonies that in 1777 he deserted his legal apprenticeship and persuaded his cousin John Brevitt to run away from home with him to fight for American liberty.[11] Arriving in Paris a few days later, they located an American agent, Arthur Lee, from whom they hoped to obtain appointments as American officers.[12] Lee, however, demanded a letter of recommendation.[13] When the boys suggested John Wilkes as a source of such a letter, Lee readily agreed. So Richard and Brevitt therefore wrote to Wilkes on 28 October 1777, seeking support. They admitted, "as Englishmen, it may be urged that we are not altogether Justified in taking arms against our native Country," but, they suggested, the present "Tyrannic Government" had alienated its colonial citizens. They then compared the English-American hostilities to the Roman civil war which pitted Octavius and Antony against the autocratic Brutus and Cassius. The runaways closed by asking Wilkes to reply to the Hôtel de la Reine, Rue des Bons Enfants, Paris, as soon as convenient.

Wilkes responded—but not to the young revolutionaries. He instead informed their respective parents, who dispatched agents to overtake the fugitives and return them to London forthwith. John Booth then wrote Wilkes, apologizing for the rash actions of his offspring and nephew. He further reminded Wilkes he had worked for the politician's election at Brentford and offered him a piece of silver plate in tribute.[14]

Richard's adventure over, he returned to his legal studies. By 1790 various London directories listed him as an attorney at 20 Walbrook in the City of London, where he remained through 1793. His father had died in 1787; his mother lived till 1801.[15]

On 23 September 1795, Richard married Jane "Elizabeth" Game, who traced her ancestors to a hero of Agincourt.[16] The newlyweds set up housekeeping near the Adam and Eve Inn, on the west side of Tottenham Court Road, near Euston Road, and their first child, Junius Brutus Booth, was born on May Day, 1796. The young couple had two other children, Algernon Sydney, born in 1798, who died at age five, and a daughter, Jane, born about 1800, whose birth proved fatal to her mother.[17]

The names Richard chose for his two sons indicated that his admiration for the United States had in no way diminished. Between January 1769 and January 1772, a famous series of letters appeared over the signature "Junius" in the *London Public Advertiser.* These letters sharply criticized the British government, including King George III. The writer, thought to be Sir Philip Francis, also used the pen names "Lucius" and "Brutus," thus completing the name of Lucius Junius Brutus, a Roman patriot. During his lifetime, Junius Brutus Booth would often be called Lucius Junius Brutus Booth, although that name appeared in no official record, nor did Booth himself ever use it. Nor was Richard's son the first Booth to bear the name; a Junius Brutus Booth from St. John's Square was buried at St. John's on 7 August 1787.[18] Similarly, Algernon Sidney (or Sydney) (1622–83) fervently advocated the cause of Parliament, fought in Cromwell's army, and was beheaded for participation in the Rye House Plot to assassinate Charles II. Thus both of Richard Booth's sons bore the names of ardent populists and political activists, as would his grandson, John Wilkes Booth.

If Richard and Jane Game Booth married 23 September 1795 and their first child arrived slightly over seven months later, let us not imagine such a chronology unique. Of more significance was the pattern of Richard's movements. After beginning as a single man in the City of London, Richard married, then moved to Bloomsbury, a popular area for young professionals.[19] After his wife died in childbirth about 1800, Richard again changed his residence, finally settling in Queen Street.

Years later, Junius Brutus Booth recalled his Bloomsbury childhood.

> May 1st, 1796, I was born at as nearly as can be judged by parental record, a quarter before 2 P.M.—a day which ushered into existence one who has witnessed some most extraordinary vicissitudes, and endured a little in this big world, if my memory serves to recall many past events, is most certain. . . . 'Tis strange that although certainly old enough to identify and retain knowledge of my mother I have not the slightest shade of remembrance of either her person, features, or form. My grandmother, i.e., my father's mother, is the earliest link in Memory's chain which I can trace, next, my father—then two or three casual faces—my brother—again a lapse until five years of age when I can form a remembrance of a sister.[20]

According to Asia Booth Clarke, Booth "received a classical education and early showed a decided taste for drawing and literature." She suggested that Booth studied at Eton College, but Eton has no record of him as a student.[21] He learned French from a Madame D'Ambique and remembered that lady fondly in later years. Of his youth, Booth further recalled,

> Prior to my going on the stage I was destined by my Controllers first for the Printing office, then to be an architect, then to be a sculptor and modeller, then a lawyer, then a sailor, of all these I preferred those of sculptor and modeller. The premium required for these professions was greater than my father would give and I was induced not to go with Blyth, a gallant fellow who commanded the Brig Boxer on board which vessel I was to be, or was rated a clerk and midshipman in my nautical turn or desire, because the vessel was changed from the Mediterranean to the American coast with which country England was at war. My father who was what is called then a hot headed Yankee or American being resolved that I never should be at odds with the Country which he in his youthful days had formed in his mind's eye as being the grand desideratum or Heaven of all men.

Although Richard Booth had not yet found his way to the New World, he had lost none of his enthusiasm for the Great Experiment. His son went on to describe his father's passion for democracy.

> The idolatry . . . which my father always exhibited towards any and all things appertaining to America, tended in a great measure to render him unpopular amidst the circle of those who but for that would have been his patrons. The picture of General Washington that hung up in our parlour and which was as 'twere a rarity amongst many of the Londoners was an object all around him, friend or foe, he insisted should be looked at with hat off and bowed to occasionally. No wonder then that my own prospects as respects the Navy were instantly frustrated when the destination of our vessel and its object were made known. My uniform etc. were sent to Portsmouth—I was served with a subpoena as a witness to some cause in London and the Boxer sailed minus one of its or her complement. I remained in my father's office merely copying or transcribing from his dictation dry declarations.

Booth's casual mention of a subpoena actually referred to a paternity suit filed against the seventeen-year-old by, as an early biographer put it, "a frail nymph," charging that "deed of darkness which her situation could no longer conceal." Sex had come oozing down Queen Street, and Junius Brutus Booth had answered the call.

Richard unsuccessfully defended his son in court. Apparently the precocious boy had faced these charges before; the same biographer suggested a similar indictment made in 1810 when Junius was not quite thirteen, costing Richard thirty pounds.[22]

Clearly, this youth's energies needed, indeed demanded, some more appropriate outlet. Richard apprenticed his son to "Old Piggot," a printer on Old Street who specialized in publishing the antemortem speeches of criminals executed at Tyburn and Newgate Prisons.[23] Booth later described Piggot as also dealing extensively in "ballads, tales of wonder, and stories of fairies and goblins." Booth and his father quarreled following his unhappy amour, their relations taking an "acrimonious and vindictive aspect," so the errant son signed on for a voyage to Rio de Janeiro as a cabin boy on the *John-of-Gaunt*. Richard discovered the flight, found his son at Downs where the ship awaited favorable winds, apprehended him, and signed him on with Captain Blyth and the *Boxer*. But then new orders sent the *Boxer* to North America, and Richard could not allow his son to bear arms against the United States. The younger Booth nevertheless yearned to leave Queen Street, and Richard was evidently more than ready to let him go.

But Junius Brutus Booth had no idea what to do. Several professional possibilities already lay behind him, and any young middle-class Englishman in 1813 confronted a very bleak future indeed. The British economy and government teetered on the brink of disaster; the French Revolution had severely shaken the aristocratic establishment. England's population had just swelled some 14 percent from 1801 to 1811 to over ten million persons. Booth's country had warred with France almost steadily since 1793 and America since 1812, triggering a wildly fluctuating economy. Between 1792 and 1813 the cost of living had skyrocketed over 90 percent; artisans' wages had risen until 1813, when they stood at about thirty-six shillings per week. A young man without a profession could contemplate only dismal prospects.

But then Booth attended a production of *Othello* at Covent Garden, and a new possibility dawned.[24] The theatre deals in dreams, and Booth was in the market. As a strolling actor, he could surely stroll far from Queen Street and parental disapproval. And a performer could achieve great fame and wealth, were he to claw his way to stardom.[25] Furthermore, the young find the instant gratification of applause and the glamorous veneer of the theatre most attractive, far more seductive than reading law or working as a printer's devil. What matter if actors were less than men and actresses the playthings of the aristocrats? Actors will happen in the best regulated households, and Number 4 Queen Street, Bloomsbury, hardly qualified.

An aspiring actor needs a role, and Booth found his as Frank Rochdale in the now-forgotten script, *John Bull; or, The Englishman's Fireside*. Not, of course, at Covent Garden or Drury Lane, or even in a regular theatre. Like most actors, Booth began as an amateur, debuting in a temporary theatre at Pancras Street, Tottenham Court Road, just a few blocks from Queen Street.[26] There he appeared with various similarly star-struck milkmen and glaziers in a hayloft converted into a rude theatre.

Such amateur theatres polluted London at the time; these so-called spouting clubs reflected a craze for theatricals at all social levels. The particular group joined by Booth was led by the cow shed's owner, Mr. George, a milkman with dreams of glory. Audiences climbed a narrow staircase to witness performances on a makeshift stage lit by a wooden hoop with tallow candles in lieu of a chandelier. Nothing so grand as an orchestra pit separated audience and players, although the actors might have benefited from some such barrier. Once, while Booth perpetrated Buckingham to Mr. George's Richard III, a gentleman near the stage, noting Booth's unhappy configuration of leg, cried out, "Ah! you're a pretty fellow to stop a pig!" Booth did not join the ensuing merriment; he was indeed somewhat bowlegged.

Booth soldiered on; his only other recorded role at this thespian nursery was Collooney in *The Irishman in London,* in which he substituted when a regular cast member failed to appear. Still, Booth received regular and frequent applause; his performances won praise for their emphasis and propriety; and he cast his eyes about for professional employment in his new vocation.

Such employment came quickly, far more quickly than usual in the theatre. A pair of third-rate managers, a Mr. Jonas and Samson Penley, offered Booth a job at twenty shillings a week. Twenty shillings constituted one pound sterling, but miserly managers then quoted salaries in shillings to make them sound larger. A working-class family at the time might survive, if not prosper, on forty pounds a year, but actors had to pay for their own costumes, properties, and traveling expenses.

Booth thus joined the Jonas-Penley Company at Deptford, a Thames River dock town of sordid reputation. If he still acted on crude and temporary stages, he now at least received a salary. His professional debut, beginning a career that would last nearly thirty-nine years, presented "Mr. Booth" in the walk-on role of Campillo in John Tobin's *Honey Moon,* 13 December 1813. A little over three years later, Booth would challenge Kean for the dominance of the London stage. For now, he followed Jonas and Penley to Peckham, another depressing river village, where he performed miniscule roles until March 1814.

Since Booth's entry into professional acting had excited no one, his retirement for several months with a severe case of jaundice also went unnoticed. His pittance of a salary (Booth later recalled it as five shillings, not twenty) compelled him to live on one meal a day. Booth had never enjoyed a robust constitution, and so illness and poverty forced the budding thespian back to Queen Street and bed rest.

Dreaming of stardom, Booth would have avidly read the accounts of London's newest star, Edmund Kean. On a bleak, snowy day—26

January 1814—Kean made his first London appearance at Drury Lane as Shylock. Only a third of a house braved the filthy weather; only two critics attended, and the Drury Lane company anticipated disaster, but Kean achieved a triumph almost without equal in British theatrical history. Nothing resembling him had ever been seen on the London stage.

The revolution Kean brought to English acting had political as well as aesthetic roots. As the middle classes rose to political significance in the eighteenth century, various writers championed their cause—Rousseau, Goethe, Schiller, Keats, Shelley, Byron, Voltaire—as long a list as one cares to assemble. The old order, born in the medieval period, fostering the aristocracy and emphasizing the divine right of king and court, would no longer serve. First in America, then in France, the people manned the barricades, stormed the Bastille, dumped the tea, chopped heads, and infant democracies rose from aristocratic ashes.

England had barely managed to avoid armed revolution, but individual rights and the middle class improved markedly. To reflect this upheaval, the old neoclassic stage heroes—kings, princes, emperors—gave way to rebellious outlaws and political radicals, championing the people, not the aristocratic establishment. The decorous and formal style of acting, exemplified by John Philip Kemble and Sarah Siddons at the turn of the century, passed from the scene, replaced by Kean's explosive, emotional outbursts. Icy rationality melted in the furnace of passion, and Kean swept away all competition. Samuel Coleridge likened his performances to reading Shakespeare by flashes of lightning, and a stunned Lord Byron cried out, "By God, he is a soul!" All things became possible, not to those of affluence, but to those of genius, however eccentric.

Meanwhile, Richard Booth no doubt thought he had his prodigal son back for good and again set him to studying the law. Improved diet and rest facilitated Booth's recovery, and as soon as the young dreamer had regained his health, he again succumbed to the theatre's siren call. Jonas and Penley planned a Continental tour opening in Amsterdam; they invited Booth to join them.

And so this young man again left home, as young men will, as indeed his father had before him, to try his luck far from home. He struck out with the confidence and ignorance born of youth, sired by hope out of dreams, with no more adequate preparation than any of us has when we enter the arena. He was just four days past eighteen years old, no stranger to the charms of women, adequately educated, and a theatrical neophyte. He would return to London eleven months later, far wiser in the world's wanton ways.

Booth did not inform his father of his intentions; he merely "packed up his bundle," as he put it, booked passage with the company on a packet ship, the *Three Brothers,* and sailed for the Continent. However dazzled he may have been by his prospects, he retained presence of mind enough to keep a diary of his adventure.[27] In it he described a rough crossing, beginning at midafternoon on Friday, 6 May 1814, from Simpson's Ways, Limehouse, a dock area east of London. In a heavy rain the *Three Brothers,* captained by Hinrig Block, laden with treacle and actors, arrived at Fiddler's Reach and tied up for the night.[28] The ship proceeded to Gravesend for provisions, there detained till three o'clock that afternoon by petty bureaucrats demanding a passenger list. Eventually the ship took on a pilot to take them to Harwich, then arrived at the Nore, a sandbank in the Thames estuary.

One of Booth's fellow travelers described the youth sitting astride a barrel in the hold, devouring a meat pie, declaiming in full voice, "By Holy Paul, I will not dine before his head be brought me," a quotation from Nicholas Rowe's script, *The Tragedy of Jane Shore.* The exhilarated Booth was practicing being an actor, the curse of neophytes. Booth said of his first evening aboard,

> I observed, for the first time, the setting sun, which went down in all its splendour, leaving the world to the influence of luna, till the morn. The Admiral's ship fired the evening gun, followed by the rest, and the music played God save the King.—After contemplating the beauties of the evening, and reflecting on my situation till dark, we betook ourselves to the hold, the cabin being kept for the ladies, and slept on a box all night.[29]

The admiral's ship lay at anchor off the Nore, with the rest of the British fleet poised to defend England from invasion by the French. Booth, his head stuffed with visions of stardom and seeing the world, had sailed blithely into the last of the Napoleonic Wars.

After crossing the North Sea, the *Three Brothers* sighted the coast of Holland on Monday, the ninth, but could not land because of unfavorable winds. Booth spent another night in the hold (he complained of sharing space with a sick Prussian reeking of garlic), but the roaring of the wind and sea soon waked him. Again the ship failed to reach shore; the wind was in their faces, and Booth suffered a second miserable night, improvising a bed out of casks and boxes.

At daybreak, winds and waves still prevented a landing. Some fishermen tried unsuccessfully to put through the surf to reach the ship. Booth and his companions pleaded with Captain Block to put in at Rotterdam, but the Dutchman insisted on Amsterdam. Booth and nine fellow travelers signaled the shore for help, and eventually a fishing boat came alongside. The Dutch fishermen demanded ten guineas to take the party three miles to shore; after some bickering, they settled for two. To the cheers of a small crowd huddled on the shore, the fishermen fought their way close enough to the beach to carry the actors, one by one, to land. Booth learned they had landed near Camperdown, a tiny village eight miles north of Alkmaar.

The actors ate before starting to walk to Amsterdam, but Booth's feet grew so sore he could not continue. One of the actors stayed behind with him while the rest of the group continued. At six o'clock the two reached Alkmaar, Booth cursing his folly for ever leaving England. The next day, with Booth still unable to walk, the two men went by boat to Saardam (Zaandam), a city Booth found delightful, six miles northwest of Amsterdam. They arrived in Amsterdam on the twelfth. There Booth claimed his baggage and changed clothes for the first time since leaving London, six days earlier.

On Wednesday, 18 May 1814, the company opened to a good crowd at the High German Theatre with *The Honey Moon* and Ludvig Holberg's *The Weather-Cock*, Booth playing Campillo and Gardner.[30] His feet, still throbbing, incapacitated him for the next two days.

Booth described none of the other performances in Amsterdam; most of his diary entries dealt with local architecture, the French theatre, and local customs. He supplemented his income by selling songbooks and lived fairly well, in his youthful opinion. He mentioned being somewhat repulsed by the natives' habit of "sacrificing to Cloacina," or relieving themselves, in public. Nevertheless, after the rough crossing, the Amsterdam engagement went fairly well. The company's repertory and talents lacked distinction, but with no competition, audiences had little choice.

No newspapers seem to have reviewed the productions. However, a Dutchman with some theatrical experience, Johannes Jelgerhuis, saw two performances by the company, although Booth appeared in neither.[31] Understanding no English, Jelgerhuis could barely follow the scripts, but he regarded the actors as reasonably accomplished. He found especially noteworthy the absence of a prompter. As a graphic artist, Jelgerhuis commented more specifically on the scenery, which he judged remarkable in its "natural, [but] visibly ordered confusion," quite distinct from the more formalized and symmetrical practices of the French and Dutch stages. As for the costumes, he considered them modern and unremarkable, but he included a few sketches and watercolors. Jelgerhuis did not see Booth and thus made no specific comments about him.

After three months of what Booth called "tolerable success," two Englishmen named Astley and Richer took over the Amsterdam theatre for an equestrian show.[32] Booth saw Alexander, the Russian emperor, make a royal visit to Amsterdam, then, as strolling players ever must, he moved on to the next engagement. He arrived in Antwerp on Friday, July twenty-second, awed by the detritus of war he saw everywhere, blasted trees and shattered buildings.

By this time, Booth had begun to doubt the wisdom of a theatrical career. He had visited several churches, claiming they filled him with such religious awe as to give him second thoughts about his new profession. No doubt the youth had grown homesick; one of the company's actresses, a Mrs. Benyon, gave him a poem her late husband had written, and Booth copied it into his diary, commenting, "it struck me . . . forcibly, reminding me of a circumstance which once occurred to myself." The turgid verses described a homesick and repentant youth.[33]

Booth entered nothing in his diary about the company's Antwerp engagement, and only a few of the playbills have survived.[34] He left early in the morning on Sunday, August fourteenth, by a diligence, or coach, and proceeded to Brussels, again noting the recent war's devastation of the countryside. Completing the trip by covered wagon, Booth sat beside "the loveliest girl" he had ever beheld, but they parted upon reaching Brussels early that evening.

Jonas and Penley had picked a propitious time for a Brussels engagement. Wellington's defeat of Napoleon at nearby Waterloo on June eighteenth had swelled pro-British sentiment in the Netherlands; at no period in its history had Brussels so esteemed the English. Although the majority of the city's population spoke no English, a British theatrical company could expect to draw from some five thousand Englishmen recently arrived in the city. Even Lord Wellington, the hero of Waterloo, attended the performances by his countrymen.

Meanwhile, Booth needed lodgings. Military personnel had commandeered all hotels and public housing, leaving the actors to fend for themselves. Booth secured a room near the theatre in a widowed milliner's house for seventeen francs a month, noting, "the people keep early hours." He would regret his Brussels' housing arrangements for the rest of his days.

Booth enjoyed the 25 August festivities celebrating the birthday of the Prince of Orange. The company canceled its performance that night; two of the actors failed to appear. Booth found himself with a free evening and "took the opportunity of escorting some fine girls, who were waiting my return, at my landlady's, as I had conjectured that there would be no performance." Perhaps he took the "fine girls" to the fireworks exhibition. Very likely the girls were daughters of his landlady, Mme Delannoy. Booth found one of her four daughters—Adelaide—"finer" than the other girls, although four years his senior.[35]

Meanwhile, the company's fortunes at the Théâtre de la Monnaie fluctuated.[36] The celebrated English actress Dorothy Jordan arrived and performed three nights with them. Mrs. Jordan drew full houses, with the Prince of Orange in attendance each evening. At the same time, Charles Kemble, the younger brother of John Philip Kemble and Sarah Siddons, performed at another theatre and later appeared with the Jonas-Penley Company. Booth struck up an acquaintance with Charles Kemble, who encouraged the young actor. Booth in turn considered Kemble "a perfect gentleman in every sense of the word" and acclaimed his Shylock as superior to Kean's.[37]

At the same time, Booth's own professional stock began to rise. As a new actor, he needed a breakthrough role on this track toward stardom. For Booth, this role was Megrim in the younger George Colman's play, *The Blue Devils.* William Oxberry, never a great supporter of Booth's, reported his success, saying, Booth's "performance of *Megrim,* at Brussels, was attended with great success, and has been represented to us as a finished effort. Mr. Samson Penley . . . was the 'great creature' of that company; but, after that gentleman, Mr. BOOTH had his choice of parts, and he became a favourite amongst that land of exiled Englishmen, shattered demireps, and retired swindlers."[38] Booth's role as a suicidal, jaded traveler ("Russia's too cold, Italy's too hot, Holland's too dull, France is too gay") augured some of the dark and villainous roles in which he would later succeed.

While in Brussels, Booth witnessed the public guillotining of three prisoners, including M. Moucheur, a criminal condemned for a long history of atrocities and jailbreaks. On another platform across from the scaffold, Booth noted two women and five men chained by their necks to stakes. This punishment reminded Booth of the British pillory, and English citizens constituted the majority of the crowd taunting the seven wretches. No doubt this experience contributed to Booth's later insistence that all life-forms are sacred, not to be destroyed under any circumstances.

On the eighteenth of October, having been in Brussels for over two months, Booth wrote his father a long letter, suggesting he might abandon acting. As later events show, he penned a masterpiece of evasion.

> Dear Father—
>
> Penley is a Scoundrel—we are here in Brussels without knowing how to get out of it. The Dresses [costumes] have been seized by the Administration of the Grand Theatre who have a claim on us for a fifth of our Profits, and only by the greatest Entreaty and paying up the Arrears, was it settled. A Mr. James, a very respectable Man who is by business a Jeweler & who has brought over with him on Speculation several articles in that line, has been advised to set up in business here, and he on account of my knowledge of the Language, in which I have . . . made a wonderful Progress, so much that in many Places they take me for a Fleming, has kindly offered to instruct me in his business, if I can get some things to work upon which must be brought here & we then would open a shop for the Sale of Jewelry. Now in order to do this it is necessary to have the Sinews of every enterprize, Money which if it please you venture, as I intend quitting the Stage in toto; I find it a life of so much Idleness and care, too & no money to be got at it, that if I can establish myself in the line aforesaid, or procure any permanent

Situation I will strive every nerve to succeed in it and endeavor to become a respectable Member of Society. The theatrical mania that raged within me begins to die away, I perceive now the folly of it, yet do not regret this last Freak of going on the Continent as it may be a means of doing something for me.

The Living is so cheap in Brussels that a man may board and lodge handsomely for 12/– a week and I have cultivated the acquaintance of many respectable people here whose Assistance I could ensure myself if once I made a beginning—

You may weigh this in your mind and I pray you don't consider it, my dear father, as the whim of a moment, as I have other reasons for quitting the itinerant Life than those I have mentioned. Though I never meant leaving the Stage till an opportunity showed itself for doing something better. I should have no Apprenticeship to serve which will be a great thing at least not for the term of Seven Years.

I remain

Dr Father,

Your son, restored to
his senses,

JB Booth

No 1159. Sect 5
Rue des Fripiers
a Bruxelles
Oct 18th 1814

P.S. I beg of you to think me serious and if you can spare as much as £5 to throw into a concern which I am sure will answer, do it for Heaven's sake.[39]

Any reader who has ever had a son, been a son, or had to do with sons may well imagine Richard's thoughts as he read this epistle. No record informs us if he sent the money; his son desperately needed additional funds, but one can doubt he ever seriously considered becoming a jeweler.

Booth left Brussels for Ghent (Gand) on November twenty-fifth. He had been in Brussels for 104 days, but the company gave only thirty-six recorded performances, so the young actor had abundant spare time. And apparently he used it, for he left Brussels with Adelaide Delannoy, his landlady's daughter, nicknamed "Mimi." Years later, Booth gave a reporter a lurid account of this escapade, colored by the intervening years and by Booth's highly developed sense of the romantic and dramatic.

> To a union, as well as to the elopement, the friends of the milliner were most decidedly opposed, and every effort was made to prevent them the one and the other. . . . The lover, and the beloved, were resolved;—neither bolts, bars or gates, could oppose them;—the gods aided their efforts, and whilst Booth leaped with his bundle from the second floor of the house, in which his mistress lived, and thus escaped, she scaled the walls that surrounded the domicile; and uniting her fortunes with those of her gay Lothair, "fled from the home of her ancestors." A seat was provided for her in the Belgic Diligence; Booth closely followed on the road side, eluding the vigilance of his pursuers, and evading the demands for passports that were made of him, till he reached the village of Alost, where he joined the Diligence and arrived safely at Gand. He remained at Gand for a few days, and played there with success, and was on the point of being wedded to the maid he loved, when he discovered that he was pursued by her friends and parents. Finding it imprudent to remain any longer in the "enemies' country," like Xenophon, he made a hasty retreat, and took up his line of march for Bridges;—from thence he proceeded to Ostend, and was in that city, when Louis the XVIII made his public entry, after his flight from Paris. His pursuers, keeping up the track, overtook him at Ostend;—the parties again attempted to escape, but were taken back, by those who had pursued them. They now availed themselves of a fortunate opportunity, that accidently presented itself, and fled to England, where they were clandestinely married.[40]

Booth and Adelaide had left Brussels on Thursday, 25 November 1814, hotly pursued by her relatives, arriving at Ghent the next morning. They found rooms at the Hôtel d'Angleterre, a handsome lodging near the theatre in the Place d'Armes. The company gave only six performances in Ghent with Booth performing Iago for the first time.[41]

On Monday, December eleventh, the couple went by boat to Bruges, a city Booth found exceptionally dull. Apparently they had given the pursuing Delannoys the slip; they remained in Bruges till New Year's Eve. Booth closed with Othello, and the couple departed for the coastal city of Ostend on 2 January 1815.[42] Booth had visited Ostend before to prepare for the company's arrival there; he found the city frigid from its proximity to the North Sea and the theatre "a most wretched place." Again, the city teemed with English tourists, potential theatre patrons.

The lovers lodged on the Place d'Armes for twenty-five francs a month, and the company began its last engagement. By the end of the month, they had begun to play a round of benefits, determining the order by lot. Booth's benefit fell on Monday, 13 March 1815. A Colonel Hammerton was his patron, and Booth chose Richard III as his vehicle, with *Matrimony* as the afterpiece.[43] This bill drew a total house of twenty-three pounds, with Booth clearing eleven pounds after paying Jonas twelve for expenses.

Booth's status as a star increased in Ostend; besides Richard, his roles included Sir Edward Mortimer and Iago. He would play these roles regularly for the rest of his life.

In mid-March, Booth wrote to his father to notify him he would be returning to London soon. He described his benefit and also remarked that word of peace with America had reached Ostend. No further mention was made of leaving the acting profession.[44]

Booth also failed to mention his new traveling companion. But if he could postpone dealing with Richard, there still remained Adelaide's mother in Brussels, who had offered to obtain Booth a position as clerk's stationer in the Department of the Dyle. Booth wrote to her at 1159 Rue des Fripiers, Brussels:

> Ostend, March 17, 1815
>
> Madame and Dear Friend—I have received your dear letter of the 4th inst., and I am delighted that you have partly succeeded in the matter of the place you were trying to get for me. I should like to know how much the place is worth. My salary as an actor brings me thirty-five francs a week, with a benefit in each town if I like to take it, and I assure you it is none too much. But as I should like to be in Brussels I should not care much about that. I have written to my father for the letters of recommendation. I am, meanwhile, waiting your reply, as also the information concerning when I should leave here. Believe in my entire gratitude, I embrace you with all my heart. Also my uncle and my future sisters-in-law.
>
> J.B. Booth
>
> I believe you are angry, but there is no cause for it.[45]

After arriving in England, Booth described recrossing the North Sea in his diary.

> We left Ostend the day after, Friday, 3 o'clock, P.M. by the London packet, Captain Small, in company with Anthony Pasquin,

> Esq., Mrs. and Miss Watson, Burton, &c. After a beautiful passage, we found ourselves at Gravesend, Saturday evening, where we were obliged to go to the Alien-Office, and not having passports, we should have been rather awkwardly situated, had it not been for the kindness of Dr. Williams, who generously gave his name to the commissioners, and we reached the Hermitage Wharf, Monday, April 3.

Anthony Pasquin and Dr. Williams were one and the same, a minor celebrity who promised to use his influence to secure Booth an engagement at Covent Garden.

Perhaps Booth intuited the changes in his life that lay just ahead as he pondered his circumstances:

> I must here remark that ingratitude is the most odious of all the vices: while at home and on ship-board my heart seldom blessed those who had reared me from infancy, but was filled with fantastic images of the future. I never reflected on the pain and anxiety I had caused, what faults I had committed, and for which too frequently others suffered. The only thing that reminded me of home was the difference of treatment, and being compelled to associate with those I abhor. I do not mean to include all the performers, but by the narrowness of our finances we were constrained to associate chiefly together, and there certainly is in theatrical life greater friendship or greater malice than in any other. When obliged to disguise the feelings of disgust and coercion, life becomes miserable.
>
> Les passions les plus dangereuses quand l'esprit n'est pas bien employé se levent en fermentation et le produit est une coterie d'idées excentriques et des desires irreguliers.[46]

He had deserted his home as a bit player and a bachelor. He returned having played leading roles and with, if not quite a wife, certainly a significant relationship. Returning to London meant, first, explaining Adelaide to his father, then securing an engagement and chasing stardom.

Adelaide was three months pregnant.

2

Showdown at Old Drury

Two stars keep not their motion in one sphere.
—*1 Henry IV,* V, iv, 65

Booth first had to inform Richard Booth of the impending new generation of Booths. What explosions rocked Queen Street when the prodigal son introduced his pregnant Adelaide to Richard we can today only imagine, but some uproar seems likely. On the other hand, Booth had demonstrated his potential as a starring actor and had the doubtful advantage of Pasquin-Williams' patronage. In any event, when the air cleared, Booth and Adelaide took up temporary residence on Queen Street and began looking for work.

On 10 April 1815 Booth received a note from Dr. Williams, suggesting the actor call the next day on Henry Harris, then manager of Covent Garden, using Williams' name to gain entrance.[1] Booth accordingly applied for a position to Harris, who promptly showed him the door. Booth immediately wrote to Williams for further assistance; on 9 June Williams replied from Brussels, "I have received your letter.—As to interfering further between you and Mr. Harris, I have only this answer to return; namely, that he is, and will be, the governing judge of what concerns his theatre; and that I have done all that I can, at least immediately, do, by introducing you to his notice.—The rest remains with yourself."[2] Williams also urged Booth to play his best roles that summer at Brighton, suggesting Richard III, Norval, and Sir Edward Mortimer, all roles Booth had acted on the Continent. He further urged Booth to study the role of Achmet in John Brown's *Barbarossa; or, The Captive Queen,* but not to write him in Brussels again. If Williams got Booth through the manager's door at Covent Garden, he could expect nothing more, and the actor began to realize patrons varied widely in their influence.

Meanwhile, Booth and Adelaide were married on 8 May 1815 at St. George's of Bloomsbury, a parish church just around the corner from Queen Street.[3] Richard Booth surely attended his only surviving son's wedding; certainly he must have strenuously encouraged the hasty ceremony. After a few weeks of tantalizing silence, Adelaide finally wrote to her mother in Brussels to reassure her about marital propriety.

> May 26, 1815.
>
> Very Dear Mother—It is with the greatest pleasure in the world that I inform you that I am married to Booth since the 8th of May, and am the happiest of women.
>
> He was engaged at the Theatre Royal of London for five weeks, but does not commence before September next, consequently he takes a place meanwhile at another theatre, but this appointment does not suit him, and I do not wish to leave his father. I am in a millinery store, where they are well satisfied with me. I work during the whole week, and on Sunday Booth comes for me and I return on Monday. The day of our marriage I did not wish it to be known, and I returned immediately after the ceremony and worked the same as usual.

Adelaide enclosed a copy of the marriage certificate to placate her distressed parent, emphasizing its cost of twelve francs. She closed, "Tell me, mother, if you are well, also all the family, and embrace them for me and say to my uncle that some time we will be married by a Catholic priest, that is to say, when our finances are better. . . . I am as well as I can be, and I am getting as fat as a great beast."[4]

Booth added a note, expressing the hope that their marriage consoled Mme Delannoy and asking her to tell Williams to write him.

In a later letter Booth told her he had on May fourth signed a five-year contract with Covent Garden, beginning at forty francs (eight dollars) a week, doubling by the fifth year.[5] In the meantime he accepted a summer position at Brighton. Booth offered his best regards to his in-laws and advised Mme Delannoy to write to him in English.

Adelaide accompanied Booth to Brighton for his engagement with Mr. Thomas Trotter, manager of theatres in Brighton and nearby Worthing.[6] Booth earned thirty-five shillings a week, an improvement over his income from Jonas and Penley but hardly enough to support a wife and imminent dependents. He spent the summer with Trotter, playing roles of no great distinction. No reviews mentioned him; he evidently did not particularly distinguish himself as he learned his craft.

The newlyweds returned to London for the birth of their first child, Amelia Portia Adelaide Booth, 5 October 1815, baptized by Curate Forth at St. George's on January seventh of the next year.[7] On the baptismal form, Booth listed his profession as solicitor. Again, the parental presence seemed to hover in the background; Richard Booth still dreamed of bringing his son to his senses and out of the theatre.

But Booth had an engagement pending at the Theatre Royal, Covent Garden, where he would face a London audience for the first time. Harris, however, postponed Booth's debut from September until 18 October 1815. Booth finally appeared in *As You Like It,* not in the leading role of Orlando but as the simpleminded rustic, Silvius, little better than a walk-on. Booth played the sheepherder four times, then in November he performed Harcourt in Mrs. Hannah More's *Percy*, an equally small role, for four performances. In December he did not appear at all, then in January 1816 he performed Glenalcon in John Home's *Douglas; or, The Noble Shepherd,* at Brighton, a role he repeated on 24 February, again at Brighton.[8]

Back at Covent Garden, Booth played Davila in *Pizarro* on 19 February 1816, then did not reappear until May. On the sixth and thirteenth of May he performed Pindarus in *Julius Caesar* and on the last day of the month played Lovel in *Henry VIII* for the benefit of Charles Kemble and his wife. Appearing infrequently in minor roles, he could hardly attract attention from either the public or the press.

The next month saw little improvement, and Booth finally realized Harris had no intention of allowing him to star; for whatever reasons, the manager intended to shelve Booth and keep him from the public eye. In June Booth played Davila twice more and Silvius once.

As the 1815–16 season drew to a close, Booth played his best role at Covent Garden that year—Henry in the afterpiece, *The Magpie or the Maid*—and ended his first London season as Cadwall in *Cymbeline*. In nine months in London, he had performed only eighteen times in insignificant roles, receiving no critical notice. Actors can live with bad reviews, but being ignored completely they simply cannot tolerate.

Booth returned to Brighton and Worthing with a slight increase in salary. He had received one pound, ten shillings per week in 1815 at Brighton and two pounds weekly during his lackluster season at Covent Garden; but in 1816, he signed on with Trotter again for two pounds, two shillings a week, plus a benefit, serving as acting manager.

According to Asia Booth Clarke, after her father became something of a local favorite as Fitzharding in Marie-Therese Kemble's comedy *Smiles and Tears; or, The Widow's Stratagem,* he quarreled with Trotter and left the company.[9] A brief engagement at Windsor failed, forcing him back to Trotter, who accepted him but cut his weekly salary to one pound, five shillings.[10]

Booth completed his provincial apprenticeship as an actor between 20 July 1816 and 4 February 1817. After playing roles of little or no distinction, he began to assemble a repertory in his line of business, that of leading tragedian.[11] Several characters became mainstays for Booth for his entire career. During the next few years, for example, the role of Fitzharding in *Smiles and Tears* won him great favor. Octavian, the mad lover in George Colman, the younger's, *Mountaineers,* remained a Booth standard for decades, as did a similar role, the archvillain Sir Giles Overreach in *A New Way to Pay Old Debts,* an Elizabethan revenge tragedy by Philip Massinger. The title role in C. R. Maturin's *Bertram* supplied another starring vehicle for Booth, as did Jaffier in Thomas Otway's *Venice Preserved.* Similarly, Booth often played Othello, but he won far more applause as the scheming, revenge-driven villain Iago. He was now a tragedian, and he would remain one till the day he died.

For a change of pace, the role of Jeremy Sneak in Samuel Foote's afterpiece *The Mayor of Garratt,* a sniveling, henpecked wretch of a husband whose wife cuckolded him gleefully and often, offered

Booth a chance to show his versatility. Indeed, Booth played the role cross-eyed, a technique described as "very difficult to maintain and inexpressibly funny."[12] For the actor, fresh from some bloody tragedy or melodrama, the role closed the evening as a romp, a piece of dramatic fluff tossed like a bonbon to the audience.

Thus Booth began to attract attention and to accumulate a favorable, if provincial, reputation. That reputation mushroomed when at Brighton on 25 September 1816 Trotter announced Edmund Kean as Sir Giles Overreach, one of Kean's most successful roles. For some unknown reason—one suspects an attack of brandy—Kean never arrived at the coastal resort, later claiming he had contracted no such arrangement. Trotter brought Booth the few miles from Worthing to Brighton to take the role on short notice for a hostile and disgruntled audience.

Every would-be star dreams of being suddenly thrust into the limelight, and the cliché sometimes contains a kernel of truth. As Booth began to perform Sir Giles, the audience forgot his presumption and began to express surprise and delight. The neophyte had risen to the occasion.

His breakthrough as Sir Giles preceded a comparable reception as Bertram, after which the delighted audience called for him. The next day the Honorable Lady Jane Chambers offered her patronage, insisting Booth's Bertram bore no scrap of resemblance to Kean's.[13] Booth had already received a highly complimentary letter from Douglas Kinnaird of Drury Lane, who wished to see him play a villain, but who promised to see him in any role. Booth's star had begun to rise, and he had begun to attract patrons far more influential than Pasquin-Williams.

He also received unexpected support from his father.[14] On 16 October 1816, Richard Booth wrote to the Drury Lane Committee, solemnly requesting a tryout for his son. In a four-page letter, Richard stated his case, attached his son's Brighton reviews, and suggested an "Exorbitant Salary will not even be wished for." Richard closed by noting he had always voted the Whig party. However, nothing came of this ploy. No doubt the Drury Lane Committee chortled over the attorney's temerity. Richard personally delivered the letter, but professional theatre managers customarily loathe stage parents and ignore amateurs.

Back in Brighton, although the performance excited no unusual interest at the time, Booth played Iago to Kean's Othello on Christmas Eve, 1816. They would repeat these roles together early the next year at Drury Lane.

Apparently Lady Chambers, Lord Erskine, Sir William Garrow, and others had more impact on Covent Garden's manager, Harris, than had Williams alone.[15] Together with Charles Kemble, they persuaded Harris to give Booth a "trial night," a performance to test his metropolitan appeal. Harris tried to notify Booth of his engagement for 12 February as Richard III, but Booth was already bound for London in a stagecoach, the Comet. After he had arrived he discovered to his astonishment his name already posted in the Covent Garden bills.

Booth went to rehearsal the next morning, only to be greeted by sneers and predictions of failure by the resident company. One actor remarked, "Why, I declare! It's little Silvius of last season, come to play Richard the Third, in opposition to the great Kean!" And another, expressing amazement, asked, "I wonder, now, if the manager expects respectable actors to play secondary parts to *him*!"[16]

The small audience's reaction to Booth's first performance as Richard III at Covent Garden, described earlier, buoyed his spirits considerably. He repeated the role the following night to a larger house, and although one observer considered his death scene "the worst," much of the audience, especially those in the pit, demanded he repeat the part. Booth then entered into negotiations with Harris for a longer engagement.[17] Harris recalled paying Booth two pounds a week the year before, so he offered him five pounds a week for the remainder of the season. Booth rejected the offer (the *London Sun* later reported he had asked for fifteen pounds), requesting that Harris not bill him as Richard III the following Monday.

And then all histrionic hell broke loose. Kean correctly recognized Booth as a dangerous rival, then discovered Covent Garden and Booth could not come to terms. He immediately leaped into his carriage, found Booth dining with Trotter, told him he had an engagement for him, and took him to meet the Drury Lane Committee.[18] Lord Essex, Richard Wilson, and George Lamb greeted him. Brandy circulated.[19] A hastily written contract appeared, and Booth signed with Drury Lane to open as Iago to Kean's Othello. Booth thus found himself more or less engaged by both patent houses, leaving himself vulnerable to all manner of tribulation. Testing his powers against the more experienced Kean constituted another indiscretion. He would pay for his misjudgments many times over.

On Thursday, 20 February 1817, London theatregoers witnessed the showdown between Booth and Kean. Nothing had so titillated them for years as this confrontation between novice and star.

Booth lost. Most accounts suggest that Kean acted Booth off the stage, driving him out of London and to America. While not exactly the case, Kean took the palm for the evening, and London theatregoers never again considered Booth a rival to Kean, even after the older actor fell from public favor.

Newspapers delightedly covered the controversy, reviewers swarming into Drury Lane to record their impressions. The next day the *Sun,* considering Kean unsurpassed as Othello, maintained, "on this occasion he exerted himself more than he ever did before. His energy was great, and his execution of many touches very fine. Indeed the whole third Act was a masterpiece in his style." The reporter regretted Kean was from time to time interrupted by his "obstreperous friends" (the Wolves) with their hysterical raptures. As for Booth, his Iago was dubbed "a fair specimen of dramatic powers, but certainly not of the highest order." He was "generally correct, but seldom forcible, though a few of his speeches were well delivered, and in Kean's best scenes he played well up to him." The *Sun* showed rare insight into the situation, suggesting that Booth appeared "not as a rival generously promoted, but rather as a foil ingeniously cast upon a vain competition."

The *London Morning Post* echoed the *Sun,* stating Booth received "a thunder of applause" upon his entrance and "commenced his performance with great success. His voice is, in some respects, better than that of Mr. Kean, and of this he availed himself with much felicity in his first scenes." Well begun, but "as the play advanced, Mr. Booth lost the high ground on which he had stood at its commencement; and the comparison which the audience were unceasingly called upon to make, was not very favourable to him. His *Iago* . . . was a creditable performance, but it was nothing like what a too [sanguine] public had fondly anticipated it would prove."

Booth's singing (during the scene with Cassio) the *Morning Post* considered "one of the oddest substitutes for harmony we have ever heard." Booth was often very fine, they thought, but never transcendent, but Kean had produced "a more powerful effect" than the critic had ever seen. The review concluded, "With another actor . . . the *Iago* of the evening might have been thought great, but by the side of Kean we could discover in him nothing strikingly original in thought, vivid in conception, or brilliant in execution." The *Morning Post* did note that Booth had to perform in strange circumstances, among a cast with whom he had never worked, and added that he received strong applause upon his final exit.

By far the most prejudicial critique appeared in the *Champion* for 23 February. The reviewer found Mr. Booth a clever young man, as young men go, but praised Kean lavishly. The critic felt, "Mr. Kean's *Othello*, on this occasion, was one of the most surprising achievements that genius ever perfected. We will venture to assert that there never was a grander and more pathetic piece of acting on the English stage,—of course on no other stage." Furthermore, "Kean beat his antagonist hollow. He played Othello from his very soul,—and he sent the fierceness and misery of the Moor into the hearts of all his hearers. Kean played himself into a state of absolute exhaustion more than once." This critic recognized what was at stake, saying, "Mr. Kean always played *Othello* with a beautiful earnestness,—but on the other evening, he seemed to feel his fame snatched at by a stranger hand, and the consequence was that he put forth all his energies and arose on the wings of genius like an eagle above his opponent." The same writer dismissed Booth by saying, "Mr. Booth has evidently seen Mr. Kean in *Richard* and *Othello*;—but when the *imitator* and the *imitated* come together we see the difference pretty plainly. . . . He will make an admirable second to Kean. . . . But Mr. Booth must endeavour to keep his little body together,—and gather up his mind into one parcel;—at present his arms and his faculties dangle about like a lady's ridicule [reticule]."

The *London Times* reacted similarly, considering Booth "highly respectable," adding, "he poured his poisons with dextrous and smooth hypocrisy into the imagination of the credulous Moor." But again the higher praise went to Kean, who "excelled on the present occasion all his preceding efforts; he not only threw a stronger light than ever on the terrible workings of *Othello*'s mind, but he shed a new light on many passages that had hitherto been sunk in obscurity. . . .

Kean was the very soul of passion." Overall, the *Times* felt, "There were scenes in this play which we had never yet beheld so ably represented; and there were improvements in Mr. Kean's acting of which we did not think the tragedian's art had been susceptible."

William Hazlitt, as usual, had the last word. In the *London Examiner* the lord of London critics opined, "there neither is nor can be any idea of competition," and as for Kean's Othello, Hazlitt considered it "beyond praise, . . . perfect tragic acting." The Olympian jury had sent down its thunderbolts, with Kean the clear victor.

If Booth, a young actor with a young actor's fantasies of glory, had entertained some hope of toppling Kean, such was not to be. In that regard, he had failed. True, he had forced the greatest actor of his day to the full transcendent exercise of his powers, but second place remained second place. Some magazine reviews later judged Booth more kindly, but the damage was done.

Booth's problems had only begun.[20] The Drury Lane management informed him that they would not allow him to perform Richard III, Hamlet, Sir Giles Overreach, Bertram, or any other of Kean's leading roles, adding that they had cast him for the next Thursday in the subordinate role of Richmond to Kean's Richard III. At the same time, Harris informed Booth that he did not consider their negotiations completed; Covent Garden still held a claim to his services.

All this controversy quite overcame Booth; he had acted only slightly more than three years, and he now found himself torn between the two leading theatres of the English-speaking world. Faced with this dilemma, he needed time to sort things out. At half past 3:00 P.M. on Saturday the twenty-second, Booth sent a note to Alexander Rae, the Drury Lane stage manager. "Mr. Booth presents his compliments to Mr. Rae, and is sorry to inform him that he finds himself so extremely ill from the agitation he has suffered during this last week, that it is totally out of his power to perform this evening, and that he is gone a little way out of town to endeavour to restore his health."

Booth fled to Tottenham, a suburb six miles north of London Bridge, by the Edmonton coach, arriving about 5:00 P.M. at the house of a Mr. Pope, solicitor. He remained there until early Sunday afternoon. James Salter had accompanied him but, having business in London, returned on horseback, then went again to Tottenham Sunday morning to travel with Booth back to London.

Almost for the first time since arriving in London, Booth had time to consider his future. At Drury Lane he would have no chance to perform his leading roles, would have to play characters for which he was not prepared, and at all times would pale by comparison to Kean. At Covent Garden he would have an unlimited range of characters of his own choosing. The salary mattered less than one might think; what counted was a London reputation, leading to summer engagements in the provinces. Kean, for example, had acquired twenty-four hundred pounds in twenty-four nights while on tour, and after Booth first appeared as Richard III at Covent Garden, a provincial manager offered him twenty pounds a night for six performances.[21]

None of this mattered to Rae or to the Drury Lane audience on 22 February; they expected to see Kean as Othello and Booth as Iago. Rae had received the note from Booth in sufficient time to have posted new bills or to have erected signs around the theatre announcing that Booth would not perform that night—Rae did neither. If Kean had a part in all this, he said nothing but offered to act Iago to Rae's Othello, an arrangement the audience accepted, applauding Kean loudly and often during the performance.

Before the show ended, however, another letter over Booth's signature, this time to the Drury Lane Committee, arrived at the theatre.

> Gentlemen, In an unguarded moment I quitted Covent-garden Theatre, (where the most eligible situation for the exertion of my professional talents was open to me) to go over to Drury-lane Theatre, where I have since found, and felt to my cost, that every character which I was either desirous or capable of playing, was already in possession, and that there was no chance of my appearing in the same. What occasion, therefore, could you have for me, unless to crush any talent I may possess in its infancy? I have now seen through my error, and have therefore renewed the negotiation which was so unfortunately interrupted with the proprietors of Covent-garden Theatre, and have just signed a regular article with them for three years; consequently I have no longer the power of appearing at Drury-lane Theatre, and you will have the goodness to take my name entirely out of your bills.
>
> I have heard, Gentlemen, that your treasury has benefited considerably from my appearance on Thursday last: I ask no pecuniary recompense for it. I only request that you will not seek to persecute or molest a young man, just entering into life, and who

> cannot afford either to be shelved (according to the theatrical phrase) at Drury-lane Theatre, or to be put into such characters as must infallibly mar all his future prospects.
>
> I have the honour to be, Gentlemen,
> Your very obedient humble servant,
> J. BOOTH.

Apparently Booth and Covent Garden had come to terms before he left for Tottenham inasmuch as the following placard appeared around the theatre: "The public are respectfully informed, that Mr. Booth has satisfactorily arranged his differences with the Proprietors of this Theatre, and is engaged by them for three years. He will perform King Richard the Third on Tuesday next, Feb. 25, which character for two successive nights, he had the honour to be called for by the audience to repeat."

The battle joined, charges and countercharges clogged the London papers for the next several days. Drury Lane struck back; on Monday, 24 February, a circular appeared, widely reprinted in the newspapers. Drury Lane set forth the chronology of the matter fairly accurately, quoted Booth's note to Rae, and asked the public to make their own judgment about the conduct of Mr. Booth.

Henry Harris and Covent Garden responded immediately. First, they accused Drury Lane of ignoring a long tradition of the two houses: confirming with one another the status of a performer's contract with the other house. Second, Covent Garden claimed that they would have let Booth play at the other house, but he was too ill to make the attempt. Third, Harris piously hoped that the "usual candour and liberality" of the English public would prevail.

The circular appended a letter from Douglas Kinnaird corroborating the agreement between the two houses. Kinnaird further claimed each administration had agreed to wait a year before entering into negotiations with any performer who had previously appeared at the other theatre. Finally, Covent Garden accused the Wolves of trying to drive Booth from the stage. When Covent Garden attacked the Wolves, Kean himself entered the fray, and the leading newspapers and journals printed the following letter over his name:

> I think it my duty, in justice to a society of which I once had the honour of being a member, to refute a most malicious piece of calumny. The *Wolf Club* seems to have been the foil with which the

> friends of the *rival theatre* have for the last two years parried the public censure against their unsuccessful candidates. I wish, therefore, through the medium of the public prints, to inform their *fears,* that such a society is no longer in existence, has not been for the last nine months, and when it was, the principals of the institution were founded in integrity and *universal philanthropy.* The misrepresentations with regard to this society laid before the public, rendered it unjustly an object of reprobation, and in acknowledgment of my duty to that public, I resigned it.
>
> With regard to Mr. Booth, that I have the highest opinions of his talents I gave proof when I recommended his engagement to the Drury Lane committee. If any one shall assert that I would, individually or accessorily, do anything detrimental to the interests of Mr. Booth, or any brother professional, I should be happy in person to tell the propagator of such a report that it is A FALSEHOOD.
>
> I remain, sir, with the greatest respect,
> Your obedient humble servant,
> EDMUND KEAN.

Also on Monday, 24 February, the Drury Lane Committee filed a bill in Chancery against Booth and Covent Garden for an injunction to restrain Booth from acting anywhere except Drury Lane. The next day, however, the plaintiffs petitioned to have the bill dismissed. Drury Lane had to bear the court expenses, a trifle.

Booth's dream of London stardom was souring rapidly. The next day, the twenty-fifth, with Booth scheduled to reappear at Covent Garden as Richard III, another circular appeared in the vicinity of that theatre. This one, the London theatregoing public read wearily, reprinted a deposition by James Salter, swearing Salter had delivered the letter to Rae at three o'clock the previous Saturday. An hour later, Salter claimed, he and Booth proceeded to Tottenham, where Booth remained ill for the rest of the day.

The same day the London press published a letter from the proprietor of a pub, the Coal Hole, claiming the Wolves, while formerly meeting at his establishment, had disbanded several months earlier. The contention continued; everyone seemed to be right; no one was to blame for anything.

But Booth had returned to Covent Garden, and the time had arrived for him to reappear. He performed Richard III on Tuesday, 25 February, less than two weeks after his arrival in London.

London had seen many theatre riots before; they were about to enjoy another. The house filled to capacity, though neither Boothites nor Keanites seemed to hold a clear majority. When Booth appeared, simultaneous roars of applause and condemnation filled the hall; the audience shouted, blew whistles, rapped their sticks on the floor, and shook their fists. Booth tried to wait them out to apologize for any disappointment he had caused, but his detractors would suffer no word to be heard.

Finally, Booth bowed and exited. The stage manager, John Fawcett, entered and similarly waited vainly for the riot to abate.[22] Several men threw notes on the stage, but Fawcett mimed the impossibility of reading so many. With no opportunity to speak, Fawcett also left the stage.

The other actors began the show, performing unheard over the mob's rising fury.[23] The din increased when Booth entered; he walked down to the footlights, but again the rioters drowned him out completely. He exited for the second time, then reentered with a standard bearer carrying a sign reading, "Grant Silence to Explain." Fawcett entered, led Booth to the front of the stage, implored the audience to hear them, was again rebuffed, and again exited.

The actors struggled on while fistfights broke out in the audience. During the second act, an actor brought out a placard reading, "Mr. Booth wishes to apologize," to which several in the audience roared out, "No more lies! No more lies!" Fawcett again led Booth forward to no avail. Another placard appeared, reading, "Can Englishmen condemn unheard?" But the mob was in full cry, having left rationality far behind. Finally, the performance halted completely, and again Fawcett brought his star forward. Not only screaming and yelling greeted them, but a shower of oranges and orange peels, driving them once more from the stage, Booth seemingly overcome with grief.

Even under these conditions, the show must go on, so the company began the afterpiece, a farce. As they started, a man in one of the boxes tried to address the audience, triggering yet another outburst. The crowd demanded Fawcett throw the rabble-rouser out, but the manager replied, "This whilst I am manager of the theatre I cannot do; if the person has offended you, it is in your own power to turn him out."

Things quieted somewhat (Booth did not appear in the afterpiece), and upon its conclusion, most of the audience remained, so Fawcett spoke to them. He informed them that Booth had waited until "a late hour" to address them but finally gave up and went home. The manager also pointed out that the dispute between the two theatres was now left to the law courts; the public would have to wait for their decision, and the managers would have to abide by it. Most of the remaining audience were pro-Booth, calling out as they left the theatre, "No shelving," "No Wolves," and "Booth forever!" The last of the audience departed about midnight.

Another spate of bills and placards appeared the next day. First, Covent Garden attached the following to their bills for Wednesday:

> Mr. Booth last Tuesday made his third appearance at this Theatre, in the character of *King Richard the Third.* After repeated attempts to give an explanation to the audience, and implore them not to suffer an humble individual to be made the victim of disputes between the two Theatres, no hearing was allowed him;—but, as far as the Proprietors could judge from the cheering at the dropping of the curtain, a vast majority of the audience was in his favour.—Mr. Booth will therefore perform *Richard* again on Saturday next, and throws himself upon the mercy and liberality of Englishmen.

Then the Drury Lane Committee published their own views on the matter on the twenty-fifth. Citing the case of a Mrs. Glover during the previous season, the Drury Lane Committee observed actors could certainly move from one theatre to another freely; otherwise they could be shelved for an entire year, an unthinkable situation. In closing, Drury Lane swore to ignore all further "insinuations, mis-statements, or calumnies, from whatever quarter they [might] come."

Londoners breathed a sigh of relief—prematurely, for on the twenty-sixth, Booth made a personal and lengthy appeal to the public.

> MR. BOOTH'S APPEAL TO THE PUBLIC
>
> It is with feelings of the most poignant grief, that I found, by my reception at Covent-garden Theatre last night, that I had incurred the serious displeasure of a large proportion of that audience. As far as I could judge, from my own observation, and that of my friends, the accusations against me were,
>
> First—My having left one Theatre, to renew my engagement in another. And, Secondly,—A want of respect to the public, in not

performing at Drury-lane on Saturday last. In regard to the first cause of complaint, I humbly submit, that most unexpectedly entangled as I have been, between the two Theatres, and involved in a contest that older and wiser heads than mine might have erred in; and as the whole matter will shortly be explained in a court of law, I earnestly entreat the public to wait for the result of that decision. Respecting the second, and, to me, by far the most serious charge, if I had been allowed the honour of a hearing, I think I could have satisfactorily explained to the audience that, in my delicate situation, between the clashing interests of the two rival Theatres, I never could have been such a fool, or a madman, as to have done a *wilful* act to offend the public, by whose favour and support alone I was to exist in my profession.

For the cause of my absence from my duty on Saturday, I am ready to make the same affidavit which has been made already by Mr. Salter, who was with me at the time, viz. "That on Saturday morning last, I did complain of severe indisposition, owing to the anxiety of mind, and the great fatigue I had suffered during the last week; and that I was so seriously indisposed, that I found myself totally incapable of making the exertion necessary to perform that evening; and that I wrote the same to Mr. Rae, which letter was at Drury-lane Theatre by three o'clock on Saturday afternoon, which was time sufficient to have had hand-bills printed, to apprize the public of my incapability to perform, and prevent my being the cause of any disappointment to the audience.

Had I thought that such an unfair advantage would have been taken of my illness, and that it would have been insinuated from the stage, that my indisposition was feigned, rather than have been ungrateful to my benefactors, I would at all hazards have performed, even though death had been the consequence. But as in every month, and every week in the season, instances of apologies for performers on the score of indisposition are accepted, I could not imagine, that on that plea I should be made the first dreadful example of public indignation. My punishment has already been severe; and surely a British Public, a name synonymous with generosity, will not, for an involuntary error, combine to deprive a fellow-citizen of the means of supporting himself and family.

And again, I most earnestly conjure the public, that, if they still think me guilty of a fault, they will kindly bring to their recollection it is my *first*; and should they graciously grant me their indulgence, I pledge myself, that it shall be the *last*—I will dedicate my whole life to their service, and ever remain

Their most devoted and attached servant,

J. Booth.

Doubtless some readers wondered what part Booth actually had in drafting his appeal, but it appeared over his name, and most of the London public assumed he wrote it. His plea, however, did nothing to resolve the matter. Covent Garden (Harris) realized the publicity value of the controversy and so issued an undated circular about the same time, accusing the Drury Lane Committee of being an "Amateur Theatrical Sub-Committee," with no responsibility and only temporary power. Harris further implied this aristocratic committee, with their independent fortunes, could abolish laws and annul agreements by whim, while he, Harris, bore personal responsibility for his debts "like other Traders in this great commercial country." To uphold the drama, then, Covent Garden had to act in its own self-defense.

The newspapers had just about had enough of this; one journal cried out, "A plague on both your houses!" But the issue remained unresolved.

Whatever the feeling, sooner or later, Booth had to go back onstage and face the monster he had helped create—or find some other way to make a living. On Saturday, March first, he braced himself for a fourth performance at Covent Garden as Richard III.

Covent Garden theatregoers found Booth's appeal to the public in every box and scattered through the pit and galleries. Drury Lane had taken the easy way out by swearing not to reply to any further accusations. Someone, however, had placed anonymous tracts in the theatre and along the neighboring streets. They were signed by "A Lover of Truth" and contained seven specific questions directed at Booth. Did he not inform the Covent Garden managers to remove his name from their bills on the seventeenth? Did he not inform the Drury Lane managers his negotiations with Covent Garden were terminated? Did not the Drury Lane Committee accept his terms, and did he not sign a three-year contract with them? Did the Drury Lane Committee use any improper means to induce him to sign? Did Booth tell Drury Lane he was underage, which assertion he now used to avoid his contract with them? Did not Covent Garden then offer Booth triple his previous salary there? And was not *that* why Booth did not appear on the twenty-second? Then this "Lover of Truth" appended yet another deposition, this one by a William Edwards, who swore that he had seen James Salter, supposedly with Booth in Tottenham, in a public house at ten in the evening the same day. All charges went unanswered; the resolution would take place on the Covent Garden stage.

The audience gathered, ready for a brawl, as described by the *London Courier:* "The audience were no sooner assembled, than the cry of 'Booth for ever,' resounded from all parts of the Pit, the occupants of which stood on the benches. This was answered by the call of 'No Booth,' and the parties immediately joined issue, and proceeded to try, if not the goodness, the strength of their cause, by clapping, by hissing, by shouts, and by groans." Boothites hoisted a placard reading, "He has been punished enough. Let us forgive him," but the Keanites shouted them down. The theatre that evening was no place for ladies, but the few who attended seemed predisposed to Booth.

More signs appeared: "Hear Booth, of Old Drury, in his proper place"; "The Pit forgives him"; "No persecution"; "We pardon him"; "No playing in London for three years"; "Booth has done enough to appease John Bull"; "Contrition purchases repentance even in Heaven"; and "Beware! the artillery of Drury-lane is in Covent-Garden!" All this among shouts equally divided: "No Booth," "Booth for ever," "Turn out the Wolves," and "No hirelings from Drury-lane!" Booth saw the previous Tuesday's debacle replaying before his eyes.

Eventually the tragedy began. Once again no one could hear a word of it. Booth's first entrance elicited garlands of laurel from his supporters and a barrage of orange peels from the Keanites—a decidedly mixed review. After vainly attempting to speak to the audience, Booth began his first soliloquy, and at last he began to take command of his audience. His shift from humble and apologetic actor to stern and tyrannical villain so struck the onlookers that he won considerable applause, although silence remained elusive.

As the next scene began, the indefatigable John Fawcett stepped forward to address the audience. Most wanted to hear him, but a raucous minority prevented it, and Fawcett retired.

From the second row of boxes, an anti-Booth partisan hurled an orange into the pit. One of the Boothites seated near him launched a right cross, and the fight was on. The original aggressor was eventually thrown out of the theatre, losing a shoe. The Wolves then invaded the box, which was already full of patrons; the rest of the house cried, "Out with them," and then repulsed the invaders, who spent the rest of the evening beating their walking sticks against the box doors.

The show limped along. During Richard's wooing of Lady Anne, a note was passed up to Booth, who duly read it and left the stage. Fawcett led him forward yet again and asked, "Is it the wish of the house that Mr. Booth should be heard?" Some in the house cheered, some groaned; Booth stepped forward and said, "Ladies and Gentlemen, I have endeavoured all in my power to atone for the disappointment of which I was the cause in another place. I have apologized for my conduct on that occasion, and have endeavoured to explain the circumstances. I now again most humbly and sincerely repeat my apology." But few could hear Booth, so his apology had little effect. Fawcett and his star tried again at the beginning of the third act, coming forward with a placard reading, "Mr. Booth craves your silence to explain and apologize." Booth then said, "Ladies and Gentlemen, I have done every thing in my power to express the sense I entertain of my offence, and I am willing to do so again in any way you shall suggest." Not many heard him, so the play staggered on, still punctuated by sporadic fistfights in the audience.

At the beginning of the fourth act, the audience, hearing Mrs. Faucit for the first time, applauded her vigorously. Chaos then resumed its empire, continuing to the end of the performance. Loud cries for "Booth! Booth!" filled the theatre, and again Fawcett and Booth trudged out, with an employee carrying a placard reading, "I have acted wrong; I have made a sufficient apology and throw myself on the candour of Englishmen." While cheers outweighed boos, Booth again had to exit without speaking.

The afterpiece being completed, the audience demanded Fawcett and shouted various suggestions to him. When a semblance of silence fell, Fawcett asked, "May I not interpret this call on me to be a request on your part to know what the play is to be on Monday?" Booth's friends roared out, "Yes," "Yes," "Booth," and "Richard." "Then," said Fawcett, "bowing as I always do to your command, I beg to announce that on Monday (with your permission), the play of this evening will be repeated."

One might think that enough would have been quite enough, but this amusement simply would not subside. The next day several papers wrote, "We understand that the Lord Chamberlain has intimated to both Theatres that if the present dispute is improperly prolonged, he shall consider it his duty to prevent Mr. Booth from appearing on either stage."[24]

Emotions continued to run high. The matter did not escape the wits of the town, evinced by this widely circulated street ballad:

THEATRICAL SQUABBLES,
OR
A BOOTH IN COVENT GARDEN
-1-

Have you heard the mighty row,
Of late so much the go,
Bout the little Actor Man
How amaz'd the people ran,
They were planet struck no doubt
  Such a wonder was never seen O!
  Hob a nob! What a mob!
  Squeezing crushing crowding pushing,
    Pit full what a pull!
    O rare! let's stare!
  Hey down! ho down! derryderrydown
    Oh! dear! what a farcical scene O![25]

As Macbeth says late in the tragedy, "And the cry is still, they come!" More of this moving paper fantasy appeared in the press; Harris wrote to Kinnaird on 27 February 1817, citing the case of a T. Cooke as evidence of the treaty between the two theatres. Kinnaird had the letter published in the newspapers, commenting that, since only two of the Drury Lane Committee had acted for the whole, he would use these means to "refresh the memory" of the other three members.

Still more followed, but the end finally came into sight. Drury Lane sent a letter to various editors of London papers on March third, apologizing for breaking their self-imposed silence. They included a note from Lord Essex, denying any knowledge of T. Cooke. And on the same day, Fawcett of Covent Garden sent *his* letter to the papers, accusing Rae of Drury Lane of coming to Booth's performance to speak to the audience. Fawcett suggested that no one from a rival house should dare appear in the other.

Slowly, things began to return to something like normal. Petty sniping continued, but Booth had secured his position at Covent Garden and would remain there for the season. As for salary, the *Morning Post* on March first reported that Booth had not returned to Covent Garden for higher pay, that he received the same money there as he would have at Drury Lane: eight pounds a week for a year, nine pounds for a second season, and ten pounds a week for the third. While the accuracy of these figures may be questioned, they correspond roughly to standard salary practices of the time.

Booth repeated Richard III on March third and again on the sixth. The *Morning Post* reported on 4 March the production's reception as relatively calm and the audience as large and approving. No more than three or four persons tried to disrupt the evening, but they were quickly silenced and thrown out. Some of the audience again threw laurel branches upon the stage at the performance's end, but King Richard no longer waded through orange peels.

The last published word on the entire Booth-Kean squabble came from the ubiquitous James Salter; on 7 March several of the London papers ran his letter in which he insisted on the truth of his previous statements about Booth's illness on the night in question. The Kean camp made no rejoinder; they no longer considered Booth a serious threat to Kean. As for Booth, he damned Mr. Salter and Mr. Pope as "My evil genius" and "Satan's aid-de-camp," adding, "My offence was trifling,—being the effect of a grateful impulse and imagined incivility; but Salter's and Pope's of magnitude,—for never were wretches more assiduous in their attempts to corrupt the morals of youth."[26]

And so, finally, Booth was allowed to get on with it and pursue his career. He was starring at one of the two leading theatres in England, and, though Kean had quite overcome him, he could still reasonably expect a substantial career on the London stage, supplemented by high-paying forays into the countryside.

Booth's Richard III had run its course; he now needed to appear in some other role. He chose Sir Giles Overreach on the eighth of March, a role in many ways comparable to Richard III, and again one of Kean's more successful personations. An overflow audience turned out for his Sir Giles, as described by the newspapers, who though split along party lines in their evaluations of his effort, on the whole treated Booth's Sir Giles positively. The *Morning Post* found his resemblance to Kean "most striking" but noted, the similarity "arises more from a coincidence of genius than from an imitation of style," giving Booth his due. Others still accused him of imitating Kean. The audience itself sent forth peals of applause, and the pit gave Booth a standing ovation, shouting and waving their hats. Of the magazines, the *Theatrical Inquisitor and Monthly Mirror,* a pro-Kean publication, attacked most viciously:

A PROCLAMATION

WHEREAS it hath been humbly represented unto us, The Theatrical Inquisitor, that between the hours of seven and ten o'clock in the evening of Saturday, the 6th instant, *Sir Giles Overreach,* knt. was stopped in his journey through Covent-garden Theatre, and inhumanly murdered:

And WHEREAS Junius Booth the younger, now of Queen-street, Bloomsbury, comedian, stands charged upon oath on a violent suspicion of having wilfully and feloniously attempted to kill and murder *Richard Plantagenet, Duke of Gloucester,* on Wednesday the 12th day of February last; and the said Junius Booth also stands charged, on vehement suspicion, with having committed divers other high and atrocious theatrical offences; now, putting these specific charges together,

For the more speedy apprehending and bringing to justice the said Junius Booth for the offences aforesaid, The Theatrical Inquisitor is hereby pleased, acting in the name, and on behalf of his readers, to promise to any person or persons who shall apprehend, or cause to be apprehended, the said Junius Booth, the sum of FIVE HUNDRED *thanks,* to be paid by the Commissioners of the Editor's Treasury, upon the said Junius Booth being apprehended and lodged in any one of the Monthly Magazines.

March 23, 1817. INQUISITOR GENERAL.[27]

All this furor further stimulated interest in Booth's personal life, and about this time the first book-length biography of the new star appeared: *Memoirs of Junius Brutus Booth, from His Birth to the Present Time; with an Appendix, Containing Original Letters, From Persons of Rank and Celebrity, and Copious Extracts from the Journal Kept by Mr. Booth During His Theatrical Tour of the Continent.*[28] This anonymously authored treatment of the twenty-two-year-old actor amounted to only eighty-six pages and sold for four shillings. Whoever wrote it had Booth's full cooperation, manifested by large portions of his 1814–15 diary and several supportive letters. The dedication, dated 22 March 1817, was to Lord Erskine, with thanks for his patronage of Booth. Appended letters by Pasquin-Williams, William Godwin, Lady Jane Chambers, and Douglas Kinnaird all praised Booth most fulsomely.

Only one review of the *Memoirs of Junius Brutus Booth* appeared; in April 1817 the *Theatrical Inquisitor,* ever pro-Kean, roasted it vehemently as a "barefaced attempt . . . to impress the imbecile, the wavering, and the credulous." Pasquin-Williams was dubbed a "hackney-scribe" and "a literary cur, whose critical praise is poured upon every object prepared to sustain its filthy collision." The *Inquisitor* had never heard of the Honorable Mrs. Jane Chambers and hoped not to again. As for Booth, the *Inquisitor* sneered, "We trust . . . that a firm boundary will be adjudged to his unlicensed career, and the rude progress of Mr. Booth be arrested by critical impediments, as the rush-light expires at the cross pins, appointed to extinguish its despicable brilliance."

Another volume, undated, anonymous, and consisting of only twenty-seven pages of large print, appeared about the same time: *Memoirs of Mr. Booth, Containing A True Statement of All the Circumstances Attending his Engagements at the Rival Theatres, with a Few Remarks upon his Conduct; by an Old Actor*. This biography claimed Booth had been born in Hackney, mentioned his "amatory pursuits" with a neighbor's maidservant when he was thirteen, and sketched his early career. Again, the writer must have had the actor's confidence, for he described Booth's flight with Adelaide from Brussels, as well as her pregnancy. The author excused Booth's simultaneous dealings with the two patent houses, but on very flimsy grounds.

In any event, the unextinguished Booth pressed on, playing more roles at Covent Garden. On the ides of March he performed Posthumus in Shakespeare's *Cymbeline*; for the first time in London, Booth starred as a nonvillain in a role in which Kean had not appeared.

Posthumus did not become one of Booth's more successful roles; the character is, as several newspapers pointed out, a "finished knight," and most observers considered Booth lacking in the requisite social niceties and grace. Both the *Times* and the *London Courier* commented on Booth's "strange habit of shuffling his feet, and, as it were, sliding along the stage." The *London Morning Herald* thought Booth had "some talents, but we think of a very limited compass," calling much of his work "devoid of propriety and expression." Similarly, the *Sun* decried Booth's lack of experience, although mentioning his genius for the stage, saying his Posthumus exhibited "the same jumble of vigour and debility, of talent and dullness, as most of his other performances." And the *Champion* put it in a nutshell, saying, Booth performed with "immense labour and bustle," showing "how easily passion could be counterfeited," adding, "Mr. Booth is by no means the gentleman enough in voice, step, or action, to perform *Posthumus*."

Booth must have picked up the *Theatrical Inquisitor* with fear and trembling; that journal seldom hesitated to pillory him. In the March 1817 issue:

> Without hesitation or concealment, we avowed the most rooted abhorrence of those arts by which this young man has been raked out of his native insignificance, and having analyzed the successive endeavours, with the closest attention that disgust could allow, into which Mr. Booth has been shuffled, we are prepared to stigmatize the whole tenor of his efforts as fraught with every blemish, obnoxious to the most aggravated correction. . . . the errors of Mr. Booth in *Posthumus* are beyond amendment, and even if they were not, can never again come within the scope of our own observations.

The *Inquisitor* again lay in wait as Booth presented another new role, that of Fitzharding in John Tobin's potboiler *The Curfew*, on 27 March. Of Booth's latest effort, they sneered,

> We harbour no anxiety to sift his bushels of chaff for a solitary corn, and especially when the chances of success are against the picking up of that miserable grain. . . . Mr. Junius Booth squatted in an arm-chair, with his mouth open, and a hand upon each knee, so warmly were his feelings aroused by the urgencies of the character. . . . for trepidation, his fingers dangled like a bunch of radishes from a green-grocer's stall, or the sham-candles, in a high wind, at a tallow-chandler's door. On the whole, these and other exquisite instances, coupled with the admiration of his half-play supporters, presented a loathsome subject for ridicule and disgust.

The newspapers commented briefly on Booth's Fitzharding as being nothing special, and apparently the audience, which included the duke and duchess of Gloucester, found neither play nor performance particularly attractive. The *Morning Herald* noted the script had "some passages . . . which, in the hands of a superior actor, would have reached to the deepest recesses of feeling." Booth, they felt, had talent, but not so much as his friends seemed to believe. After a sea of ink had been spilled about Booth, his London reviews began to shrink, as did his popularity. So, Booth took to the countryside, cashing in on his new fame while continuing to act intermittently at Covent Garden. Harris surely realized that Booth could not compete with Kean, that he had other actors, such as William Charles Macready, who were far more likely to achieve stardom than was Booth.[29]

Booth could and did demand large sums on the road; he would for the rest of his career. Between 31 March and 5 April 1817 he played four performances at Woolwich, as recorded in an account book he began keeping at this time. Booth divided the box-office receipts equally with the Woolwich manager. If indeed Booth received eight pounds a week at Covent Garden, the appeal of the provinces clearly emerged as he cleared nearly forty pounds during his Woolwich engagement, almost five times what he would have earned in London.

He then returned to Covent Garden for two weeks to do two new roles. The first was Sir Edward Mortimer in Colman's *Iron Chest,* a tatterdemalion melodrama extracted from Godwin's *Caleb Williams* and mercifully retired later in the century. The role, which became a favorite Booth vehicle, suited his acting style exactly. The *Courier* considered Booth's talents "still disputed," but felt, "This choice has been justified by a success far exceeding our expectations; for we have not seen Mr. Booth to such advantage in any former character as in that which he assumed last night." Still, Booth was not Kean, and the reviewer continued, "he was deficient in that delicate discrimination and richness of colouring which so peculiarly belong to [Kean]." The *Times* similarly found him an inferior imitation of Kean.

Booth's other new role was Rinaldo in William Dimond's *Conquest of Taranto; or, The Eve of St. Clara,* a turgid bit of dramaturgy having to do with Moors and Spaniards. After the new script was read backstage at Covent Garden, Macready, cast as Valentio, offered Harris thirty pounds to release him from the part, but the manager refused. Macready coveted Booth's role as Rinaldo, considering Valentio "one of the meanest, most despicable villains that a romancer's invention ever teemed with." Macready mentioned his dismay to Booth, who replied, "I think your part is as good as mine." "Will you change with me?" Macready begged. Booth merely smiled in reply.[30]

The Conquest of Taranto hung on for a few more performances. The *Times* felt that the script needed pruning and that Booth needed to avoid "so much bustling and ranting, and redundancy of gesture." Although Booth had only two months earlier taken London by storm, the metropolitan audience now judged him second-rate.

On Saturday, 19 April 1817, Booth played a multiple engagement. He performed Sir Edward Mortimer three times in one day in three neighboring cities: at 11:00 A.M. in Cirencester, at 4:00 P.M. in Gloucester, and at 8:00 P.M. in Cheltenham. Again, he took as compensation half the box-office receipts, totaling twenty-seven pounds, ten shillings for the day, more than three times his weekly salary at Covent Garden. That stunt over, he returned to Covent Garden for three performances of *The Conquest of Taranto,* then he went on the road again. His account book notes two performances at Croyden, one at Bristol, and three at Bath.

Booth's Bath engagement met with some unfavorable reviews in the *Bath Chronicle;* a gentleman signing himself "T.Q." wrote to the editor of the *Bath and Cheltenham Gazette* praising Booth. He also offered the first extant description of the young actor in *The Mayor of Garratt.* Booth often chose this short play as the afterpiece for his benefits, and apparently it played quite well. T.Q. stated that the audience did not recognize Booth at first, "so completely had he disguised himself by the quaintness and propriety of his dress," and added, "The Cockney dialect was hit off admirably, and he threw into the part all the broad rich humour of a first-rate comedian, without any buffoonery or grimace."

The Bath manager took the first sixty pounds of receipts, then shared anything over that with Booth. They divided his benefit ticket sales equally. The first three performances, including Bristol, brought him just over 54 pounds, but his benefit drew a box office of almost 165 pounds, giving Booth a share of over 82 pounds, or a total for four performances of over 136 pounds, a very tidy sum indeed. So, too, at Liverpool, receiving half the receipts above 65 pounds and taking half his benefit, Booth received almost 160 pounds.

After Liverpool, Booth played one-night stands at Manchester, Croyden, and Guildford. He went back to Covent Garden on 25 June for his benefit, playing Richard III and Jeremy Sneak, his income there being unrecorded. He then returned to the road and, by the end of the year, calculated his provincial receipts for 1817 at more than £1,124—doubtless more money than he had ever imagined earning in any other profession.

Still, Booth's dream of London stardom lay shattered. Years later, Booth would insist fame meant nothing to him, he only wanted the money he could earn from acting.[31] He had earned large sums but found his treatment by critics and managers somewhat abusive.

Then, too, his first child by Adelaide, Amelia, died in infancy, although no record survives of the exact date. Things simply were not working out. His disenchantment nearing totality, Booth suddenly decided that acting was a mug's game and that he would join the army. He would leave theatrical glory to those willing to pay the price—he should have known better.

3

This England

I must unto the road, to disembark
Some necessaries.

—*Two Gentlemen of Verona,* II, iv, 187–88

Booth was playing against a stacked deck. If acting had earned Booth a great deal of money, the profession had also treated him shabbily. He had starred on the two leading stages of the English-speaking world, but the London critics, led by William Hazlitt, had dismissed him as a second-rate Kean. And London audiences followed their leaders: Kean reigned supreme; Booth represented merely the latest pretender to the throne. Booth might dream of fame and fortune in his hometown, but he would never receive it. In 1818 he did not yet realize that simple fact.

He proposed joining the army in a letter to Adelaide on 2 February 1818, while she visited her relatives in Brussels.[1] On the fifteenth she replied sympathetically, insisting that, although she had married him as an actor, he need not remain one on her account. She then begged Booth to be certain he wanted to change his profession, gently suggesting he did not really prefer the simple military life and in fact avidly sought distinction. She warned him against change merely for the sake of change, pleading with him to write to her soon. If he did, the reply has disappeared. Booth remained a leading tragedian, plying the provinces with an occasional foray into London.

Booth did not appear onstage in 1818 until a single performance at St. Alban's on 11 February as Shylock earned him three pounds, eleven shillings. He had opened the Covent Garden season on 3 November 1817 but did not appear there again for slightly over a year. From March to November, Booth again toured the country towns with varying degrees of success and financial gain, usually for somewhat less than he had earned in 1817.

Almost immediately, Booth again appeared in court—but this time as the injured party, not as the precocious sly seducer of Queen Street housemaids. The case appeared in the Court of King's Bench on Wednesday, 17 June 1818, and the *Theatrical Inquisitor,* Booth's unflagging critic, cheerfully recorded the events, chronicling the high-handed ways of managers with actors.

It seems the manager of a temporary company of actors at Stamford, a Mr. T. W. Manley, wrote to Booth on 7 March, suggesting a two-night engagement the following week.

> My dear Sir,—This is our fair-time—we fill good houses without stars—better with them. Come and play Tuesday 10th, and Wednesday 11th, and share half after 10£. each night. It may be 25£. or 30£; nay more—just as they bite! And there ends our bargain. If you say *aye,* wrap it up in a letter—if *no,* adieu! 'And for my love, I pray you wrong me not.'—Shaksp.—*Iago,* Sir Giles, or Richard III.
>
> Yours,
>
> T.W. Manley.[2]

Booth agreed to this proposal, asking Manley to secure lodging for him, and arrived in Stamford to perform on the tenth. Upon arrival Booth learned Manley no longer required his services, either then or the next night. The marquis of Exeter had arrived in Stamford and demanded performances of his two favorite scripts; neither contained roles for Booth.

Booth stayed through Tuesday, ready to appear if called, then he paid his lodging bills and returned to London. He wrote Manley, requesting his travel expenses, to which Manley sneeringly replied,

> Sir—You have indulged your humour by conduct more nearly allied to absurdity than folly, and which I believe is without a parallel in the history of theatrical concerns. Acknowledged genius and admired talent may have its pardoned weaknesses, but an actor of your humble kind can have no pretence for giving himself the airs of a popular favorite: when he does, it becomes provokingly ridiculous. You came down here by stealth to play two characters, which shows your precarious tenure in London, &c. Novelty, however, was in request with us, and I thought that you would take for your trouble what I offered: it is scarcely to be believed that you refused twenty guineas for playing three nights. No; Master Booth weakly thought that we dared not to do without him. Weak little man! Now, Sir, as your actions were full of unmannerly and coarse arrogance, I think it necessary that Mr. Harris should be made acquainted with the circumstances, and as there are two excellent papers published here, I shall fairly give it to them: it will put country managers on their guard, that they may view such stars as you without winking or alarm. If you say you were a little tipsy, it may be forgotten, and that will be your best excuse, &c. After a respectable family at my request opened apartments to receive you, you left them without any remuneration. Is this the great Mr. Booth, the fearful rival of Mr. Kean?
>
> T.W.Manley.

Booth, the lawyer's son, took matters to court, where Lord Ellenborough ruled the terms of the engagement insufficiently specific, suggesting Booth should have awaited a reply from Manley before leaving London. Each party had to pay his own costs.

As for Manley's threat to tell Harris of the matter, the Covent Garden playbills for this season find Booth appearing only on the opening night, as noted. Booth was drawing a small salary from the London theatre, but he did not enter it in his account book. Nonplussed, Booth forsook the boards until 6 April 1818, when he voluntarily appeared at Wolverhampton for J. Vining's benefit, receiving no payment whatsoever, a common practice among actors of the day.

Booth did not play as often or as profitably during the summer season of 1818 as he had in 1817; he had clearly lost his drawing power from the previous year after the confrontation with Kean. For his engagement in Glasgow from 29 June to 4 July, for example, he shared the receipts after thirty pounds and received all the second-best night's receipts. Since only two performances drew over thirty pounds, he earned only the box-office income for one night, slightly more than thirty-three pounds.

Booth made similar arrangements in Edinburgh, his next engagement. There he shared seven nights' receipts after fifty pounds and took his best night clear. Of his ten performances, however, only four drew over fifty pounds, but his best night (as Hotspur) earned him over sixty-five pounds. For the rest of the engagement, Booth received under two pounds; he had badly overestimated his appeal in Scotland.

True, he played to cheering audiences, even the newspapers admitted that. But the critic for the *Edinburgh Reflector* found little in Booth to praise and much to condemn. Said he, "His acting consists of a palpable but extravagant imitation, or rather burlesque of the style of [Kean], without any of his excellencies. The appearance, gesture, tones, and most minute peculiarities of Mr. Kean are affected by this gentleman to a nauseating degree."[3]

Such treatment enraged the young actor, and his letter to the *Caledonian Mercury* on 11 July revealed both his contempt for critics and his vain attempts to quell the comparisons with Kean. Booth had imitated Kean doing certain scenes, then performed them in his own style, asking the audience to judge to what degree he was aping the older actor. His letter:

> *To the Author of the articles called "The Drama," contained in the First Numbers of the Edinburgh Reflector.*
>
> "I do despise them,
> For they do prank them in authority
> Beyond all noble sufferance."—SHAKESPEARE.
>
> It was with an intention to falsify the assertions, and *evidently* to repel the attacks of people like yourself, (who, through the medium of some publication, wish to palm themselves upon the world as Judges and Dramatic Censors,) that I *condescended*, for the first time, to give an imitation of your Leviathan. By this mode only, it was suggested to me, I should be exculpated in the public mind, and throw malevolent and ill-founded attacks on my professional attempts to the ground. In the opinion of those present, *to my own satisfaction,* I convinced them my efforts *were* original, (or *more* so than your *vile copied* trash of Hazlitt's).

> I am too proud—too impatient to descend to an imitation of any actor I have yet seen, but for the purpose of refuting *hired* calumny. My personal resemblance to the reigning actor of the present day is by me considered a curse, as it has proved a bar to me in my profession, in affording a *clue* for the hirelings of the press to *form* their attacks. . . . *I here directly avow* there is not a word of truth or judgement in your articles on theatrical criticism. It would behoove the editor or publisher of the Reflector, to chuse a writer who comprehended what he wrote about, without being biassed by a *good dinner* or *half a guinea*. . . . Wishing you may experience good for evil, . . . I remain your obedient,
>
> J. Booth[4]

In London, the *Theatrical Inquisitor* seized the opportunity to print both the reviews and Booth's letter, adding,

> not all Mr. Booth's enemies, if he is of sufficient significance to have any, could wish to add a single word to this production. If any insidious adviser, anxious to crush him for ever, had tortured his ingenuity, he could never have conceived a more effective plan for obtaining his end. We were desirous that Mr. Booth's London *supporters* should have this fresh subject for admiration.[5]

Still, managers continued to use the rivalry with Kean to draw audiences. In July 1818, for example, Booth played a week in Perth, advertised as "the only one in the profession capable of entering the list of competition with Mr. Kean." From Perth, Booth went on to Hull, where he had negotiated to receive half the receipts on the first and last nights of his engagement and to share seven nights after thirty pounds. Four nights failed to draw thirty pounds, so for those performances he received nothing. Nevertheless, for those two weeks he earned more than sixty pounds.

Three more provincial engagements followed; then on 9 November 1818 Booth appeared at Covent Garden as Gloster in Nicholas Rowe's sentimental "she-tragedy," *Jane Shore*. Macready, who played Dumont, considered the production powerfully cast—except for Booth. According to Macready, Booth's Gloster was so poorly executed and received that Covent Garden and Booth parted company, Booth being replaced by Daniel Egerton.[6] He would not return to either patent house for well over a year.

In his account book, Booth entered, "Quitted Cov. G. Theatre Nov. 14th, 1818." He added a further note in January 1819: "In the Cash Acct of 1817 or 1818 I have not included my Covent Garden Salary from Feb. 12 of the first year to Nov. 14 of the second, when the Engagement for three years was cancelled by the Proprietor paying me 182.10. The third of my Salary in advance from Nov. 14 to Feb. 26 1820." Booth had started his account book to record only his provincial income, but his circumstances had changed drastically. He had risen to minor provincial stardom then had blazed into London's attention; now he was again only a provincial star. London had put the upstart in his place.

After three performances in Whitehaven in late December, Booth calculated his 1818 income at just over £383, slightly over a third of what he had earned on the road the year before. On 11 November he recorded the receipt of 218 pounds, 10 shillings from his grandmother's will. Elizabeth Wilkes Booth's legacy no doubt helped Booth's young household, but Adelaide expected a baby in January. Booth's expenses rose, yet his income plummeted.

Booth's next round of provincial wanderings had only begun when on 21 January 1819 Adelaide bore her second child, Richard Junius, a son who would have considerable impact upon his father's life in later years. Booth was performing Macbeth at Sunderland when the child was born.

To its credit, the *Theatrical Inquisitor* reprinted favorable reviews of Booth in Sunderland, the local critic saying, "whatever quarrel you may have against him in London, we venture to say he is a very clever young man and gave in Sunderland much satisfaction to every audience he had, and in return was gratified with much applause and good houses."[7]

Seeking income further and further afield, Booth next invaded Ireland, specifically Dublin, for an engagement for a mere five pounds a week and half a benefit performance. As his income steadily decreased, he chose what became one of his most popular benefit combinations, Hamlet and Jeremy Sneak in *The Mayor of Garratt*. This time it netted him a little over sixty-six pounds, a substantial if not a stellar sum.

While Booth was in Dublin, his sister, Jane, married on 10 February 1819 one James or Jimmy Mitchell at St. George's, Hanover Square.[8] Mitchell had been a sort of flunky, or kitchen boy, for the Booth household on Queen Street.[9] Jane's father was furious, feeling Jane had married far beneath her station. They would all cross paths again, far from London.

After Dublin, Booth played an engagement in Bridgnorth that apparently so captivated the city fathers that they made him a freeman of the city, the equivalent of being given the keys to a city today.[10]

He then played Chester, during that city's annual races, then Newport before arriving for a seven-week stay in Bristol. Booth failed to record the engagement in any detail in his account book, but some startling events offstage no doubt distracted him, events that contributed richly to the growing legend of Booth's aberrations.

The Bristol Theatre Royal management had just been assumed by William M'Cready, a veteran manager and the father of William Charles Macready of Covent Garden. M'Cready, seeking to rehabilitate the Bristol Theatre, hired Booth for a month in mid-May. In early June the manager also hired Il Diavolo Antonio, a well-known performer on the slack rope. The bills described Antonio's jumping through a balloon twenty feet above the stage, all the while blowing a trumpet, or his accompanying the orchestra with the trumpet in a "select part of the OVERTURE to LODOISKA" while on the rope. Audiences swarmed to behold his artistry.

Booth and Antonio were on a collision course, although published versions vary. To begin, the following story appeared in the *Bristol Gazette* on 17 June 1819, quoted in the *Bristol Mercury* two days later.

> On Sunday evening about nine o'clock a rather novel scene took place in Queen-square: a person was shot in the face from a pistol, but whether from an assassin, or from a *Friend,* has not yet been discovered. The ball has been extracted, and the party are likely to do well. We recommend Gentlemen, who have an inclination to decide affairs of honour or dishonour, in this style to chuse less frequented places; and another day beside the Sabbath would be as well.

A week later this letter appeared in the Bristol papers:

> To the Editor of the Bristol Gazette.
> 34, Queen Square, June 19, 1819.
>
> Sir,
>
> Understanding that the unpleasant affair which lately occurred between us has occasioned some undo animadversions, and may

ultimately prove injurious to our separate interests, we owe to truth this public declaration, that whatever temporary inconvenience may have been sustained from an unpremeditated conflict, every symptom of hostility between us has been amicably extinguished, to the satisfaction and the entire approbation of our mutual friends and acquaintance.

ANTONIO
J. BOOTH

According to Kathleen Barker, on Sunday, 13 June, Booth, Antonio, and James Jones (a celebrated clown) took a country walk along Kingsdown, a nearby high ridge. With them were Mrs. Jones and Mrs. Antonio, the latter described by Booth as "a woman of unusual charms, and possessed of all the rare qualities of an Italian education." Barker suggests that Booth began to press his attentions on Antonio's wife; a quarrel arose; and a challenge was flung. A local innkeeper restored peace, and the party returned to Bristol. That evening, however, shots echoed in Queen Square.[11]

Rumor intertwines with fact at this point. Antonio may have been shot in the right eye, and his return fire supposedly brushed Booth's aristocratic nose and then lodged in a lady's handbag.

The next Tuesday, the fifteenth, bills announced Booth as Colonna in Richard Sheil's *Evadne; or, The Statue,* for M'Cready's benefit, but the curtain rose late. M'Cready addressed the audience, as quoted by the *Bristol Observer* on the seventeenth, "Mr. Booth had been at the theatre about a quarter of an hour before, but had left it, and was not then to be found: though he could not account for his absence, he felt assured that Mr. Booth would not wantonly attempt to injure him—he had been frequently engaged in his company, and always conducted himself with strict propriety."

After the letter from Booth and Antonio appeared, Booth volunteered his services as Richard III for Antonio's benefit on the twenty-fifth, received boos on his first entrance, apologized, and Bristol audiences forgot the matter.

Booth later gave his own version of the story, claiming he boarded in the same house as Antonio and his wife and discovered them quarreling violently in their rooms one evening, Antonio finally striking the woman in the face. Booth started to leave, maintaining he could not remain where "a woman could be publicly insulted with impunity." Antonio took Booth by the collar and demanded an apology. Booth returned to their apartment and sent for his dueling pistols, but a terrified servant pretended not to find them. The actor and the slack-rope dancer reconciled their differences and parted.

The next night about midnight, according to Booth, he heard screaming and discovered Antonio beating his wife in the street. Booth drew his pistol and exclaimed, "Release that woman in an instant, or you are a dead man." Antonio continued his violence, whereupon Booth shot him in the head and fled the resultant uproar. When he at length arrived at his boardinghouse, he learned that little hope remained for Antonio's recovery. Antonio, however, rallied, while Booth continued performing in the Bristol Theatre. A few nights later, as he prepared to perform in *Evadne,* word reached him of Antonio's impending death. Booth again fled, walked the twelve miles to Bath, and departed the next morning for London.

Booth next claimed he planned to leave England for Germany when a letter arrived saying Antonio had recovered completely and wished to see Booth. Armed, the actor left for Bristol, there to be met by his victim, who forgave all. Booth then played for Antonio's benefit and paid his medical expenses.

Eleven eventful years had passed since the incident by the time Booth recounted his version, and we receive it secondhand. We might do well to recall that Booth was not only an actor who specialized in melodrama but that on several documented occasions he would "guy" critics and members of the press. Perhaps his version contains some of the truth; more likely, he merely "remembered big."[12]

Nevertheless, Booth did perform in Bristol, and reviews appeared. The *Bristol Mirror* on June fifth suggested that Booth resembled Kean in almost everything but felt that, if Kean had followed rather than preceded Booth, "the former would have been considered the counterfeit resemblance." So, too, the *Bristol Journal* said, "Nature has been unkind in forming him so like Kean in figure; and Fortune doubly cruel in letting Kean appear before him!" The *Observer* stated, "His pauses are too frequent and too long, though his look and action certainly supply the vacuum, and keep the sense suspended; and he is overfond of allotting 'emphatic study' to epithets." A number of patrons saw fit to write letters to the editor; without exception they praised Booth lavishly. Given his offstage antics, Booth's popular success no doubt reduced the engagement's trauma.

And so Booth continued 1819 on the road, still fantasizing about London stardom. From Harrowgate he wrote to Robert William Elliston, who had on September eighth leased Drury Lane for fourteen years. Booth recommended to Elliston a pair of performers: Mr. and Mrs. Tyrer. Apparently Elliston considered hiring them. In Booth's 22 August letter to Elliston, he made one of his few recorded comments about his profession and its requirements.

> May the septre you hold, never prove barren!—A l'egard da Madame Tyrer you ask—is she short?—no—tall?—inching to be so—dark—with a commanding Eye—expressive face, and well moulded figure—possesses considerable Energy & a powerful voice, without ranting—If you were to write what opening you would make for her and on what conditions, she can use her reason & need not be effrayee [startled]—Either I mistake your remark, or am totally wrong in my ideas of acting, that mediocre Talent will appear to greater advantage with bad Performers than good ones. With the former, in my humble conception—the highest Talent must be depreciated—and mediocre Talent stands more in need of ability in its Supporters to keep the Ball in motion—It must be innate & great Merit that can shake off the Trammels, the injustice of neglect of the world so readily load it with—Je suis qu'un Acteur ambulant et pas un chevalier.
>
> Adieu!
>
> Yours truly
> Junius B. Booth[13]

With a new manager at Drury Lane, Booth hoped to curry favor and win a place in the patent house. Life on the road had its vicissitudes, including gun fights with Italian rope dancers, and the top of the profession remained in London. Even so, Booth had had a fairly lucrative year in the provinces. His income amounted to almost six hundred fifty pounds, a vast improvement over the preceding year, although not approaching the heady sums of 1817. Nor was the season without its ominous notes, harbingers of horrors to come. The *London Times* reported on 1 October 1819,

> Whilst Booth was acting *Brutus,* at Newcastle-under-Lyme, in the last scene he strained the jugular vein so much whilst beholding the

> death of his son, that a vast quantity of blood was thrown into his head, and produced a similar effect to apoplexy. He was falling upon the tribunal seat, when two of the company imagining he had over balanced, from relying on there being a back to it, assisted him, and by bending him forward, circulation was restored, and he awoke as from a dream. He had just strength and memory sufficient to repeat the last line of the tragedy. No ill effects have occurred from it.

The ill effects would be along later.

Booth returned to London and his family. His next engagement in the metropolis again starred him as Richard III, but not at Covent Garden, not even at Drury Lane, but at the Royal Coburg Theatre, south of the Thames, a new theatre which had opened on 11 May 1818 as a house for melodrama.[14] Located near the Cut, a seedy area off Waterloo Road, the Coburg failed to attract the gentry from the Thames' north shore, but it soon won a large and faithful audience from the working classes.

Although together Drury Lane and Covent Garden still held exclusive rights for the legitimate drama in London, various managers sought by fair means and foul to break the patent houses' domination. London's population had doubled during the eighteenth century, making it the world's largest city with one million inhabitants. Increasing population brought increasing demands for entertainment, so several nonpatent theatres obtained permission to produce shows—but only if they did no legitimate drama. Such a theatre was the Royal Coburg, licensed to John Joseph Glossop, James Jones, John Thomas Serres, and James Dunn to "exhibit entertainments of music and dancing for the public recreation."

By signing on with Glossop, Booth embroiled himself in yet another theatrical squabble. He enacted Richard III six times during the week of 27 December 1819, but then he and the Coburg management had a falling-out. After three performances, Booth signed a blank piece of paper, offering himself at any terms to the rival Surrey Theatre, complaining that he had been so ill-used by the Coburg he would never appear there again.[15] But he was bluffing; he completed the run of *Richard the Third,* then created the role of Horatius in a new melodrama, *The Horatii and Curatii,* for seven performances. Being presented in a minor theatre, neither production received newspaper notices.

Glossop then learned the patent houses planned to sue him for producing *Richard the Third,* so he wrote long, impassioned letters to the newspapers, denouncing the plans to suppress him. One such letter, comprising almost two full columns on the front page of the *Sun* for 8 January 1820, presented Glossop's views. First, he felt the public should not have to settle for whatever the theatres royal chose to offer, "however insufficient." Second, Glossop pointed out the patentees had not previously complained about the minor theatres, thus giving them "silent consent." Third, Glossop calculated those dependent on the Coburg, on the Surrey, and on Astley's theatres at no less than three thousand individuals, including their families, but not counting those hired by the other minor houses, the Olympic, Adelphi, Regency, Sadler's Wells, and East London theatres. Fourth, he cited the population of Paris at six hundred thousand, that population supporting twenty-five theatres, while London with its one and one-half million had no more than eight at any given time. Fifth, he accused Elliston, the new Drury Lane manager, of producing the same melodramatic version of *Richard the Third* while managing the Surrey Theatre.

Glossop had an ax to grind, and he honed it to a razor's edge, using his advertisements to plead his case. In the *Morning Herald* two days later, Glossop thanked the public for supporting him and Booth, accused the patent houses of trying to "crush emulation," and solicited continued public patronage. Four days later, another Glossop letter appeared, this time forswearing any hostility toward the patent houses, but arguing on the grounds of "right, justice, propriety, expediency, and practicality" that London's theatres grow in proportion to its population. Glossop even evoked Elizabethan London, claiming London had supported more theatres in 1600 than in 1820. Finally, Glossop asked the patent houses to explain why they objected to Booth's appearance when they had already rejected him.

Booth, after playing his London benefit, left for Dover for four performances then returned to the Coburg to star as Brutus in *The Judgement of Brutus; or, Tarquin and Lucretia.* His scheduled opening on Monday, 24 January, was postponed due to the death of the duke of Kent, the father of the future Queen Victoria. Booth opened the next day, Tuesday, but no reviews appeared; then on Saturday evening, 29 January 1820, England's mad monarch, George III, died, and the theatres closed for several weeks.

A king's death did not close the courts, however, and on 9 February, Glossop, accompanied by Booth, appeared at Union Hall to face charges brought against him by the patent houses. A Mr. Pollock for Covent Garden and a Mr. Turton for Drury Lane represented the prosecution; Mr. Adolphus and Mr. Dowling, the defense. After a few preliminaries, Pollock for the prosecution put forth the simple question, had or had not the law been violated?[16] The law in question demanded a fifty-pound fine for anyone producing dramas without a license from the Lord Chamberlain. The prosecution read Glossop's license into evidence, stoutly claiming that it gave him no permission to produce plays. Mr. Adolphus for the defense pointed out that the Coburg license listed four men as proprietors—Glossop, Jones, Serres, and Dunn—while only one was charged, hence the court should drop the charges. Magistrate Chambers ruled against him, and the proceedings continued.

John Doobey, a box-office assistant at Covent Garden appeared next. He stated he attended the Coburg on 29 December, witnessing *Richard the Third; or, the Battle of Bosworth-field.* Doobey then maintained that the production corresponded very closely to *Richard the Third* as performed at Covent Garden. He had taken a script with him (implying he attended the Coburg specifically to gather evidence) and marked the passages and musical interludes, stating that while the music did not always correspond to that at Covent Garden, often it did. The defense pointed out some differences between the two versions but to no avail.

Magistrate Chambers called Booth, who testified that he had applied to Glossop for an engagement there to perform in a "melodramatized" *Richard the Third.* From the transcript:

> MR. CHAMBERS: What do you mean by a performance?
> BOOTH: To recite speeches; to personate dramatic characters in a stage-dress.
> MR. CHAMBERS: Then you are not engaged as a dancer?
> BOOTH: *(with evident indignation)* No, sir, I am not engaged as a dancer.

Booth admitted he had spoken to Serres and Dunn, the other Coburg managers, about his engagement during a rehearsal the morning of the twenty-seventh. Dunn, the Coburg treasurer, referred

Booth to Glossop for his money; Glossop paid Booth with a personal check bearing only Glossop's name. Booth added that he had made a fresh engagement with Glossop to commence the following Easter. The prosecution rested.

Adolphus began the defense by noting Elliston's absence from the court, since Elliston had, while managing the Surrey Theatre, produced *Macbeth, Bold Stroke for a Wife,* and, indeed, *Richard the Third,* legitimate dramas all. Next Adolphus cited the patent houses' bills which urged the public to arrive early to obtain seats in the "overflowing" theatres. These, the lawyer added, were the parties come to annihilate Glossop and his little theatre, reminding him of Caractus' appeal to the Romans, "How can you, possessed of such splendour at home, envy me a little cottage in Britain?" Further, few patent-house managers had prosecuted the nonpatent managers since 1780; the magistrates had relaxed the severity of the statute, but now because of a public informer they must revive and enforce it.

Adolphus insisted that Glossop had used music during the play, although it was, admittedly, inaudible to most of the house. Then, after a few technical matters seemingly designed to cloud the issue, the defense rested.

Magistrate Chambers ruled that under the statute Glossop's offense was disjunctive; that the other three proprietors might be individually sued; and that the defendant was guilty as charged of causing the play *Richard the Third* to be performed without proper authority, for which he was liable to the penalty of fifty pounds.

Glossop immediately appealed to the Quarter Session, and the case finally reached resolution on 27 June 1821, the King's Bench confirming Glossop's conviction. Half the fifty-pound fine went to the informer and the other half to the poor of St. Mary Magdalen's parish. Booth escaped without a fine, although according to the statute he was equally guilty. Harris fully intended to sue Booth if his case against Glossop failed.[17]

A page is missing from Booth's account book at this point, but he next appeared in Aberdeen for eight performances in mid-March, then returned to London for the engagement at the Coburg, beginning Easter Monday, 3 April 1820. He played five nights in *The Crusaders,* a lavish spectacle based on *Jerusalem Divided,* all full of enchantresses, storms conjured up to sink sailing ships, and the conquest of the Holy City. The *London Morning Herald* reviewed the production but ignored Booth, who received eight pounds, six shillings for the week's work.

Booth then entered into his account book, "Obtained leave to play Lear at Cov. Garden on cond[iti]on of resigning salary at Coburg." Shakespeare's *King Lear* had not appeared on a London stage since 1810, nor had Nahum Tate's alteration of it, which most of the English actors would have performed.[18] George III's madness, which had led the hedonistic Prince of Wales to serve as regent since 1811, made dramatizations of insane and dying kings at best a bit indiscreet, and the Lord Chamberlain therefore forbade any production of *King Lear*. With George III dead, however, both patent houses rushed to revive the piece. Elliston at Drury Lane had Kean, but Harris eagerly sought to beat Drury Lane to the punch. He offered the role to Macready, who refused such a hastily assembled production. A Mr. Terry likewise rejected the role, after which Harris negotiated with Glossop for Booth to appear as the mad king. Booth leaped at another chance to star in a London theatre royal.

He played Lear, arguably Shakespeare's most difficult role, three times at Covent Garden for twenty pounds per performance. Significantly, he entered the role in his account book for six performances but crossed out the last three. Booth's public and critical receptions were melting away to nothingness.

Once again the *Theatrical Inquisitor* led the attack, vehemently expressing its disapproval not just of the production but of both the patent houses. The *Inquisitor* accused Elliston and Harris of seeking only power and money and of ignoring the higher values of the drama. As to *King Lear*, the *Inquisitor* told its readers, Booth was "the exploded puppet of a hundred hidden wires," now making Lear "the victim of his ignorant distortion and unshrinking audacity." Reminding its readers of the 1817 Booth-Kean controversy, the periodical insisted that, even though Kean's talents were "in direct opposition to intellectual endowment," "illiterate and unthinking," they were still superior to Booth's. Booth they condemned as a "cautious plodder, just dull enough to think upon the subject he wants faculties to investigate, and . . . hampered for power to express the notion he may properly conceive." The *Inquisitor* blamed Harris for using Booth, adding, "We profess our conviction that Mr. Harris would put a pug dog in the part of *King Lear,* if such an experiment could tend to recruit his coffers, nor do we see, essentially, that the innovation is less violent in the case of Mr. Booth."[19] Even Sally Booth, with whom Booth had had the encounter over the spelling of his name in 1817, drew critical venom: "If mediocrity be the safest condition of human nature, Miss Booth is a lucky little woman, for a more mediocre effort than her *Cordelia* it has seldom been our lot to discuss." Only one actor survived the *Inquisitor*'s diatribe; as Edmund, William Charles Macready, who would later himself star as Lear, won praise for his energy and discrimination.

The newspapers were a bit more forgiving. The *Morning Post* considered Booth's Lear "perfectly correct," noting loud calls for the star at the curtain. The *Morning Chronicle* found it a respectable effort, much like Kean would probably do it when he played the role, an opinion shared by the *Morning Herald*. The *Sun* felt Booth lacked the "dignified deportment" required to play a king, and the *Mirror of the Times* reminded its readers that the role had been first assigned to Terry, then transferred to Booth, suggesting that the lack of rehearsal time no doubt injured the effort.[20]

Booth's Lear failed, but Kean's deranged king, when he opened in the role on 24 April, drew wide acclaim. Booth had by then returned to the Coburg to star in a strange and melodramatic script titled *The Lear of Private Life,* written by one of Glossop's resident script manufacturers: William T. Moncrieff.[21] Booth had no more regard for Moncrieff than he did for Glossop. In an undated letter to Montague Chambers, an aspiring playwright, Booth referred to "the perverseness of Glo——p & chicanery of M—ri—eff" then referred to Glossop as "Monsr. Girouette" (French for weather vane).[22]

Booth's account book becomes suspiciously incomplete at this point, but he recorded his opening at the Coburg in *The Horatii and Curatii* on the twenty-fourth. Extant bills indicate he appeared in *The Lear of Private Life* 24–29 April and 1–10 May, then he played two weeks of Horatius and Fitzarden and *The Lear of Private Life,* all for a relatively trifling ten pounds a week.[23]

In 1820 Booth started another diary, now lost.[24] In it he noted, "A pistol fired at me in Oakley Street, Thursday night, May 11th, 1820." Booth appended no other comment. Evidence does indicate that Booth had moved into the Lambeth area, which included Oakley

Street, and had taken up residence at 10 Pratt Street, south of the Thames.[25] But who shot at him and why we have no idea.

Booth soon left London for another tour. In June he appeared at Norwich, in July at Rochester and Maidstone, then two pages are sliced out of his account book. He resumed the account on 25 July in Cheltenham, beginning a provincial tour that continued till mid-August 1820 with disappointing receipts.

He then appeared in the theatre seemingly least likely to engage him, Drury Lane. Elliston had his reasons for hiring Booth; Kean was planning a series of farewell performances before his first American tour. On 14 August Elliston offered Booth £140 plus a benefit to perform supporting roles for Kean.[26] To sweeten the offer, Elliston also offered Booth a year's engagement for 1820–21 at twelve pounds a week, with Booth to appear at the Olympic Theatre as well as at Drury Lane. Booth would perform roles as directed by Elliston at the patent house but could play his principal characters at the Olympic.

Elliston rightly feared a season without his star, Edmund Kean, so he made two expedient moves: first, he squeezed every possible pound and pence out of Kean's farewell engagement, and second, he hired Booth and other actors to bolster his company for the season ahead. In addition to Booth, the manager would star John Cooper, making his London debut, and James William Wallack, returning to Drury Lane after a three-year absence.[27]

Booth eagerly seized the opportunity; with Kean out of the country, he might yet win stardom in the English theatre. He fulfilled the engagement Elliston had proposed. The manager cleared some two thousand pounds during Kean's farewell performances, while Booth received four to six pounds for most of his performances. For his part, Kean, before leaving for the American el dorado, presented Drury Lane with a plaster bust of himself, which Elliston enshrined in the greenroom.[28]

The newspapers naturally concentrated on Kean, dismissing Booth with a few comments. Booth's Pierre in *Venice Preserved,* for example, the *Sun* considered too boisterous and violent in expression, commenting that, if a person had bawled out treason in the streets of Venice as Booth had done, the conspiracy would have been discovered and stopped by the second act. When Booth finished his eight performances at Drury Lane, he took once more to the provinces—Reading, Surrey, Weymouth, Plymouth, and Dock—before the fall season at Drury Lane opened.

Booth's Drury Lane engagement, which he and Elliston terminated on 15 January 1821, was a disaster. London audiences now longed for the absent Kean, and Wallack, Cooper, and Booth combined could not draw as well as the absent star. Elliston tried everything, but when Booth as Lear on 17 November drew a paltry fifty-seven pounds, the end drew near.

Cooper won favorable if not rave reviews with his Othello, but Booth's Iago was not even mentioned. A few days later, when Booth performed Lear, the *Morning Chronicle* suggested London had seen enough of the play for the time being, Kean having played it for twenty-six performances. The critic found Booth "positively clever, and effective, without the merit of originality or great depth of manner . . . unquestionably an imitator of Kean." The *Mirror of the Times* thought he had improved somewhat since his underrehearsed previous version but still found him lacking in royal dignity. Booth's first appearance as Lear brought barely respectable box-office receipts of £126, his second attracted slightly over fifty pounds; he played no third performance.

Elliston next revived "Monk" Lewis' *Adelgitha* to indifferent critical comment and slackening houses. He had slightly better luck with *Pizarro* with Wallack as Rolla and Booth in the title role. The papers accused Booth of merely walking through his part, and for the second presentation Booth appeared as Orezembo the Peruvian. He continued in that role for the remainder of his engagement.

Elliston still hoped Shakespearean productions would attract crowds to Drury Lane and so produced *Julius Caesar* with Booth as the lean and hungry Cassius, Wallack as Brutus (originally Booth's role), and Cooper as Antony. The *Sun* accused Booth of overacting, of "out-Heroding Herod," and the tragedy closed after only two performances. Elliston desperately brought forth *Pocohontas; or, The Indian Princess,* with Booth as Opechan, performed, according to the *Morning Chronicle,* with "ample justice." Cooper played Captain John Smith. One wonders just how Englishmen in 1820 staged a show about American Indians—*Pocohontas* enjoyed a brief run.

But without their star, Drury Lane's season careened steadily downhill. An anonymous critic for the newspaper *John Bull* laid waste to Drury Lane and all concerned on New Year's Eve, asserting,

> the coolness with which they act tragedies, without one tolerable player, is perfectly comical. What an idea of a London audience Mr. Elliston must have, now that he is not in the habit of seeing them, to suppose that they could endure Pizarro as acted last week. . . . Mr. Cooper, transformed by the classical air of Liverpool, from an underling at the Haymarket, to the hero of poor old Drury; and Mr. Wallack, who has lost, by his association with American vulgarity, all he had gained before he left England, are, in themselves, repellents strong enough to keep away the least fastidious audience in the world. And when to these is super-added Mr. Marc Antony Tiberius Caesar Booth, who can wonder that there are seldom half a hundred persons in the theatre.
>
> Mr. Booth, who is endowed with all Mr. Kean's faults and deformities, without one redeeming quality, is (always excepting Elliston himself), the most illustrious specimen of the ridiculous in Tragedy now living. . . . Were he sewed up in a skin to act a Hog in a pantomime, he would act a Hog with six legs better than a hog with four.[29]

Bad times had come to Drury Lane, and worse lay ahead, but Elliston had one more script to try before he abandoned drama for opera. On 8 January 1821 he opened John A. Court's *Montaldo,* something of a travesty of *Othello*, in which Booth played Durazzo, an Iago-like character. The critics roasted it, and after four performances *Montaldo* disappeared.

So did Booth. In his account book, after the payment of twelve pounds for the week of 13 January, he appended, "Closed with Elliston by Agreemt. on above Date." He had finally achieved a second starring engagement at Drury Lane, but London theatregoers still had no interest in him. On the same page, Booth wrote, "Engt. pending with Glossop from Easter Monday till 'I don't know when' nor does he." And at the bottom of the page is written, "Penalty £200," implying Booth had to settle with Elliston to obtain his release from old Drury. As Booth's London career lay in shambles, so, too, did his marriage.

Booth's account book contains a marginal note for 9 October 1820, a night he played Lear in Reading. Someone other than Booth marked the date with an *X* and inserted, "The night Mother first saw my father." This note refers not to Adelaide Delannoy Booth but to Mary Ann Holmes, a flower girl working like Shaw's Eliza Doolittle around Covent Garden.[30] She was young, beautiful, even voluptuous, and, best of all, she was not Adelaide.

Mary Ann Holmes' exact genealogy remains shadowy, as do accounts of her background and introduction to Booth.[31] Some substantial information comes from the diary of James Winston, appointed by Elliston to hire actors and negotiate salaries and conditions of employment at Drury Lane. Winston worked in this capacity during Booth's 1820–21 engagement there. On 17 February 1821 Winston entered, "It appears that shortly after Booth got leave of absence from Drury Lane a few weeks ago he set off for America with [a] shopkeeper's daughter in the night-time." And on 14 March Winston's entry bristles with clues.

> A Mrs. Holmes called to ask if I could direct her where to find Booth. She said her husband, Mr. Holmes, who keeps a seed shop [in] Bridge Road, Marsh Gate, [died] of a broken heart, his daughter having eloped with Booth about seven weeks ago; [she said] that they found in her room ninety-three letters from Booth and a dark lantern. His [Booth's] father has since called on Mrs. Holmes and wished her sanction to let her daughter live with Booth. The father said Booth's wife had left the country, and she was allowed £50 a year.[32]

The address—Bridge Road, Marsh Gate—matches an entry in *Johnstone's London Commercial Guide and Street Directory* for 1817 for a Robert Holmes, corn chandler and seedsman, at 7 Mount Street, Lambeth. And John Lockie in his *Topography of London* (1810) situates Mount Street in Bridge Road, Lambeth, not far from Pratt Street and Booth's new residence.[33] Genealogical records for the Holmes family of Lambeth reveal an entry for Mary Ann Holmes, christened 29 August 1802, the daughter of Robert and Sarah Holmes, Lambeth, in the parish of St. Mary.

If Mary Ann had left London with Booth "about seven weeks ago," as Winston maintained, they would have departed around the first of the year, at which time Booth was still appearing at Drury Lane. As for the ninety-three letters (long since disappeared), if Booth in fact met Mary Ann in Reading on 9 October 1820 and ran away with her on the next New Year's Day, he would have written the ninety-three letters in eighty-three days. Young men in love, even young married men, have done far stranger things in pursuit of ladies, still. . . .

And the account book interpolation of their meeting in Reading remains problematic, Reading being thirty-six miles from Covent Garden, where she was selling flowers. Further, Winston's statement that the ninety-three letters were found "in her room" implied Mary Ann lived with her parents in Lambeth. Given the Winston evidence, perhaps Mary Ann did indeed meet Booth just after he had played Lear, but it is more likely that they met during his three unsuccessful performances at Covent Garden the preceding April. Or, perhaps Mary Ann had seen the April Lear but did not meet Booth until October in Reading, but why she would have been in that city is anyone's guess.[34]

Booth's settlement with Adelaide of fifty pounds a year became much later a matter of legal contention, but he appears to have paid her that sum annually for almost the rest of his life.

Asia Booth Clarke maintained that Booth married Mary Ann Holmes on 18 January 1821 at the residence of the Honorable Mrs. Chambers, the woman who had encouraged Booth in his early career. Later developments cast considerable doubt on this "marriage," which could not have been a legal union anyway; by then English law demanded weddings be held in churches. Asia and the other American Booths understandably clung to the myth.

Asia further asserted that the couple briefly visited Bologne-sur-Mer and Calais, then returned to England, when Booth decided to tour the West Indies professionally. They sailed from Deal, a seaport near Dover, where Booth bought a piebald pony named Peacock. The ship stopped at the Island of Madeira, where, Asia claimed, the island's beauty so charmed the young couple they remained there for several weeks. Booth rejected offers to perform in Madeira, and he and Mary Ann, with Peacock, booked passage on a schooner, *The Two Brothers,* for North America. For the next forty-four days the young lovers crossed the Atlantic: Mary Ann was two months pregnant.

4

An Object of Interest

Happy star reign now!

—*The Winter's Tale,* I, ii, 363

Doubtless Booth thought he was leaving most of his problems behind when he sailed from England to North America. He had no more idea of what lay ahead than he had the first time he left home, but he had youth, talent, some money, a woman who loved him, and a pretty good horse—assets vastly superior to what most immigrants imported. The New World offered the young actor a new start, far from Adelaide, Kean's Wolves, managerial wranglings, and the slings and arrows of London critics.

Many English had made the trip before him; the new nation offered people seemingly infinite space and opportunity, although not all immigrants were pleased with what they found. Booth left an England with twelve million citizens crammed into slightly over fifty thousand square miles. On 30 June 1821 he and Mary Ann stepped ashore at Norfolk, Virginia, and into a twenty-three-state nation with a population two million fewer than England's but with fifteen times the land area. No insane king or dissolute regent ruled here; presidents were elected by white male citizens. The United States was forging itself; the people were determining their national character; and Booth would contribute his own small influence.

Newspapers announced the arrival on 2 July 1821 of "Mr. Junius Brutus Booth, of the Covent Garden and Drury Lane Theatres, and lady." Booth immediately set about securing an engagement in Richmond, hoping to begin his American career by opening on the "glorious Fourth" of July, an idea from which the Richmond manager dissuaded him.[1]

A correspondent to the *Petersburg Express* recalled meeting Booth at Osbornes, a small village on the south side of the James River, fifteen miles from Richmond. He discovered an immense stack of luggage on the veranda of the local hotel, each case labeled "J. B. Booth," of whom the reporter had never heard. He soon met Booth at dinner, finding him intellectual, free and affable in manner, and "of a very convivial disposition."[2]

For the next few weeks, Booth remained at the hotel in Osbornes without revealing his profession. The *Express* reporter then discovered a Richmond playbill announcing Booth as Sir Edward Mortimer in *The Iron Chest,* "his first appearance in America," and confronted the young actor. Booth complacently admitted his identity and invited the reporter to see his performance in Richmond.[3] The reporter accepted and recorded the "manifestations of approval" won by Booth as Sir Edward Mortimer and Richard III.

While Booth rusticated at Osbornes, he heard the landlord asking an assistant to secure a new lodger's boots, which the guest in question would not surrender. When Booth asked the proprietor why he so anxiously sought this footwear, the owner explained that he could thus prevent boarders from sneaking away without paying their bills. The next morning the lodger proved to be Thomas Abthorpe Cooper, a distinguished tragedian from England who had moved to the United States in 1796.[4] The two expatriates struck up a friendship which continued until Cooper's death in 1849.

Booth stayed at Osbornes while acting in Richmond and at the Bollingbrook Street Theatre in Petersburg, continuing to record his engagements and terms in his account book. He alternated engagements in those two cities until 24 September. Mary Ann, however, remained at the hotel.

Noah Ludlow, later an important manager, then a young actor, met Booth during these early engagements and later recorded his impressions in his autobiography.[5] Like many of Booth's biographers, he eventually referred to the English actor as "*the* Booth."

Booth applied to Charles Gilfert, the Richmond theatre manager, but failed to produce any letters of introduction. The crafty Gilfert, wondering if the man before him was in fact Booth and not some clever imposter, hired him for one night with a conditional extension of the engagement. That was all Booth needed.

Ludlow was then appearing at Petersburg under the management of Richard Russell. Russell, hearing of Booth in Richmond, went to that city, hired him for a one-night performance of Richard III, then for a longer engagement later. The company assembled at 10:00 A.M., the usual hour for rehearsal, but Booth failed to appear. Russell rehearsed the scenes not requiring Booth, who arrived after the cast had reached the fourth act. Ludlow described the ensuing events:

> a small man that I took to be a well-grown boy of about sixteen . . . came running up the stairs, wearing a round-about jacket, and a cheap straw-hat, both covered with dust, and inquired for the stage manager. I pointed across the stage to Mr. Russell, who . . . hurried towards us, and cordially grasping the hand of the strange man, said: "Ah! Mr. Booth; I am glad you arrived; we were fearful something serious had happened to you." I do not think any man was ever more astonished than I was just then in beholding this meeting. Is it possible this can be the great Mr. Booth, that Mr. Russell says is "undoubtedly the best actor living?" and I began to think Russell was trying to put off some joke upon us all. I observed, however, that when the small man came upon the stage to rehearse his scenes, he was quite "at home," and showed a knowledge of the business of the character that a mere novice or pretender could not have acquired. He ran through the rehearsal very carelessly, gave very few special or peculiar directions, tried the combat of the last act over twice, and said, "That will do," and the rehearsal was over. He then told Mr. Russell that he had been a few minutes too late for the stage-coach that left Richmond early in the morning, and that he soon after started on foot, and had walked all the way,—*twenty-five miles;* that his wardrobe had been sent to the stage-office before he was up; had been taken by the coach, and he supposed was ready in the city for the proper claimant.[6]

Ludlow, unimpressed, waited for the evening performance. Booth, he said, strolled upon the stage, ignored the applause, and delivered the "Now is the winter of our discontent" soliloquy in the manner of a schoolboy reciting a lesson, seemingly heedless of the words' meaning. The audience did not applaud his exit.

W. H. Benton, an old actor playing King Henry that evening, asked, "What do you think of him, Mr. Ludlow?"

"Think," Ludlow replied, "why I think, as I thought before, that he is an imposter! What do *you* think of him?"

"Why, sir," said Benton, "if the remainder of his Richard should prove like the beginning, I have never yet, I suppose, seen the character played, for it is unlike any I ever saw; it may be very good, but I don't fancy it."

The rest of the company quickly agreed; only Richard Russell persisted in proclaiming Booth the greatest actor he had ever seen. Ludlow also despised Booth's scene with Lady Anne, calling it "tame and pointless," recalling the stunning effects George Frederick Cooke had achieved in the same scene.[7]

Not till the fourth act did Booth unleash his full powers as he hinted at the murder of the young princes. Ludlow called Booth's acting from that point on "unique and wonderful," triggering a burst of applause at the curtain, both from the audience and from the rest of the cast, more applause than Petersburg had ever heard. After he became a manager, Ludlow frequently hired Booth and often wondered why the actor always walked through the first two acts of *Richard the Third* with such indifference. He assumed Booth sought to save his energies, psychic and physical, for the more demanding last three acts.

The local newspaper, the *Richmond Enquirer,* also compared Booth to the late Cooke, saying: "Gentlemen who have seen Cooke in this part, do not hesitate to pronounce Booth superior to *him*, and others, who have lately seen Kean in the same character, aver that, in some scenes, he is equal, and in others, the most trying of the play, superior to that celebrated actor."[8] Kean had just triumphed in America, and Booth, still smarting from his second-rate reputation in England, doubtless savored these comparisons.

The actor had finally found his audience. When Booth returned to Petersburg, Ludlow played Wilford to his Sir Edward Mortimer in *The Iron Chest,* including a scene in which Mortimer discloses a guilty secret involving an earlier murder. Ludlow recalled that Booth's passions were

> so terrifically wrought up and so magnificently portrayed that I was brought to a "stand-still" upon the stage, in wonderment at the man's great tragic powers, and only recovered my self-possession when Mr. Booth said, in an undertone, "Go on, go on!" I never had such an effect produced on me by any other person's acting, in the whole course of my dramatic career. Mr. Booth had at that time the finest stage-face I ever met with . . . and his eyes, of which he made great use in acting, were brilliant and expressive,—as *Hamlet* says, "an eye like Mars, to threaten and command."[9]

Booth had finally won critical and popular success, but, more to the point, he earned over twelve hundred dollars for sixteen performances in Richmond and Petersburg. Booth found this New World much to his liking.

He played New York City next, then a community of under one hundred twenty-five thousand. A prestigious new theatre, the Park, had just opened, replacing an earlier house of the same name, which had burned the year before. Booth arrived in New York 2 October 1821, and the Park's manager, Edmund Simpson, immediately engaged him to open on the fifth as Richard III.

New York's reactions to Booth's opening night exceeded all expectations: audiences cheered him long and lustily, and the newspapers heaped praise upon him. Again, Booth's tent scene drew cheers and provoked bursts of applause from the house. The critic for the *National Advocate* found the closing death scene especially laudable.

> The desperate valor, the haggard look, the madning [*sic*] thrusts, the rage and fury with which he rushed upon Richmond, whom he attempted to bring to the ground, after receiving his deadly wound; and finally the Satanic smile which played upon his lips when in the last agonies of death, must be witnessed to be felt and understood. The effect produced was such as to exact loud and continued applause from a numerous and respectable audience; indicative of the high opinion which they entertained of the talents of this eminent performer.[10]

The *Advocate* critic, "Thespis," claimed to have seen Booth in Brussels and in London. He found many points of difference between Booth and Kean, especially in the tent scene and the closing fight with Richmond.

Booth, acting for ninety dollars a night, attracted gross receipts for seven performances of $5,523; Simpson rejoiced in his new star. Kean, the previous year, however, had acted with the Park company for fifty pounds sterling for seven nights, then half a clear benefit, an engagement he repeated. George C. D. Odell estimated that Kean in Philadelphia, Pennsylvania, received a total of £1,354 for fourteen nights, an average of almost one hundred pounds a night.[11] At that time, no actor had drawn so well in America, nor, in fact, would Booth.

To close the engagement Booth chose his favorite benefit roles, Hamlet and Jeremy Sneak. A reviewer from the *New York Post* recounted the delighted audience calling him forth for a curtain call. The reviewer described Booth as overwhelmed with gratitude, not knowing how to express his feelings for this unexpected honor but swearing never to forget the audience's kindness to him.[12]

Booth had not spent those years in the English countryside for nothing; he knew how to work an audience.

He next opened on 1 November 1821 in Baltimore, Maryland, a city with which he will forever be associated. Six performances earned him slightly over four hundred dollars, more than half of it coming from his benefit on 7 November. William Wood, the manager, later described his new star's subsequent career.

> The violent enthusiasm of a part of the audience on his first night led to great expectation of future success, but it was never realized. This excellent actor suffered the misfortune to be overvalued by some persons, and undervalued by others. He was seldom justly appreciated. An attempt to elevate him above Kean, and to claim for him the *originality* of a peculiar style of acting practised by both, could not fail to create a prejudice against him, and he suffered from it afterwards in every part of the Union. . . . I must say that with all his follies and attempts at singularity, this really fine actor was an object of interest to all who can appreciate genius and study.[13]

Whatever the case, Booth went south for the winter, playing Norfolk, Virginia; Charleston, South Carolina; New Orleans, Louisiana; and Savannah and Augusta, Georgia, over the next few months.[14]

In his memorandum book, Booth recorded his departure from Charleston on 15 December, noting he took twenty-two days to get to New Orleans, arriving there on 6 January 1822.[15] The memorandum book contains only sporadic entries, beginning on New Year's Day, when Booth inserted, "Reached the Bier and X'd it on Mississippi River." For the next three days, he entered only a single word, "Warping," suggesting he drank to pass the time. In those early days, he could still do so with few ill effects.

Arriving in New Orleans, a city soon to become a favorite of his, Booth helped to celebrate the seventh anniversary of the Battle of New Orleans and noted that the next day the city first began to pave its streets. During his engagement he visited the battleground, five miles from the city.

Of more importance, on 23 January Booth entered in his memorandum book, "Received news of Mary Ann's delivery by a Letter . . . from a gent. in Charleston." They named the infant Junius Brutus Booth, Jr.[16]

Once again, the ubiquitous Noah Ludlow, who had seen Booth in Petersburg, appeared. Ludlow had followed manager James H. Caldwell to New Orleans for the season and thus witnessed Booth's debut as Richard III in the Crescent City.[17] The company grew apprehensive; they knew the New Orleans theatregoers to be quick and impulsive in their reactions. Ludlow sneaked out front to see Booth's first scenes, the same ones he had thrown away in Petersburg.

After Booth had plodded through his opening scenes, a few audience members approached Ludlow, demanding, "Mr. Ludlow, what does all this mean? Who is this man? Does Mr. Caldwell imagine he can palm off . . . this fellow as a great actor?"

Ludlow responded, "Gentlemen, be patient; when the tragedy is ended, if you do not pronounce him the greatest actor you have *ever seen,* I will give you leave to rail at me as well as him, to your heart's content."

"Well," replied one, "if what you say prove to be the case, I'll give up my judgement on acting hereafter, and forever hold my peace."

By the opening of the third act, some of the audience hissed Booth, to Ludlow's horror, but by the death scene Booth had again quite conquered the audience. The hissers rose, applauded with all their might, and roared out "Bravo!" Ludlow recorded Booth's premiere as a perfect triumph over first prejudice and a great success.[18]

Many French citizens in New Orleans had attended Booth's first performances, although few of them understood English. During the second week, a French deputation called on Caldwell, asking him to feature Booth in some tragedy more familiar to them, although they much admired Booth's Sir Giles Overreach and Sir Edward Mortimer. Booth informed the gentlemen that he could perform Orestes in *The Distrest Mother* by Ambrose Philips, an English version of Jean Racine's *Andromaque,* and that he would be most pleased to perform it for a French audience. Since Caldwell's company performed only four times a week, the French emissaries and Booth settled on a night for his Orestes during his third week.[19] Ludlow acted the part of Orestes' companion, Pylades.

The capacity audience understood little of the English version but knew the plot from Racine's version. Booth received immense applause throughout the performance, and upon his death scene in Pylades' arms at the end of the play, Ludlow recalled the audience rising to their feet, crying out "Brava! Brava!" and "Talma, Talma, Talma!" For the French to liken Booth to Françoise Joseph Talma was high praise indeed; Talma, a friend of Napoleon's, is still considered the greatest of all French actors. As for Ludlow, he felt he had never seen such a splendid effort of tragic effect, even surpassing Booth's Mortimer in Petersburg.

Booth thus progressed rapidly in both his old profession and his new country. But again he contemplated leaving the stage for another vocation. Perhaps the birth of his first child by Mary Ann suggested the need for a more stable career and relative seclusion. Possibly he had simply begun to outgrow the theatre, that particular honeymoon being over. He decided he would forsake fame and money for a quieter and more contemplative life.

He revealed his thinking in notes he made 12 February 1822 as he traveled.

> Spoke to Mr. Blunt, one of the passengers, about Cape Hatteras Light House. He turned out to be a collector of customs. He offered it to me with the dwelling house, and twenty acres of land attached with a salary of $300 per annum for keeping the light. Government providing oil and cotton. Grapes, watermelon, cabbages, potatoes, carrots and onions grow in abundance there. Rain water is the only drink, and a cistern is on the premises for that purpose. Firewood is

> generally procured from the pieces of wreck found on the shoals. The proprietor of the woods, half a mile off, only allowing the branches to be lopped off the trees, which must be done without injury to the trunk. Mr. Blunt to write me word if the office can be given me next April, from his seat at Washington, N.C. The office is for life and will only be taken away through [unclear]. Abundance of fish, wild fowl, and pigs, sheep, horses and cows find good pasture. . . . Flour bought for $5, sometimes $4 a barrel. House thirty feet from the light, which is seventy-five feet high, and requires trimming every night at 12. By digging ten or twelve feet, well water may be had. No taxes whatever. One dollar per day is the charge per man for board in cases of wreck.

There follow six heavily crossed out lines, then Booth apparently wondered if Mary Ann would leave "the social world with me for this desert place, thought I? Will she not pine, at losing those amusements which present themselves in so many shapes, in populous towns, and be reconciled to live alone with Junius? No, I cannot expect it of her."[20]

Rural life strongly attracted Booth; in the same diary he noted that public lands cost only two dollars an acre, payable over four years, or $1.64 an acre, cash, and he included a list of eastern land offices. He also recorded what he had learned of planting practices in this new land, for example: "Rule for Virginia planting: Indian corn should be planted early in April in rows four feet apart—the seed along each row being eight inches asunder on sandy loam—three grains in each hole about two inches deep, with a small piece of cob for the ants to work on and so save the seed from attack, are sufficient." Booth also studied the Southern dialect, recording several local mutilations of the King's English, such as "had not ought"; "Kyow, for cow"; "This here and that there"; "Toat them there things along"; "Hominy for hasty pudding"; and "Engine is sounded en-*gine*."

Booth would find his rustic retreat, but not quite yet. Legend has it that theatrical managers lured him back to the stage with large sums of money; perhaps Booth sought to accumulate enough cash to settle his new family in something more comfortable than a lighthouse. At any rate, he went to Charleston, a journey of nineteen days, for which he collected sixty-two dollars from Gilfert for travel expenses. His notes also include receiving $680 from Gilfert during the engagement.

Booth recorded various financial transactions in his memorandum book, some of which were for considerable sums. On 4 March 1822, for example, he entered, "Sent two 6p. Receipts to Crawford in Washington for 1260 [pounds]," and on the seventeenth he sent $110 to "R.B." (surely Richard Booth). Booth was receiving $90 to $120 per night for his performances at this point in his American career.

After Charleston, Booth played engagements in Savannah and Augusta, then sailed for Boston, Massachusetts, on the fourteenth of April, arriving in Newport, Rhode Island, on the twenty-sixth and Boston the next day. He bought forty-three dollars' worth of clothes from Whitson and Taylor there out of the apparent $680 he had earned from his benefit on the twentieth. Booth was always a favorite of the sophisticated Boston audiences. Two days later he opened in Providence, Rhode Island, for a week and a half, taking his benefit on the third of May.

On 5 May he sailed for Norfolk, arriving on the thirteenth at 5:00 P.M., after which he took "bilious fever" and was sick for five days. On the twenty-second he managed to get to Osbornes but remained ill for four more days, till 29 May. During July he wrote letters to his father and also obtained a judgment against Gilfert for $1,005 plus costs, presumably for nonpayment. On 25 July he left Osbornes for Richmond, then to Washington, D.C., to open on the first of August 1822—the first time a Booth appeared in Washington, though not the last. The sole surviving review, from the *Daily National Intelligencer* for 13 August, sharply contrasted with London receptions.

> The predominant excellence of Mr. Booth's acting is chasteness; for, though he possesses ample powers for the display of the stormy passions, he never introduces them out of place; he uses no trick to catch applause, never descends to the rant and mouthing, or even the strut, which always distinguish the inferior tragedian; but seems to remember that kings and heroes can walk and talk like other people. . . . He has the rare art to conceal all art.

Booth left Washington almost immediately after his closing performance, having sent for his trunks from Osbornes. He then took a room at Knight's Tavern, eleven miles north of Baltimore, which was at that time gripped in a yellow fever epidemic.[21]

Booth now had a family—indeed, he had two—but he needed a home, a base from which to tour. On 19 August 1822 he made a down payment of $265.50, one-third of the purchase price, on 150 acres of land three miles from the town of Bel Air in Harford County, Maryland. He bought the property on time; his memorandum book contains an entry reading, "five dollars an Acre—1st pay one third in cash, second in twelve months & the last in two years." Booth did not record exactly how he chose Harford County, but he had been in Baltimore the previous November and doubtless looked up his father's cousin John Brevitt. Brevitt had married a Harford County girl in 1784 and thus knew the area.[22]

In Harford County, Booth dealt with Elijah B. Rogers, who had a "tenant," or log house, for rent. According to Rogers' wife, Booth completed an engagement in Baltimore, after which he rented the log house on the Rogers' farm. Booth then made the down payment to William Hall, a physician, for the 150-acre farm next to the Rogers'. Since the land was unimproved, Booth bought the Rogers' log house, hired men, horses, and oxen, and moved it across the intervening fields on rollers. This practice startled the local citizens, who had never seen a house moved without first being dismantled.

Wrote Mrs. Rogers about her new neighbors:

> Mr. Booth was a gentleman in every sense of the word. And Mrs. Booth was a lady also. They did not visit but a few of the neighbours, but was very kind and generous, and every body loved them. When they came or moved up to our farm they brought three very large dogs as protectors, . . . Bosen [Boatswain], Florah, [and] Carlow. They were kept chained in daytime, let loose at night. They were very savage dogs. They brought a beautiful little horse, Peka [Peacock] by name. His color was in blocks, white squares, with bright bay squares, which Mr. Booth rode back and forth to Baltimore. He was small. Every horse was scared that met with him.[23]

Mrs. Rogers' account indicated Booth sought solitude, both to have peace from theatrical maelstroms and to isolate Mary Ann and their growing family. As for Booth's new estate, Asia Booth Clarke later described her childhood home as 150 acres of dense woods, adjoining a great forest on one side. A crooked lane wound from the Bel Air Road to the Booth log house, which stood in a clearing surrounded by huge oaks, sycamores, and poplars. Booth's daughter then rhapsodized about the area,

> The forest scenery is romantic and beautiful. There are huge rocks with tiny cascades; streams and springs of delightful water gushing out in the most remote places. Natural bowers of flowering vines, and groves of tall interlacing trees, wild flowers of every shape and hue, from the simple field-violet to the spotted lily and scarlet lobelia of the marsh. Long copses of hazel-bushes and old English hips and haws, and nuts of various kinds abound. Away off in the great forest, where the light seldom penetrates, is the "Dismal Swamp," covered with gorgeous lilies and bright grasses, and here on the smooth sward are those magical fairy rings, on which no grass ever grows. Here, too, is the old well-trodden foot-path of the Algonquin Indian; and, winding far away through the dark, still woods, the ground is strewn with the memorials of these lovers of warfare and the chase. Arrowheads of every dimension, axe-heads and tomahawks and curiously cut stones are thickly buried in the marshy ground, as if for all time these solemn woods should keep their memory. Here in these wild forests my father made his home, far removed from the turmoil of city life, and surrounded by his growing family and faithful servants, among whom he labored with the zeal of an anxious farmer.[24]

Booth also added granite ledges and steps to a natural spring under some thick trees on his new property. In this spring lived an immense green bullfrog who totally charmed the Booth children; they imagined him to be one hundred years old. Near the spring Booth erected a dairy. He also laid out an orchard and had a barn and stables built, as well as a cider press. Separate quarters housed the black hired hands, whom he needed to help make his new farm productive.

Although Booth detested slavery, his children recalled later that he bought a female slave after he gave up hope of hiring an obedient servant. The slave threatened to beat Mary Ann's brains out with a fence rail three days after her purchase, so Booth freed and dismissed her.[25] He replaced this woman with a black woman named Hagar, whom he leased for ten years. After three years, Hagar asked for her release, which Booth gave to her when she promised to return to her owner, Judge Bond of Harford County. Hagar promptly disappeared, leaving Booth to pay for her. Eventually, he hired Joe Booth (or Hall, his former owner's name).[26] Hall remained Booth's employee for many years; Mrs. Rogers referred to him as "a faithful old creature" who married Ann Hall, the slave of Rowland Rogers, Mrs. Rogers' father-in-law. Later Booth hired Henry, a black man, and George Brown, the latter to look after the horses and to serve as a companion to young Junius.

Mrs. Rogers understood that Booth and Mary Ann had married on 18 January 1821 at the residence of the Honorable Mrs. Chambers in London; the Booths no doubt supplied that information. Mrs. Rogers also knew, at least in 1886, of Adelaide, whom she referred to as "a French lady" who "was not pretty," and mentioned their son, Richard. Mary Ann she considered "the hansomest [*sic*] woman I ever saw . . . and a good loving wife." None of the deeds or leases, however, referred to Mary Ann as Mrs. Booth. Booth would travel many miles and many years before that matter would reach resolution.

Booth's memorandum book for this period contains several puzzling items. One expects him to have sent money to his father, as he did, but he also included such items as, "Sent per ship Mary, to Rotterdam a Bill for 137 guilders & 10 styvans," on 10 September 1822. On 9 October, "Sent 2d of Exchange on Rottdm by ship Arcthusa—to B=x=lls [Brussels] on Packwines Donepaal & Co." And on a half sheet in December, "Send to Br + s—'Frailty, thy name is Woman'." Later he mused, "Wickedness is a social malady. Man is good when he is alone." Something, as usual, was troubling Booth. On the last page of entries he had written, "1174 Rue des Fripiers a Bruxelles," the address of the milliner's house from whence he had taken Adelaide to London, a hasty marriage, and two children. Booth was sending money back to Adelaide, having settled a separate maintenance; the full details would surface some decades later.

In the meantime, Booth combined acting and farming; his notes describe his agriculture far more than his performances. He visited the farm at Bel Air on 12 September 1822 and on the twenty-first hired a Richard Boneramp to work there for nine dollars a month and board. Booth also contracted with the Baltimore manager, William Warren, for an engagement to begin the thirtieth, but he had to wait until the visiting star, Charles Mathews, completed his successful engagement.[27]

On October first his goods arrived from Osbornes via Richmond; three days later he sowed two acres of rye. He stayed at Knight's Tavern, recording regular payments there of from ten to twenty dollars. On October first he began an engagement in Baltimore and later in the month sent a thousand feet of pine planks to Bel Air for improvements to the log house.

Professionally, Booth was prospering. A Baltimore paper during this engagement praised him unstintingly, calling him "one of the finest actors in the world—chaste, natural, and full of deep passion." His Lear they considered unrivaled, the equal of Kean's Othello and Cooper's Virginius, high praise indeed. The critic "X.Z." added, "For noble tenderness and melancholy, Mr. Booth has the best face that we know of."[28]

On 29 October 1822 Booth entered into his memorandum book: "Mr. R. Booth came to Balto by steamboat from Philada." The actor's father, the long-widowed Richard Booth of Bloomsbury finally achieved his dream of coming to America; he would remain until his death. Booth often asked his father to look after the Bel Air farm during his road trips, his requests meeting with varying results.

Booth played Baltimore in October and November 1822 and appeared in Richmond in November and December. But his memorandums until mid-November concerned the farm; he fired Boneramp on 5 November, continued to pay Knight's Tavern small sums, arranged for his steamboat passage to and from Richmond, bought various supplies for the farm, and purchased livestock. The Harford County farm had become Booth's solace from the rigors of the road; Mrs. Rogers recalled that Booth was "very industrious," that when he returned from his travels he would take off his shoes and stockings and hoe in the fields. Booth, she added, "did not eat any meat nor wish his family to eat anything that had life in it. He thought it was a sin to take life. He would not nor his family when he was at home. He could repeat the Lord's Prayer with more fervor than I have ever heard any one. I believe Mr. Booth has gotten safe to heaven, he was very charitable, good to the poor, a kind man, and Mrs. Booth was also." For an actor to so impress his farming neighbors in a new land speaks well for the man.

Booth had secured his sanctuary, designing it to suit his tastes. Asia described the facilities as simple and rough: a corner cupboard, a looking glass, a spinning wheel, and a Dutch oven. More important to Booth, his library was in place: Shelley, Coleridge, Keats, Racine, Alfieri, Tasso, Dante, Milton, Locke, and, above all, Shakespeare. The walls bore three engravings: "Timon of Athens," "The Roman Matron

Showing Her Husband How to Die," and the "Death of Bonaparte." He subscribed to and carefully filed a weekly magazine on farming to learn his new avocation. Perhaps from it he learned to use ground bone as fertilizer, Booth being the first farmer in the area to do so.

Early in 1823, Booth attempted a short engagement with Francis Wemyss in Philadelphia, but his appearances were indifferently attended.[29] Wemyss canceled Booth after three performances and substituted Charles Mathews. Booth tried again in early April 1823, playing a short engagement, and his shrewdness in selecting his new home became evident. His Harford County farm put him near many of the East's theatrical centers, and Booth usually drove himself in a "carryall," drawn by Peacock in tandem with Captain, a much larger horse. Thomas Abthorpe Cooper used a similar conveyance to move from theatre to theatre; the two tragedians often met on the road.[30]

Booth's first Philadelphia engagement had won him no laurels. Philadelphia had dominated the American theatre from the beginning but was now losing that leadership to New York. Charles Durang recalled of Booth's premiere,

> Junius Brutus Booth made his first bow to a Philadelphia audience with very poor prospects of success. Nobody knew anything about him, nor did anybody seem to care for him. His reception was extremely lukewarm. The house was poor, the applause was poorer. A few saw merit. The verdict of his jury was "No go!" . . . he played with his usual excellence, winning moderate applause from those who were present, but not drawing large houses, such as were due his merit and great excellence.[31]

Booth's day would come in the City of Brotherly Love, but perhaps the Philadelphians in 1823 had too vivid memories of Kean from a few years earlier. Then, too, Booth again had to compete with Charles Mathews, who packed the house at the nearby New Theatre for seventeen nights. Booth retreated to his farm and played Philadelphia again in April with little more success.

He did not appear again until July, when he played a week and a half in Washington, D.C. Most theatres closed during the summers; patrons would not endure the heat. Booth returned to his farm for the birth of Rosalie Ann Booth, born 5 July 1823. Twelve days after Rosalie's birth, Booth opened in Washington as Richard III. The

Early drawing of Junius Brutus Booth. Artist unidentified. From the author's collection.

Johannes Jelgerhuis watercolor of costumes worn by the Jonas-Penley Company in Amsterdam during Booth's first tour of the Continent. Courtesy of the Rare Book Room, University of Amsterdam.

Edmund Kean, Junius Brutus Booth's nemesis. From the author's collection.

1817 drawing of Junius Brutus Booth, based on an unspecified painting. From the author's collection.

Junius Brutus Booth as Fitzharding in *The Curfew*. From the author's collection.

William Charles Macready, Booth's co-star and rival at Covent Garden from 1817 till Booth's departure. From the author's collection.

Junius Brutus Booth as Guiscard in *Adelgitha*. By permission of the British Museum.

Junius Brutus Booth as Posthumus in Shakespeare's *Cymbeline*, ca. 1818. From the author's collection.

Mary Ann Holmes Booth, attributed to Sully. From *Harper's Weekly*, 14 June 1893.

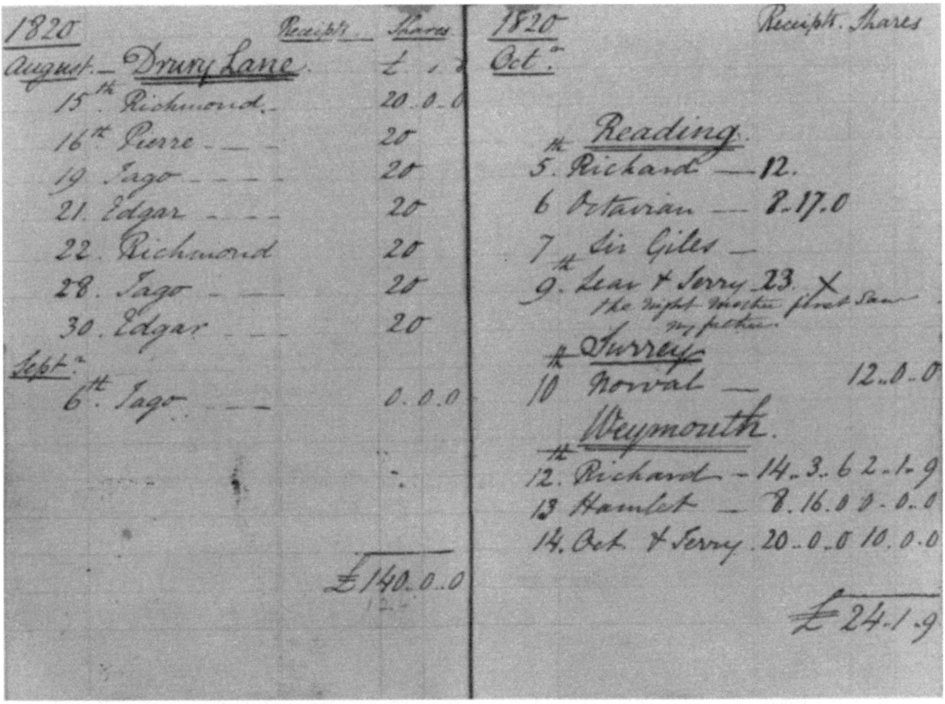

Four pages (*above* and *facing page*) from Junius Brutus Booth's account book, the first two from 1820, listing roles and income. The second two pages (*facing page*) cover the period when Booth left London and includes his first engagement in Richmond, Virginia. Note the deterioration of Booth's handwriting. Courtesy of the Rare Books and Manuscript Division, New York Public Library, Astor, Lenox, and Tilden Foundations.

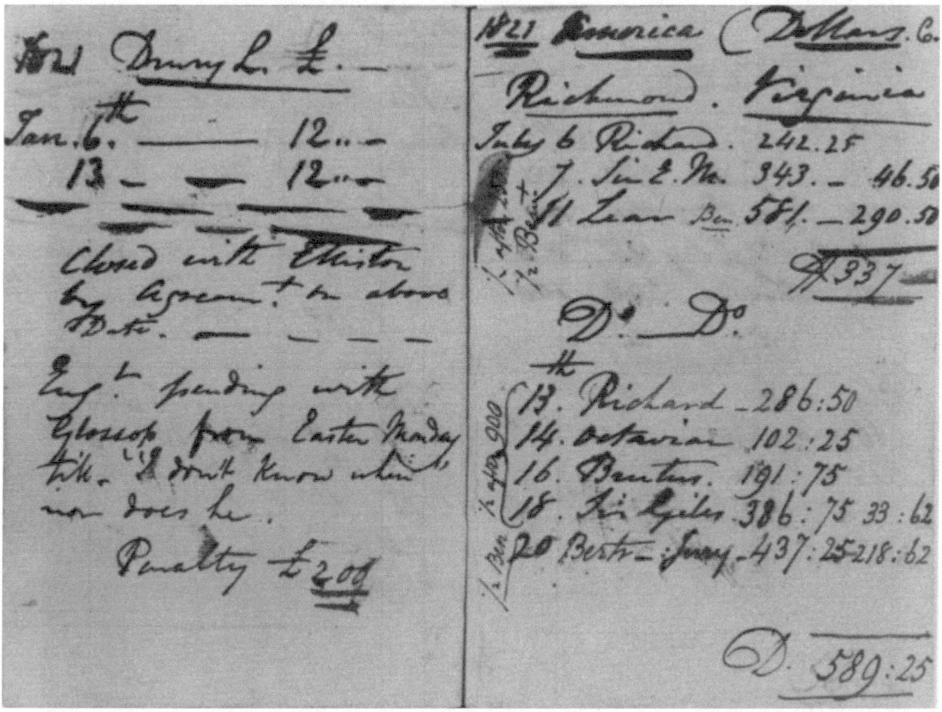
No 21 Drury L. £. —

Jan. 6th — 12.. —
13 — — 12.. —

Closed with Elliston by Agreem.t on above Date. —

Engt. pending with Glossop from Easter Monday till — "I don't know when", nor does he..

Penalty £200

No 21 America (Dollars. C.

Richmond. Virginia

July 6 Richard. 242.25
7. Sir E. M. 343. — 46.50
11 Lear Ben. 581. — 290.50

½ after 250 ½ Ben +

D. 337

D.o — D.o

13th. Richard — 286:50
14. Octavian 102:25
16. Bertram 191:75
18. Sir Giles 386:75 33:62
20 Bertr — Jerry — 437:25 218:62

½ after 900 ½ Ben

D. 589:25

Junius Brutus Booth as Hamlet. Edwin Booth placed this portrait over the fireplace in the Great Hall of the Players. Courtesy of the Hampden-Booth Theatre Library at the Players.

Washington Gazette, after scolding the audience for talking loudly during the production, complimented Booth, but noted he had received "little or no profit" for his engagement. Whether patronage increased on his benefit on the twenty-sixth we have no record.

Booth rested during August then traveled to New York for another Park Theatre engagement. Cooper was appearing there, as were John and Mary Ann Duff, so the engagement proved both amiable and profitable.[32] Again, Booth retired for two months. Then he appeared for a few performances in Boston. He included in his benefit on the first of December his demonstration of Richard III's soliloquy, "Now is the winter of our discontent," in his own style, then in imitation of Kean. Booth still suffered from comparisons to his old nemesis and sought to refute them with this ploy.

On that last night in Boston, 1 December 1823, he was called for by the audience, and while he did not always answer such calls, this night he did. The audience insisted he play one more night in their city, but they suspected Stephen Price, a New York manager, wished others to appear (a Mrs. Holman and a Mr. Pearman), so amid the calls for Booth were cries of "No New York managers here!"[33] Booth had played tougher houses, so he retired to consult the managers, reappeared to assure the audience he would perform the next evening, but did not. Boston audiences took their revenge on Holman and Pearman, patronizing them sparingly.

Booth stopped at the Park Theatre to play Orestes to Mrs. Duff's Hermione for her benefit, then again played Philadelphia the last half of December, this time with moderate success, playing to a $381 average and a benefit of $1,038.[34] He repeated his presentation of the Richard soliloquies à la Kean and Booth. But after closing his regular engagement in that city on December twenty-ninth, he volunteered to play Hamlet on 7 January 1824 to raise money to help the Greeks in their war of independence against Turkey. Philadelphians apparently felt considerable sympathy for a nation fighting for independence. The house filled with an unusually intellectual audience, who had never seen Booth, did not care who played Hamlet, yet paid $922 to see it. Booth acted them to an astonished standstill; after that he drew enthusiastic and large audiences in Philadelphia.

An uneventful engagement in Baltimore in late January followed. After Booth played Othello, a patron, writing over the name "Spectator," praised him highly and painted a vivid word picture of his Moor.

> Mr. Booth . . . was from meek-eyed love poisoned into hatred, festered into fury and distorted into madness; by the baleful breath of the green-eyed monster he was gradually swollen from the first ruffle, raised by the emphatic word *indeed*, into a lawless storm of contending passions. At *his grim laugh,* the summit of the pathos, the blood seemed to be chilled with wild sensations, the brows knit in black despair, the eye blazed with vengeful ire, and the whole man was horrified into merciless jealousy itself!!![35]

A newspaper puff for his benefit suggested that, since Booth resided near Baltimore and spent his money there, it would "suppose a want of good feeling, as well as good taste, were a full house not to be anticipated." For his benefit Booth played Geoffrey Muffincap in *Amateurs and Actors,* the first time Baltimoreans had seen that afterpiece. Newspapers reported an overflowing house.

Booth returned to the Park Theatre in New York in late March to good houses and reviews, did two performances in Philadelphia the next month, then went back to Baltimore in late April 1824. Not only did he appear with the lovely and talented Mrs. Duff, but the manager had also booked Thomas Hilson for the week, giving Baltimore audiences three stars to contemplate.[36] The *Baltimore American and Commercial Daily Advertiser* reported that a scene in *The Apostate* between Booth and Mrs. Duff elicited "*nine distinct rounds of applause*." Baltimore theatregoers had taken Booth to their hearts, where he would remain for a long time. For one thing, Baltimoreans considered Booth one of their own. During this engagement, "An Observer" wrote to the editors the following:

> As Mr. Booth is now playing at the Holliday street Theatre, I consider it but an act of justice to mention what fell the other day under my observation. I had business in the neighborhood of the farm in this state, purchased and occupied by Mr. Booth, and observing that several alterations and improvements were going on in the farm, in building, &c. &c., I made some enquiries, from which I learned, that his industry is laborious and incessant, and that by much the greater part of the money he obtains by his profession as an actor, is expended in improving this property. That his fortune is usefully employed in the state of Maryland, and not, as by other actors, carried away to contribute to the wealth of another country. I hope the Baltimoreans will recollect this at his benefit.[37]

A letter from Booth to his father, dated 9 May 1824, however, indicated trouble on the farm.

> I am sorry you refuse to take any interest in my affairs, even to so small a charge, as overlooking the Servants and Labourers, that I may not be cheated and robbed on every side—.
>
> However, Argument with you is out of the question.—I do not at all mean or wish to offend you, but to beg you for your own Sake, to refrain from that destructive and Sense-depriving Custom of getting intoxicated. Madness will be the result if you persist—I have witness'd often with regret the terrible ravages it has made both on your Mind and Body—Even the occupation of looking now and then after the Garden, or any part relative to Agriculture (not laborious) would I sho'd think, give you greater pleasure than feeling every faculty besotted—I had no idea you have left the Negroes the option of doing as they pleased in my absence, or Sampson either—These people are receiving my money and eating as 'twere the Bread that I earn. . . . I do not ask you to work, but I ask you to see that they work. Surely the request is not very exorbitant.
>
> Look at the folly of that Man Curtis!—on my return—I shall not continue him in my Employ. Drinking made him break the Carry-all. Whatever tends to deprive Man of his Reason, of his Memory, of his Nerves and physical Powers, and render him pro-tempore in some lamentable instances, for ever, Idiot or a Maniac, ought not to be drunk as Mother's Milk.
>
> Yours affectively,
> J. B. B.[38]

That Booth should warn his father against drink and potential madness was most ironic, given his own growing propensities for both. At this point, Booth drank but still seemed able to function.

On 4 June 1824, Booth made the final payment on his farm.[39] The terms were $733.20 to Richard W. Hall for a one-thousand-year lease, with ground rent of one cent per year, payable upon demand. These strange arrangements stemmed from Maryland laws forbidding aliens to own property; not till 1826 could land be legally held by noncitizens. On 15 March 1825, Booth similarly leased a small sliver of land from Henry Woolsey for four dollars and one peppercorn annual rent.

So, less than four years after his arrival in North America, Booth had established himself as a leading tragedian. He had secured a rustic retreat and had started a second family; all seemed well. But cracks soon began to appear in his facade.

The same day that Booth leased the bulk of his land, he acted Othello at the Park. Some parts of his Moor were "inimitably fine," but others seemed to be played as a tragic burlesque. Newspapers reported that, although he excelled himself in the death scene, just before the curtain fell, he rolled over, put his head in his hands, and said to the audience, "There, what do you think of that?" A strange thing for an actor to do, but worse followed.

The next morning, just before noon, while chatting with another actor, Jacob Woodhull, in the Park lobby, he calmly asked, "I must cut somebody's throat today, and whom shall I take? Shall it be Wallack, or yourself, or who?" The unfortunate Henry John Wallack chanced by at that moment, and Booth whipped out a large dagger and tried to stab him, but as Woodhull cried out, Wallack turned and thus avoided the blow. Booth chased Wallack into the street and slashed at him again; Wallack stumbled and fell, and again Booth missed. Bystanders disarmed and secured Booth, took him to a friend's house, and calmed him.[40]

The next day the *New York Evening Post* described the fit as temporary, relieved by a single night's sleep. Then the paper inserted a most puzzling statement: "There was not the slightest ground for the report respecting his domestic loss." A rumor of Mary Ann's death had spread, more rapidly than seems possible, for James Winston, the Drury Lane prompter, inserted in his diary for June seventh, "New York—Booth is affected with mental derangements here for the loss of his wife and is obliged to be put under restraints." And on 2 July, the *London Times* ran the following item:

> Mr. Booth.—(From a New York paper of June 7.)—We regret to state that this gentleman, whose great improvement as a tragedian has of late become so conspicuous, has been affected within these few days with mental derangement. It is said that this has been occasioned by the sudden death of his wife. It has been found necessary to place him under restraint, to prevent him from doing injury to himself or friends; but it is hoped that by the kind attention of the family under whose charge he now is, his recovery will be speedily effected.

Mary Ann Holmes Booth did not die in 1824; indeed, she survived her husband by many years. Surely if Booth had believed these strange rumors, he would have cut short his engagement and returned to Harford County. Details of this episode are few, but the taint of madness had entered the Booth history, never to leave.

As for Booth's relationship with Mary Ann, although Booth was obviously something of a womanizer in England, no hint suggests he ever philandered after setting up housekeeping with Mary Ann. Actresses are an occupational hazard for men in the theatre, and vice versa, but apparently not for Booth. Mary Ann had enough to worry about—nineteenth-century farm life was nothing if not strenuous—but Mary Ann made the farm a home. To her eternal credit, she raised the children, oversaw the hired hands, did what she could with her father-in-law, and established a life for herself as an actor's wife. Stars shine brightly, and lesser figures live in the shadows by reflected glory.

Booth, his fit over, returned to the Park on June ninth. He made no recorded performance for the next four months, time spent, no doubt, on the farm, recuperating from whatever demons had beset him. On 22 October 1824 he resurfaced in Baltimore in *The Apostate* as Pescara for William Augustus Conway's benefit, with Mrs. Duff as Florinda.[41] Slightly over a month later he appeared for another single performance in the same city as Lear for Mrs. Duff's benefit.

Booth began to appear less frequently, not acting again until the following March in Charleston. All we know of him in the meantime is an excerpt from a letter to his father, begging him to see that all the farm's animals were cared for and that Henry, a hired man, be not so fond of using the whip on them.[42]

Of Charleston in 1825, during his first appearance there in four years, he commented, "There is a hot moisture here that relaxes the system dreadfully—it is, however, of this benefit that there is a greater suavity of manners than can be found in the Northern States—and were it not for the unnecessary and wicked treatment of the colored people the Carolinians would have few blemishes."[43]

A two-week engagement in Baltimore concluded with a conglomerate performance of Act IV of *The Apostate,* Act II of *The Iron Chest,* the last act of *Brutus*, with *The Mayor of Garratt* as an afterpiece. Booth and other actors would from time to time arrange bills of this sort; audiences came to see stars, not plays.

During his engagement in Baltimore, the Chestnut Street Theatre in Philadelphia staged a script Booth had written for the Wallacks,

Ugolino. Booth was performing in *The Iron Chest* and so missed the premiere. *Ugolino*, Booth's only attempt at dramaturgy, was in the flamboyant tradition of the times, and although revived for a few performances by Booth's friend John R. Scott (usually billed as J. R. Scott), it failed to win a lasting place on American stages.[44]

From his next engagement in Albany, New York, Booth wrote to his father, the "gentlemen employed in raising the barn must use more expedition," lest they try to hang on for the rest of the year, in which case Booth threatened to replace them. Apparently Booth was still in litigation with Charles Gilfert for the thousand dollars owed him; Booth mentioned, "Gilfert behaves very well, but I fear will not be able yet awhile to keep his promise in cancelling the old debt."[45]

As he continued to improve his property, Booth opened an account at the Hays General Store in Bel Air; he advised his father to secure whatever goods he might require there. Hays' account book from 1824 to 1834 has survived, offering a detailed description of Booth's farm life for that decade.[46] If Booth and his father were drinking men, the price was right: a quart of whiskey cost twelve and one-half cents, a gallon nineteen cents, and peach brandy ran twelve and one-half cents per half gallon. Booth purchased Spanish cigars from Hays for a penny apiece. The black servants often collected the goods necessary for the farm, such as candles, soap, chamber pots (thirty-one cents), writing paper (twenty-five cents per quire), a pair of shoes for Junius, Jr. ($1.50), molasses, peppermint, pins, needles, cloth, thread, sugar (four pounds for fifty cents), coffee, and so on. Postage on a letter from New York, however, was fifty cents. Booth's indebtedness fluctuated, running as high as three hundred dollars while he was out on tour. Apparently he kept his credit in order.

In another letter to his father about this time, Booth also described his visit to a Shaker settlement, revealing some of his thoughts on organized religions.

> I have visited the Shakers who have a settlement a few miles from Albany, and I was much gratified. They are the most singular people I ever beheld. They have more simplicity and apparent primitive Christianity than all other classes of Christians. Sexual intercourse is prohibited, and they would become extinct, but for converts who continually are joining them on Earth before they will be received among the Elect—They are the best farmers and gardeners in

> America. Marriage is considered by them a sin. Bible Societies are the Instruments of Satan. They place little faith in a future state, and maintain that Christ is again on Earth. Their cleanliness is excessive, and their deportment full of suavity and mildness. There is nothing to disgust—much to admire in them, and their ceremonies whose description would excite ridicule, produce a very contrary effect in witnessing. They are the best of Christians for they don't prosecute, and are harmless. All they desire is to live and die unmolested—but they are often insulted by the foolish and thoughtless.[47]

Booth closed with an admonition: "Tell Curtis I hope he'll be steady & not drink. Burke the actor died from it a few days ago."[48] Booth and his father continually warned one another of the evils of drink, with mutual lack of effect.

Booth's life and career now took a sharp turn. He still dreamed of London and stardom, and recent news from London gave him reason to think Kean no longer posed a threat. He packed up Mary Ann, the children, and one black servant girl and sailed for Liverpool on or about 22 August 1825.

The Booth entourage arrived in Liverpool on 20 September, only to encounter none other than Kean himself, as Booth described in this letter to his father:

> At last we are arrived after a passage of twenty-nine days. . . . To-day we go to London through Leicester. Kean sails the day after tomorrow, by the "Silas Richards" for New York. Strange that he should meet me here—he ready to embark, and to the very country I have just left! He has been quite ill, and looks wretchedly. I passed an hour with him last night at his quarters, and reconciled our ancient misunderstanding. . . . I really wish he may meet with success. He has been all along a victim to sharpers and flatterers, who buoyed him up with the notion of omnipotence, which now he awakes from, and perceives the hollowness of those on whom he mostly relied. Macready is sick, Young is gone to Italy for his health, and Elliston is reported to be dying.[49]

Booth no doubt thought this a propitious time to claim what he considered his rightful place in the London theatre. After Booth left London in 1821, Kean began an adulterous and protracted affair with an alderman's wife, one Charlotte Cox. In January 1825, the scandal reached the courts, and the lord chief justice found for the alderman in a lurid case, which the London press exploited with fiendish glee. The *Times*, for example, castigated Kean upon learning that he planned to return to the stage.

> When every person who can read knows that Kean's offence is aggravated by the most shocking circumstances of indecency, brutality, obscenity, perfidy and hypocrisy—we do say that the public . . . ought not to be insulted by his immediate obtrusion before them, as a candidate for their applause. Let him hide himself for a reasonable time; his immediate appearance is as great an outrage to decency, as if he were to walk naked through the streets at mid-day.[50]

Nevertheless, Kean appeared on 25 January 1825 as Richard III to a rioting audience at Drury Lane. The theatregoers calmed down after a few weeks, as they had for Booth, but Kean found himself ruined socially and ridiculed professionally, the butt of jokes and semipornographic London street ballads.[51] During his next several London appearances Drury Lane audiences roasted Kean by shouting lines from his unprintable love letters. In April he toured the provinces, only to receive hoots, jeers, and showers of orange peels. In September Kean fled England for his second North American tour.

None of this ado had escaped Booth's notice; he arrived in London in October for a one-week engagement at Drury Lane. Professional opportunities aside, he could contemplate seeing Adelaide and Richard Junius after a four-year absence. Exactly what arrangements he made with his two families we can only surmise. When he later wrote to various London newspapers, he listed his address as "79, Lower Thames-street." At some time while Booth was in London, a Mr. Williams painted a family portrait of Booth, Adelaide, and their son. Whether Mary Ann and the family stayed in London is unknown.[52]

The London newspapers and periodicals perceived Booth's sudden arrival as an attempt to replace Kean as the leading London star. As the *Times* sneeringly put it in its first review,

> This gentleman has, for a considerable time, been sojourning in America, where report has settled him comfortably on a farm, cultivating cotton and tobacco, and perfectly careless about theatrical laurels. No sooner, however, was Kean's intended departure from England noised abroad than the latent ambition of the rival

> Roscius burst into flame: he quitted his sylvan retreat; and, anxious to fill the abdicated chair, hastened across the Atlantic. . . . Mr. Booth has returned to London, as might be expected, quite unimproved in the histrionic art. America is the very last place where a player is likely to throw aside a vicious propensity to rant (that propensity being the most striking feature of Mr. Booth's performance).[53]

Booth's other London reviewers gave him no more encouragement. The *Morning Herald* noted the moderate applause throughout and commented, "He does not seem to be at all improved by his Transatlantic expedition." Nor did the *Morning Chronicle* admire him, saying,

> If Mr. Booth would, in the technical language of the profession *keep down* the part a little more, reserving his efforts for occasions which demand them, instead of endeavouring to give a false importance to every passage by the mere force of lungs, he would impart an intellectual charm to his performance, of which it is now destitute, and avoid the painful uniformity of incessant declamation.[54]

So, too, the *Morning Post:* "His style continues to be marked by the same extravagance, and, excepting a few points, the performance exhibited nothing of the power of genius, or the discrimination of judgment."

Booth would not be intimidated. The crowd called for him loudly at the end of the play, but Booth chose not to appear. The ovation continued, till finally James William Wallack appeared to say, "Ladies and Gentlemen: The curtain had not been down one minute before I sent to Mr. Booth and informed him of your wishes, but he declined the honour. I not only sent, but finding the call unanimous, I went to him—he still, most respectfully, declines the honour."[55] This was hardly a discreet ploy for an actor seeking the support of London audiences, and Booth received a few scattered hisses when he next performed. Adelaide must have attended this performance, for she wrote Booth a note advising against such cavalier treatment of Londoners. Booth sent her tickets for his first two performances; apparently Mary Ann and the American children did not attend.[56]

Booth again failed to win the London press or public; the *Morning Post* dismissed his Richard III quickly, saying, "The performance in the early acts presented nothing remarkable, as they were played with a seeming listlessness, which rendered them generally insipid. In the tent scene, and the last, however, Mr. Booth made ample amends for any previous want of exertion, by going to the last degree of extravagance."[57] Several papers reported a few calls for Booth at the end of the play, but finding no support, they soon died away.

A thin house attended Booth's Othello, his third and final performance at Drury Lane in 1825. Again, hisses mingled with cheers. Some preferred Booth, some preferred Kean, most Londoners no longer cared one way or the other. Booth had stimulated no excitement professionally, but he had incurred more substantial problems with the London press.

On 16 October, a week after Booth's arrival, the *London Sunday Monitor* took him to task, not as an actor but as a husband and a father. The writer dipped his pen in venom, and his accusations fairly dripped with sarcasm.

> Mr. Booth, finding that Mr. Kean had been driven from Drury-Lane, determined to recross the Atlantic,—and as the most virtuous and unsullied character yields the surest passport to public esteem,—as the man who would shrink with horror from the crime of deserting his wife and child in a foreign land,—stripping them of even common necessities,—and seducing from the roof of a father an infatuated girl to follow a traitorous husband to another quarter of the world, leaving a wife and offspring as objects of professional charity,—as these are peccadilloes not likely to be overlooked by the same virtuous public that anathematized Kean,—we repeat, as these are errors from which the town would turn with abhorrence, Mr. Booth, from his exemplary conduct and well-known rectitude of principle,—from the amiability and good feeling with which it is notorious he fulfils the separate relations of husband and father,—is eminently calculated to fill the vacuum made by the departure of the never-sufficiently-to-be-reprobated Mr. Kean. What if Mr. Booth lacks some portion of the inestimable talent of his predecessor, does he not more than requite such a want by the innumerable evidences of the spotlessness of his private life? We can now visit Drury-Lane and enjoy ourselves, since the departure of Kean, and the engagement of Booth. . . . While listening to Mr. Booth, we know that the language of the stage-husband is but a more lofty and poetic description of the feeling he nurtures at home-that the display of paternal affections on the boards, is the same with the aspirations breathed over the cradle at his own domestic hearth. . . .

> Mr. Booth is in every way angelic! Many circumstances have shewn the excellence of his heart—it holds no black drop, but is, indeed, a vessel which enshrines the purest and brightest endowments of nature. How can we, then, but rejoice at the departure of Kean and the arrival of Booth? . . . If our readers should wish to know why we have as yet abstained from making any notice upon the acting of Mr. Booth, we must inform them, such a task is reserved for a future occasion, our present purpose being to illustrate the virtue of that public who has chased to a foreign shore the desperately vicious Mr. Kean, and its *consistency* in patronizing the much-respected Mr. Booth; a man so utterly incapable of the vicious actions enumerated above. We have in this article merely acted as essayists on public consistency and taste-criticism will come anon. Mr. Booth may be certain we shall not neglect him.

Booth could hardly let such accusations go unanswered. First, in a letter published by almost all London newspapers, he took the dramatic critics to task, calling them "gin-drinking, frothy, self-elected arbiters of public taste," insisting he sought to imitate not Kean, but Joseph Grimaldi, the clown. Booth added, he regretted that "men, who should evince some knowledge of theatricals, appear to be so consummately ignorant of everything relating to the stage." Warming to his task, Booth then counterattacked the *Sunday Monitor*, suggesting that his private life had no bearing upon his theatrical career, concluding,

> He [Booth] therefore distinctly and unequivocally declares, that the statement relative to his leaving a wife and child *destitute* on his departure for America, is a gross and wilful falsehood; and that, though circumstance and family disagreements for years, may have occasioned a separation between himself and the Lady alluded to, she has always been a participator in his fortune. He has further to observe, that with respect to any other part of his conduct, which may seem to require his doing so, he is ready, to those who are *entitled* to demand it, to afford any explanation in private.[58]

On the next Sunday, 23 October, the *Monitor* replied with a broadside worthy of Admiral Nelson. After apologizing to his readers for wasting their time on so trivial a subject, the journalist asked if it were not "*notorious* that when he left his wife and child, and fled to America with *Miss H.*—was not Mrs. Booth left *so very* destitute that many of the performers of the [Royal] Coburg Theatre entered into a *public* subscription for the relief of herself and child?" The full column concludes, "We regret to hear that Mr. Booth should be driven into exile; but we have little doubt that it will not be *for ever.* If his *talents* should induce a London Manager to whistle him back again, we may again be astounded by the *phrenzy* of his genius." Booth had finally had enough; he hied himself to the provinces.

After an engagement in Liverpool, he returned to a scene of former glory, Brighton, for four performances. While the audiences thronged to see him, the newspaper critics were divided in their opinion of his acting, and Booth moved on to Manchester and into a local theatrical imbroglio.

The Manchester manager, Thomas D. Lewis, had dismissed a local favorite, Mrs. McGibbon (as well as her husband), after a decade's faithful service. Local audiences were incensed; the newspapers attacked Lewis' petty bureaucracy. The dismissal took place only a few days before Booth arrived, and the papers ignored him to print Lewis' excuse that he was only following London theatre practices to which Mr. and Mrs. McGibbon refused to conform.[59]

On 28 December 1825 Booth once again faced a rioting audience, but, for once, they cared not a whit about *him*. The audience hoisted placards reading, "The Managers ought to be fined 100£ for not suffering Mrs. McGibbon to play her character this evening"; "What ruined Macready? discharging favourites"; "Six hundred frequenters of this Theatre will not be seen here after the 2d January"; and, the worst threat of all, "£2 10s. houses," hinting at the depths to which receipts could fall. The next night the stage manager spoke to the audience, promising a resolution of the matter. Friday, after Booth's Richard III had begun, the stage manager interrupted the performance to announce that Mrs. McGibbon had been rehired, causing the audience to cheer vigorously for several minutes, after which the show resumed. Booth went on to less tempestuous engagements in Sheffield, Bristol, and Dublin.

In April 1826 he returned to London, to neither of the patent houses, but to the Royalty Theatre.[60] Booth opened as Richard III on April tenth. At 1:30 A.M. the next morning, the theatre burned to the ground, ignited by some smoldering fireworks used to represent Mount Etna. As the *Sun* reported, not five pounds' worth of property survived. Of Booth's costumes and properties, he found only three charred links of his Richard III coronation collar. Some two hundred persons lost their income; and James Dunn, one of the proprietors, estimated his loss at three thousand pounds.

Somewhere, somehow, after passing his thirtieth birthday, Booth gathered together some more costumes and appeared the next month in Amsterdam at the German Theatre. It had been here on Amstel Street where he had opened with Jonas and Penley in 1814.[61] Booth played only four performances as a guest star: Hamlet on 11 May, Othello on 18 May, Shylock on 22 May, and Macbeth for his benefit on 29 May (see the Appendix). The brevity of the engagement was probably just as well; the manager, Joseph Smithson, abandoned the company a week later.[62]

Booth wrote a friend, Henry Monk, in London, on 20 May, from Amsterdam. The first paragraph hearkens back to 1814–15: "A Scene similar to one we were once years back engaged in at Antwerp occurr'd here a day or two since—but the Revolt was most unjustifiable, therefore the Simile fails." Booth then described to Monk several available situations, paying from sixteen to twenty guilders per week, Smithson being the manager seeking talent. Booth had recommended Monk, as well as several others, and urged him to come to Amsterdam: "The steamer gets to Rotterdam from the Town in 24 hours—at 5 o'clock in the afternoon of every Day, a Coach leaves the Hoosstraat for Gouda, & you arrive next morning in Amsterdam—The Expense from Rotterdam to Amsterdam is 4s & 6d." As always, Booth advanced sobriety: "Can you recommend a leading man? Qualities—clever, intelligent, handsome & above all, sober; for by G–d, this concern has nearly been broken up by the drunken folly of a parcel of boys—."[63]

Booth completed his engagement and returned to London for three performances at the Royal Coburg. On 10 June 1826 he packed up his blighted London aspirations and sailed from Rotterdam on the *Draper* for Baltimore.

Booth had experienced rather a strenuous half decade—though the worst was yet to come. Having failed in London, he abandoned Adelaide and his infant son, Richard, transported a new lover to a new land, and almost immediately established himself as a major star. He secured land and a new home, sired two children, and set about carving a life out of what was little more than a wilderness. Kean's public castigation lured him back to London, but only to meet another torrent of rejection, even public humiliation. He could have had no idea the New World would remain his home, although he would visit his native land once more.

5

The Fire Must Burn

There are stars indeed.
And sometimes falling ones.

—*Henry VIII,* IV, i, 54

Booth sailed from Rotterdam on the *Draper,* commanded by Captain Hilliert. The tragedian spent much of the forty-nine-day trip learning Italian, memorizing a list of words each day. An insane passenger, considered harmless, heard Booth repeating his Italian lesson, concluded the actor was a conjurer practicing black arts, and threatened Booth with an ax. Booth stared down the maniac, who lowered his weapon and backed away.[1]

The *Draper* arrived in Baltimore 15 August 1826.[2] Booth first returned his family to Harford County, checking to see how his father had supervised his property in his absence. He then set about securing his career in North America rather differently than he had upon his arrival in 1821.

Booth signed on at the Chatham Theatre in New York as stage manager under Henry John Wallack.[3] On Christmas Eve, 1826, he wrote to his friend George Holland, an English actor, offering both an engagement and his assessment of the American theatre at that time.

> Theatricals are not in so flourishing a condition in this Country as they were some two years ago. There are four Theatres in this City, each endeavoring to ruin the others, by foul means as well as fair. The reduction of the prices of admission has proved (as I always anticipated from the first suggestion of such a foolish plan) nearly ruinous to the Managers. The Publick here often witness a Performance in every respect equal to what is presented at the Theatres Royal D.L. and C.G. for these prices. Half a dollar to the boxes and a quarter do[llar] to the Pit and Gallery! . . . Acting is sold too cheap to the Publick and the result will be a general theatrical bankruptcy.
>
> Tragedians are in abundance—MACREADY— CONWAY—HAMBLIN—FORREST (now No. 1) COOPER— WALLACK—MAYWOOD and self with divers others now invest New York. But it won't do; a diversion to the South must be made—or to Jail three-fourths of the Great men and managers must go.[4]

Considering Booth had usually performed for one hundred dollars a night when he had first come to America, his offer to Holland reeked of managerial parsimony.

> Now, sir, I will deal fairly with you. If you will pledge yourself to me for three years, and sacredly promise that no inducement which may be held out by the unprincipled and daring speculators which abound in this country shall cause you to leave me, I will, for ten months in each year, give you thirty dollars per week, and an annual benefit which you shall divide with me. . . . and I should expect the terms on which you would be engaged to remain secret from all but ourselves.

Booth then asked Holland to engage a pair of actresses he had seen the previous January in Exeter; to them he offered fifteen dollars a week and travel (not board) to America. Their travel costs he planned to deduct from their salaries at three dollars a week. He offered this advice to Holland, advice he might well have taken himself:

> Let me recommend you to Economy—see what a number of our brethren are reduced to Indigence by their obstinate Vanity—I have here Mr. D—who was once in London the rival of Elliston, and is now a better actor—approaching the age of sixty, and not a dollar put by for a rainy day—too proud to accept a salary of twenty dollars per week in a regular engagement—he stars and starves. Many have been deceived and misled in their calculations in coming

> to this country—some have cut their throats, &c., from disappointment—Mrs. Romer (once of the Surrey), Mrs. Alsop, Mr. Entwistle—Kirby the Clown—are all on the felo de se list. . . .
>
> The temptations to Drunkenness here are too common and too powerful for many weak beings who construe the approval of a boisterous circle of intoxicated fools as the climax of everything desirable in their profession.[5]

During Booth's New York stint, he had to compete with two of his old London "colleagues": William Charles Macready, who before leaving London was rising to prominence there, and Edmund Kean, who had remained in America during Booth's abortive visit to England. The newspapers gave much more space to the visiting Englishmen than to the transplanted Booth, but Booth, as ever, soldiered on.

He played Albany to bland notices but large crowds, going thence to Philadelphia, after passing through New York to play three performances of *Sylla,* a new play of no great virtue. In Philadelphia for over a month, Booth failed to appear as Lear on February sixteenth. He then returned to Harford County, from which he wrote Francis Wemyss on 17 April, rejecting an invitation to play in Wemyss' benefit in Philadelphia. Booth claimed, "This is the beginning of my busiest part of the Season, and my absence would throw all aback, as I have this year assumed the whole direction & could not leave, without hiring some one competent to superintend for me." Booth did not remember Philadelphia fondly. "My acting for you unless in conjunction with others of greater note, would not I fear draw you one dollar more than you would have without me—I became stale with the Philadelphians after my first performance—and I owe my big Benefit solely to Mrs. Duff & Mr. H. Wallack:—to prove this compare all the other Receipts with those of the great Creatures, yclept Singers, &c."[6]

Booth seems to have passed the summer of 1827 on the Harford County farm, with only one engagement between March and September, that being two weeks in Baltimore in May. Advertisements do not indicate that Booth was still stage managing at the Chatham Theatre, so what his "direction" might have been remains in doubt. Booth clearly did not want to do Wemyss' benefit, so any excuse would suffice.

Booth returned to Philadelphia in September and October, before beginning a southern and western tour, including Nashville, Tennessee, Cincinnati, Ohio, and ending in New Orleans, where he took up stage managing again, this time at the American Theatre for James H. Caldwell.

Sol Smith, who played support to Booth during this engagement, recalled it as "highly successful," adding, "I should say these were his best days. It was my luck to support him as the Physician in 'King Lear,' the Lord Mayor, in 'Richard the Third,' and one of the shouting citizens in each of the Roman pieces. After his engagement at our theatre was finished, he performed Oreste twice in the Theatre D'Orleans to crowded houses, and [to] the great delight of the French population."[7] Apparently during this engagement, not the previous one, Booth performed in French as Oreste in Racine's *Andromaque*. Although historians have argued whether Booth acted in French, the evidence indicates he did.[8]

While Booth succeeded in New Orleans, manager Caldwell lost at least ten thousand dollars, according to Smith. He was back East by May 1828, scheduled to play Othello at the Park for James Hackett's benefit, but he failed to appear. The theatre substituted *Henry IV*, and nothing was said of Booth's nonappearance. He appeared as scheduled the next month, though, performing Shylock for Mrs. Mary Hill's benefit on the fifth, then playing a two-week engagement at the Park.

On the fifth of July, he wrote a puzzling letter from New York to a Baltimore lawyer, Wilmot Hall. "You will oblige me by making a Freehold Conveyance of the Property I purchased near Bel-air, to Mr. Edwin Forrest of Philadelphia. This Deed to be given from yourself and family to him—Any extra Expense such a measure may bring, I will cordially defray."[9] We can only speculate as to Booth's motives for placing his property under Forrest's name, especially since on 11 February 1826 Maryland had passed a law allowing aliens to own property. At any rate, Edwin Forrest had become America's first native-born star a few years before, noted for a robust, noisy, and virile style of acting. He and Booth were professional rivals but good friends; indeed, a few years later Booth would name a son after Forrest. Evidently Booth considered Forrest trustworthy enough to look after his business matters.

In the fall of 1828 Booth again took a managerial position, this time at the Tremont Theatre in Boston; the touring tragedian seemed to be trying to find a place to settle down. Booth ran the following advertisement in the *Boston Daily Advertiser:*

> The association for conducting this establishment, respectfully inform the public that the extensive alterations and embellishments being nearly complete—the Theatre, under the management of Mr. Booth, will be open for the season on Monday Evening, Sept. 1, with a favourite Comedy and other entertainments as will be enpressed hereafter.
>
> They have during the recess made arrangements for an accession of talent, both permanent and auxiliary, of the first order, and whose merits are fully known and appreciated by the patrons of the various theatres in the United States, and the combination of such talent as will be named, it is hoped may serve to realize the expectation of the management in obtaining complete success for the present season.[10]

The advertisement then listed the luminaries to come, including Booth himself, Edwin Forrest, Mr. and Mrs. Joseph Cowell, Thomas Hamblin, Mr. and Mrs. Edmund Simpson, Mrs. Duff, and Miss Eliza Placide.[11] Booth and the management had indeed assembled a distinguished company. For two months, Booth managed the theatre, taking three days in mid-October to perform at the Bowery in New York with Forrest. The two actors alternated as Iago and Othello for two nights.

Another Booth mystery first surfaced in the *Boston Daily Advertiser*, 23 October 1828. Caldwell was appearing in one of Booth's favorite roles, Reuben Glenroy in *Town and Country*, but the advertisement read further, "Mrs. Booth's 2nd appearance on any Stage." A few flimsy theatrical legends had it that Mary Ann Holmes Booth did attempt to act a few times, and she was between children, as it were, in late 1828.[12] The newspapers printed no reviews, nor does any Boston stage history mention Mary Ann as an actress. Later appearances of a Mrs. Booth further suggest someone other than the tragedian's wife.

But Booth had other engagements, and so Joe Cowell succeeded him as the Tremont's manager. The Tremont Theatre Association awarded Booth a silver cup and plate, value one hundred dollars, inscribed, "The Tremont Theatre Association, in token of respect to J. B. Booth, Esq. Boston, October 28th, 1828," along with the following letter: "The association for conducting the Tremont Theatre, regretting that your previous arrangements prescribe your engagement for so limited a period, tender you their grateful acknowledgements for the able and satisfactory manner in which you have discharged the duties of the management."[13]

This marked Booth's high point as a manager; he was an actor, not an administrator. He penned a brief and graceful reply.

> Mr. Cowell has presented me your kind reward for my humble endeavours to serve your interests during my sojourn in Boston. I can only assure you of my continued good wishes, and flatter myself that, should fortune ever bring us again together, I may be able to return in some shape or other, the urbanity evinced towards
> Your most obliged and obedient servant,
> J. B. Booth.

The *Theatrical Censor* for 4 November 1828 reprinted both letters from the *Boston Bulletin;* perhaps Booth saw them there and read in the same issue that Covent Garden had engaged Edmund Kean to perform two nights a week for an annual salary of two thousand pounds. Kean had broken with Drury Lane as a result of a quarrel with Stephen Price. Charles Kemble, the brother of John Philip Kemble, was managing Covent Garden and hired Kean to bolster the theatre's slumping income.

But Booth was off again, to New York in November, then to Cincinnati, and finally to New Orleans. The audiences there welcomed him as usual, braving the streets turned to quagmires by heavy rains. Of his Shylock, the *Louisiana Courier* said, "We think Mr. Booth excels any other actor that we have ever seen attempt the personation of that character." For his benefit the house was crowded with "youth, beauty and fashion."

Booth left the city for two weeks in Natchez, his first recorded appearance there. Caldwell had built the Main Street Theatre in the midst of an abandoned cemetery on the south side of Main Street between Pine and Rankin Streets. Caldwell sent many stars to Natchez; during this particular season he sent Forrest, George Holland (whom Booth had tried to hire for the Bowery), and a child star of "prodigious versatility," Louisa Lane.[14]

Booth returned to New Orleans on the *Lady of the Lake* and played the Crescent City for the next three months. Of particular interest was Booth's creation of a new role, that of Malcour in *The Gambler's Fate*. The *Courier* said of it:

> Every person who was witness at the *Gambler's Fate,* on its first representation, must be gratified to see that it is to be brought forward again this evening, with a new and very interesting cast of

> the characters. The united efforts of such actors as Mr. Booth and Mr. Caldwell, must be interesting in such parts as the two principal characters in this piece affords. The *moral,* the *sentiments* and the plot of this piece are unquestionable. We truly wish it may meet with cheering success. Every thing seems to promise well, to a full house.[15]

The *Courier* then heaped praise on this thunderbolt of morality, giving Caldwell high marks for his staging as well as for his acting, and saying of Booth that he "showed *Malcour* to be as horrible and depraved a wretch as *crime* can make, or as the votaries of *roulette* could wish to see." One wonders if any American city of the time accommodated more gambling than New Orleans.

Thomas Abthorpe Cooper, Booth's friend since their meeting in 1821, joined the company for an engagement, Booth and Cooper appearing together in several bills. Booth was to act Othello to Cooper's Iago on 14 March 1829, for example, but the *Courier* ran a note saying, "It will be seen by the advertisement, that in consequence of the indisposition of Mr. Booth, the fare for this evening has been altered; and that the excellent comedy of *The Honey Moon* is to be represented." The nature of Booth's indisposition was not specified; but, his later actions raise doubts about his sobriety on any Saturday night in New Orleans.

During this engagement, Booth played Fontaine to Miss Placide in *Therese, The Orphan of Geneva,* one of John Howard Payne's lesser works. Then Booth played Richmond to little Louisa Lane's Richard III; Miss Lane was but nine years old at the time. Child stars were all the rage in the early nineteenth century, both in England and in America. Children played most of the great tragic roles, audiences finding their innocence comparable to the Romantic ideal of the unspoiled savage. Booth had never before appeared with an "infant Roscius," nor would he again.

Shortly after Cooper closed in New Orleans, Forrest arrived to perform with Booth and Miss Placide. The *Courier* compared Forrest as a tragedian to Cooper and found him lacking, but Booth they mentioned not at all. Booth closed his engagement by playing unusual roles for him, including King Henry to Forrest's Richard III. Friends they may have been, but playing second fiddle to Forrest must have tried Booth sorely. Perhaps this competition contributed to Booth's "eccentricities," as Sol Smith charitably termed them. Smith claimed Booth's drunken capers "interfered somewhat with the interests of the theatre."[16] Later, Smith amplified his comments.

> I was acquainted with . . . Booth for about a quarter of a century. When I first knew him (in 1827) he was a truly great actor, and continued to be so until he fell into bad company in New Orleans, and took to hard drink. Then he became undependable, and, "putting an antic disposition on," made many believe that he was crazy. *I* never believed him to be a crazy man except when he was excited by liquor, and that was pretty often—nearly all the time, in fact.[17]

Booth closed in New Orleans on 12 May 1829; in mid-June he appeared in New York in a single performance of *Richard the Third* for Mrs. Cowell's benefit at the American Opera House. (James Hackett had taken over the Chatham Gardens Theatre in 1829, renaming it the American Opera House for one season.)

While he was in New York, an operetta titled *No!* was performed at the Park Theatre. Booth made no mention of it in any of his letters or notes, but the next year R. H. Elton, a New York publisher, brought out an edition of it listing Booth as its author. *No!* is at best a trifle, hardly in the tradition of Booth's acting, but there were other problems. The same script had been produced three years before, at the Edinburgh Theatre Royal on 30 November 1826. There it had been listed as adapted from the French by William Henry Wood Murray (1790–1852).

Dramatists in the nineteenth century enjoyed no such luxury as copyrights, so if indeed Booth did write the script, he did not commit plagiarism in the modern sense. Still, one wonders why it appeared over his name. He made no effort to attend the Park Theatre production on 15 June 1829, and nothing came of the matter.

Before leaving New York he wrote ahead to Albany to manager William Duffy to confirm a brief engagement there.

> My Dear Sir: Please write to me in Boston on receipt of this, for I am told you've announced me, and I was so damned drunk when we parted that I cannot recollect what was said or done by
>
> JUNIUS B. BOOTH
>
> N.Y., June 20th, 1829.[18]

He played his engagement in Boston, another in Albany, then retired to Harford County for the summer, appearing again in late September in Philadelphia. His alcoholic demons hibernated until his next engagement in Boston, beginning 16 November 1829. When he failed to appear at the theatre, the *Boston Daily Advertiser* ran on November eighteenth: "The public is respectfully informed that intelligence has been received of the sudden and severe indisposition of Mr. Booth in New-York. The earliest notice will be given of his ability to perform." And on the twenty-third, the same paper announced, "The public is respectfully informed that Mr. Booth having recovered from his late severe indisposition, is now in Boston, and will have the honour of appearing before them as Richard Third." But Booth was teetering on the edge. He played a new role, Richard II, on the fourth of December—no review appeared—and then was billed for his benefit on the seventh as Ludovico in *Evadne* and Geoffrey Muffincap in the farce *Amateurs and Actors.*[19]

Actors have nightmares about breaking down onstage; the horror came true for Booth in *Evadne*.[20] The various versions of the event agree to an unusual extent. Booth had been under a physician's care for several days after his arrival in Boston, but several friends swore he had not been drinking. As *Evadne* began, Booth was careless and hesitant in his delivery, and his face lacked its usual expressiveness. He interjected speeches from other scripts into the dialogue and often ran to the prompter's side of the stage, the prompter giving him lines enough to continue, although the audience in the balconies could hear them clearly.

Booth staggered through the first two acts. The overflow audience gaped and gasped at this display and began to protest mildly. The worst was yet to come; early in the third act Booth shared a scene with the King of Naples, during which he quit acting entirely and merely chatted with the other actor, saying to him, "Upon my word, sir, I don't know, sir," and the like. The audience sat stunned, then Booth turned to them and said, "Ladies and gentlemen; I really don't know this part. I studied it only once before, much against my inclination. I will read the part, and the play shall go on. By your leave the play shall go on, and Mr. Wilson shall read the part for me." This aside triggered a burst of hissing, while Booth grinned at the audience. Then he broke into laughter.

The stage manager, W. H. Smith, rushed onstage and led Booth off, while the actor cried out, "I can't read—I am a charity boy;—I can't read. Take me to the Lunatic Hospital!"

Smith tried to placate the audience, telling them that Booth had for some time suffered from partial insanity and that the management would take a few moments to consider what they might do next. Backstage, Booth told the managers he would redeem himself if they would only let him act Sir Edward Mortimer or Iago, claiming he was more perfect in those parts than in any others. This he said so calmly that the managers almost agreed, when another fit came over Booth, and a substitute farce, ironically *The Poor Gentleman,* was performed.

Smith announced this change to the nearly rioting audience, then a quartet came out and sang "Old King Cole," and the audience subsided. Smith entered a third time and swore that, while Booth had not been drinking, he had been ill of late.

Friends took Booth to his lodgings, his disorder intensifying in severity. The Wednesday following that Monday, his friends thought it best to place Booth in an asylum and so went to fetch him. Booth had escaped. Inquiry revealed he had applied for a seat on the Providence stagecoach, but it had left without him.

Booth's distracted mind compelled him to walk from Boston to Providence, Rhode Island, some forty miles distant, through a New England winter. A stage driver encountered him between Dedham and Walpole, Massachusetts, on foot, without his outside garments, indeed without any extra clothing at all.

On Friday, 11 December 1829, the *Providence Journal* ran a brief item that stated, "Mr. Booth, the celebrated tragedian, arrived in town yesterday, in a state of mental derangement, having traveled on foot from Boston.—His feet were much swollen, and it is said he slept in the woods on Wednesday night, covering himself with the leaves of the forest. He is now in the care of his friends, and we are happy to add, appears to be recovering from his illness."

According to Charles Blake, a Providence stage historian, Booth discarded his shoes along the way and upon his arrival in Providence went immediately to Deming's boardinghouse for sailors at the corner of South Main and Wickenden Streets. Word soon spread that the mad and miserable tragedian had arrived. A friend of Booth's, Colonel Josiah Jones, went to see the actor, who greeted him calmly enough but asked Jones for his boots. Jones complied, Booth put them on and left Deming's without a word. Jones borrowed a pair of shoes from the landlord, overtook Booth, who was hurrying down the street on some imaginary errand, and took the distraught actor to Jones' house on Aborn Street.

For some days Booth alternated fits of madness with perfect lucidity, while Jones entertained curious visitors, among them some religious types. One Sunday morning, Jones asked Booth to read something for his visitors. Booth asked for a Bible, chose a passage, and began. By the time Booth finished, no eye remained dry; never had the listeners heard the sublimity of Holy Writ so illuminated. When he finished, Booth took the opportunity to condemn the soulless mumblings of pastors who found reading an onerous task.

Eventually Booth demonstrated sufficient stability and was transported to New York for a few days' rest under Edwin Forrest's care. The editor of the Providence *Literary Subaltern* accompanied him and attempted to interview Booth, who supplied him with all manner of wild stories. The next month the nonplussed editor published the following:

> It was our fortune, to accompany Mr. Booth to New-York, after his late affair at the Tremont theatre, Boston. On our passage up the sound, I said to him, "Booth, when you are dead, I intend to write your biography."
>
> "If you do," said Booth, "I beseech you to be careful to relate one or two facts, which will otherwise be lost to my friends, and they are of infinite importance. I will write them down for you," he continued, "that you may not forget them."
>
> He then wrote the following, which was the only decided evidence we had of his insanity, whilst we were with him.
>
> "Booth once drank an excessive quantity of laudanum, in order to destroy himself, because a woman would not suffer him to eat off her left ear. Afterwards, he went and dug up a grave and carried home in a bundle, a skull and bones, which he used to sleep with; and his nocturnal visitations have often created alarm to the numerous wanderers of the night, who might be returning to their peaceful homes. It has been asserted, though the fact has not been sworn to, that he and the Devil, were seen one moonlight night in close communion over Lieutenant Smith's grave in Potter's Field, Philadelphia."
>
> At this period of Booth's acquaintance with Peters, it was believed and accredited by a celebrated Alchymist, that on the night of the

> ninth of August, at twelve o'clock precisely, these two unfortunate human beings, bound themselves by an irrevocable and damning oath to the service of Beelzebub. The oath was drunk in blood, out of a horse's skull, upon the Miller's tomb, three miles from Worthing, in Sussex, whither Booth and Peters went to visit certain Gypsies on a non-play day.
>
> The Miller's Tomb, is a celebrated place or kind of ancient Golgotha, where a Miller was entombed, according to the legends of antiquity. It is in Sussex.[21]

The editor described Peters as "the celebrated Antipodian, of 'celebrated celebrity.'"

Apparently Booth recovered quickly; on 23 December he played Octavian, the mad lover in *The Mountaineers,* "to great satisfaction," and "it was announced that he would appear again in three weeks."[22]

He did indeed return to the stage, even sooner than announced, in Philadelphia on 29 December 1829. For four nights things went well, then on 4 January 1830 Booth again had "a crazy fit"; R. C. Maywood substituted for him as Sir Giles.[23] Nevertheless, Booth reappeared in Philadelphia on the thirteenth of the same month and worked steadily for the next six weeks in Philadelphia, Boston, and New York. In Philadelphia between February tenth and March twenty-second, he played the Chestnut Street Theatre, the Washington Amphitheatre, the Arch Street Theatre, and the Walnut Street Theatre, indicating the complexity of his arrangements with managers at that time.

Booth's correspondences during this period reflect a certain defensive arrogance. From Washington, D.C., Booth wrote to Joseph Robinson at the Baltimore Circulating Library declining to perform in *The Lady of the Lake* as Roderick Dhu for William Warren's benefit.

> I am astonished at the request. My terms of course would be unmentionable.
>
> The Play itself is a most pitiful attempt of Sir Walter's. His Grub Street Elegance would not induce me to commit one line to memory.
>
> Roderick Dhu was parrotted into me when a boy, or I never should have condescended to study it.
>
> My time is engaged, therefore cannot have the pleasure of aiding Mr. Warren on the occasion of his Benefit with my services.[24]

While Booth's American career threatened to disintegrate, London still festered in his mind. He wrote from Baltimore during an engagement in late April 1830 to John Rowland Durrant, Royal Exchange, London, "I have just learned that you are the Lessee & Manager of Drury Lane Theatre for the next Season. If suitable with your arrangement I should like to form one of your Company. I would return to England, if an Engagement could be given me of fifteen pounds per week for one or more seasons. Your reply will oblige."[25] Booth wrote to the wrong man; Alexander Lee took over the management of Drury Lane for the 1830–31 season, succeeded by Alfred Bunn until 1841.

Booth had a bad season in 1829–30. Whether he contacted Lee we have no record, but he would not return to London for several years. Another Booth letter, undated and to an unknown recipient, asked for fifteen pounds per week for three to five years for which he would arrange to revisit the London theatres. After suggesting he would need at least six leading characters to establish his name, he added, "The salary I ask is not equal to what my Exertions can obtain in this Country—but there is a hankering for the old Soil which being gratified, would overbalance the deficiency."[26] Once a Londoner, always a Londoner.

In the meantime, he continued orbiting around the East Coast, plying his craft in the larger American cities. Philip Hone saw him in New York on 31 May 1830 and recorded his reactions in his diary.

> I went this evening to see Booth play Iago to Cooper's *Othello*. . . . I do not remember to have ever seen Booth, and was rather disappointed in his performance. It was respectable, but wanted spirit, raciness, and point; but I do not wonder at it, for Cooper is a perfect wet blanket resting upon all around, flat, stale, and unprofitable. O most lame and impotent conclusion! Is this the man whom I remember to have seen in my boyish days at the theater then in Greenwich Street? We have both grown older and I am only a looker-on in Verona, and am not compelled to obtrude my infirmities upon the public notice. *Tant mieux pour moi*.[27]

Cooper was in his mid-fifties when Hone saw him and had been acting in America since 1796.

Booth next tried management again, this time closer to home, in Baltimore.[28] He leased two theatres, the Adelphi and the Holliday, with his old friend Tom Flynn as acting manager. The season opened on 11 September 1830; Booth acted intermittently, then left his concerns on October eighth for several performances in Philadelphia, traveling back to Baltimore for a single performance on October twelfth. He appeared in Baltimore once more, closing the season on 22 November 1830.

The stars Booth imported for the Holliday Street Theatre included Charles Kean, the son of his old London foe. The elder Kean had not intended his son for the stage, but when Kean broke with Drury Lane in 1827, the management offered his son an engagement which he accepted. Three years later the younger Kean arrived in the United States for his first American tour. Booth naturally sought this attraction for his theatre, possibly out of curiosity but also as a definite box-office enticement. On 29 October 1830 Charles Kean performed Hamlet at the Holliday; Booth supported him as the Second Actor.

For Booth to accept, let alone volunteer, for such a small role had almost no precedent. Moreover, Booth gave the thankless role his full powers and artistry, as Asia Booth Clarke later recorded from an unidentified review. "Booth gave the actor's speech with great effect. The audience rose *en masse,* and cheered him . . . as much for the beauty of its delivery as [for] the modesty which induced him to select the subordinate character, thus bringing into effect the entire strength of his company, and extending every advantage to the distinguished stranger."[29]

During November a mysterious "Mrs. Booth" appeared at the Holliday. Advertisements listed her as Jessica in *The Merchant of Venice* during Kean's engagement, later as Barbara in *The Iron Chest,* with Sir Edward Mortimer performed by "a young gentleman from New York," rather than by Booth. Newspapers made no mention of her relationship, if any, to Booth. Considering that neither of Booth's daughters went on the stage, that Asia claimed to hate actresses, and that the father sought diligently to keep his sons from going into the theatre, it seems most unlikely that Booth would have suffered his lady to enter so tarnished a profession. Several unrelated Booths, none of them significant, appeared on various American stages in the first half of the nineteenth century.[30]

Booth forsook management soon thereafter for a long and uneventful engagement in Philadelphia, sharing the bill with Forrest for *Othello* on 20 December 1830. He also created the title role in a new but undistinguished script, *Sertorius,* written by a local lawyer. Wemyss described the premiere:

> Booth played the hero in a manner which would have commanded success for any piece; the beautiful poetry of this play, flowing from his lips, must have gratified the fastidious taste of any author—how, then, must it have delighted the audience. The play wanted *action*—there was too much declamation. It was received by a fashionable audience with every mark of success, and repeated several times, being withdrawn only by the termination of Mr. Booth's engagement.[31]

Booth next went to Richmond, arriving New Year's Day, 1831, and wrote to his father in Maryland—a long letter—two days later.

> I am once more in Richmond after an absence of more than eight years. In Philadelphia I encounter'd some difficulty in obtaining my money from the Manager & have been obliged to employ the Author of Sertorius in his legal character to collect the greater part of the Sums due me.
>
> I arrived in this city the day before yesterday, afterward I played Richard to a very good house & if the weather would only become fair, my Engagement here will be lucrative. Mercer, my Tenant of the Adelphi, is in Balto Jail. The Theatre consequently is at present closed.
>
> Sally on her return told you of Mary Ann's having had the scarlet fever. Cassandra Brevitt has had the Small Pox & was nearly dying. Junius was very weak when I left Baltimore & I sincerely hope Henry & Rosalie, with yourself, enjoy good health.
>
> Tell Joe to take care of the Horses & Cows & to water them at least twice a day, as he is apt to leave the Stable shut & forget that Horses are in the Stalls. Let Boatswain have clean straw at least once a week. Tell Sally and Hagar to mind that.
>
> I shall leave here for Washington about the 15th. Give my love to the children.[32]

Booth's concern for his animals, indeed, any animal, was central to his life, but he felt his father needed frequent reminders. As for his troubles with the Philadelphia managers, a lawyer's son knew how to deal with them, and so he wrote from Petersburg to attorney David Paul Brown, the author of *Sertorius*.

> Your letter was delivered me this morning. The intentions of the Chestnut Street Managers are evidently fraudulent, and I beg you

> will now mánifest no indulgence, but proceed as the Law allows instanter.
>
> The Travelling by Land & Water from Richmond may be considered at an end, except to this place. I am obliged to pass my time at one Town or the other & must continue to do so I fear till Spring. Stages and Steamboats are now useless. The Poor in Philadelphia must suffer dreadfully this [January] Weather if Fuel be as difficult to obtain as it is here.[33]

The remainder of 1831 and most of 1832 passed without incident. Booth traveled the eastern cities, staying relatively close to home: New York, Philadelphia, Boston, Baltimore, and Washington, D.C.

But Booth was far from content with his lot. On 12 September 1832 he wrote to a John Finlay, hoping to rid himself of the Adelphi Theatre in Baltimore. "Owing to a severe illness which has rendered me incapable of attending to my affairs I have at the earnest intreaty of my family, dispos'd of my property and shall shortly leave the United States for my native country as I am unable to cope with the buyers and sellers of managers who have nearly stripp'd me of all."[34] Booth went on to complain about a Mr. Chapman who rented an apartment in the theatre building, but who was upwards of four hundred dollars in arrears. Booth was fed up with his profession.

The old Booth propensity for trouble and disappointment arose again toward the end of October 1832. He played at the Arch Street Theatre in Philadelphia for six performances, closing on 27 October as Old Norval in *Douglas* in a benefit for the widow of the elder William Warren. Booth volunteered his services and appeared with the younger William Warren, who here made his first appearance on any stage.

The next Monday, the twenty-ninth, Booth was to play the Bowery Theatre in New York but failed to appear. The next day the manager published his apology in the *New York Evening Post*. "From the great disappointment evinced in consequence of Mr. Booth not having arrived from Philadelphia, and the uncertainty attending his present engagement from his severe indisposition, the Manager feels himself compelled to withdraw his name from the bills of engagement, but pledges himself to the engagement being fulfilled immediately." Booth's irregularities had now begun to interfere with his career, but the public forgave him time after time. One wonders how cold-bloodedly Booth cast himself in the role of a lunatic and how much was real.

In all fairness, production quality in the American theatre at this time would have made a saint swear. How incredibly bad it could get was described in detail for a performance of Booth's in New York at the Bowery Theatre to celebrate Evacuation Day, the anniversary of the British withdrawal from New York on 25 November 1783. Booth and T. D. Rice were to be the chief attractions.[35]

> Booth played Richard the third, and the house was crammed to such an extent that an *avalanche* of spectators broke from the pit, and covered the orchestra and the greater portion of the stage. By reasonable computation there were about three hundred persons on the stage and wings alone—soldiers in fatigue dresses—officers with side arms—a few jolly tars, and a number of apple-munching urchins. The scene was indescribably ludicrous. Booth played in his best style, and was really anxious to make a hit, but the confusion incidental to such a crowd on the stage, occasioned constant and most humorous interruptions. It was every thing, or any thing, but a tragedy. In the scene with Lady Anne . . . the gallery spectators amused themselves by throwing pennies and silver on the stage, which occasioned an immense scrambling among the boys, and they frequently ran between King Richard and Lady Anne to snatch a stray copper. In the tent scene, so solemn and impressive, several curious amateurs went up to the table, took up the crown, poised the heavy sword, and examined all the regalia with great care, while Richard was in agony from the terrible dream; and when the scene changed, discovering the ghosts of King Henry, Lady Anne, and children, it was difficult to select them from the crowd, who thrust their faces and persons among the royal shadows. The battle of Bosworth-field capped the climax—the audience mingled with the soldiers and raced across the stage, to the shouts of the people, the roll of the drums, and bellowing of the trumpets; and when the fight between Richard and Richmond came on, they made a ring round the combatants to see fair play, and kept them at it for nearly a quarter of an hour. . . . This was all done in perfect good humor, and with no intention to make a row. When Mr. Rice came on the stage to sing his celebrated song of Jim Crow, they not only made him repeat it some twenty times, but hemmed him in so that he actually had no room to perform the little dancing or turning when appertaining to the song; and in the afterpiece, where a supper-table is spread, some among the most hungry very leisurely helped themselves to the viands. It was a rare treat, indeed, to the audience.[36]

Audience members sitting onstage had been common in the English theatre till David Garrick (1717–79) drove them back into the pit in the eighteenth century, as Voltaire did in France about the same time. People who enjoy the theatre today and those who work in it owe a great deal to the pioneers of the past, Booth among them.

Booth revealed something more of his seething mental state in a letter written from Baltimore to William Jones, manager of Philadelphia's Arch Street Theatre, 5 November 1832:

> Most reverend and illustrious Signor, How fare the showmen? I have absconded, alas left my name in the Bill and I understand the Devil's to pay in consequence thereof, but Jones—is it not [?] to act on Friday. Jesus Christ & Mahomet died that Day, Adams and Jefferson also—many other great men have also made exalted Exits on that remarkable Day: it should be devoted to Prayer and Meditation.—Sunday, the Day of the Resurrection should be a time of rejoicing and pastime and good Deeds—I am willing to play gratuitously on that Day, provided the Surplus Proceeds of the House's Expense be given to the Relief of Orphans & Widows, the Deaf & Dumb Asylums & the Emancipation of Negroes by Societies who may form for that laudable purpose.
>
> Second my project and hereafter instead of being angry at my abrupt running away, you will say that I was right. A moral and retributive Agency is at work & what the Million may have called, or christened Insanity, I fear will prove Truth. . . . I am an Alien—not an Enemy & will become a citizen when my Master Andrew Jackson commends me to do so: till then I am in politics neuter.
>
> Or if you like crazy.
>
> My next appearance on the Arch St. Boards I wish to be on a Sunday night for Mr. Warren's Widow's benefit. On Friday preceding it I should like to preach in the Penitentiary with permission of the Authorities. . . .
>
> J B Booth
>
> celebrated actor[37]

Booth did not appear again until the following March; Jones must have looked upon the preceding letter as the ravings of a lunatic. But in mid-November, Booth performed a trouble-free engagement at the Bowery. Indeed, the *Spirit of the Times,* a weekly journal devoted to sports, horse racing, and theatre, applauded him vigorously.

> During the absence of Mr. Hamblin and Miss Vincent, the attractions at this theatre are kept up by Mr. Booth. On Monday he

> appeared in Richard before a full house. The celebrity which he has acquired in this part, had raised the expectations of the audience to that height which none but Booth could have realized. His performance gave general satisfaction, and although evidently suffering from the effects of his late illness, he surmounted all difficulties, and rendered the points of the play in a most masterly manner.[38]

Perhaps Booth perceived his career's delicacy and insecurity. He signed, at any rate, a year's engagement with Thomas Hamblin. The contract simply read, "16 Nov 1832—Agreement, Junius Brutus Booth and Hamblin. Engaged for one year, beg. 19 Nov, to perform, but never on two successive nights. Terms $6,000, 120 @ week."[39] The actor would pay his own travel expenses. It was a seemingly harmless document but one that Booth would regret. He played Boston and New York as 1833 began, then he returned to Baltimore; 1833 would contain some of the lowest moments of Booth's life, professionally and personally.

The year began innocuously enough. Thomas Hamblin advised manager "Nosey" Phillips to hire the Richmond Theatre for his new star, then Hamblin, Booth, Miss Naomi Vincent, and a company of supporting players began the trip south. On the road from Philadelphia to Baltimore the stagecoach broke down, leaving the company afoot. Booth offered the entire troupe accommodations at his farm; thither they trudged. A night's rest and a good breakfast put them all in better spirits.

Then Hamblin asked, "Why, Booth, how do you manage to kill the time, without company? You must be solitary here."

"I am never without company," replied Booth. "I am surrounded by congenial spirits; I converse and hold counsel with the great and good of all ages. Look—there are Shelley, and Byron, and Wordsworth; here are 'rare Ben Jonson,' Beaumont and Fletcher, and Shakespeare and Milton; with them, time never wearies, and the eloquent teaching that fall from their leaves, are counsellors and guides. These are my companions," said Booth, pointing to his beloved library, "and I am never *less* alone, than when alone."[40]

The company continued to Richmond for their engagement, and Booth's life began to fall apart.

In February 1833, Booth's fragile grip on sanity was put to the test most severely. A cholera epidemic started in Baltimore and swept through Maryland. By this time Booth and Mary Ann had six children; within a month—a little month—the disease killed three of them: Elizabeth, Mary Ann, and Frederick. Once when one of his horses had died, Booth thought Mary Ann could restore it to life by her prayers. Neighbors helped wrestle Booth into bed for a day's sleep, after which he returned somewhat to normal. The loss of his children put Booth teetering on the edge.

Mrs. Rogers described his anguish, recalling that when Booth returned from Richmond, abandoning his engagement, to find his child Mary had died and had been buried in the small cemetery on the farm for over a week, he had the body dug up and brought into the log house. He hoped somehow to bring her to life again, maintaining she would never have died had he been at home.[41]

Grief is a private matter, not publicly recorded. Booth's first extant comments appeared in this letter to Flynn:

> Mrs. Booth's health is so far impaired that it is essential I should remain with her for some time. The child was buried to-day here. It died on the 4th. On the 5th I played Hamlet, and a child's skull was thrown by Hadaway out of the grave in the fifth act.[42]
>
> Junius is still sick.
>
> It will not be in my power to resume the engagement till the 1st of May. Of course I must lose the intervening salary. It would be unjust to expect you to pay for services not rendered.
>
> Yours respy
>
> J B Booth[43]

While mourning his lost children, Booth still had to deal with Hamblin, who had threatened to sue him for nonappearance; Booth had abandoned his engagement when the first child died. He tried reasoning with the manager in an unusually long letter from Baltimore on 3 March 1833. Booth first tried to convince the manager that steamboats could not operate until the weather changed and that there were no stages running in time for him to fulfill his obligations. Booth then offered a counterproposal.

> I do not wish to quarrel with you, but your Disposition & mine unfortunately can never again harmonize therefore a long continuance or endurance of each other's society which must be the case if you persist in the unlucky Engagement made between us &

which you find often as inconvenient as I do—for instance the disposal of the nights—the risk of accidents & detentions, which seem to have (as a fatality) attended this Contract, in spite of every endeavor to keep it holy. For you to have broken it, as perhaps I shall be compelled to do by not arriving in time now.

I therefore beg you to consider the following proposition: "I will act Ten Nights in Boston, Twenty in Philadelphia, and Thirty in New York: Say to be classed for occupation of time as One Engagement at Boston, Two in Philadelphia, and Two in New York—and during such Engagement I do not wish to play more than three nights per week. You may use the name for benefits and choose the dates for commencing such Engagements between now & the first of November next. To apprize me within one month of the plan, that no Disappointment may occur—."

For this you will pay me ($3600) in nightly installments of sixty dollars nightly & every night of acting during said sixty nights.

Believe me you'll get more by this than by hostile measures as I have already made over my property, which no doubt was the object aimed at when a Suit was threatened: however I wish you safe out of Danger, your Interest, as well as Principle. I further will agree not to act in any other Theatre in New York during said terms of 60 nights Engagement between us.

Booth described specific possible business arrangements, then begged for understanding.

You are become cold, selfish, unfeeling and ________. I will not say more—your own reflexions in the hour of adversity will supply the blank. For Adversity you will encounter be sure—. You are surrounded by people more your Enemy than Friends. I can no longer be the latter: the former I seek not to be unless openly.

This letter you will not if you please, submit to the perusal of others—Act from yourself, as you did, and used to do some months past.

After repeating his terms and asking for an advance on his salary, Booth closed:

I am sick, Thomas Hamblin, and the contemplation of this pestering contract between us does me no good—I can't afford to hire Physicians, and I look upon them as useless except in cases of Fractures—Wounds, &c neither of which I have & yet am sick.

If you agree to what I here submit try and allow me a day or two to rally: but let me not be pestered with conversations from & with others in your Employ as to the Engagement. Pay the sum named yourself or by an Order on the Managers of Philada or Boston.

Speculate not with my feelings & I will not harm yours. Should you do so, my lord, then count me dangerous. We have gone far enough & I do not wish the Rubicon pass'd by either.

Awaiting your reply
I am
J B Booth[44]

Booth had reached his nadir in the spring of 1833. In an undated letter to Wemyss, he revealed something of the strain on his faculties and the impact of her children's deaths on Mary Ann.

My father is gone instead of me to Philadelphia, and as you are a Father & know how severe is the loss of a beloved child, I request you to meet Hamblin with him, and try to change the nature of a very silly Engagement I have with him, which now on my way to fulfil, I am prevented proceeding to, by the very dangerous state in which another Child lies who so forcibly reminds me of poor little [Otto?] that it induces me to appeal to you to wait with my father on Hamblin, who has I believe intentions to sue me for breach of contract. He has behaved rather unfriendly to me of late since the news of my poor child's Decease tore me from Richmond to prevent its Mother following it to the Tomb which but for my arrival in Balto would; or the Mad-house have been her lot. She is now sick as also myself. He (my father) will explain further to you and shew you the letters from Hamblin to self.

I have received no salary from Hamblin since March 4th. He owes me for the week I played afterwards, to the 11th. I have committed no wilful breach of Engagement and his cool behaviour towards me, with the attendant circumstances, considering he has made money by the Engagement thus far; & I have not much more than cleared myself, ought to have some weight in inducing him to defer the future performances, and if he have any feeling, to change my Agreement to the Shape I have proposed to him in my recent Letters. As you are well acquainted with Theatrical matters, it is my particular request that you will do all you can at this Interview to serve my interest. . . . If the engagement can be cancelled altogether I should still prefer it to my other arrangement. My respects to your family.[45]

Booth and Wemyss came to some understanding or other while the fever swept through Harford County. Booth employed his old friend and playwright David Paul Brown to deal for him and wrote him on 23 March 1833:

> Yours is received but today enclosing $50 from Mr. Hamblin. He only owed me ninety dollars, therefore I cannot understand his paying you for me $150. As I know his liberality springs from some policy I only wish you to retain of some forty dollars, which he owes me, & in doing this please give him back his balance. . . .
>
> Owing to the peremptory way in which I was hurried from my home by his letter from Balto another of my children has perished.
>
> Mr. Hamblin, however he may feign to others, or even to myself, I have found too late is a designing bitter enemy. I am in his power and must go on of course with the Engagement.
>
> Tomorrow I shall leave on my way to Philada and hope no more fatalities may arise & intercept my performance of the bitterest and most losing Engagement I ever was duped & inveigled into.[46]

Whatever Booth's naïveté about business dealings, he remained true to his word and did indeed play eight performances in Philadelphia for Hamblin, often costarring with him, in late March and early April. He appeared once in New York as Richard III, then there is no recorded performance by Booth till mid-November 1833, a hiatus of some seven months.

Booth was at the farm on the first of November, as he wrote William Duffy in Philadelphia about some newspaper subscriptions he wanted canceled. Booth presumably summered on the farm, consoling his grieving wife, who was soon expecting to deliver her seventh child. On 13 November 1833, Mary Ann gave birth to a boy, Edwin Thomas Booth. Edwin had apparently been conceived the previous January, just before the deaths of the three children. He was born in sorrow; he was destined to be a child of sorrow. The elder Booth named his new son after two friends, Edwin Forrest and Thomas Flynn.

Edwin Thomas Booth was born during a meteor shower with a caul, or membrane, over his face, causing the servants to prophesy a charmed life. In fact, the mid-November meteor shower occurred annually on the East Coast, but the 1833 display was especially spectacular.[47]

Perhaps Booth saw the display, but he missed Edwin's birth; he was playing Richard III at the Bowery. For two weeks he alternated performances between the Arch Street Theatre in Philadelphia and the Bowery Theatre in New York. The battle with Hamblin dragged on, as Booth described in a letter to Wemyss from Philadelphia on 16 November 1833.

> Your letter has reached me & I thank you for the good-will therein expressed. Perhaps Scott has told you of my present dilemma. Hamblin sent on Flynn with power of Atty, legal Proofs of the [Damage?] . . . as I was packing up my trunks for the Stage Office & ready to depart in the morning, so on Saturday night in walks the Agent with Attorney &c—Russell suffers a disappointment and I scarcely know how to arrange matters for all. I wish you & Russell could accommodate each other as regards the time.
>
> Hamblin cancels his claim for damages as well as the old Contract for 8 months on condition of my acting now at the Bowery 2 weeks and six weeks beginning the seventh day of April: the interim must be devoted to the West if no fresh accident prevents it.
>
> I was engaged to Russell for 7 nights in Cincinti [*sic*] beginning 18th of November; then 7 nights in Louisville & 8 nights in Orleans. If you and he are on terms try and settle so I can play your six in Pittsburg during the vacancy stated. I may be able to reach Cincinnati by the 9th of Dec. is what I wrote to Russell in my hurry on the night of my arrest, however if it can be a few days later I shall prefer it. So that I can safely [convenience?] in New York by the 7th of April is all that I wish yourself & Russell to arrange for me. Direct your answer to Arch St. Theatre where I have to appear the alternate nights of the Bowery Engt. a precious fatiguing Job I can tell you for one not long recovered from sickness.
>
> Wishing you success
> I am
> D. Wemyss
> Yours truly
> J B. Booth[48]

On 1 December 1833 he wrote to Duffy from Bel Air and two days later to Wemyss from the Baltimore stagecoach office, confirming the Pittsburgh, Pennsylvania, engagement.

> I am, as the French say, en route, and hope to reach Pittsburgh in time to begin on Monday night—bar sickness, my lord judge, and other delays. Messrs. Managers of the West, you are partly the cause of ______. Had you not announced Mr. Booth as being engaged in Pittsburgh and Cincinnati, Hamblin never would have cotched me

here as he did. It is best, in my humble opinion, not to announce until the beast arrives.

Your's as in duty-bound,

J.B.

Good!—commence with I am—conclude with J. B.—
he conjugates—the villain![49]

Booth played engagements in Pittsburgh and Cincinnati uneventfully and tried to get to his next engagement in Louisville, Kentucky, but the "state of the river" made him late. After his arrival, Booth wrote his father that his engagement progressed nicely, then brought him up to date on his latest business venture, his religious views, and how he lived on the road.

> I have just purchased two Egyptian Priests of the God Apis (Mummies) and hire them for exhibition at the Museum, for which I receive 12 dollars per week.[50] Perhaps this is as good an investment as the stock in some of the more tottering banks at this juncture. They (the Priests) are in good preservation and yet neither eat nor drink; they are direct from Thebes and have only been in the Union 4 months. The Papyrus Mss. are in excellent and legible order, but unfortunately the Literati have not been able to translate their meaning. A Frenchman named Champolion published a work explanatory of Hieroglyphics, but these seem of greater antiquity than those he describes. Languages like Nations and Religions take their turns and all seem to prove the constant mutability of Nature.
>
> I pity that Hindoo for relinquishing his creed lately in England. Although practical Christianity is a beautiful type of Man's approach to perfection, yet he is not so near it as is the poor despised and unavenged Hindoo. So thoroughly am I convinced that these Asiatics are nearest the Truth, that were I acquainted with their language and living in Hindustan, I should most conscientiously and devotedly become a worshipper, not of Fire, but of those Images, which every minute satisfy the Hindoo who and what he is himself and also of his relative position in the World, which the vain European, the brutal American and the ignorant African have long forgotten.
>
> I have written a letter to June [Junius, Jr.] and one to Mary Ann and hope they and the whole family are in enjoyment of health. I lived here some days at the Hotel which as far as magnificence and comfort thoroughly English go, certainly has not its equal in the United States. I moved from it and occupy a room in the Theatre and live much more to my notions of Luxury: viz: there is nothing I

> use that has cost aught its life. My fire is of coal, my lamp either of olive, cotton, or flax-seed oil. I get water cresses and [surrey?] grass with sea biscuit or brown butter or white sugar in it there is blood and the other two are generally obtained at the cost of Life to the wretched Calf. I use sweet olive oil to my soaked biscuit and with tomato ketchup or catsup and salt make a good and wholesome food and incapable of producing bile or acid on the stomach. An orange or an apple, or a slice of Cocoa nut added, a stalk of celery or a radish and my meal is good enough for an Emperor.
>
> I abstain from Eggs, Oysters and all those putrefying substances which engender fevers and constipation. A glass or two of wine ór beer after my dinner which of course is also vegetable.
>
> A bed of straw and a straw pillow which is sweeter than a feather one as there is no stench of carrion about it and I sleep sound, feel very little cold and am in better and more elastic spirits than half the people I meet with. Give my respects to Mr. Woolsey and his family and my kind love to the children and my wife. . . .
>
> Your affectionate Son,
>
> J. B. Booth[51]

Noah Ludlow recalled Booth's lunacy in Louisville, describing his attempt to sell eviscerated rats to people going to the market, claiming rats were much more tender than squirrels and cleaner than hogs. Booth made no culinary converts, according to Ludlow.[52]

A fellow player, T. D. Rice, told Ludlow a tale about being with Booth one afternoon in a hotel, when a clergyman called on Booth at his request. Said the preacher, "Mr. Booth, I have come to perform the last rites of our church over the deceased, as you desired I should."[53]

Booth led the clergyman and an astonished Rice into the next room and pointed to a small coffin, which the preacher opened.

The preacher expressed amazement, asking Booth, "Pray, sir, what is the meaning of this?"

"Of what, sir?" countered Booth.

"Of this. You requested me to come here and perform the funeral rites of the dead, and you present to my astonished senses a poor *pigeon.*"

"Well, sir," said Booth, "is it not dead?"

"Truly said; but it is not a human,—it has no soul."

"How do you know, sir, that it has no soul?"

The preacher, who had edged to the door, said, "I will not suppose, sir, that you brought me here to insult me, and I hope your friend will find a strait waistcoat for you as soon as possible." With that, the clergyman fled the scene.

Booth did not mean this episode as a joke. Before he left town he wrote the clergyman a letter.

> My Dear Sir: Allow me to return you my grateful acknowledgments for your prompt and benevolent attention to my request last Wednesday night. Although I am convinced your ideas and mine thoroughly coincide as to the real cause of man's degradation, yet I fear, human means to redeem him are now fruitless. The fire must burn, and Prometheus endure his agony. The pestilence of Asia must come again ere the savage will be taught humanity. May you escape. God bless you, sir.
>
> J. B. Booth[54]

Ludlow related yet another yarn about Booth's getting so noisily drunk one night he was thrown in jail. Left to himself, Booth began to sing "The Poachers," a popular English song. This roused the prisoner across the way, a man using the name George Lovett. Lovett, a great fan of Booth's, introduced himself, and the two prisoners chatted till dawn, Lovett being a highly educated criminal. He was about thirty and under sentence of execution for highway robbery and murder.

The next day Booth sent for Ludlow to bail him out. By the time Ludlow arrived, Booth had talked the jailer into letting him into Lovett's cell, in which Booth introduced the criminal to his manager. Booth left Louisville, but Rice remained, and after Lovett's execution he secured the thief's head and took it to Philadelphia and Booth. Booth prepared the grisly relic and used it for Yorick's skull in the gravedigger scene whenever he played Hamlet.[55]

Another letter indicating Booth's state of mind before he left Louisville has survived. This one he addressed to Joseph Cowell, Esq., Clarke's Store, Whitewater Township, Hamilton County, Ohio:

> Year of the Christ
> Feb. 3. 1834 — Exterior of Louisville Jail
> of the Planet
> 5994
>
> Praise be to Allah!
>
> Your loving communication has been just delivered after my third incarceration in the above for carrying on solely an unprofitable and disgraceful business: namely—telling the Truth to Scoundrels. I have

> suffered much what is called physical pain—shamed more and feel (I wish I did not) more supreme contempt than ever for my own race. I wish I could pity—I can not. I can not say 'Forgive them, for they know not what they do!'
>
> Per advice I hear you intend to make money by sale of Hog's blood—in which is the life. It is none of my business—only be sure blood calls for blood: your horticultural notion I prefer, only be gentle in thy operations even then for there is a never dying worm. The Hindoo religion is the only one I believe to be at all like the Truth—I feel so certain of it that were this my last moment & Death hanging over me on the very eve to stifle what tiny spark was lingering in my heart I would declare myself Hindoo versus quasidum.—Had there been no fish there would have been no Crucifixion—do you take? Excuse bad pen, hurry—dirty hands torn papers and Steamboat about to go. . . .
>
> Yrs ever
>
> J. B. Booth[56]

Booth next played Cincinnati, although the records are incomplete. On 22 February 1834 he wrote Wemyss' wife from Wheeling, Virginia (later West Virginia), the letter accompanied by two fine Kentucky turkeys.

> I hope you are in full enjoyment of health, and that your lamp, fed with vegetable oil, burns well and clear. I take the freedom of making you a present of two handsome turkeys—pets of mine—which I transfer to you on condition that you will not have them killed, but let the children now and then give 'em bread to eat and water to drink, or pulse, as Daniel calls it, and let them live until the great Jehovah of the Christians causes them to die of a good old age.[57]

Booth usually carried little or no money, except when traveling, and then only enough to cover expenses. Two days after the turkeys arrived, Wemyss received a letter. "Please pony up, and pay my attendant and companion, John, enough to settle with the captain for his passage, as I have only by me some silver and 1400 dollars in two large lumps, one for a thousand, t'other $400. I hope your wife received her turkeys." Wemyss thought the turkeys looked delicious.

Two days later Booth roared into Pittsburgh with Sam Houston, then governor of Tennessee.[58] As Wemyss said, the evil spirit was upon him. Booth played Pescara in *The Apostate* with Mrs. Duff on 27

February 1834, then departed for the east with Houston, Booth painted and dressed as an Indian chief.

Once safely back at the farm, Booth again wrote to Wemyss.

> Please forward me by the earliest opportunity a large Mattress I left at Weaver's on his Landing place near my Room (No 6) the day I left Pittsburgh with Governor Houston, also a Richard's Sword & red Sash.
>
> I left at Mr. Forrest's lodgings my Pescara's Dress with a request that he would place it in his Trunk & bring it to me when he came northward: the melancholy event respecting his brother may have prevented him so doing—I must therefore beg you to make inquiry concerning this as well as the former matter & write me the particulars. Ask Mr Adams . . . if a Dog I lost in Pittsburgh on board the Ohioan has been recovered, take care of him if so, for my sake, till I write to you or see you & forward all the other Articles by my performance coming eastward.[59]

Booth had apparently littered Pennsylvania with various lost items while under the influence.

The next two months he spent in Philadelphia and New York, accompanied by the young Junius; on April twelfth he wrote to his father, still pleading for his attention to the farm.

> I hope things go right, the Rows in New York are alarming.[60] We are well. If you are arrived at the farm I wish you to tell Joe to take all care of the live things left in his charge & not to sleep away from the house. If he is forced to go to Mill or Store, please do you oblige me by staying at the house during such, his one or two hours absence as it is not prudent or safe to leave the premises entirely deserted. It is time to sow some more Peas & the Squash Seed I gave him. He may also plant some pumpkins in the Peach Orchard & he must finish the pales round the parlor window. I hope you enjoy good health. I shall be home May 22nd. June sends his love.[61]

Booth had borrowed some money from William Duffy, the Albany manager, and now wrote him to arrange an engagement as payment. Booth offered his services for four nights, asking for a third of the receipts for three nights and half the fourth, or a flat fee of three hundred dollars; other managers paid Booth comparable sums.

That summer Booth stayed at the farm, from which he wrote a chatty letter to his friend Flynn, on 6 August 1834.

I return you many thanks for the variety of news sent us. I was obliged to visit Philadelphia & on my return found June going home with your letters & the newspapers. I have had a letter from Louisville saying George Lovett was condemned to be hung for murder on the 1st of this month: if such were true, his earthly troubles are by this time over. . . . During my few hours sojourn in Philada I saw Forrest. Who were the 2 performers in Tom & Jerry that got to fighting as the phrase is? Some short remark was in the Boston Galaxy about it & as far as I could make head or tail of it they were two Englishmen—Anderson & Farren.[62]

All Offences I suppose will from the growing dislike and jealousy be set down to the English. Holy Jasus!!! We've had a Camp Meeting on the verge of the farm & the splendid yelling &c actually prevented me from getting my nocturnal rest, therefore I stroll'd to Philada. Brower's Hotel is now about the best in that City. Your theatre will open too early to do much if this hot weather lasts. I hope Mrs. Flynn does not suffer.

. . . Farren actually forced me to play that Oroonoko the last time I was in New York at the time of a row in Chatham Street Chapel respecting one Brown, a Negro from Liberia, and the lumber fell on his own sage shoulders, about the time of a second religious row. Hamblin must have been insane to create him the representative. Talent he has none & Tact enough to make himself disliked by all in the theatre. As a Dry Goods Store Keeper or Bacon Dealer he might do well in the West Indies—as Manager of the Bowery Theatre & as an Actor on its stage for my own part I congratulate Hamblin; he has discharged him. If he wants to do well, he'd better engage you as Manager as if Cowell joins Simpson, which is likely, Hamblin will want an active Lieutenant or he'll go down—down—down—. . . .

J B Booth[63]

In mid-September Booth's script, *Ugolino,* starring J. R. Scott in the title role, appeared for seven performances at the Bowery, but Booth apparently did not attend it, as he had begun another season's wandering up and down the East Coast, foregoing his customary trips to the South.

The next indication of Booth's growing mental distress was recorded by a Philadelphia physician, James Rush. Rush, who had married into a fortune and dabbled in literature and drama, had just written a play about Hamlet which took place before the murder of Hamlet's father. Rush often treated Booth and recorded the actor's latest escapade in his diary for 25 March 1835.

> This evening Booth the Actor called upon me in a state of Derangement and left upon my plate the following note—
>
> > "I am delighted with your Hamlet. The scene with the Gipsy is excellent—you are the Shakespeare of this day. You know where I put up in N. Second Street.
> >
> > In passing through this 'great temaqueous slave market' perhaps you'll condescend to see me. Excuse my stealing your pocket handkerchief—
> >
> > Yours J.B.B."
>
> My handkerchief was lying on the table upon which he wrote, which I suppose suggested the idea of his stealing it, but it was not taken.[64]

In July Booth began a series of correspondences revealing disturbances welling up within him. The first he directed to no less a personage than the president of the United States, whom he much admired, Andrew Jackson.

> Brower's Hotel, Philadelphia
>
> July 4th, 1835
>
> You damn'd old Scoundrel if you don't sign the pardon of your fellow men now under sentence of Death De Ring & De Soto I will cut your throat whilst you are sleeping. I wrote to you repeated Cautions—so look out or damn you I'll have you burnt at the Stake in the City of Washington.
>
> Your Master
> Junius Brutus Booth
>
> You know me! Look out![65]

Booth was only joking; in 1834 a presidential assassination was both unthinkable and unprecedented.

Later in July 1835, Booth wrote from his farm to Duffy at Buffalo, New York, to reject an invitation to go there.

> Your offer is generous & at the same time, excuse my vanity, correct. It is really so remote from my summer haunts, that <u>same</u> Niagara, and at the <u>same</u> time I understand so very eccentrically noisy & obstreperous in its <u>still</u>-vaulting & lofty tumbling that it might drive me crazy to look at the stupendousness of its restless aqueous body—argal—during the Dog-days, had not I best avoid all which might induce Hydrophobia?

I wish you success most cordially and when our planets cause us to meet each other, I trust a Mint Julep and a squint at Demogorgon will amuse us as we sing cigarro tella mano. "It's our delight of a shiny night, &cetera."[66]

A week later he turned down James H. Caldwell in New Orleans, again making a ridiculous excuse.

Your letter I have received but would not reply to for reasons I wish the Publick to know—viz: a certain Law has been sanctioned by the Populace of New Orleans to detriment the Interest of Gamblers in consequence of such a law being approved of by the Mob I shall not condescend to degrade myself by acting on the stage when my Patrons have & do suffer persecution. I therefore declare to you that I break my Engagement.[67]

And on 28 September 1835, Booth's Philadelphia doctor, James Rush, entered into his diary:

This day on visiting Booth's child, now sick at Browers in Second St where his wife is staying. I had after leaving the room a long conversation on the stair and afterwards at the street door of the Hotel, with Booth himself on the subject of his habit of drinking—and said those numberless things of both warning and encouragement, which a sober man may and ought to say to one with naturally good feelings and high powers in an art, but of habits that are rapidly reducing him to imbecility of mind and to crookedness of passions. This drinking has taken most of his appetite away, and he lessens even the little chance of his getting nourishment through a foolish freak, of eating no meat,—which he fell into from reading Shelley, one of your vain, wish-to-be-remarkable poets, and good-for-nothing idle and mean complainers of the injustice of the world. I advised Booth to drink nothing but water, for I knew if he did so he would soon come to his senses sufficiently to think it would be neither an evil to him nor cruel to animals to eat their flesh,—for I ought to add that this poor fellow, who has for years past kept his wife in misery, and his friends in fear by his outrageous threats & acts has bothered his acquaintances by vexatious importunity, till they bolt their doors against him—this fellow I say in his mad humanity, will not eat meat forsooth because it encourages acts of suffering to animals.—But to return, as I said, upon advising him to take to water, and he would soon come to good sense, he promised to abstain and I left him, as I had often done before after the same advice, with not the least confidence in his promise to regard it, accordingly in less than four hours afterwards, I found the following short epistle on the slate which hangs within my office door.—

> "Thanks for the advice of being temperate; I've broke my promise, and am again intoxicate.
>
> Yours ever
>
> J. B. Booth."[68]

Something wild was building up again in Booth, and in less than a year it would erupt. But for now he resumed his eastern circuits. When on 18 November 1835 Mary Ann Booth delivered a daughter, Booth wrote from New York, "Call the little one Asia in remembrance of that country where God first walked with man, and Frigga, because she came to us on a Friday, which day is consecrated to the Northern Venus."[69] The parents had considered naming the new baby for Sydney Bateman, the wife of their friend H. L. Bateman, and Asia signed her early letters Asia Sydney. In point of fact, Asia was born on a Thursday.

Booth played a long engagement at the Bowery Theatre in November, marred by another incident. In his diary, Philip Hone recalled Booth as billed for Iago on November ninth. The house filled, the curtain rose, and Hamblin as Othello waited for his costar; Booth crossed the stage, left by a back door, and disappeared for two or three days. On 13 November Hone entered: "Poor Booth now comes out with a humble apology for the 'sad and unconscious act,' the excuse for which he says is 'a serious visitation, affecting and enfeebling my nerves, and a long deprivation of sleep, acting on a body debilitated by previous illness, and a mind disordered by domestic affliction, occasioning a partial derangement.'"[70] Both manager and public forgave him yet again, and Booth went on to star as Sir Giles Overreach on the fourteenth.

Booth completed this New York engagement—without further recorded incident—then had a brief engagement in Philadelphia. On 26 November 1835 his performance as Sir Giles was announced as a "farewell benefit prior to his departure for Europe"; Booth was planning another London engagement.

From Baltimore Booth wrote to Wemyss to arrange a Philadelphia booking.

> Mr. Rice informs me you wish us both to re-appear at the Walnut Street Theatre. For myself I have no objection, provided you can let us have Thursday night next on the following terms, viz: to all us the first fifty dollars received, and then to halve the surplus—one moiety or half part to be yours, the other ours.
>
> This is my proposal: Mr. Rice coincides with it & if you do the like you may announce me for Pescara or Octavian and Mr. Rice for Bone Squash Diavolo.[71]

Booth played in Washington at the American Theatre; Wemyss recalled it as a profitable engagement, for both the actor and the manager. Wemyss' only memory of the engagement was the Irish actor Paddy Field playing the Ghost of the elder Hamlet while so drunk he staggered out the wrong entrance. Booth went on, after laughing with the audience; Wemyss supposed him to have a "fellow-feeling for a fellow-failing."[72]

While the Irish were not the only hard drinkers on the stage, such mishaps regularly plagued touring stars. Some years later, according to the *Memphis Daily Express,* an Irishman substituted as the Ghost of the elder Hamlet at the last minute in a small town. Save for his brogue, the substitute managed to get through the first scene with Booth as Hamlet. By the closet scene, however, the Irishman had been "looking into a green bottle until everything looked blue," and the following exchange was made:

Enter Ghost

Hamlet—Save me, and hover o'er with your wings,
You heavenly guards!—what would your gracious
Figure?
Queen—Alas! he's mad.
Hamlet—Do you not come your tardy son to chide,
That laps'd in time and passion lets go by
Th' important acting of dread command?
O, say!
Ghost—Hamlet, me boy, don't forget!
This visit that I'm paying ye—
Off-stage voice—Come off! come off! You'll kill
the performance!
Ghost—I've come on here to play the ghoust,
And by the Holy Mother I'll finish it.
To Hamlet—This visit is to whet your purpose!
But look at yer muther, ye blackguard,

> Don't you see the amazement sitting on her?
> Go quick and get betwixt her and her frightning
> Soul! Consate and wicker baskets!
> Spake to her, ye villain!

The curtain crashed down as Booth drove the sodden Ghost off the stage with the flat of his sword. Such were the vicissitudes of touring in nineteenth-century America.[73]

Apparently Booth held no ill will toward the Irish; John W. Oliver late in his life recalled seeing a crowd gathered one rainy day in Baltimore. When he investigated he discovered Booth, "in the very ecstasy and recklessness of intoxication," teaching an Irish ex-bookbinder (who had left his trade for the stage) to recite King Richard's soliloquy, "Now is the winter of our discontent," in a brogue. Oliver thought it the funniest thing he had ever seen, as did the crowd, who paid no mind to the storm, while enjoying watching Booth full of Baltimore whisky.[74]

Wemyss recalled a brilliant farewell engagement in Philadelphia by Booth, his Richard playing to eight-hundred-dollar houses twice, being repeated by audience request. "Such," mused Wemyss, "is the hold this wonderful man possesses over the minds of his audience, and such was the estimation of his talents during this engagement."[75]

But this success preceded yet another outrage. Booth played two farewell engagements in Washington in February 1836. On 26 March 1836, the *Spirit of the Times,* admittedly a sensational rag, published on page one a lurid tale of Booth's "usual attacks of eccentricity." Booth was supposed to have been onstage when he turned up drunk in Bladensburg, Maryland, just outside the District of Columbia. A friend took him home and gave him a bed, but at midnight, so the story went, Booth evaded the servants and escaped. The startled servants heard him in the stable yard, naked, declaiming lines from *King Lear* in a raging snowstorm. Also according to the *Spirit,* on another occasion he wandered about all night and was found early the next morning passed out in the road, completely senseless. A physician stayed with him for an entire day and at length allowed him to leave for Baltimore and his family.

Booth was not done yet. On 16 April 1836, the *Spirit* reprinted a lengthy story from the *Baltimore Transcript:*

> It appears that Mr. Booth had for some time past been seriously indisposed, so much so as to be noticed by the newspapers in the District of Columbia, . . . although he elicited the unanimous approbation of the critics at the time, each account of his performances agreed that he was laboring under severe indisposition. In this state of bodily infirmity he arrived in this city, where he has been confined ever since to his private dwelling. On Monday morning, 28th, during the absence of his wife from his bed side, and while laboring under a mental aberration he attempted to immolate himself by hanging, in which he had partially succeeded when discovered by his wife, who released him from his perilous situation, and sent for medical aid, upon the arrival of which, had somewhat recovered, and although not entirely sane, there were some moments when the cloud seemed to be dissipated, and his countenance would beam with the utmost complacency, which brightened the hopes of his family and friends. It was during one of these returns to self-possession, immediately after the arrival of medical aid, that he burst into tears and exclaimed in the most feeling manner, "My God—my God! what could have come over me!"[76]
>
> We publish the above, in order that it might do away with any false impressions that may have been created as to the cause of this unfortunate affair, and in conclusion would remark that as Mr. Booth abstains altogether from eating any food which has had animal life, and lives only upon vegetables and light diet, his physical form has naturally become much debilitated, and rendered unable to sustain the working of his gigantic mind, which, when brought into full play in the arduous duties of his profession, often dethrones reason and leaves "a wreck behind."

Few other papers seem to have dealt with the incident, although the *Baltimore American and Commercial Daily Advertiser* had on 30 March 1836 noted, "We have never seen the time when self-destruction was so common as it is now. The newspapers are positively burdened with accounts of hanging, throat cutting, and the blowing out of desperate brains. It is becoming unfashionable to live, and the rage is, to die."

A little over a week after the supposed suicide attempt, Booth wrote to Flynn, intimating awareness of mortality but not referring to suicide.

> I have been rather unlucky since I saw you and am only just about again from the Hospital where it was thought my leg would have to be amputated. It must be nurs'd yet for some days. My reason for

> writing is to beg you will purchase a [?] for me at the Life Insurance Office for the Children. It will cost much less in New York than here. For your advance I will pay you with Interest. You may insure either my life or yours for $2000 to be paid the Children on their reaching the ages of 21: or say insure $500 each on Junius Brutus Booth (15), Henry Byron Booth (10), Rosalie Booth (12), Edwin Thomas Booth (2), & Asia Sydney (4 months). I understand you can in New York effect it by one general Installment or Policy without the annual payments which are so troublesome.
>
> If you can spare the change or Hamblin will do it I will soon repay you as some money is due me from Philada & I shall soon resume my Engagements. The whole amount you'll have to pay will not exceed above $250 or $300. Do it instantly & oblige your friend & well wisher.
>
> J B Booth
>
> P.S. If any thing should occur to me, Tom, take care of my Children & I will assist your family in their need if it should ever so happen.
>
> Write by return or come with the Policy in person & if well enough I'll travel with you. My respects to Mrs. Flynn, your brother & sister.[77]

Throughout Booth's life, rumors and exaggerations about his various activities abounded. No more details surfaced about his attempted suicide in 1836, nor about a nearly amputated leg, but Booth, about to turn forty, had stared into the face of his own mortality, perhaps for the first time.

In mid-May and early June he continued touring. He went with Boston's Lion Theatre Company to Providence for a pair of two-performance engagements. The *Spirit of the Times* commented on Booth's support in Boston, revealing something of the conditions under which Booth performed and of the growing public suspicions about him.

> He had a very successful engagement, so far as concerns himself, but has been with one or two exceptions wretchedly supported. To cap the climax of absurdity, the actor to whom was assigned the character of *Gomez* in "The Apostate," did not know a word of his part, and attempted to cover his ignorance by "splitting the ears of the groundlings," and reciting verse "shreds and patches" of other plays. The good natured audience had borne a great variety of glaring faults very patiently, but this went far beyond that point where patience ceases to be a virtue, and they very unceremoniously

> gave the delinquent the "big bird." This was at the close of the third act, where the interest of the piece begins to be developed. The curtain fell, and after a "wait" of about fifteen minutes, the manager came forward, and stated that one of his actors, on whom considerable depended, had taken "French leave." The general cry was *"Who is he?"*—"Give use his name," but the manager very modestly refusing to answer the interrogatories, a voice from the boxes cried out *"Is it Booth?"* "No!" was the prompt reply, and the excitement soon after subsided. Some time having elapsed, the curtain again arose, not however for the continuance of The Apostate, but for a Fancy Dance—think of the inconsistency! "Pescara's Masterpiece" introduced by a *fancy dance.*[78]

Something of more substance took place while Booth appeared in Boston, but exactly what remains a mystery. On 20 May 1836, the *Boston Post* ran an advertisement for Booth in *Richard the Third.* William Barrymore, the stage manager, however, appended a note.

> The public is most respectfully informed, (and to allay all unnecessary excitement) that the prosecution of Mr. Booth for $3,000 damages, was instantly met by a spirited number of friends—and good and substantial bail promptly tendered. The merits of the case will be submitted to the tribunal of the country, and to the decision of an impartial jury. In the mean time, Mr. Booth, free from all the perplexities that have surrounded him, will have an opportunity of exercising those transcendent talents which he so eminently possesses.

The litigant was one Thomas Barry, but the nature of the suit is not available from the Boston civic records.[79] The matter was evidently internal; Barry was a former stage manager at the Park Theatre in New York who became a Boston manager in 1833, bringing a highly respected reputation with him. The nature of his quarrel with Booth has not survived.[80]

Booth at least got out of town to Providence for two nights, then played an engagement in Philadelphia from 30 May through 11 June 1836. He next went to Baltimore and Harford County to plan the details of his upcoming return to England. The details of his plans he sent in a letter to his father on 20 August 1836.

> I have expected some time an answer to my letters that I sent you from Boston where all my difficulties were adjusted with Barry by my consenting to give him three nights performance gratis on & during my next Engagement at his Theatre—Pelby paid me—and

> Hamblin proposed the trip to England for this winter, as he relinquished rebuilding the Bowery, which is now let to Dinneford of the Franklin Theatre in New York. Had time allowed I should have tried to bring all on to the farm to see you before our departure which takes place today for Liverpool. Write to me, care of [Silverad?], whom I will find on my arrival in London where Hamblin & I shall be acting together until April and shall then come back—Don't be alarmed for us on acct. of the long journey; it is not 500 miles further than to New Orleans & not half as dangerous. What you want, get in my name from Hays & let Joe mind the Instructions I left with him on going away. Any letters that may come to me, lock up in your Trunk for me and with sincere wishes for a continuance of Health, & contentment to you, believe me, dear Father, your grateful Son. I should like to send you the Keys of the farm, but I suppose you would still prefer remaining at Mr. Woolsey's to whom present my respects. Such attention to my Interest as he can spare & give during my absence I shall be thankful for & will repay. We all desire our loves to you & pray for your welfare. I shall expect to visit you in May next, until when God bless and protect you.
>
> Your affectionate Son,
> J.B. Booth[81]

Affectionate or not, Booth misled his father: Francis Wemyss reported that Booth played Richard III on 22 August 1836 to a house of $556. Indeed, he played New York, Philadelphia, Boston, Albany, and New York and Philadelphia again before his departure. His last American performances in 1836 were well received; the *United States Gazette* of Philadelphia referred to Booth as "unquestionably the best tragedian that has of late years appeared amongst us," adding that, "when he chooses to exert his surpassing powers, [he] can convey to his audiences a nearer impression of reality in his tragic delineations than any actor we have seen."[82]

Finally, on 20 October 1836, as reported by the *United States Gazette* the next day, Booth, Mary Ann, Junius, Jr., Rosalie, Edwin, Henry Byron, Asia, and their longtime servant Hagar set sail on the *Susquehanna* for Liverpool under the command of Captain Cropper. Thomas Hamblin evidently made other travel arrangements.

Across the Atlantic waited Adelaide, who was—as inconceivable as it may seem—still unaware of Booth's American circumstances, and his only legitimate son, Richard Junius Booth, now seventeen years old.

6

An Apparent Heir

I would forget it fain,
But, O, it presses to my memory.
—*Romeo and Juliet,* III, ii, 109–10

As he sailed toward his next London offensive, Booth kept a detailed journal.[1] Upon arrival, he settled his family at 7 King's Row, Pentonville, just north of Clerkenwell. If he had any apprehension about Adelaide and Richard Junius, he need not have; they had gone to Brussels to visit her family.

Booth arrived in London just after Edwin Forrest had opened with moderate success at Drury Lane. Forrest, the first American-born actor to star in London, opened with some trepidation on 17 October as Spartacus in *The Gladiator*. Forrest's roughshod acting won cheers on his opening night, plus a few shouts of "Give us Shakespeare!" William Charles Macready, now London's leading actor, unimpressed with Forrest, nevertheless led the round of parties to welcome the American.[2]

No such welcome greeted Booth, who opened on 21 November 1836 at Drury Lane as Richard III. The *London Sun* noted he received warm, even enthusiastic applause upon his entrance, but

> soon gave proofs that the character is not one in which he is at all calculated to succeed. In the first place, he wants physical strength; secondly, he wants understanding. Except, perhaps, in one or two scenes in the fourth act, he totally misconceives the part of Richard, who was not a mere common-place blustering tyrant, but a laughing, reckless man of the world, of consummate address, infinite readiness and energy, and with wit and caustic sarcasm at will. All these qualities we missed in Mr. Booth's Richard.
>
> His courtship of Lady Anne was not marked, either in manner or look, by anything even approaching to what Kean used to achieve in this scene.

Furthermore, Booth could hear a few scattered hisses under the applause. Nothing had changed for him in London—even three years after his death, Kean still thwarted Booth.

The other newspaper reviews commented on Booth's lack of physical power, his tameness in the early scenes, and how much better Kean used to perform the same role. At the end of the performance, however, the audience clamored for Booth, demanding a curtain call. John Cooper announced that Booth had retired to his dressing room but that he would go fetch him.[3] Cooper then reappeared to suggest Booth had in fact left the theatre. The audience let the matter drop.

Booth contracted with Alfred Bunn, the Drury Lane manager, to appear for twenty-five pounds per night, opening as Sir Giles on 24 November, but he failed to appear for reasons unknown.[4] He performed for the last time at Drury Lane on the twenty-fifth as Iago to Edwin Forrest's Othello. Forrest had succeeded handsomely in London, although many Londoners considered him merely a talented barbarian, a brute confused by a grain of genius. No English newspaper condescended to review the combined appearances of America's two leading tragedians.

After the Drury Lane performances, Booth wrote to his old friend Wemyss, describing his opinion of London theatricals:

> I've played now about six nights since leaving Philad. Entre nous, theatricals in England are gone to sleep—with all their puffing of full houses, I don't believe that more than two Managers in London got even enough to pay for what they individually eat.
>
> Mr. Bunn broke his Engt with me after the 1st night—it was then modified & made with Mr. Cooper who broke his in imitation of his master—they owe me £100 & I must sue them both to obtain it.

> Forrest has the town entirely with him, but I don't think gets much except Fame. His greatest house, Cooper tells me was under £300 & he has acted to several under £100—Why he remains wasting his time & labour I don't know. The Gladiator didn't exactly do—but the Million insist that the only Shakespearean Actor is E. Forrest! & his Lear, Macbeth & Othello elicit universal praise.
>
> Charles Kemble is much more highly esteemed in London than formerly—his tragedy is put before all others by the elite & he gets about £20 per night for it—He is the only Tragic Man making money in the country. . . .[5]
>
> A particular reason induces me to trouble you with this—A Relative whom I had considered to be eight thousand miles away, I found in distress the other day, & a letter was sent about two weeks back by her to my father directed Mr. Rich Booth, or Mr. Booth Sen, care of Mr. Booth junr Philadelphia.[6] As by such an address it never can reach my father, I beg of you to get the letter & enclose it in an envelope to Mr. Richd Booth Bel-air Maryland. These little expenses I will repay you on my return in April.
>
> Yours truly
>
> J B Booth[7]

Booth obtained an engagement at the Surrey Theatre in Lambeth with a Mr. Davidge, described as a miserly curmudgeon of a manager. Since newspapers did not often carry advertisements for the nonpatent houses, and since the bills have only partially survived, we have an incomplete record of Booth's work there. He appeared at the Surrey December fifth through December twenty-second, then ushered in 1837 with six performances at Birmingham.

The new year brought a new family catastrophe. Booth revealed it to his father in a letter from Pentonville dated 28 January.

> We have at last cause and severe enough it is, to regret coming to England. I have delayed writing till time had somewhat softened the horror of the event. Our dear little Henry is dead! He caught the small pox and it proved fatal—he has been buried about three weeks since in the chapel ground close by. Guess what his loss has been to us—So proud as I was of him above all others. The infernal disease has placed Hagar in the hospital, but she is recovering and the two youngest who were inoculated are also getting well. Junius and Rosalie have been vaccinated—so had Henry—but on him the vaccine had not taken effect and his general health being so excellent caused us to forget the danger he was liable to.

> I shall return (God willing) by the Packet of April 8th to Philadelphia as theatricals . . . turn out to be not so prosperous as they seemed on my arrival. I played at Drury Lane for £25 per night but was forced to sue Mr. Bunn the manager and he is now paying me the hundred pounds he owes me by weekly installments of £1/10 each. I afterwards acted at the Surrey with tolerably good success and was honorably paid. Since then I've been to Birmingham where I was when the melancholy news alluded to reached me. I expect to play a few nights more in London at one of the minor theatres and at Edinburgh before I return. Forrest won't play any more, at least he says so now—Hamblin is here—so is Barrett of Boston, Ternan of Philadelphia, and Rice—the only one it appears who really has bettered his fortune by London is he. Jim Crow would have thought the cockneys could not understand, but contrary to all calculation, it is the mania . . . amongst them.
>
> Rosalie goes to school and is improving very fast. Junius is gone a few miles in the country with some friends for a week or two.[8]

Booth closed by mentioning he had tried unsuccessfully to contact "Mr. Silberrad" (or Silverad), the caretaker of Booth legal matters in London. The sudden death of his beloved son cast Booth into deep melancholy for many months until the birth of his next child, John Wilkes Booth, in 1838.

On 25 March 1837 Booth again wrote Wemyss.

> Your favor of Feb. 22d arrived here this morning and I thank you for forwarding the letter to my father as requested. I have had cause to regret coming to this Country as it has cost me the price of a Son's Life. My poor Henry died Dec. 28th of the Small-pox, & it unhinged the requisite energies for coping with the Tricksters of London.
>
> I shall soon return, perhaps by the Susquehanna which is now at Liverpool. The news of Rowbotham's Death had not reached me till your announcement of it. With regard to the Theatres through England it is I can plainly see "a great cry and little Wool."[9]

Booth played a few more times at the Surrey then returned to America on the *Ontario*. He would never see England again.

Booth had narrowly missed a confrontation with Adelaide in London. In 1839 Adelaide wrote a long and illuminating letter to her aunt, a Mrs. Nichols, telling of her relationship with Booth and describing events in 1836–37. She derided Booth for not having secured an engagement before leaving America for London, thus allowing the London managers to take advantage of him. And that they did, by not paying him and, Adelaide suspected, paying such papers as the *Court Journal* to publish devastating reviews. Adelaide referred to Jane Booth and "her seven children, applying to her brother for assistance." She expressed great sympathy for her sister-in-law, quoting Booth as saying Jane had tried to "prejudice my father." Adelaide said she had expected to see Booth during the 1836–37 visit, Booth having vowed to see her at Brussels. But while she waited in Brussels, Booth and his Maryland family set sail for America, Booth promising Richard Junius he would be back in two years to "look after his success." While Adelaide considered her relationship with Booth friendly, and Booth was most prompt in sending her money, she heard nothing from him after a letter dated 16 May 1838. She therefore caused "a person in Philadelphia who knows Junius intimately" to investigate his whereabouts. She closed by describing Richard as a little larger than his father, "not very light built and quite strong" as a result of gymnastic exercise.[10]

Booth had missed her, but they would meet again.

Booth had left two sons abroad—Richard Junius, alive; Henry Byron, buried—now, some of England joined him at the farm. After his return to Baltimore, he sent money to his sister Jane so that she and her children could emigrate to America—on condition that they leave her husband, James Mitchell, in London. When they arrived, however, Mitchell accompanied them, and the entire tribe took over the Booth household.[11] Richard, furious at having the scoundrel who ruined his daughter once again sharing his household, never thereafter spoke to any of the Mitchells. Mrs. Rogers recalled Mitchell as having done nothing to support his family, not even chores on the farm.[12]

Booth now had nine Mitchells, his own four surviving children, Richard, and Mary Ann to support, plus his servants. He resumed his engagements, but the loss of four children and the disruption of his household seemed to plunge him ever deeper into melancholy and madness, soon leading to another attempted suicide.

He took up his American career again in New York on the Fourth of July 1837 as Richard III at the rebuilt Bowery Theatre. Asia maintained that he received two hundred dollars for the single performance. He then did four performances in Philadelphia later in the same month, then recommenced his old pattern of restless movement from city to city, from stage to stage.

Wemyss invited Booth to open his season at the Walnut Street Theatre in Philadelphia; Booth played Hamlet to a house of $344. At about the same time, William Wood considered Booth to have "become wholly unattractive."[13]

Attractive or not, Booth kept working and earning a living. He revealed the nature of his arrangements in a letter to the Bowery manager, William Dinneford, dated 18 November 1837.

> In reply to yours of 16th just come—Ecce! your arrangements I perceived could not be conveniently made for my appearing at the Bowery and I have therefore made an Engt. with Mr. Willard & Mr. Blake for a few nights which tho I hope will prove attractive, will not it is my wish & belief injure the Receipts of the Bowery. In your Letter you have not said aught concerning Woodworth's benefit, and the Newspapers differ so widely in Dates that I cannot rely on them for correct information. If it should take place on Tuesday the 21st, I shall be happy to give my services, but if protracted as some Papers say until the 28th my other Engagements will prevent me aiding Mr. Woodworth. The inclemency of the weather prevented me calling on Major Noah & my desire to return to Philadelphia in good order, kept me from venturing out too much on Tuesday. My precautions were futile as I caught a most awful cold, thank Providence![14]

As 1837 closed, Booth played Philadelphia and Baltimore. At the Walnut Street, Wemyss recorded that Booth failed with his engagement, and the management lost $356 for the six nights.[15]

As Booth's American career resumed, he no longer insisted on playing only three nights a week. Perhaps the need for money to feed his household horde forced him into more lucrative arrangements, but he began to perform regularly six nights a week. This added to the strain on his faculties and led him to further disasters, both onstage and off. Acting is hard work; only dilettantes find it easy. And Booth's style was especially strenuous.

Booth returned to the Bowery Theatre on 18 February 1838, only to find the theatre had burned down the night before. Booth secured an engagement with the Wallacks at the nearby National Theatre.

Then he got himself into trouble at the Park Theatre almost at once; later the *Spirit of the Times* raged:

> Among the "novelties" . . . this week, the *Booth humbug* at the *Park* stands pre-eminent. On Tuesday evening [27 February] a benefit was given at the Park to the sufferers of the destruction of the Bowery; the play selected was "The Merchant of Venice," in which Booth was to have played *Shylock*. When the curtain rang up, that interesting "babe of grace," Mr. Booth, as usual, was nowhere to be found, though he had been vagabondising about the theatre from the time of rehearsal until it was time to dress. An apology was made to the audience, and Clarke went on in the part. The receipts . . . amounted to $375. . . . The amount received is a pretty clear evidence of the attraction of Booth; and though he played at the National last night, we doubt if a single person who attended the Park the evening when he was so *particularly* drunk or crazy, took the trouble to go and hiss him.[16]

Asia delicately reported her father had abandoned the Park for a fire on William Street, where he labored at pumping water on the flames to try, as he put it, "to save people's property from destruction."[17]

Perhaps, but Booth was building up for another misadventure as he went to Charleston for the first time in fourteen years. The *Charleston Courier* for 12 March 1838 reported the beginning of Booth's next freak.

> Mr. Booth went on board the . . . packet, in company with his friend, Mr. Flynn, the well known Comedian, on Wednesday evening last [7 March], and on the passage showed evident symptoms of insanity, but being carefully watched by his anxious friend, had no opportunity of escaping his vigilant eye, and appeared to improve gradually under Mr. Flynn's friendly care, until the afternoon of Friday last when 36 miles N.E. of Frying Pan Shoals, during dinner, when Mr. Booth excused himself from the table, took advantage of his friend's absence, and lowered himself from the promenade deck, which attracted the attention of the men.
>
> Capt. Pennoyer, Mr. Flynn, and the rest of the passengers being called from dinner, endeavored to persuade him to return on board, when he not only refused, but immediately plunged into the ocean. Capt. Pennoyer instantly stopped the boat, which was then going at the rate of eleven miles an hour, and by his prompt exertions and presence of mind, a safety buoy was thrown over, and a safety boat

> immediately launched. The gallant Captain took the helm, and Mr. Booth, though then half a mile from the boat, was rescued from a watery grave.

Booth had asked Flynn to notify him when they reached the point at which William Augustus Conway, the failed tragedian, had drowned himself. As Flynn pulled Booth into the safety boat, Booth warned, "I say, Tom, look out: you're a heavy man,—be steady; if the boat upsets we'll all be drowned." A closer guard was placed on Booth, and eventually the steam packet *Neptune* arrived in Charleston after a trip of slightly over sixty hours, setting a speed record for the journey. The papers rejoiced at the prospect of seeing Booth perform, but he had not yet recovered and soon went to war again with his demons.

The *Courier* for 14 March 1838 described the new horrors, widely reprinted by other newspapers. As the *Courier* reporter described the events, Booth and Flynn had gone to the theatre on Monday evening, then returned to the Planter's Hotel, where they shared a room. Flynn retired, but somewhere between one and two in the morning he was awakened by receiving a tremendous blow over his right eye. He sprang to his feet, only to discover Booth aiming another blow at him with one of the andirons from the fireplace. Flynn dodged and received only a glancing blow over his left eye, which drove him from the room, Booth in close pursuit. Booth caught Flynn and grappled with him, but Flynn, who was absorbing considerable punishment, called for help, and Booth was placed under restraint.

For many, this was the last straw; Booth had degenerated from heavy drinker to problem drinker to suicidal and finally to homicidal. The *Spirit of the Times* reprinted the story, referring to Booth's "tomfooleries," adding that, "in his last freak, it seems he came near using up his man-Friday—TOM FLYNN."[18]

Booth had reached a crisis, but many felt he merely feigned madness. In a later story, the *Spirit* mentioned that Charles H. Eaton, a rising young tragedian, was about the only person in the profession who considered Booth's insanity genuine. The *Spirit* added, "There is too much 'method' in it to excite anything but disgust with those who know him best." One should note, however, that Flynn stayed with Booth through good times and bad. The *Spirit* then appended a letter from Eaton.

> I have just heard of Booth's attack upon poor Flynn . . . and shudder, as it recalls to memory the opportunity he had about three years ago to make me participant in a *real* tragedy. We were playing an engagement together . . . at Baltimore, and reversed Pierre and Jaffier, Othello and Iago. On the second night he played Othello (a part he seldom personates) to my Iago. After rehearsal, he came to my lodgings and requested me to go through the parts with him again. "Iago," said he, "you must do your d— —dest to-night or I shall play you down." There was a singularity in his manner which I had not observed before, and I confess that I felt considerable fear that he might fall into one of his melancholy paroxysms and do me some harm. We adjourned to an oyster-room, and every time an oyster was opened he cried out "murder," in various tones, with apparent horror. Night came. He played Othello *splendidly*, and drew down thunders of applause. In the last act, after the death of "gentle Desdemona," it seemed as if all hell was raging in his heart; his eyes displayed the fierceness of a tiger's, and his thrust at me, I verily believe, would have been fatal had I not suddenly stepped aside to avoid it. The audience were as hushed as death; my heart beat audibly, and it was a minute or two before I could recover my self-possession.
>
> A short time after this I passed a few days beneath his hospitable roof, and was entertained with great kindness by him and his amiable lady. One night I was awoke by a tremendous crash in the next room. I hurried on my dressing gown and ran into the entry to see what the matter was. It seems that Booth had wound a sheet around him, and with a light in his hand, had gone to his aged father's room; but the old gentleman, who happened to be awake and heard him coming, had dashed the bowl and ewer upon the floor at his feet as he entered, and effectually frightened him out of his mad freak. "Ah, Junius, Junius," said the venerable old man, "will you never have done with these mad freaks?" Alas for Booth! alas for the prostration of genius![19]

This incident would have occurred after the death of Booth's three children in 1833 but before his trip to England in 1836.

Theatrical and Booth-family legend held that Flynn, in defending himself, broke Booth's nose, not only marring his patrician profile but for a time damaging his voice, that essential tool for any actor. Asia Booth Clarke mentioned the "accident" in passing, then quoted Thomas R. Gould on the matter.

> The accident by which his nose was broken, spoiling forever his noble profile, threatened for a time the more serious disaster of a permanent injury to his voice. Immediately upon recovery, he began to play. To those who, during these first performances, recalled the perfect features and the resonant tones of former years, the sight and sound were indeed pitiful. But instead of humoring this vocal infirmity he spoke with all the old mastery of motive, and let the results take care of itself. By this persistent method, in less than two years after the accident his voice had completely recovered its original scope, variety, and power, as we can attest by close, solicitous, and comparative observation.[20]

A pitiful case, to be sure, if it happened.

Gould wrote his tribute to Booth in 1868, sixteen years after Booth's death and thirty years after the incident in question. One wonders why the Charleston newspapers would make much of Flynn's injuries and not mention physical harm to the extent of a broken nose to Booth.

Within a week, Booth was back on stage. The local *Mercury* ran a note on March 19 stating, they were "most happy to learn that the great Tragedian is at large again—sane and regular, and that he will appear . . . to-night in the character of Sir Giles Overreach." And appear he did. If his voice and looks had been ruined, the *Mercury* nevertheless poured out a tribute to him while fully aware of his "late indisposition." First, the anonymous writer summed up Booth's career to that time.

> No man has ever appeared on the stage in this country, who has excited more enthusiasm, than Mr. Booth. We are used to consider him not only as the ornament and glory, but in some sort the *victim* of his profession. To other men it has been only the consummation of education, the gradual development of talent or taste, the result of some one of the many necessities that make the destiny of man, or the accident of whim and fancy—to him it was the deep and uncontrollable impulse of nature, rising above habit, breaking the chains of education. . . . The first outbreaking of his genius showed what he was—it came from him as a thing he could no more help, than the mountain gorge can keep back its swelling and bounding torrents. The stage became to him a real world—its painted scenes turned to solid castles, frowning forests and bustling streets, and he himself stepped into the shadows of the poets' dreams, as no simulated hero. If this be not literally true, there is at least, we

> believe, enough of truth in it to have made Mr. Booth's histrionic career a life of wild excitement to himself, and to throw around him in the eye of the world, a mystery and romance altogether peculiar. The public have forgiven in him eccentricities which would scarce have been tolerated in another; for they have ever considered him as the creature of a strange idiosyncrasy, or of nerves so sensitive, that they were jangled by the ecstasy of their own intense sympathies. Every where Mr. Booth is welcomed with enthusiasm, and who would wish it otherwise? Not we.[21]

The *Mercury*'s comments are more valuable as a revelation of the Booth public image than as a delineation of his disturbed mind. Acting, especially in the intense style of a Booth or a Kean, strains the psyche and can indeed exhaust the performer. But to suspect that Booth lost himself in his roles only indicates the *Mercury* journalist had little knowledge of acting. Perhaps during his periods of madness Booth deluded himself thus, but no actor can survive for long periods of time under such conditions.

The reporter makes no mention whatsoever of any disfigurement of Booth. The same article described the supposedly battered Booth as Sir Giles (emphasis added).

> So great was the anxiety to see the hero of the night, that a hum of uneasy curiosity almost drowned every thing till he appeared, and then such an uproar of applause, beginning without moderation, and ending in a shock of utter stillness, like a cataract frozen in an instant, (that figure is Byron's) as if every one's fate depended upon *hearing the first tone of his voice. His classic face,* slight figure, and brilliant eye, are eminently calculated to realize to those who saw him for the first time, the fame of his fiery and enthusiastic character. He had not recovered from his late indisposition, and did not put all the intense ferocity into Sir Giles, which would be expected of him in his full vigor. His performance was chastened down even almost to tameness in some parts, yet to us it had a strange witchery—the character seemed in his soul and its wild struggles to be checked by strong self-command. What a chill sunk on the spirit as he whispered his monitory "Remember!" in the ear of his daughter, wrapping up in one word the foul import of all the maxims with which he had sought to corrupt her pure character. . . . Although we think Mr. Booth's Sir Giles Overreach fairly open to the exception we have taken above, yet from the suggestive power which even very subdued action, joined with true conception of the

> character, always has over the imagination of the spectator, we never felt more deeply the terrible strength of that great poetic creation, than on Monday night.

The review, quoted here almost in its entirety, is much longer than usual for provincial newspapers in the nineteenth century, yet we read nothing of a broken nose or a ruined voice. Later in the same engagement, the same critic found Booth's Iago superior to Cooper's, and on the twenty-seventh of March said, "Mr. Booth is quite recovered, both in body and spirits."

Whether Flynn broke Booth's nose or not remains unresolved. On 30 March, this same unusually articulate critic, in a lengthy discourse on Booth's Richard III and Lear, spoke specifically about Booth's voice:

> To call his voice in the expression of passion, penetrating, is feeble—it occupies you, it thrills on every nerve, it seizes frame and mind, and consciousness, it fills the whole present, and shuts out memory and anticipation. And how beautifully does he relieve the wild energy of passion, in the common development of the character. No man exaggerates less. In the quieter parts of dialogue, his words glide through the mind like a current of light, full of rich beauty and meaning.

Yet Gould had referred to Booth at this time as "pitiful."

One other critic wrote in Charleston at the time, for the *Courier*, and while he did not rhapsodize as much as the *Mercury*'s, he did indeed call Booth's Richard "a most masterly display of the histrionic art . . . not witnessed on the Charleston boards since the days of Kean. . . . perfect. It was an intellectual feast—it was a vivid and beautiful picture; and convinced all who saw him that he possesses talents of the highest order."[22] Nineteenth-century newspaper reviews luxuriated in flattery and puffery; to be sure, very few negative reviews ever appeared. But the Charleston reviewers leave us guessing about the state of Booth's nose.

Sol Smith deepened the mystery when he wrote to his partner, Noah Ludlow, on 11 April, saying, "If what you surmise about Flynn is right—if he wouldn't let Booth have a fair shake at his wife, I think Booth served Flynn right—Flynn was unreasonable, and <u>ought</u> to be killed—the rascal!—and Booth was not as insane as the papers make him out to be."[23] What exactly happened remains lost to us, but another component of Booth's tarnished reputation fell into place.

After appearing in Richmond, Booth returned to Baltimore, where he was billed to perform Pescara for the benefit of Charles Ward. He failed to appear, and two days later (3 May 1838) the *Baltimore Sun* savaged him.

> BOOTH AGAIN.—Is this man a maniac? or is he not more a fool than a madman? On Monday, he was announced to appear at the Holliday Street as Pescara; but when the hour of the performance arrived, the little eccentric was returned *non est*. "Booth is a genius," is the cry; and he has heard it reiterated so often, that he imagines his vagaries will be overlooked; but we can inform him that in this city he is eternally disgraced, by insulting an audience that have ever treated him with signal marks of approbation—and the only favor the Baltimoreans ask at his hands is, that he, as a citizen of Maryland, will never again *promise* to appear upon the stage. The trick has become stale; the "gaggery" won't do; this *affectation* of madness may be a "good point" sometimes, but to make a *business* of it is disgusting.

Booth had more important matters to consider; Mary Ann was again pregnant and on the tenth of May delivered her fifth son. They named him after the old Clerkenwell republican and political activist, John Wilkes.[24] Apparently Booth was present for this birth; he played a short engagement in Baltimore five days later, and the *Sun* forgave him, saying, "Having recovered from his late indisposition, and being anxious to regain the good opinion of the Baltimore audience, there will, we are assured, be no disappointment this time."[25]

After Booth opened, the *Sun* reported his benefit as "a perfect *jam*" and a "thorough . . . manifestation of cordial appreciation." The writer then proposed, "Indeed, there is something so closely allied to the association of this gentleman's name with a Baltimore audience, that it is almost inherent in our very nature to forgive his repeated transgressions." The *Sun* then castigated the *Spirit of the Times* for their attacks on Booth, adding, "we of Baltimore will always extend to him the right hand of fellowship, and revere his worth as a tragedian."[26]

Hand of friendship or not, the *Sun* noted that Booth's acting had been good but that it had been eroded by more imperfections than they had ever before noticed. The *Sun* also commented on Booth's having to be prompted several times, wondering if his memory had begun to wane. Still, they forgave him. Again and again, they forgave him.

The next day (22 May), however, from Washington came a letter to the *Sun*, signed "The People."

> Let me whisper to Mr. Booth, that his *eccentric* and METHODICAL *madness* is doing a great deal to injure his popularity as an actor, and that had it not been for his late unjustifiable "freak" of playing the murderer in reality, he would have been greeted by an overflowing house last night; but sensible people are disgusted by the "game he plays." There is yet time to redeem all he has lost.

Booth rested on the farm during June, then toured the eastern cities till mid-October before beginning a southern sweep, returning to the East in mid-May 1839. Perhaps the birth of his new son did somewhat reduce Booth's melancholy; his freaks seemed to abate.

Before he left for the South, Booth began making his arrangements with Ludlow (the same Ludlow who so admired him in 1821) and his managerial partner, Sol Smith. In August 1838 Booth quoted his terms to the two managers as being a clear third of each night's receipts, plus a clear half of his benefit. Two months later he wrote them again from Pittsburgh, suggesting he could join them in St. Louis, Missouri, on 21 November 1838 for one hundred dollars a night for seven nights and half the receipts of his benefit. Although the engagement never came to pass on this tour, Booth still commanded substantial financial returns for his services.

Something of the nature of theatrical bookings emerges from Booth's letters to Ludlow and Smith over this period. He agreed to an engagement to begin in Mobile, Alabama, on 18 February 1839.[27] He penned a testy letter on the fifteenth: "I have written twice to you since my arrival in New Orleans and have received no reply. That such a circumstance should occur I can attribute only to design on the part of some malevolent person, unless you have made different arrangements to what you had settled with me. I close here tomorrow." The arrangements for the eighteenth did not work out, so Booth stayed in New Orleans and played five performances at the Camp Street Theatre in competition with Mme Celeste, a French dancer who replaced him at the St. Charles Theatre.

During his Camp Street Theatre engagement he received a complaint from Ludlow and Smith that they had received no word from him since late November 1838 from Louisville, explaining they could not engage him for 18 February 1839. Forrest was also touring the area and was booked until the fourth of March. Booth opened on 7 March, as it turned out, doing so well that Ludlow and Smith reengaged him for three more performances. But on 30 March, after Booth had left to return to New Orleans, Smith wrote to Ludlow, "Curse that Booth! He may go to the d— —l for me hereafter."

Ludlow's comments were maddeningly unspecific.

> Booth . . . followed Forrest in an engagement of a certainty of one hundred dollars per night, but he got into one of his insane or drunken frolics . . . and ruined the engagement. He had but two full houses—his first night and the night that he performed *Richard III*. Mr. Booth, in this instance, was guilty of an act of great injustice toward us. He started with an excellent promise of a remunerative business to the managers, and as they were bound to pay him one hundred dollars per night, he was bound in honor to do what he could to prevent their losing money, when they agreed to give him all that he asked for his services. But the *fiend* had got possession of him, and reason and justice had been driven out.[28]

Booth and his fiend returned to the East via Natchez and Jackson, Mississippi, and Louisville.

In her autobiography, actress Louisa Lane recalled a Booth shenanigan about this time.

> We were playing Hamlet one night in Natchez and during Ophelia's mad scene a cock began to crow lustily. When the curtain fell upon that fourth act the crowing became more constant and when the manager could not find Mr. Booth to commence the next act he looked up and saw him perched on top of a ladder which was the only way to reach "the flies" in that primitive theatre. The manager ascended the ladder and had quite a lengthy discussion with Booth who at last consented to come down on condition that he should resume his high position after the play and remain there until Jackson was re-elected President. He had some very odd ways at times.[29]

Lane was then billed as Mrs. Henry B. Hunt, just coming into her own as an actress. Apparently Booth shared the wide public disapproval of Martin Van Buren, who had succeeded Jackson as president in 1837, just as the United States' first great depression struck.

After Louisville, Booth apparently rushed back home; his last son, Joseph Adrian, born in February 1840, was evidently conceived in early May 1839. After his grueling and only partially successful southern tour, Booth sharply curtailed his touring engagements. Between May and the end of 1839, he had only one two-week engagement in Philadelphia and two brief appearances in Baltimore.

Apparently the rest did him good. For the first Baltimore engagement, the *Sun* commented on his good houses and said, "He seems to be completely renovated, and his warmest admirers were astonished at the undiminished vigor with which he sustained the arduous parts of Hamlet and Richard the Third."[30] His engagement included a benefit on 26 October 1839 for his son Junius, who appeared as Diggory in the afterpiece *The Mistaken Eathers*.

Asia Booth Clarke later reminisced about her father's life for the next several years, writing,

> During the last ten years of his life the elder Booth passed a considerable portion of his time in the midst of his family, occasionally making professional tours with a careless disregard of fame, which may be accounted for by the depressing consciousness of the accident which marred his face and voice. It was, however, a marked peculiarity of his entire career that he would consent to perform at any theatre regardless of its pretensions, and was equally unconcerned about the costliness or grandeur of his wardrobe, so long as it was correct in point of fashion and of date. He played annually in Boston and New Orleans, in which places he was an established favorite, and, having removed his residence to Baltimore, made periodical visits to the farm during the oppressive heat of summer.[31]

But in the summer of 1839 the Mitchells were still at the farm, and Booth's father, Richard, had moved to a Baltimore tavern operated by a Dr. Braritta. There the irascible old man passed away on 29 December 1839. According to Asia Booth Clarke, her grandfather died alone in the night while Junius Brutus Booth was away on tour. The undertaker, a Mr. Weaver, cared for Richard Booth's body, cutting off a lock of hair, which he later presented to Booth. The undertaker kept Richard Booth's body in his own vault until the actor returned in

June 1840, when he arranged for the burial. According to Weaver, Booth first asked the coffin to be opened, then bent down and kissed his father for the last time. He then clipped a lock of hair himself, which he carried in a small Bible thereafter. Weaver recalled the inscription over Richard Booth's grave as being in Hebrew, reading:

> I take my departure from life as from an inn—
> Thee I follow to the infernal kingdom of
> The most renowned ruler—
> Thence to the stars.[32]

Booth soon secured a town house in Baltimore, primarily to provide his children access to better schools. He rented for a time, somewhat like his father moving around the Tottenham Court Road area decades before. In June 1840, for example, Booth wrote Mary Ann at North High Street, near Gay Street. The 1842 *Baltimore City Directory* listed "J. B. Booth, tragedian, east side High, north of Gay." In 1845 the Baltimore directory included, "Junius Booth, actor, 72 North Front Street." Later he would purchase property on North Exeter Street.

But for now he was still touring from the farm in Harford County. As 1840 began, he was in New York, then returned to Baltimore and was thus present for the birth of his last child, Joseph Adrian, 8 February 1840. Booth's last child by Mary Ann was named partially in tribute to his first; Junius Brutus Booth, Jr., had been strikingly handsome as Adrian De Mauprat in *Richelieu* as he began his acting career.[33] Two days later Booth opened in Washington, D.C., then went back to the road.

While Booth was in Philadelphia, Wemyss reported that he failed, for the first time in all their engagements, to appear.[34] Wemyss substituted Charles Thorne as Richard, and none other than Charles Kean attended the show.

Kean hated the performance and during the third act turned to a tough-looking young citizen and asked, "Is that gentleman who is playing Richard, Mr. Booth?"

"Booth be damned," replied the citizen, "no, by Jasus; it's Charley Thorne, my sucker. To be sure he has not so big a name, but he's a damned sight better than all the Charley Keans and Booths to boot, and can beat 'em all to blazes, easy, by Jasus!"

Kean wrapped his cloak around himself, rose, and went home.[35]

Booth accused Wemyss of appearing in James E. Murdoch's benefit at the Chestnut Street Theatre and not attending to business. Booth would not appear without Wemyss; so their engagement ended. Moreover, Booth wrote to Wemyss on 6 June 1840 one of the strangest letters he ever drafted, setting up another engagement. After dating it "Die Saturine PM Sextus Junii AD 1840 & werry off," he proposed,

> Recollect when I wrote to you, quoting the Edinburgh usual terms, I stated the Engt would be for six nights, putting $75 per Night shown as the Sum to be held by the Manager & all surplus that, to be equally divided between him & the Auxiliary. I meant then that six nights were to be employed here: & six in Philadelphia on similar terms. The four nights at $75 would be $300 to share after.—
>
> If performances for twelve nights be played, the extension weakened & you would incur a loss if you'd allow me, to divide ten Receipts after a deduction for the gross total of only $300.—
>
> Say you try six as first proposed then should it answer, six more and you can take the best Receipts clear of the second Engagement & I'll take the next best,—which will equalize profits more fairly inter Amicos.
>
> Do you thoroughly accept my meaning? If so, say you do accept my Services on them 'ere Terms? You ought to! we had a better House but the Weather was so wet & that blasted [Cider?] so queer & you'd drink nothing else or my notion is they would have turn'd out double the Amount.
>
> "Willie brew'd a Peck of [Marst?]
> Better luck Stranger next Tack—
> Lets hae thy news soon.
> Characters you know.
>
> Richard 2d can it be ridicrius [*sic*]?—likewise Riches—Bertram—Oroonoko—& the Distressed Mamma? the Addenda to them you have on your Bill files.
>
> Richelieu I reserve & then only an Act or so, at the first or 2d Benefit. I wish you'd have a bumper, honour bright!
>
> Yours
> J B. Booth[36]

This missive surely raised suspicions in Wemyss, but he booked Booth to open as Hamlet on the fifteenth of June. If he had trepidations, they were to be fully justified.

Wemyss later described his exasperation as nearing the breaking point.

> Booth, who promised reformation, and professed penitence, played Hamlet on the 15th of June; and on the 24th, Oroonoko, in bare feet. His benefit, on the 27th, Octavian, Shylock, John Lump, and the first act of Richelieu. Throughout this engagement, he had been crazy; and his Richelieu never will be forgotten—imperfect, drunk, and dressed like an English chimney-sweep—on the 1st of May. I found I could no longer place the slightest dependence upon him. He kept faith with me, when he had broken it with almost every manager on the continent; and when taxed with his folly, would say—Ask Wemyss if he believes these stories—he knows I never break engagements. Alas! Mr. Junius, I can no longer, with truth, assert you never did. His twelve nights yielded, including his benefit, $1412, or $117 per night, for which I paid him, as usual, taking the proceeds of the benefit, $1200. Quere; how much did I gain by the operation?[37]

Booth avoided such statuesque roles as Richelieu, feeling he was too short for them. When Wemyss insisted he play it for the manager's benefit, Booth replied, "No, sir! No. The Cardinal was tall and gaunt; I cannot look like him. Nonsense! Announce me as Jerry Sneak or John Lump—not Richelieu."

But Wemyss prevailed and found an old and shabby red gown for Booth's costume. And the performance began, hitched and halted for a bit, until Booth seized another actor in his arms and waltzed him around the stage. Wemyss tore the hair of his wig and rang the curtain down. Booth coolly asked the frantic manager, "Well, my boy, how d'ye like my Richelieu?" Booth then disappeared for several days but was yet again forgiven upon his return.[38]

From Philadelphia, Booth wrote back to Mary Ann, his first extant letter to her. Dated 23 June 1840, the letter reads:

> Junius has brought me the Gabardine which I return you a thousand thanks for, but regret its giving you so much trouble. Last night the Orestes dress arrived and was brought to the theatre. The play is to be acted this evening, so you must almost have guessed the time I should need it. Houses have been very slim. Don't hurry yourself about Bertram, if you have not already got the cloak made. The pen I am writing with does not obey the hand enough, and you

will find difficulty in deciphering my writing, I fear. Junius tells me he could not find the two volumes of Virgil. . . .

I took a slight cold which has rendered me rather hoarse but am nearly recovered from it. I hope the children are quite well. Kiss them for me, and give my love to each and all from Rosalie down to Joey. The time seems long when away from you and them; and I almost regret having made so protracted an engagement. By this, your health is restored, I sincerely hope. In the parcel you sent there was no letter. Did you write one? Let me hear from you by return and believe me ever and affectionately to be

your husband and worshipper,
Junius.

You know June is still here. We went out Saturday and I wish I'd taken the opportunity of journeying to Baltimore that day to see you. God bless you! Adieu![39]

A week later, Booth opened in New York at the Chatham Theatre, the *New York Herald* noting it as his first appearance since his indisposition in Philadelphia. Then, as an afterthought to the review, the *Herald* tossed off a comment found in no other paper, a tantalizing possible explanation for some of Booth's freaks.

Never have we seen him more ably sustain the character [Sir Edward Mortimer] than on this occasion, it reminded us of Booth of former years. We cannot recollect a more powerful representation of the character than on this occasion; it appeared to us that he had at once risen to his former powerful faculties, and upon conversing with some friends we were informed that he had undergone an operation in Philadelphia, by an eminent dentist of that city, for what is called a *diseased antrum,* which had for years affected his nervous faculties to such a degree, that at times he was incapable of retaining his memory, and was the cause of frequent aberrations of mind, which has been the cause of so many disappointments to the public. . . . We subjoin the following certificate, from a letter received by Mr. Thorne, from Dr. Houpt, an eminent dentist in Philadelphia:

This is to certify, that I attended M. J.B. Booth, for what is called a *diseased antrum,* which, in my opinion, has been the cause of his nervous affections in the head, and also swelling of the glans of the throat, which has incapacitated him from performing the arduous characters of his profession.

DR. C. J. Houpt,
Surgeon Dentist, Philadelphia.[40]

An infected antrum, or sinus, may well have driven Booth to deaden the pain with brandy. Booth, like his son Edwin, smoked heavily.

Medical records hardly exist for the early nineteenth-century United States, but some records indicate he had been treated around 1830 by Dr. James Rush of Philadelphia.[41] In late March 1830, Booth wrote Rush to thank him for "the valuable medical aid" he had received and to inquire about the cost. Rush sent Booth a note thanking him for a "very valuable and elegant Piece of Plate" on 20 April 1830. And slightly over two years later Richard Booth wrote to Rush on a different matter but referred to his son as feeling he owed his very existence to Rush's medical skills. No mention was made of the specific nature of the complaints. The wealthy Rush did not conduct a regular practice; Booth must have exercised his considerable charm to curry favor and to receive treatment. Rush admired Booth as one of the few actors of quality he had ever seen.[42]

Booth suffered no freaks for the rest of the year, implying his Philadelphia operation had some beneficial effect upon him. He played various engagements, including one in Norfolk in April 1841, under the management of Miss Virginia Monier, a successful actress and one of the first female managers in the United States. He had acted with her on several occasions.

Booth ran into trouble once more in May 1841, again with the long-suffering Wemyss, this time at the National in New York. Wemyss had announced Booth as Iago, J. R. Scott as Othello, Miss Clarendon as Desdemona, and a rising new star, Charlotte Cushman, as Emelia.[43] Scott, who had promised to play in Philadelphia that night, 10 May, failed to appear. Scott, according to Wemyss, went to Philadelphia Sunday morning, only to return that night to tell the manager he would not be at the National in New York the next night. Wemyss recalled, "Booth was evidently not himself, and the information I had to impart to him was not calculated to improve his state of mind." Booth refused a curtain call at the end of the show. Wemyss called the whole thing a disgrace, the worst performance presented at the National under William E. Burton's management. The last-minute Othello, a Mr. Wilson, put the audience to sleep; Booth was almost as bad, and Mr. Shaw as Cassio and Cushman as Emelia were the only salvations for the evening.[44]

Booth next went to Boston but not without incident. The *Spirit of the Times* printed a report from that city. "Booth . . . was to act at the Tremont, has broken his engagement (as usual), and went to Pelby at the National. There he played four nights, and, I learn, with more than his recent excellence, and to crowded houses. . . . Mrs. Booth, Jr. (late Miss De Bar) is also a favorite there."[45] One assumes some business disagreement or other occurred, at least nothing is said of Booth's drinking or mad freaks. And the next month he returned for a performance at the National in Boston. He then played a brief engagement in St. Johns, New Brunswick; a few days in New York; a few in Philadelphia; almost two weeks in Baltimore; then he did not again appear until late April 1842.

When he did reappear, however, so did his old affliction. For the first time since his Philadelphia operation, the papers made note of his drinking. His engagement started well; Philadelphia's *Dramatic Mirror,* on 2 April 1842, found Booth admirable as Richard.

> Since the days of Garrick, Richard III has been the peculiar property of little men, and in the person of Mr. Booth we have it most aptly illustrated, nor do we remember ever witnessing a more beautiful display of histrionic talent than we did on Wednesday evening . . . the opening soliloquy was masterly—the various scenes wherein Richard's peculiar character is portrayed, were faultless—the tent scene called up all the master qualities of the actor, and we question if Booth ever acquitted himself better than he did on this occasion.

The paper went on to decry Flynn's staging of the battle scenes, in which Richmond's army numbered about five men. On April sixteenth, however, the same paper printed a summation of Booth's latest appearance in that city.

> *Mr. Booth*—This gentleman has been fulfilling an engagement at [the Walnut Street], and has acquitted himself in such a manner as to elicit from a good audience much applause. Our readers must not however infer from this, that the palmy days of Mr. Booth have returned, on the contrary, the applause he received, was drawn forth from the fact that he played a *little* better than he did on a former engagement at this theatre. His Richard was the only good piece of acting we witnessed. His Iago was not subdued enough, he made the hypocritical, and cunning *ancient,* too busy, too stirring, always

on the move, reminding us of an automaton figure at the mercy of the wire mover, compelled as it were to jump and start at his option. Such is not the cool, calculating Iago of Shakespeare's creation.

His Hamlet had some beautiful touches, but as a whole was bad, the scene with his mother was passionate and overdone. His Sir Giles . . . might be excused, from the fact of those who acted with him, acted too much, and tried to out Herod Herod.

He repeated Richard III on Wednesday evening, the 6th inst. For his benefit, he was so drunk that we could not make out what he was trying to say, and yet a *judicious audience applauded* his beastly maudlin attempts to enact one of the most difficult characters in the range of drama. How long will this state of things last?

The acting of Mr. Booth *now* seems to us like one who endeavours to make an impression, pushing what remains of his genius to its utmost limit, thereby overstepping the bounds of nature, and marring those very beauties we once so ardently admired.

Mr. Booth still retains the vigor of other days, [but] out of a reckless disregard of self, and the careless disregard of honour of the profession [his skills] have deteriorated much from his once powerful and excellent style of acting.

Booth did not appear after his reputedly drunken Richard for five days, then played Baltimore as Shylock to good notices. By the latter part of the month, he was back in Philadelphia, and the *Dramatic Mirror* reported, "Booth played Richard III on Monday evening, with much vigor—*he was himself, liquor was absent!*"[46] One wonders if Booth was really drunk on the sixth of April or if the critics by now took any indisposition for intoxication.

The next several months flowed by without incident. In April 1843, Booth appeared after a long absence at the Park Theatre in New York, opening as Richard; and the *Spirit of the Times* threw its journalistic hat in the air, saying, "Never, since Kean, have we seen so genuine a piece of Shakespearean acting. . . . It was a gem. . . . most splendidly portrayed." A large and "judicious" audience called him forth at the end of the performance to receive "the most cordial acknowledgments of the house." The *Spirit* praised the rest of the engagement for having the same "eminent ability, energy, and genius which characterized his Richard."[47] Forrest remained America's favorite tragedian, but Booth seemed at the top of his form.

So, too, the *New York Express,* during the same engagement: "He is *not* broken down. . . . There was not a single act of *Richard* which was not carried through triumphantly . . . never has he surpassed the acting of [the last scene]. We would have sat the whole play over again without rising. . . . it was transcendent . . . enough cannot be said in approval."[48]

But serenity and Booth remained strangers. He was acting well and had seemingly conquered his drinking problems. But then he heard from his London son, Richard Junius, who, having not seen his father since 1826, wrote of his desire to come to the United States.

In 1841 Adelaide had taken Richard to London to find employment for her son, who had developed strong interests in languages and religion. After their arrival in London, Adelaide wrote back to her sister on 5 August 1841 describing their situation.

> DEAR THERESE—England is no better than it was, poor and miserable throughout; Belgium is a land of flowing milk and honey by comparison. If I had not a letter or two of recommendation to society ladies I will not be able to be recognized. . . .
>
> Richard is satisfied at London. He is determined to remain here; he will give lessons and take any employment whatever, but for this it will be necessary to have special letters of recommendation, without which they do nothing in London. There are many English in Brussels whom the Baron knows—distinguished persons. Try to obtain some other letters of introduction from them for Richard, that he may give lessons or get other employment.
>
> Our cousin assures us that it is only in this way that Richard can succeed, and that it is impossible to do otherwise in England. Lose no time, then, my dear Therese. We are giving you, without doubt, a great deal of trouble, but if Richard should obtain employment you will not care for that.
>
> Our love to Agatha
>
> M. BOOTH.[49]

Adelaide was indeed received in society as the wife of the tragedian, but life was still difficult for her in London.[50] Richard apparently fell ill in London in 1841; on 2 June 1842 Adelaide wrote to her family to tell them Richard, now twenty-one years old, was better. She also expressed a wish to accompany her only son to America, stating, "I have firmly sworn that whatever may happen against me I will never again separate myself from him." She added that she had just received some money from Booth, "most opportunely," and closed by saying, "I have all my courage, and my powers have not abandoned me. God will doubtless pity my unhappiness. Pray for us and tell the old mother to do the same. I have great confidence in such prayers."[51]

Upon recovering, Richard began planning his trip. The dutiful son requested permission from Booth, who assented and sent him a draft for eighty pounds.[52] Exactly when the young man arrived in the United States remains unclear, but he filed his last will and testament in Brussels on 24 September 1843, probably just before departure.[53]

The only surviving account of the meeting of father and son is from journalist Frank A. Burr's article. Apparently the actor told his son nothing of the family in Baltimore, and Richard traveled with his father for "three years and more." What Booth did with his son when he returned to Baltimore we can only guess. Such a delicate arrangement could hardly endure. According to Burr, Richard's travels with his father came to a halt when some backstage person taunted the youth, accusing him of being illegitimate, pointing out that Booth had a family living in Baltimore. Richard investigated, discovered the truth, and wrote to his mother, pleading with her to come to America and establish his legitimacy. She immediately began making the necessary arrangements.

Richard left Booth at that point and found work as a language instructor in Baltimore, barely surviving. Burr described him as a quiet man, inclined to melancholy, which potential students found somewhat off-putting.

Booth continued his touring as if nothing had happened, but he was on a collision course with Adelaide. His acting, at least, was going well, although notices of his drinking increased. A critic for the journal *Brother Jonathan* on 27 May 1843 gently chided him during an engagement at the Park Theatre in New York.

> Mr. Booth commenced an engagement on Wednesday night, and if acting of intrinsic merit could attract, he would have drawn crowded audiences, for he is unquestionably the only actor of genius of the present day. It is to be regretted that his course of conduct detracts from his character and reputation, and presents an insurmountable obstacle to the attainment of that position, to which his genius and talents entitle him. The house has been well attended, but not so much as he deserved.

Later the same critic suggested that, "should Booth rise superior to the vice which has beset him, he might yet bring his career to a brilliant termination."[54] And a few weeks later, at another Park engagement, *Brother Jonathan* kept after him, saying, "His efforts have been characterized by a force and vigor calculated to astonish those who profess to consider him merely a wreck of former greatness. It will be his own fault, if he does not yet regain the laurels he has suffered to fall from his brow."[55]

Of the same engagement, the *Spirit of the Times* decried Booth's weak supporting players, who decreased the box-office receipts. Of his Reuben Glenroy, the *Spirit* said,

> There are few actors who *would* have played the character in the same antiquated style that he did, but there are very few who *could* produce equal effect, play in whatever fashion they might conceive. Most of his readings were very beautiful, and at times he electrified the house by portraying some of those outbursts of passion which are so peculiarly the offsprings of his genius.[56]

Later the same year in Boston, Booth started to play Richard III but could not finish. The *Boston Post* reported, "The National Theatre was crowded last evening to witness Mr. Booth's personation of Richard 3rd, but unfortunately *Richard was not himself.* He recited a few lines of the opening speech, but was unable to proceed, and two other pieces were substituted. . . . It is painful to see a man of such undoubted genius so weak in one point, but for which he would shine without a rival."[57] On the following evening, Booth tried it again, and the *Post* could restore him to public favor: "Mr. Booth played the part of Richard 3rd last evening to the most numerous audience ever assembled within the walls of the National Theatre. He enacted 'more wonders than a man,' and fully sustained his claim to wear, unrivalled, the 'tragic crown.'"

And so it went, with the Booth fortunes flickering. Booth plodded from city to city, staying in the East during 1844. In April he played Boston, and the *Boston Daily Evening Transcript* reported that Booth "has recently 'signed the pledge,' and, being 'himself again,' he will, as of old, stand in the front rank of Shakespeare's heroes."[58] A few days later, the same paper said, "all those who witnessed those performances declare that he never, even in his palmiest days, played with more ability and power."[59]

Booth had good days and bad. George Vandenhoff described appearing with him on 12 June 1844; he and Booth were to play Brutus and Cassius in two scenes from *Julius Caesar* for Edmund Simpson's benefit at the Park. Vandenhoff, fully aware of "Booth's irregularity in business," did not attend the rehearsal, nor did Booth. And Booth was late arriving at the theatre, so Vandenhoff did not even see him until Booth entered the stage as Cassius.

> On he came, with a brusqueness quite in character, confronted me, stopped, gave his usual long sniff—a sort of drawing-in of the breath through his nostrils, which was a habit with him—made a dead halt, glared, and—said nothing! I supposed at first, never having encountered him professionally, that it was his usual mode of commencing the scene; and that the long pause was merely the herald of the coming storm—a lull before the thunder crash. I waited patiently; but not a sound, not a word! Booth still glared on me mysteriously, with a blood-shot eye. At last, when I thought this pause threatened to "stretch out to the crack of doom," I began to suspect the cause of the mystery; and as gently as possible suggested that we had waited long enough, by giving him "the word" in an under tone: "Most noble brother, you have done me wrong!" This recalled him to himself, and broke his abstraction; he gave another of his *sniffs*—and said, *sotto voce,* to me, "Thank you!"—and cooly enough proceeded with his part—"Most noble brother, you have done me wrong!"—and so the scene went on.

Vandenhoff added that Simpson's benefit drew only indifferent attendance.[60]

During the winter of 1844–45, Booth left the East and visited Pittsburgh, Cincinnati, Augusta, and New Orleans. The *Spirit of the Times* reported Booth outdrew Macready twice over in Cincinnati, although Macready's tickets sold for double the normal price. Back in New York in April 1845, the tragedian shared a bill at Palmo's Theatre with one Hervio Nano, the protagonist in *Bibbo, or, The Patagonian Ape.*

If Booth still had a drinking problem at this point, he seemed to be holding it at bay. *The Spirit of the Times* on 31 May 1845 reprinted a review from the *Philadelphia American Advocate,* praising the tragedian highly.

> This distinguished actor has taken the theatrical public by surprise; when we say surprise, we allude to the fact that he has

> satisfied them of one thing, that he has no equal in the peculiar character he impersonates, and by his extraordinary genius, impassioned manner, and beautiful classical illustration, casts a shadow over those foreign humbugs who come amongst us puffed into notice, and palmed upon us as great, when in fact they are below mediocrity. Mr. Booth of late, owing perhaps, to this fawning of the American public upon inflated action and actors, has seemingly neglected his *role* and at times walked through glorious parts—but the whole man is now changed, and looking no doubt upon these innovators, these base tendrils around the drama's oak, as so much rubbish—he throws off that insanity, that careless disregard of public opinion, and comes forth as in the olden times, his palmy days, to make the palmiest of them all. His Sir Giles . . . the other evening was tremendous; he threw around it a charm the elder Kean could not have dispelled if he were alive; he invested it with all the powers of his manly mind, and kept the actors spell bound, who forgetting themselves and position, gazed upon him in wonder and amazement—his words seemed to be carved out, and placed within grasp; they glared like the actor upon us, to astonish and awe. The last scene in the last act was overpowering, and we arose from our seats with a convulsive movement, and left the theatre, with feelings as undefined as they are undescribable.

Even given the journalistic propensity for puffery, a rave is still a rave, and the *Spirit* had never hesitated to pillory him before. A few months later, the *Spirit* again praised the old actor, saying, "His performances bear nature stamped upon them, and although the old gentleman is falling into 'the sere and yellow leaf,' he may delight us yet many years."[61] Junius, Jr., played Hemeya to his father's Pescara; the *Spirit* found him too vehement and asked him to moderate his passions a bit.

As Booth neared fifty years of age, he began to show signs of settling down; his acting seems to have gone through a renaissance. On 20 September 1845 he purchased a residence at 62 North Exeter Street in Baltimore. The records of the transaction indicate Booth bought the property from John H. Ing for $1,480. Ground rent was $47.50 per year on a ninety-nine-year lease, and the purchase involved a mortgage to J. B. Latrobe for $820.[62]

Perhaps Booth considered farm life too strenuous, even as a hobby. Living in Baltimore would be more convenient for his professional travels and would offer better educational opportunities for his children than were available in Harford County.

The new Booth residence was "a rather stately three-story dwelling . . . rather a pretty house, a little staid and formal in its style of architecture, but solid and substantial; and, indeed, somewhat fine for those times." Exeter Street was described as "quiet and old-fashioned." Neighborhood residences were "habitations . . . with high steps, and tall green shutters, as an entrance to the vestibule, and brass door-knockers instead of the modern bell-pull."[63]

Booth remained on the East Coast until the next winter, then in December 1845, he again headed south. His terms were one hundred dollars a night, plus a clear third of a benefit in New Orleans. In other theatres managed by Ludlow and Smith in Mobile and St. Louis, Booth offered to share, taking one-third of the receipts, although he was flexible on this point.

The managers agreed, and a bargain was struck; Booth was to close in Boston on 10 October 1845, leave the eleventh, and arrive in St. Louis as soon as he could get there, assuming he could find boats ready at either Wheeling or Cincinnati. He played the Boston engagement, and a Harvard Theatre Collection note records a "severe indisposition" on the ninth. Whatever it was, Booth played again in Boston from the thirteenth through the seventeenth, then wrote to Ludlow and Smith on 22 October.

> I regret that severe sickness has prevented me from joining you in St. Louis according to our understanding, but as soon as I recover, I shall use my best efforts to visit you, although I fear you will have left St. Louis before my arrival. Do not think hard of me, as it has been my most anxious wish in making this Engagement to hold my faith with you. I shall endeavor if possible to be with you in time for New Orleans & Mobile and hope we can arrange the other afterwards. Sincerely regretting this disappointment I am
> Gentlemen
> Yours respectfully
> J.B. Booth[64]

Apparently Ludlow and Smith accepted this; Booth wrote them again from Pittsburgh on 6 November 1845.

> Mr. Chypendale call'd on me & said you wish'd me to begin at New Orleans on or about the 17th instant & that the Engt should

> run as if no delay had occurr'd from my illness & inability to join you in St. Louis. I'm just arriv'd from Baltimore & tomorrow (Thursday) shall proceed at 10 A.M. for New Orleans. I presume the Mobile Engt. will commence then on Dec. 1st as stated in your previous letters—I shall perhaps be with you as soon as this letter—however in case of accident, it's best to write to you—.[65]

Booth did in fact play New Orleans, twice, and Mobile once in November and December, returning by way of Cincinnati and an engagement there, but St. Louis had to wait to experience Booth. Booth fell from grace in New Orleans, a city that has seduced far stronger men. He failed to appear as Lear for his fourth performance, nor did he appear the next night. The *Tropic,* quoted in the *Spirit of the Times,* said that Booth had recovered from his "indisposition" but warned that another lapse "will hardly *take* in this community," adding that, "We hope nothing, hereafter, will compel us to pronounce 'Othello's occupation's gone.'"[66]

Booth returned to play Richard III on Sunday (allowed in New Orleans), 23 November. A brief advertisement announced that, in consequence of the great crowds of people who could not get in to see his Richard, Booth would repeat it on the twenty-seventh, which he did. The *New Orleans Picayune* complained, however, that Booth was again not himself: "in plain English, Booth taking it into his head to play off some of his eccentricities instead of the business set down for him—another piece was substituted." That closed the engagement, but on the last day of November, Booth signed a statement, specifying, "As a compensation for the disappointments experienced and damages sustained in consequence of my failure to fulfil my engagement at the St. Charles Theatre, I do hereby agree to act the character of Richard the Third on tomorrow night, gratuitously for Ludlow and Smith."[67]

The long-suffering managers booked Booth for Mobile, and Booth played eight performances there, apparently without incident. He then played a final three nights in New Orleans, and the new year saw him in mid-January in Cincinnati and returning to the East.

In January 1846, Booth made a short tour to Cincinnati and Pittsburgh. His propensity for recording his impressions resulted in a tattered playbill for 13 January, his opening in Cincinnati as Richard III, with these notes by Booth on the back:

> Closed in Cincinnati January night of 22d Thursday was disappointed in starting by the River on Friday afternoon & started on Sunday at 12 A.M. by the [illegible] Steam boat, from Rorbach's on corner of Front & Broadway. Fare to Wheeling or Pittsburgh was ten dollars—coming [out?] it was but four. . . . Monday 26th was very warm—cold & snow on next day part of the time as we approached Wheeling. Left Steamer here at 3 PM Tuesday & sent my large Trunk by Forsyth's Exp which was packing up for Baltimore. Put up in Wheeling at the U.S. Hotel—Wrote home to Baltimore inclosing sixteen dollars—paid Coach fare, eleven dollars for next morning, Wednesday, Jan 28th at 6 in the morning. Bill here was a dollar and a half. Wheeling has over seven, say eight thousand Inhabitants and no theatre—is 56 miles by land from Pittsburgh and 95 by the River.[68]

An actress of the time, Olive Logan, recounted yet another Booth story about this time. Booth was playing Louisville with Logan's sister, Eliza, and while Booth had remained sober during the engagement, he had "taken a little stimulant" as he prepared for his benefit as Lear. His intoxication progressed as the evening wore on; Booth and Eliza prepared themselves for the last scene, in which Lear and his daughter are discovered in prison, Lear with a wreath of straw about his head. But Booth demanded to see the property man, a Mr. Pratt, before he would allow the show to continue.

"Miss Eliza," said he, "the straw that they have made this wreath of don't suit me." He continued, "It is *wheat* straw and I require *rye* straw for the wreath! I won't finish the scene without it! I always demand rye straw for this mad scene."

Pratt arrived and claimed he had tried to find rye straw but couldn't. Thundered Booth, "Couldn't! Why not, sir?"

"Because they didn't have it, sir," responded Pratt.

"Did you go to Jonson's stables?"

"Yes, sir."

"Didn't they have it there?"

"*No,* sir."

"Did you go to the *jail?*" demanded Booth.

"Yes, sir."

"Didn't they have it there?"

"No, sir."

"Well," said Booth, turning to Eliza, "ain't that singular? When I was in that jail, five years ago, they had plenty of rye straw." Booth hurled the wreath at the unhappy property man, and the scene opened on Lear and daughter laughing hysterically. Olive Logan added that Booth had spent time in jail in place of a local thief, the actor having nothing better to do, and, besides, "he didn't like his boarding house."[69]

The next few months were relatively uneventful for Booth, then in June he contracted again with Ludlow and Smith, engaging for one-third of the nightly receipts for eleven performances. On 22 June 1846 he finally made it to St. Louis to begin an engagement. He was billed to open as Sir Edward Mortimer in *The Iron Chest,* but this time Booth confronted his fiends center stage. As Ludlow recounted the story,

> It was a rainy night, and the house not more than half filled. Mr. Booth played his first two scenes in his usual melancholy and pathetic manner,—the very embodiment of the broken-hearted man. But suddenly the demon eccentricity laid hold on him, when he dropped his gloominess and became a *leetle* too *spirited* for the consistency of the character. The audience perceived this divergency from his usual style of representing the character, and being composed generally of young men, always ready to embrace new ideas, soon entered into the *spirit* with Mr. Booth, and applauded him at the end of every speech. I think I never witnessed such acting before or since that time. When the curtain fell,—as Mr. Booth fell upon the stage, having missed Wilford's arms extended to catch him,—there went forth such a burst of applause as made the chandeliers rattle. But the play was not over yet. Mr. Booth, as I suppose, feeling complimented by this burst of generous applause, jumped up after being dead, stepped quickly forward, and made three very graceful bows to the auditors, and then quietly laid down on the spot from whence he had risen. This brought down another thundering round of applause; when up jumps Mr. B., and stepping forward as before, made three more bows, and then laid down again. Seeing what was likely to continue, I rushed through a private door, gained the stage, and had the drop lowered just as Mr. B. was preparing to go forward for the third time.

The next day Booth received the following note from his furious managers: "In consequence of your having appeared upon the stage last night in a state of intoxication, and disgracing the theatre and yourself by your imperfect personation of the character of Sir Edward Mortimer, we notify you that we consider your conduct a breach of your engagement with us & we shall hold you responsible in damages for the disappointment you have occasioned." Ludlow vowed that Booth would never again appear in any theatre under his management, and Smith hated Booth even more than Ludlow did.[70]

However, the next day, Ludlow reported that the newspapers took the whole thing as a joke, pointing out how anxious the public was to see Booth as Sir Giles and Richard III. The managers reengaged Booth not once but twice, and he completed the engagement, as Ludlow had to admit, "Never playing better at any time within my observation."

The bemused manager might have found interest in a biography of Booth published about that time: *The Actor; Or, A Peep behind the Curtain. Being Passages in the Lives of Booth and Some of his Contemporaries.* The author, Thomas Ford, once governor of Illinois, early on stated, "In the History of Mr. Booth, we know there are some facts which, although they might illustrate more particularly the various phases of his character, and prove entertaining to the reader, cannot with propriety be made public, while the subject of them is still alive, nor would the author willingly submit to the public gaze, what belongs only to the privacies of life.[71]

Ford then related bloodcurdling tales of Booth's drunken escapades, his broken nose, and attempted suicides, relieved by biographical chapters on Hamblin, Flynn, and a few others. Nothing of Adelaide appears in *The Actor,* and one suspects that Asia Booth Clarke drew heavily on Ford in preparing her own two published treatments of her father. Ford's dates are frequently wrong; he seemed to be writing from memory. Many of the anecdotes show Booth as a drunk and near-madman, but no record survives of Booth's ever commenting on any of the stories. Nonetheless, *The Actor* marked the first appearance of the names Booth and Ford together—it would not be the last.

As for Booth, he seemed not to have appeared again until October 1846, in Boston. In September, however, thunderclouds began scudding across Booth's eastern horizon, threatening retribution and lightning.

Adelaide had left England and was headed for Baltimore.

7

No More in This World

I have a journey, sir, shortly to go:
My master calls me, I must not say no.

—*King Lear,* V, iii, 322–23

Adelaide boarded the *Great Britain* in Liverpool the last day of October 1846 to start for America. On the bridge some argument arose about the accuracy of the ship's compass. Captain Hosken solemnly declared nothing wrong with the instrument and about 9:30 P.M. ran the *Great Britain* aground in the Bay of Dundrum on the east coast of Ireland.

A badly shaken Adelaide wrote an account of the wreck to her sister, describing the splendid dinner she had had and the charm of her stateroom, then the shouts of the crew as the ship ground to a halt. Not till early the next morning did boats arrive to ferry the passengers to the nearby shore, the crews carrying women through the shallow water.

Adelaide took refuge in a fisherman's cabin, ogled by the many curious who came to see the hulk and the survivors. She then returned to Liverpool, was reimbursed for her *Great Britain* ticket, and re-booked on the *Great Western,* a ship which itself had nearly sunk in the

North Atlantic a few weeks earlier. This crossing went smoothly; the ship arrived off Sandy Hook on the sixteenth of November 1846, the trip having taken sixteen days and eight hours.[1] She went on to Baltimore and wrote of her intentions for Booth to her sister.

> BALTIMORE, Dec. 17, 1846.
>
> My Dear Therese—Thank God I have at length arrived. I left Liverpool on the 31st of October by the Great Western. In spite of the advanced season and the bad weather we accomplished the voyage in seventeen days.
>
> Directly after my arrival in New York I left for Baltimore. I was in a great hurry to see Richard. It was in the morning. I took the idea to go and find him in the establishment where I knew he was giving lessons in Latin and Greek. He was there. I leave you to judge of the joy his presence gave me. He was very much moved. I had great difficulty to keep from exhibiting my happiness too much. We got into the carriage which waited for me, and Richard took me to a furnished house where he had secured a lodging for me.
>
> It was so delightful to be together. Booth was playing in New York when I arrived. He is just about to commence his winter tour. I don't want to do anything to prevent him from making money, so I shall wait until he comes to Baltimore, and as soon as he arrives my lawyer will fall on his back like a bomb. Nobody here has any notion that I am the wife of the famous tragedian. My lawyer tells me that, considering the fortune which remains to him, I may demand 5,000 francs.
>
> Whilst he [Richard] was traveling with his father Booth used to sing to him the song of the "Tobacco Pipe," and also the romances that poor sister Agatha used to sing, to the guitar. Richard has told me during the last week all about the follies and extravagances of B. He has barely escaped several times being run over by carriages whilst he was drunk. I passed through the street where the Holmes live and I saw the house. It has not a very grand appearance. I have not seen any one of that set. . . .
>
> I will give you the news of Booth as soon as the affair is settled. I embrace you, and am your affectionate sister.
>
> M. BOOTH.[2]

While Adelaide waited for another ship, Booth continued his engagements, Boston in October, New York and Boston again the following month. In New York the *Spirit of the Times* referred to him as "that old favorite and great actor," adding that, although "time has evidently impaired the strength of his voice, and subdued his former powers, still as a correct and beautiful reader or easy and graceful actor he has scarcely an equal."[3] He continued to demand and receive one hundred dollars a night.

While Adelaide fumed in Baltimore, Booth swung south, beginning an engagement in New Orleans on 9 January 1847. He opened as Sir Edward Mortimer, and a young actor, Harry Watkins, entered in his diary that the managers rode Booth around all day in a carriage to keep him sober. Even though it rained, they used the same ploy the next day. Booth caught cold; the managers dragged him from his bed to perform Lear, which Watkins thought very badly done. Later, the young actor called Booth's Brutus one of the finest pieces of acting he had ever seen.[4] Most of the reviewers commented on his hoarseness during the early performances but still considered him without a superior on the American stage.

In a note written on the Mississippi River, Booth recorded that, as he was dressing for Bertram on the fifteenth, report came to him of a man who had been shot dead in the barroom next to the theatre. "This," Booth noted, "injured our receipts materially but we played to about 57 dollars."[5] Booth returned to the East after playing a short engagement in Vicksburg, Mississippi.

He next appeared at the Baltimore Museum from 8 to 20 March 1847. Adelaide finally confronted him here some twenty-one years after last having seen him. An old manager witnessed the event and described it as "very stormy," with Booth urging Adelaide to return to Europe and she pleading for Booth to admit Richard's legitimacy. Booth refused; they parted, and the issue remained unresolved.[6]

Adelaide, with only her son for a resource, learned she must wait two years before she could sue for divorce.[7] Adamant, she and Richard rented rooms on West Baltimore Street, a shabby neighborhood. Richard supported them both with his meager earnings as a language teacher, and the vigil began. In 1849, before she brought proceedings against Booth, Adelaide wrote a pitiful description of her conditions to her sister.

421 West Baltimore Street,
Bal., U.S., Nov., 1849.

My dear Therese—Richard writes this letter at my dictation, because my sight is a little weak. I have delayed writing as long as possible. Before I quitted Brussels I told you that if I succeeded with my husband I would take care of you. I have succeeded so little that here, after more than a year, I have not received a cent. My affairs are so much embarrassed by the death of my cousin in London that I do not see the possibility of determining the time of my departure hence. Richard gives lessons for which he is frequently not paid. You see this is not pleasant.

My health is not good. Richard is very delicate. The climate is bad. The only thing which is cheap here is meat. Mutton is 25 to 30 centimes a pound, beef 40. I pay for two rooms on the second floor not furnished 25 francs, and they are still uncarpeted, the walls whitewashed; this is not good, is it? We go to the theater with tickets which are given us. Amusements are very dear. We go to mass at the Cathedral. I have nobody to help me. I do the housework alone and it is very fatiguing, seeing that I have to go up and down two flights of stairs for water and to the cellar for wood. Richard helps me a little.

You see that I am not so comfortable as I was in Brussels, but I have patience and do not fret. I give out our washing and iron it myself. Considering all these occupations, I have not much time to fret. I have also to mend for two. I make and remake my own dresses; in a word, I am always at work and never idle. I don't suppose there is another woman in the city who would take my place, who is well enough off and has servants.

I often have a very inflamed tongue, and I suffered terribly with the heat during the summer. If we have to remain here another summer we must be differently lodged. It would kill me. You see I tell you all. When I have any pleasant news you shall share it, and, in the meantime, be equally frank with us. Tell us your position; if we can do anything to help you we will do all that is possible. . . .

Richard and I embrace you with all our hearts, and we are awaiting your news. Your affectionate sister and nephew.

R. J. Booth and M. Booth.[8]

What Booth told Mary Ann Holmes of all this is not recorded. Mary Ann must have known about Adelaide when she first met Booth, and what sort of ceremony took place, if any, in the Honorable Mrs. Chambers' London home in 1821 remains a mystery. Booth and Mary Ann no doubt spent the three years after Adelaide's arrival waiting for the proverbial other shoe to drop.

After the confrontation, Booth left for Richmond and a later engagement in Philadelphia. Upon his return to Baltimore in May 1847, Booth attempted to resolve the conflict, according to two surviving documents.[9] In the first, Booth swore he and Adelaide had entered into a separate maintenance agreement in 1826 during Booth's first return to London, and he had in fact paid her seventy-five pounds on May first (Booth's birthday) every year through 1847. Then Booth agreed to modify the agreement by paying Adelaide one thousand dollars and signing over to her an annuity of fifty pounds, payable out of various London properties left to him by his grandmother, Elizabeth Booth, now administered by John Wilkes Booth of London.[10] In return, Adelaide agreed to drop all charges and claims against Booth. Booth or his heirs would pay her another thousand dollars in 1857, with the annuity to pass on to Richard Junius Booth if Adelaide died.

Booth considered the matter closed. Two weeks later, perhaps feeling a bit cramped for space, he purchased the back yards adjoining his residence on North Exeter Street, knocked down the fences between them, and settled into relative domesticity and a reduced performance schedule.[11] Certainly the lots were not expensive; land records indicate he bought them on a sublease from Ing (from whom he had bought the home) for one hundred dollars, with ground rent of three dollars to be paid every Fourth of July.[12]

Late in her life, Asia Booth Clarke recalled the Baltimore home fondly.[13] The house itself she described as "very plain, simple, and yet refined; luxury and indolence had no place in it; plain, comfortable, and homelike." Asia quoted Mrs. Pelby, an old actor's wife, as having said during a visit, "This is a *home,* not merely a habitation." Booth decorated the parlor in dark green and gold, which he told his daughter were his father's colors, and many fathers before that, and his favorites. The furniture was simple; only Booth commanded a chair with arms.

Of her father, Asia recalled that he was an early riser, customarily going through the halls, waking his family, singing, "Arouse, arouse, ye drowsy sleepers; arouse, arouse, 'tis the break of day." Booth could play no instrument but had many favorite songs.

After awakening his family, Booth would grab two large baskets and hurry off to the market house for the day's provisions, to the dismay of Mary Ann, who said of him, "he gave more than double prices for everything, and bought all sorts of things that were not really required." He demanded his household eat fish, which they disliked, and would rarely allow meat for the meals. Asia recalled vegetables and fruits in profusion, with many South American and Floridian imports. Cocoa was made immediately from the crushed kernels. Yams and guavas appeared, and on rare occasions, matte tea, a potion Asia detested, which they had to suck through a silver pipe. Strong coffee, iced or hot as the weather dictated, the family drank morning and evening. Asia grumbled that the early hours, early meals, and simple diet kept visitors to a minimum but that the entire household fared alike, young and old, black and white.

Asia also recalled that Booth retained nothing of his English life or ancestry; she had never heard the phrase "God save the Queen" until she herself moved to England. Even if Booth still might dream of London and his lost fortunes there, he raised his children as Americans. Of an evening, when Booth was at home, he might read to the family; Asia recalled his renditions of *King John* and *Coriolanus.* Booth retained a substantial personal library, which Asia inherited. It included works by Shakespeare, Coleridge, Keats, Shelley, Byron, Lawrence Sterne, Thomas Moore, and Charles Churchill. A copy of Dante's *Divine Comedy,* in Italian, Booth had purchased in Madeira as he and Mary Ann fled England. A few volumes were in Hebrew or German.

And a loving daughter recalled her father's sense of fun, his lack of temper or violence, when at his home. She remembered being bedridden once and her father serving her tea, while imitating a slave, walking bowlegged with a broad, idiotic grin on his face, smacking his lips, and affecting a ridiculous accent. She recalled inviting her mock slave, dubbed Pompey, to join her in the tea, and his replying: "Whar you tink I'se got my raisin', ef *you* tinks Pomp is corn field hand, you'se *missed* it, wasn't raised wid no po white trash, no, *indeedy;* come off *rale* plantation in ole Virginny, leddes an gemmen, *dem wus,* dat's a fac! Spec Pomp knows his place as good as ennybody!" Such racist humor in a slaveholding state reduced Asia to helpless laughter; Booth's daughter never shared his regard for human rights.

On another occasion, Asia dressed her father up as a Carmelite nun, led him into the kitchen, and said to her mother, "Mother, dear, poor sister has come out of the convent, what shall we do with her?" Mary Ann recalled a nun had indeed a few years earlier escaped the convent, raving mad, so she asked the disguised Booth a long series of questions, receiving only sighs and sad nods for reply. Eventually Booth looked up to wink at Asia, and Mary Ann detected the masquerade. She cried out, "Oh, Junius, how could you let this girl play such tricks with you!" Booth and his conspirator chortled with glee; Mary Ann went back to kneading her bread dough with additional vigor, while Asia lit her father's cigar.

Booth often carried his respect for all life-forms to extremes. Even in summer, he would not allow his children to kill the flies that swarmed about any residence, lecturing them, "You should never kill a fly, they are scavengers, and cleanse the air of many impurities which no doubt is the cause of sickness. There is some medicinal quality in flies or animals would not eat them; also in spiders, for birds, particularly caged birds, seek to get them."

Booth had taught his black servant Joe never to take animal life, but once Joe had accidently plowed up and injured a snake on the Harford County farm. When Booth learned of this, he seized Mary Ann's bonnet box, dumped out the hat, half filled it with cotton, and disappeared. He returned with the snake in the hatbox, in which he had punched air holes, and nursed the creature back to health. As Mary Ann put it:

> For nearly *three days* that fearful reptile occupied my band box and our parlour, and, struggling to get out, suddenly father opened the box, and it crept slowly away through the open door into the air, and departed forever; but many weeks elapsed before I could feel one degree of comfort about the house. I had the miserable feeling that it would come back to show its grateful remembrance of such kind treatment.

Booth's family did not share his obsessive respect for life, and one wonders what effect all this had upon the young John Wilkes Booth.

Asia also recalled that on Sunday mornings Booth attended no church but sat at his parlor window or front steps, surrounded by dogs and children, greeting the passersby. Not many of his neighbors cared to associate with an actor, but Booth had an easy friendship with the more liberal element. Asia once asked about a trio of ladies with sunshades and prayer books who had greeted her father. "Who are those strangers, Father?" Booth said he did not know. "But they know *you,*" Asia insisted. Booth replied, "Everyone knows Tom Fool." Edwin Booth later recalled a similar incident.[14]

When the Sunday crowds had passed, Booth would take his daughter and wander the desolate streets, often visiting the docks, where he knew many seafaring men. Asia marveled that all of them were glad to see Booth, shaking his hand, kissing him on both cheeks. Noting some of the swarthy sailors wore earrings, she asked her father about his pierced ears, wondering if he had ever gone to sea, but Booth explained, "I had my ears bored to wear earrings in *Othello*."

No matter how pleasant his home in Baltimore, Booth, though less often, did continue to tour, and his first American son was by now starring. In August 1847 Junius Brutus Booth, Jr., appeared in Boston as Sir Giles Overreach, and the young Harry Watkins observed that he would never make half the actor his father was. The elder Booth arrived in the same city the next month for a two-week engagement. The first week went well enough, but then the demons returned. The *Journal* sneered, "He was very hoarse—so hoarse that it was almost impossible for the actors on the stage to hear what he said. He played wretchedly as Shylock, being not only inaudible but quite drunk. In any other man it would not be tolerated. In him it is called eccentricity."[15]

Booth almost missed a performance of Lear in Boston for his own benefit. When he failed to appear at the theatre, minions scurried out to locate him. One finally found him in a drinking place near Faneuil Hall, surrounded by marketmen, enrapturing them with scenes from Shakespeare and verses from the Bible. With great difficulty, he was returned to the theatre, where the audience clamored and roared for the show to begin. Booth, hearing the row, flung the curtain aside, faced the audience, and yelled, "Shut up! You shut up out there and in ten minutes I'll give you the god-damndest King Lear you ever saw in your life!" Watkins recalled that from his first entrance, a half hour late, Booth completely captivated his audience.[16]

When Booth next took to the road, just before Christmas, Junius, Jr., accompanied him. Booth played a dozen performances in New Orleans; the *Picayune* said of him, "For many years Mr. Booth has not played [this] well in this city, committing not one act of folly to estrange his friends and admirers, but playing every part he has taken splendidly."[17]

Perhaps his son's presence had a sobering effect on the old stager; Mary Ann could no longer allow him out on the road alone.

Booth stopped for a short engagement in Vicksburg. On 29 January 1848 he was booked to play Iago to J. H. Oxley's Othello, but the previous night a fire broke out in a neighboring store, and four stores, the Masonic Lodge, several offices, and Vicksburg's new theatre collapsed into smoking rubble.[18]

Booth remained in the East until September 1848. In New York, the *Spirit of the Times* called him "the very best actor of the present day," albeit his voice and body were not so vigorous as once they were. Still, they considered him "an Atlas of the drama" and urged all to attend his performances.[19] So, too, the *New York Herald* lavished praise upon him, suggesting that, although he was on "the downhill of life," he had lost none of his fire and energy. The critic especially praised his vocal transitions in *The Apostate*.[20]

On March third Booth offered terms to the Buffalo managers for a July engagement, requesting fifty dollars a night for ten nights and a clear half for the sixth and twelfth nights, to be announced as his benefits.[21] Booth could ask only about half as much per night as he could in 1821 when he first arrived in America, whose audiences had by now seen him and his repertory for almost a full generation.

In August Booth played Albany. Someone had to go along to look after him, and for the first time Booth was accompanied by his son Edwin, then only fourteen years old. Henry Pitt Phelps described the dark-eyed youngster keeping as close watch on his father as possible, reading the play line by line as the elder Booth performed. When a scene ended, Edwin stood ready with the costume for the next.[22] Edwin would travel with his father intermittently for the next four years, profoundly affecting Edwin's development. The admiring son later recalled his father's preshow preparations.

> He used to make up at the mirror there and as he settled the hump upon his shoulders he seemed to put on the character with it. From that moment on he was *Richard*. He wished to be spoken to by nobody. If I told him anything about the house or ventured a remark about the news of the day he would glare at me like a fiend. . . . I can not say "Off with his head!" as he said it. By striking one hand into the other, thus, he would picture to the audience the

> headsman, the block and the victim so vividly that everyone shuddered.[23]

Later John Malone, who acted with Edwin on several occasions, recalled him more than once describing the elder Booth's leaving the stage during some terrific scene as Richard III or Sir Giles and, while waiting for his cue to reenter, whispering some amusing story to a friend in the wings. Edwin also refuted the legends of his father becoming so excited in the last scene of *Richard the Third* that he refused to be killed, driving his Richmond out of the theatre. As Edwin put it, "The fact is, the story is one of the myths of the stage. I've heard it located in a dozen cities by eyewitnesses."[24]

Nor did Edwin ever see fit to recount another theatrical myth about his father and Yorick's skull, seemingly a difficult property to locate. In a small town the elder Booth demanded a real skull, saying, "I have put up with a pumpkin, with holes punched in it for eyes, and I have even endured a skull made of dough, but this time it must be a real skull, or there will be no Hamlet." No such item appeared in the property room, but a local black youth, a hanger-on around the theatre, said he could supply the item for a reasonable price. A bargain was struck, and Booth had his skull. But as the engagement ended, Edwin noticed the youth following him around expectantly. Asked Edwin, "What's the matter, my boy?" "Ah want dat dar skull, wot I dun give you," replied the youth. "Well, my boy, go to the property man for it, perhaps he can find it for you, but if he can't, I'll give you a couple of dollars, and that will square it." Replied the young man, "Ah can't sell dat dar skull, dat skull 'longs to my old man, an—an—an [ah] just borrowed, from de grave, fer yo to use."[25]

Phelps also chronicled Booth's missing his benefit on 18 August 1848 because an enormous fire destroyed some four hundred buildings in Albany on the seventeenth. Property damage was estimated at two or three million dollars.[26] Booth had been staying at the Eagle Hotel, and when he learned the firemen had saved his wardrobe, he donned a red shirt and worked beside them the rest of the day.

During the winter of 1848–49, Booth traveled west and south to his usual haunts and for the first time visited Chicago, Illinois, which he described as a "tiny place." He returned to St. Louis, contracting with Smith and Ludlow for seventy dollars per night and a clear third for his benefits on the sixth and last nights of his engagement.[27] This time he perpetrated no freaks and played an extremely successful engagement.

St. Louis, however, still represented the frontier. The *St. Louis Weekly Reveille* published a long assessment of the local audiences, using a production of *The Stranger,* starring Booth, as an example. The reporter expressed astonishment that even Booth could hold the second balcony in abeyance, given their propensity for uproar. As The Stranger, Booth grew impatient with their interruptions and left the stage, whereupon one "sucker-looking" individual exclaimed, "Well, I'll swar, ain't he the alfiredest, ugly, crabbed, cross-grained critter you ever see'd—Cuss him, nothin' pleases him. . . . This little feller suits me—jest the idea of *his* gittin' mad ain't nothin' else but fun; and thar he goes agin'! Thar is no mistake about his bein' wrathy now, with the hull bilin' on 'em." As the play went on, the "sucker" began to see the point, exclaiming, "Sam I don't wonder the little feller's mad, ef he is ugly. Some cuss has run away with both his wife and money, and the loss of ither is enough to make a feller *rip*."

The *Reveille* reporter watched in amazement as Booth brought the rustic into rapt attention; as he put it, "the genius of the great actor held all before him spellbound, and his mournful tones seemed to strike the chords of sorrow in every heart. . . . Tears stood in many eyes."

As for the rustic, he summed it all up, "I'm desp'rate glad the little feller forgive her, for she looks like an amazin' fine woman, Sam, and she's awful sorry, and didn't go to do it, and won't agin, I reckon."

Sam tried to explain, "Why, they wur on'y funnin', on'y play-actin' the thing out, you durned fool, couldn't you see they wur on'y play-acting'?"

"Play, thunder!" roared the country critic, "didn't you see the *children;* thar ain't no funnin' about that, and I'll jest bet my team that the *Stranger* feller, and that thar little woman he hugged, will go, herea'ter, etarnally, now and forever, from this time out, in the blessed state of *cahoot*."[28]

Alfred Bunn supplied another example of the low level of theatregoing sophistication in the nineteenth century. He observed that Booth's Othello was much liked in America, then he described an old Yankee, who had never seen any stage performance, being taken to see

Othello, then asked if he liked it. Twanged the Yankee, "Ye-as, amazing; but cus me if I don't guess that little nigger played as well as any o' the white fellors—if not better!"[29]

After engagements in Cincinnati and Louisville, Booth spent most of January and February 1849 in New Orleans. No substantial reviews of his performances appeared, although the *Picayune* cheered his competition. In February Booth acted at the American Theatre in opposition to William Charles Macready, the same Macready with whom he had appeared at Covent Garden decades before. Macready's rave reviews called him the "first living tragedian"—and Booth did not perform for five nights, owing to an "indisposition," although the hiatus began before Macready appeared. Booth returned to the stage on the fifteenth and completed his engagement on the twenty-second.

Booth was back East by May 1849. Macready was then playing the Astor Place Opera House in New York. A long professional jealousy between Macready and Edwin Forrest became a political *cause célèbre,* with the working classes strongly backing Forrest. Rioting broke out during Macready's performances; eventually authorities called out the militia. The mob charged the armed troops; the soldiers fired; something like twenty-two citizens died in the first volley; dozens more fell wounded. The Astor Place Riot went down in history as the bloodiest theatre riot of all time. Macready smuggled himself out of New York to Philadelphia, caught the next ship to England, and never returned to America.

Booth retired to the farm for the summer, then appeared in August for a four-week Boston engagement. Of him the *Boston Transcript* said, "He appeared indeed to have renewed his energies during his temporary retirement, and gave all the well known points of his performance, with most brilliant effectiveness."[30]

A young William Winter, later an influential critic and close friend of Edwin Booth, saw the elder Booth during this engagement as Pescara, and recalled him years later. "He was a terrible presence. He seemed the incarnation of smooth, specious, hellish rapacity. His exultant malice seemed to buoy him above the ground. He floated rather than walked. His glance was deadly. His clear, high, cutting, measured tone was the exasperating note of hideous cruelty. He was acting a fiend then, and making the monster not only possible but actual."[31]

Edwin escorted his father to Boston, and the fifteen-year-old continued to study his father as he performed. On 10 September 1849 the bills announced Edwin would appear in the small role of Tressel in *Richard the Third.* While this appearance was billed as his first on any stage, Edwin had performed a bit before.[32] From this engagement, Henry Clay Barnabee recalled an illuminating incident.

> The first of many unforgettable lessons in the art of acting which I acquired at the Museum came directly through the oft-told tale recording an experience of the younger Booth, under the tutelage of his father in that remarkable debut. They say that when the boy came to his father's dressing room, dressed and made up to go on, the father asked of his son:
>
> "So you are Tressel. Who was Tressel?"
>
> "A messenger from the field of Tewksbury."
>
> "What was his mission?"
>
> "To bear the news of the defeat of the King's party."
>
> "How did he make the journey?"
>
> "On horseback."
>
> "Where are your spurs?"
>
> Edwin glanced down, and said he had not thought of them.
>
> "Forgot them, did you? Here, take mine."
>
> Edwin unbuckled his sire's spurs and fastened them on his own boots. His part being ended on the stage, he found his father still sitting in the dressing-room apparently engrossed in thought.
>
> "Have you done well?" asked the elder Booth.
>
> "I think so," replied the youth.
>
> "Give me my spurs."[33]

Booth never encouraged his sons to become actors; he wished Edwin to become a cabinetmaker, little imagining Edwin's future triumphs. In December 1849, Edwin appeared in the more challenging role of Wilford to his father's Sir Edward Mortimer in *The Iron Chest;* they shared several substantial scenes. About this time, a friend asked the elder Booth if he thought Ned (Edwin) was going to make an actor, to which Booth thundered, "Damn it! No! He'll never make anything but a nigger minstrel!"[34] Edwin had by then become proficient at playing the banjo.

In December 1849, Booth played Pittsburgh, accompanied by Edwin. A young actor, Barton Hill, cast as Horatio to Booth's

Hamlet, recalled being so ill as to have to be excused from rehearsal. When Booth heard this, he asked the young actor to come to his dressing room before the performance. When Hill arrived, he asked for instruction, but Booth said only, "Never mind, my boy; I'll tell you as we proceed with the play." Hill later said Booth told him nothing, but modified all his business whenever Horatio appeared, tenderly drew Hill's arm through his, and led him about the set and on and off the stage. For one night, Hamlet supported Horatio.[35]

Stories of Edwin's travels with his father grew into theatrical legends over the years. One of Edwin's favorites concerned an evening in New Orleans. His father appeared as Richard, supported by John Green (a gnomish specialist in Irishmen and testy old men) as Henry VI. Their scene had gone well, Booth had uttered, "Die, prophet, in thy speech!" and Green had died so well the audience applauded him. But the manager's huge mastiff wandered onstage and began sniffing at Green's upturned face. Green spasmodically rolled over, Booth assumed the *en garde* position with his sword, the audience roared, and, as Edwin put it, "doggie held the stage!"[36]

Booth toured the South as 1850 began, significantly bypassing New Orleans, and playing Mobile, Charleston, and Savannah, with Edwin again appearing as Wilford. Edwin's presence stabilized his father to a certain extent, but the elder Booth went to his next engagement in Richmond alone, to disaster.

Booth opened on April Fool's Day roaring drunk. The managers, Sefton and Chippendale, the next day informed the public that they could not allow Booth to appear again that season because of the disappointment to a brilliant audience, so they booked the popular comedian Charles Burke. The next day a letter of petition, signed by seventy-seven Richmond citizens, implored that the managers reconsider and let them have their Booth. Tactfully, the petitioners suggested:

> The infirmity of nature, which induced the accident, should not, in our opinion, deprive the admirers of eminent genius and transcendent theatrical talent, from the pleasure of witnessing the performances of one of the *brightest ornaments of the stage.*
>
> Regretting the occurrence, we feel well assured that if properly explained, it will not prevent a large and lucrative attendance at each of his performances.[37]

No doubt the word *lucrative* caused the two managers to reconsider; on the fourth they announced that they would reengage Booth to open on the eighth, on condition that both the managers and Booth should deposit five hundred dollars in neutral hands to be forfeited in case of nonfulfillment of the engagement. On the sixth, the managers repeated their terms, closing their public bill with, "The proposition was not met."

Supposedly Edwin had to leave for Richmond to locate his father, finding him on a friend's plantation. Booth borrowed fifty dollars from Sefton to return to Harford County, paying it back within two weeks.[38]

Booth played Philadelphia in May 1850, with Edwin in attendance. A week in Baltimore closed the season, but in June Booth wrote to Moses Kimball at the Boston Museum, arranging an engagement for twenty nights there for a total of one thousand dollars, to be paid in installments of $250 each Saturday morning for four weeks.[39] Again, Booth's price had dropped to about half of what it had been in 1821. And on 12 August 1850, Booth began his engagement. He played the twenty nights; indeed, he played twenty-two, but he became too ill to appear as Richard III on the twenty-first of August. By now Booth's "illnesses" evoked public suspicion, so the next day this letter appeared in the *Boston Transcript:*

> W.H. Smith, Esq.—Dear Sir: In reply to your inquiry whether it would be possible for Mr. Booth to appear this evening, I must say that it would not be proper or safe for him to do so. He has been suffering from a severe affection of the lungs, and is still under treatment.
>
> Yours truly,
> Joseph S. Jones, M.D.

Five days later, Booth returned to perform Richard, a Richard the *Transcript* called "the best Richard now in the field," and completed the engagement with no further incident.

A few weeks later in New York, the *Spirit of the Times* assessed Booth's position in the American theatre favorably but again decried the conditions under which he worked.

> Mr. Booth appears to be in good condition, and as full of energy and poetic fire as ever. We can perceive no lack of spirit, and no falling off of the extraordinary ability for which he has been and is

> justly celebrated. We much regret, however, that he has not been engaged at a theatre where he would receive some support from the characters of the play. It is true that he requires less aid than any actor we have ever seen, and is not much affected even if the theatrical people are not up in their parts; but it is exceedingly unpleasant to be a spectator of such an occurrence as we were on Wednesday. Mr. Booth was miserably sustained, and we marvel that he could brook such disrespect. He can attract the intelligent multitude in a temple where they could be comfortably accommodated, and feel some assurance that he would not be compelled to act the call-boy, the prompter, and the hero he might undertake. It is said that for faithful attendance during an engagement he cannot be relied upon, and for that reason is not sought by our first-class theatre men, but if it be true, it only illustrates a truth demonstrated by almost every man of genius of whom we have ever heard, that "To err is human." We hope to see Mr. Booth where his talents will be properly appreciated.[40]

In contrast, Harry Watkins said of him and this engagement, "It is sad to see the poor houses this great actor has drawn. He seems very much broken."[41] Edwin Booth, however, appeared for the first time in New York on 27 September 1850 as Wilford to his father's Sir Giles Overreach, and of him Watkins prophesied, "He will make a fine actor in time, should he prove studious."

About this time, a twenty-two-year-old Joseph Jefferson III played Marrall to Booth's Sir Giles, long before he was appropriate for so important a role. The struggling young actor recalled that Booth made the best of a bad bargain and, rather than annihilating Jefferson, took considerable pains to teach him the business of the part. Jefferson later described Booth's Sir Giles.

> During the last scene he beats Marrall, who hides for protection behind Lord Lovell. Booth's face, when he found he could not reach his victim, had the look of an uncaged tiger. His eyes flashed and seemed to snap with fire; his nostrils dilated; his cheeks appeared to quiver; his half-opened mouth, with its thin lips pressed tightly against the white teeth, made a picture of anger fearful to look upon. At the point where he is about to draw his sword, his arm shakes, his right hand refuses to do its office, and, stricken with paralysis, he stands the embodiment of despair; then come his terrible words of anguish and self-reproach:

> Some undone widow sits upon mine arm,
> . . . my sword,
> Glued to my scabbard, with wronged orphan's tear.
>
> His whole frame, shaken with convulsions, seems to collapse, his head sinks upon his breast, his jaw drops, and the cruel man is dead. There was no applause the night I speak of; the acting was so intense and so natural that the mimic scene seemed really to have happened.[42]

On 2 November 1850, Booth opened three nights in Baltimore; on the last night he introduced Edwin to the city's theatregoers as Titus in John Howard Payne's *Brutus*. The elder Booth next appeared in Washington, D.C., where he was supported by Mrs. Flynn and Edwin, who acted Hemeya to his father's Pescara in *The Apostate*. Another Booth played Washington for the first time.

As 1850 closed, Booth was again at the Boston Museum, appearing for fifty dollars per performance, plus benefits. The Boston Museum presented various natural curiosities, as well as legitimate drama, and one of those curiosities had an encounter with Booth. The papers delightedly covered the story.

> Booth, while playing a recent engagement in this city, received a horrible shock which might, possibly, have resulted fatally, but happily was productive of a much more ludicrous than serious result.
>
> The renowned fat girl, Miss Anna Crouse, was exhibiting herself at the Museum at the time of this engagement. Mr. Booth was to appear on Monday evening as *Richard*. He was in an exceedingly nervous, irritable and unhappy state, from some unaccountable cause, all that day. Everything seemed wrong, and by one mishap and another he was worked up to a frenzy. The time for the performance arrived—Booth grew calmer, and commenced his work.
>
> The delectable fat girl, urged by an insurmountable desire to see the great Booth as *Richard*, her experience in the drama being limited, gathered herself together, and with some difficulty succeeded in gaining the rear of the stage. Panting with the exertion necessary to get all of herself through the contracted entrances, she found the narrow stairway by which Booth would leave the stage, and composedly adjusted herself in a manner capable of obtaining all the comfort which a stair a foot wide was competent to afford. Her bulk being enormous, when sitting, (the fat having full license

to spread itself in all directions) she completely choked up the passage, and found herself securely wedged between some substantial bannisters on one side, and on the other a firm brick wall. Though somewhat alarmed as to her ability to free herself from this situation should an emergency occur, she sat patiently waiting for the grand burst of Booth in the last act, as the stricken king. It came—the death scene was executed in a most effective manner, and received the liberal plaudits of the vast assembly in the front.

As we have stated, Booth was in a frenzy previous to the opening, and his efforts during the evening made him still worse. He was distracted—his nervous system was woefully overtaxed. At the conclusion of the play he rushed from the stage to seek his dressing room, thinking to gain there quiet and relief; reaching the staircase, his glance at once met Anna's delighted and admiring gaze. There she sat quietly and calmly, while Booth, waiting to make the passage, his mind being temporarily disordered, could not comprehend this singular obstruction.

She began, however, to be quite alarmed at the tragedian's terrific look. Booth was astounded at the sight of her. (He had not chanced to see the fat girl, and knew not that such a person existed.) He imagined his vision was obscured, and that Anna was a blind fancy of the brain—or else his sight had *doubled*—and yet there certainly was a human face peering at him. He looked and looked. He assured himself that he must be mistaken in taking so huge a hill for a human being. Determined to satisfy himself, he unsheathed his dress sword merely to prove with its point the existence of this strange fantasy. The fear occasioned by this act was soon apparent. Poor Anna imagined herself slaughtered, and her struggles to escape were tremendous—those horrible eyes of Booth's driving into her could not be borne. Again and again she tried to edge away, but all was of no avail—the bannisters were fearfully stout, and the brick wall frowningly resisted her.

But when the sword was drawn, her o'erwrought sense left her—one long, loud, piercing shriek, and she swayed to and fro like the wind, and finally her head dropped on her breast; she seemed dead, the treacherous but yet friendly brick wall and bannisters alone prevented her from falling. Booth, by this time, was perfectly insane. He drove his sword fiercely towards her, exclaiming, "Out of the way, demon—hell's tortures be thy doom—way, way, or by St. Paul I'll cleave thy ruffian's skull—stand, I say—defend thyself, or flee—so that thou giv'st me way I care not." Foaming with rage, he violently thrust at her, but luckily the thick folds of her dress, and the wavering hand that held the weapon prevented aught but a mere

> scratch. That scratch, however, sufficed—"Murder, murder, murder," re-echoed through the building, coming from the revived Anna—"help, murder, oh, help, help!" Then what a scene ensued. Actors, supernumeraries, carpenters, and all the mysterious beings that dwell, invisible behind the scenes, rushed towards the spot from whence the continued and thrilling sounds proceeded.
>
> There stood Booth—pale, but calm—his eyes flashing, lips compressed, and his upright mien betokening his dauntless spirit—and there, shrinking and trembling, like an overgrown lily or sun flower, sat the Fat Girl—her features convulsed with fear, and her agitated, substantial frame, heaving with spasmodic jerks. On her fine forehead stood big drops of perspiration, and her flesh swayed to and fro like the waves of the troubled ocean!
>
> "Save me, save me!"—she shrieked.
>
> "Sathanas—have at thee," furiously cried Booth—"I'll drive my point full at thee if thou giv'st me not way. Draw, or by St. George—" Here the tragedian was seized, disarmed, and conveyed away—the terrified fat girl again placed erect through the kind offices of two of the strongest ropes and pulleys, and order was restored.
>
> Booth, when told of the incident—for he was unconscious throughout the entire night—laughed heartily, and made Anna all the reparation she would accept.
>
> But she never has been induced to witness his impersonations since; her curiosity was entirely gratified. Just and impartial, always, she considers his acting by far too vivid—too fierce—too natural. But she has recovered her calmness now—time having intervened—and still continues at the hall of the museum, looking quite stout and hearty, receiving the congratulations of visitors with an amiable suavity and a high born grace, well becoming her.[43]

Did that young law clerk in Bloomsbury in 1812 even dream of what lay ahead of him—irate Italian rope dancers, simultaneous marriages, fourteen children, the Mitchells, and a hysterical, elephantine Miss Crouse?

In early 1851, Booth offered terms for an engagement at the Baltimore Museum as either a clear fourth of five nights and a clear half of the sixth, or $150 and a clear half benefit, a lower price than he usually commanded. His star, it would seem, continued to fade.

Meanwhile, his troubles with Adelaide were far from over. On 6 February 1851, he wrote Adelaide's lawyer, L. Pennington, the following:

> I've received your Letter this afternoon, and upon consideration of all the circumstances relative to this business, I think the Agreement you made & drew up for your clients fully adequate, nay in fact more than I could afford. Owing to ill health, my Engagements for six weeks past have netted hardly more than my Expenses. I have been already put by this business to much inconvenience & I think I have already given more than I ought in the Agreement you made for them in 1847. I of course thought from your high standing, all was well, and no further Imposition by them would be attempted—if you will write fully to me what is intended & expected, I will see if I can arrange but now my health is so indifferent that I should not like to expose myself by venturing out prematurely.[44]

Annuity or not, Adelaide pressed for a divorce, and Pennington blistered Booth with his reply. On 27 February 1851 Adelaide filed a bill for divorce from Booth in the Baltimore County Court, accompanied by a marriage certificate dated 8 May 1815, St. George's, Bloomsbury. In the bill, Adelaide maintained that Booth had "without any intimation whatsoever . . . of his intention or any justifiable cause" abandoned her in London. She made no mention of any separate maintenance agreement or annuities. Mary Ann and Booth, Adelaide submitted, "had been in the habit of adulterous intercourse from that time to the present."[45]

Although he tried to resolve the matter with Adelaide, Booth never knew when his first wife (to be fair, his only wife) would confront him on the streets of Baltimore to curse and revile him. Adelaide now knew Booth sold his farm vegetables at the Belair Market in Baltimore, and that became the site of many shrieking rows.

Mary Ann soon learned to slide into a convenient side street and avoid public scandal. But at least once Adelaide made the trek to the Harford County farm to curse and berate the interloper. Kimmel claimed that the enraged Booth smashed the gravestones of his children and destroyed the family Bible and thus the birth records of his American children.[46]

While matters with Adelaide moved toward resolution, Booth played a long engagement in Philadelphia and a short one in New York. The *Spirit of the Times* again complained about the wretchedness of the supporting company at the National Theatre, adding, "Mr. Booth is undoubtedly the best tragedian in this country at the present day, and in the world, to our knowledge."[47]

Back in Baltimore, Booth's lawyer, John Green, on 26 March 1851, filed the following: "The answer of Junius Brutus Booth to the bill of Mary Christine Adelaide Booth: This respondent admits the facts as stated in said bill to be true, and assents to a decree as prayed for."[48]

Before the decree became final, Booth played a week in New York at the National Theatre, Edwin accompanying him. Perhaps the trauma of the court proceedings troubled him; perhaps he had admitted to himself that Edwin would follow him into the profession of acting. In any case, on the fifth of April, Booth and his son were preparing to leave their hotel for the theatre when the elder Booth announced he was ill and could not perform that evening. Edwin knew his father had felt fine all day and tried to get him to at least appear at the theatre, but the elder Booth was adamant. Edwin asked, "What will they do without you, Father? Who can they substitute at the last moment?"

"Go act it yourself," Booth responded, and after further entreaties, Edwin left for the National, where he met the manager, John R. Scott, his father's old friend. Edwin told Scott of the development, which the manager took calmly enough, saying, "No matter, *you* act it."

And so Edwin played Richard in his father's costumes, which were, in his words, "a world too wide." Scott paced back and forth nervously during the performance; the audience had not been warned of the switch, but Edwin won admiring applause from them. As Scott led the new star out for a prolonged curtain call, he announced Edwin as "the worthy scion of a noble stock," muttering under his breath to Edwin, "I'll wager they don't know what that means."

Edwin returned to the hotel and found his father just as he had left him. Booth coldly interrogated his son, and the matter was closed, but Edwin later suspected that his father had arranged the matter with Scott and had witnessed the performance from the back of the house. Apparently he was pleased with what he saw.[49] Both Booths returned to Baltimore, where Edwin signed on with Theodore Barton in that city to play utility roles for six dollars a week. Another Booth began to learn his trade.

The divorce decree, at last separating the elder Booth from Adelaide, became final on 18 April 1851. Booth left the next week for a Richmond engagement. Shortly after he returned, on 10 May 1851, coincidentally John Wilkes Booth's thirteenth birthday, Junius Brutus Booth and Mary Ann Holmes married in Baltimore.[50] The newspapers published nothing about the ceremony. And no Booth ever reacted publicly to the 1851 wedding. Asia, the starry-eyed romantic who once called her parents' love "perfect," understandably never mentioned it.[51] Rosalie, then twenty-eight, rarely said anything about anything. Junius, Jr., had his own affairs, marital and extramarital, to contemplate. Edwin, even when later threatened with blackmail, maintained his silence. John Wilkes and Joseph Adrian were barely teenagers in 1851. Mary Ann's extant letters, almost all of them written long after the 1851 marriage, reveal nothing, nor do Edwin's. If events in 1851 strained the relationship between Booth and Mary Ann, no evidence has survived. For that gentle lady, far worse lay ahead.

As always, Booth resumed his professional engagements. He also began to think of a retirement retreat and so began building a new house on the farm in Harford County. The house, which he called Tudor Hall, still stands today, a charming two-story brick building of neo-Gothic design, based on designs published in William H. Ranlett's *The Architect* in 1847–49.[52]

On 21 October 1851, Booth asked his neighbor John Rogers to oversee certain construction details for Tudor Hall.

> I wish the Locust Trees at the South western corner of my new cottage to remain and not to be cut down, or grubb'd up, as it is the only shade for the S.W. gable for nearly three hours of the day—If the branches are in the way of Labourers & Masoners, they may be trimm'd up. Mr. Gifford will probably be along with you by Thursday, or Monday at the latest. Edwin arrived in Philadelphia this morning at 4, and his mentioning that the cellar was dug 5 feet, and your opinion to the tree interfering with our work, has caused me to write this in order that this tree may not be cut down. All money for bricks which Mr. [Dossen?] may want, he can have by speaking to Mr. Gifford. I wish to pay by his delivery of 1000 which by his contract, I think was for five fifty, hard, $6.50 if he delivered them, which I would prefer his doing. Stone which can be quarried, previous, or before removing the chimneys I wish to be, if firm, for my foundation. If you need any supply of money for expediting the work, Mrs. Booth will furnish you with.[53]

Booth continued with his standard repertory in the eastern cities until June 1852, when he completed a "farewell engagement" at the

Junius Brutus Booth's log house, which he moved to his farm near Bel Air, Maryland. The people in the photograph are thought to be the King family, to whom Mary Ann Holmes Booth rented the farm after the assassination. The original house was the central part of the structure; Booth added extensions on both ends. Courtesy of Michael W. Kauffman.

Edwin Forrest, Booth's friend and rival in the United States, and the actor after whom Edwin Booth was named. From *Autobiographical Sketch of Mrs. John Drew*, 1899.

Junius Brutus Booth as Richard III. From the author's collection.

Portrait of Junius Brutus Booth as Brutus by John Neagle. During a visit to London, Edwin Booth presented a copy of this portrait to the Garrick Club. Courtesy of the Theatre Collection, Museum of the City of New York.

Watercolor portrait of Junius Brutus Booth. Artist unidentified. Courtesy of the Hampden-Booth Theatre Library at the Players.

Mary Ann Holmes Booth, the elder Booth's second wife.
By permission of the Folger Shakespeare Library.

Rosalie Ann Booth, daughter of the elder Booth. Courtesy of the Hampden-Booth Theatre Library at the Players.

Junius Brutus Booth and Edwin. Courtesy of the Hampden-Booth Theatre Library at the Players.

The young Edwin Booth. Courtesy of the Hampden-Booth Theatre Library at the Players.

John Wilkes Booth. Edwin Booth kept a copy of this photograph by his bedside at the Players, where it remains today. Hampden-Booth Theatre Library at the Players.

Portrait of Junius Brutus Booth as Richard III, painted by Henry Thomas. Courtesy of the Charlotte Cushman Club, Philadelphia.

Junius Brutus Booth as Richard III. Courtesy of the Hampden-Booth Theatre Library at the Players.

Photo by Matthew Brady of Junius Brutus Booth,
undated. Courtesy of the Library of Congress.

The aging Junius Brutus Booth. Courtesy of the Hampden-Booth Theatre Library at the Players.

Portrait of Junius Brutus Booth, attributed to Sarah Miriam Peale. Courtesy of the High Museum of Art, Atlanta, gift of Mr. E. B. Hollis of Washington, D.C., 61.10.

A sketch of Booth's Baltimore town house. From the author's collection.

Adelaide Delannoy, Booth's first wife, from the *New York Dramatic News*, 1 August 1891.

A drawing of the room in which Adelaide Delannoy died 9 March 1858 in Baltimore, from *New York Dramatic News*, 1 August 1891.

The aged Mary Ann Holmes Booth, second wife of Junius Brutus Booth. Courtesy of the Hampden-Booth Theatre Library at the Players.

Booth family plot, Green Mount Cemetery, Baltimore. Photograph by the author.

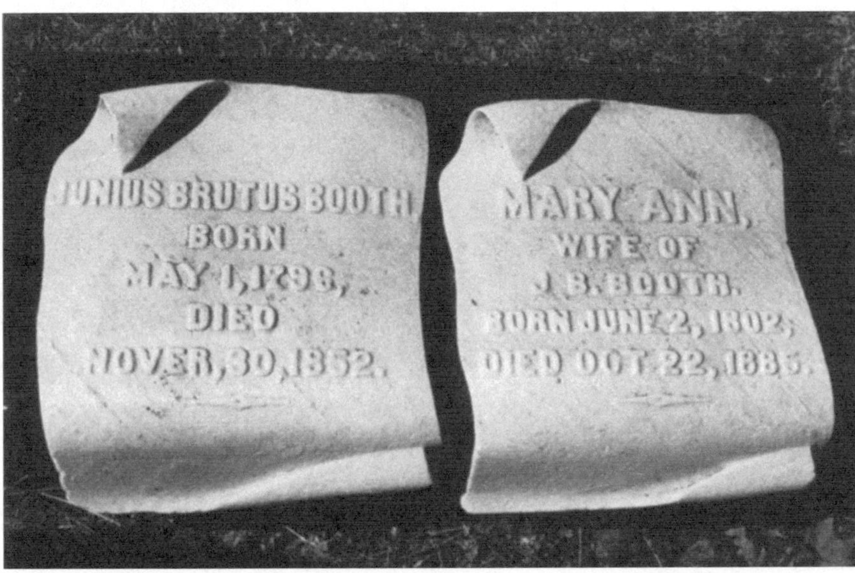

Headstones of Junius Brutus and Mary Ann Holmes Booth, Green Mount Cemetery, Baltimore. Photograph by the author.

Gravestone of Richard Booth, father of Junius Brutus Booth, Green Mount Cemetery, Baltimore. Photograph by the author.

Tudor Hall, Booth's intended retirement home, near Bel Air, Maryland. Photograph by the author.

Holliday Street Theatre in Baltimore. The irony of that advertisement became evident only later.

That spring, Junius, Jr., had arrived at the farm from San Francisco, California, where he was managing the Jenny Lind Theatre. He brought with him Harriet Mace, an actress and his current lover. When Booth realized his oldest American son had deserted his first wife for another woman, we can doubt he had much comment. The younger Booth invited the elder to visit San Francisco, where he could earn enormous sums of money as a visiting star. It took some convincing, but Booth agreed, as Asia Booth Clarke said, "more for the novelty of a trip than a desire to perform there."[54]

The eventual excursion included the elder Booth, Edwin, Junius, Jr., and Harriet Mace. They left on the steamer *Illinois* on 21 June 1852, steamed past Mexico, and landed at Colón, on the Atlantic side of Panama. They took a flatboat up the Chagres River to Gorgona, where they stayed overnight. For the rest of the trip through the jungle, they hired mules and natives, sleeping at night in a hut. Harriet slept in a hammock, while the men kept pistols at the ready. Edwin later described to Asia his sleepless nights as he watched the natives sharpening their machetes. The elder Booth predicted that someday a canal would connect the two oceans. At Panama City, the Booth party caught another ship and sailed for California. The entire trip had taken thirty-seven days, eight of them in Panama. They arrived in San Francisco on 28 July 1852.[55]

The Jenny Lind Theatre, in which Booth was to perform, was about to be converted into a city hall, but Junius, Jr., wheedled the city fathers into one last engagement.[56] Booth opened in *The Iron Chest* on the thirtieth. The next day the *Daily Alta* published substantial comments.

> MR. BOOTH—The advertisements and posters announcing that Mr. J.B. Booth, Sen., was to make his first appearance in California at the Jenny Lind last evening, brought out, as might have been anticipated, one of the most crowded houses we have ever witnessed in this city.
>
> Mr. Booth had selected one of his finest characters for the occasion—Sir Edward Mortimer in the play of "The Iron Chest." Of course, and the first two scenes dragged their weary length along, the audience was all anxiety to see the great actor. And when the

> third opened and discovered him, he was greeted with long, prolonged, vociferous and hearty applause by his many old friends in front of the curtain, an applause which at once did merited honor to the actor and credit to the audience.
>
> To attempt a criticism on the acting of such a man would be a tactless task, and entirely uncalled for, since the laurels have rested so long and so gracefully on his brow. It is several years since we have seen him, and we could not but notice that in the interim Time had not touched the old man in vain. It was with mournful feelings that we irresistibly thought of that day when Mr. Booth would tread the stage no more. We looked upon him as we would look upon a splendid ruin, aged and crumbling, but majestic and magnificent even in its decay.
>
> The enthusiasm which accompanied him throughout the performance, and which called him in front of the curtain at the close, is not to be wondered at, not only from the fact of his previous and even present splendid powers, but from the fact that California has never before seen or heard intonations so perfect, conception so just, and action so unexceptional. Mr. Booth was not in good voice, but as the play went on he warmed up finely to his part, and often equalled the efforts of his palmier days. In the more subdued portions he has lost none of his excellence, but the effects of his tedious journey were visible when the stormier reaches came on.
>
> He yet stands among the two or three at the head of his profession. The enthusiasm which is now waked up among us has something substantial and lasting about it, and he will have a brilliant and triumphant tour through California.
>
> Mr. E. Booth is a very judicious actor, and we shall take occasion to notice him more at length hereafter. He took the part of Wilford and was applauded throughout.

An auspicious beginning. During a rehearsal for *The Apostate,* in which the elder Booth played Pescara and Edwin the moor, Hemeya, the father saw fit to direct his sons. Edwin went through his part listlessly, until his father barked, "That won't do! Come, come, come!"

Edwin started over and drawled out, "The weary sun has made a golden set."

"For God's sake!" the old man roared, "*where* does the sun set? Well, show it then! Point to it! Nod your head! Do *something!*"

Booth then led his son through the part. J. J. McCloskey, who described the incident, felt Edwin showed no indication of his future greatness.[57]

When Booth closed his two weeks at the Jenny Lind, Junius, Jr., invited him to play an engagement at the American Theatre in Sacramento, California. That theatre had just failed on 29 July, the local press calling the resident company a pack of "great boobies." Junius, Jr., leased the house, and the Booth entourage opened 19 August 1852 in *The Iron Chest*.

They played to only half an audience—most of the miners and citizens preferred a prize fight between George Thompson and John Morrissey for the championship of California and a purse of six thousand dollars. Not till the eighth performance did the Booths enjoy a capacity house in Sacramento.

The elder Booth became ill, which forced a cancelation of *The Stranger*, and the company soon began doing benefits, marking the end of the engagement. Edwin took his on 2 September, as Jaffier to his father's Pierre. Jaffier traditionally wears black, and the elder Booth noted, "You look like Hamlet. Why didn't you play Hamlet for your benefit?" Edwin casually replied, "If I ever have another, I will."[58]

Booth closed with Richard III and Jeremy Sneak for his benefit, then Junius, Jr., went before the curtain to thank the audience for their support, although the engagement had nearly bankrupted him. One member of the audience roared out, "As good as we saw it in '27," implying Booth's powers had not diminished significantly.

The group returned to San Francisco by steam launch, after which Booth performed four nights at the Adelphi Theatre, closing the last day of September 1852. Many years later a correspondent for the *San Francisco Call* described finding Booth one afternoon in a dive near the Adelphi Theatre, reciting speeches from *Richard the Third* and drinking tin cups of whiskey. The reporter had tickets for Booth's Richard that night and felt he should notify Edwin of the elder Booth's shenanigans but failed to do so. Booth appeared in the street, joined the reporter, demanded drink, and barely made it to the theatre. The reporter went to the Adelphi, where the show was delayed for an hour. When it finally started, said the correspondent, Booth, obviously drunk, hissed out not his proper lines but, "I'm a gentleman, and a soldier; I'm a scholar—and (long pause)—a pirate!" The curtain came crashing down, and there was no show that night.[59]

Although Junius, Jr., had barely cleared expenses with the Sacramento engagement, his father demanded and received every penny due him. He sailed from San Francisco, alone, the next day on the steamer *Independence,* having told his sons that he intended to retire soon. He would play only one more engagement.

Edwin, with some premonition, offered to return with his father, but the old man suggested he practice his craft on the West Coast. Booth asked a friend, Dave Anderson (a character actor), to look after the eighteen-year-old Edwin, and the two became great friends.

Edwin accompanied his father to the *Independence* on the first of October and, years later, recalled their parting.

> My last experience of his vagaries was at our final parting on the ship that bore him forever from me. He asked a sailor on deck to take his luggage to his cabin. The fellow replied—"I'm no flunky." "What are you, sir," demanded my father. "I'm a thief," responded the brute. Instantly the actor assumed his favorite part of Bertram at this "cue," and said—"Your hand, comrade, I'm a pirate!" The sailor laughed and rejoined, "All right, my covey; where's your traps?" and carried the trunk to the stateroom. His influence on the lowest minds was as great as it was strong over the highest intellects with which he came in contact.[60]

So Booth traveled alone, back to Panama City, across the Isthmus of Panama, and to Colón. But before he left San Francisco, he wrote to the New Orleans managers, the long-suffering Ludlow and Smith.

> It is my intention to leave here, on the 1st prox by Nicaragua, and thence to New Orleans. If suitable with your other arrangements, you could enter into terms with me, I will perform ten nights for $1000, you taking the Benefits, or for seventy dollars per night for nine nights, and a clear half of the tenth night as Benefit—in such case, my name to be up but on the tenth as for the Benefit and last appearance of the Season.[61]

Booth eventually arrived in New Orleans, claiming to have been robbed of his California money while crossing the isthmus. He was to open at the St. Charles Theatre, sharing after $250, with a clear half on the sixth night for a benefit.[62]

The *Picayune* noted upon his arrival:

> This evening the veteran Booth makes his first appearance here for years in "Richard III." Many years have elapsed since this great

> actor first came to this country and won for himself a preeminence that the lapse and changes of Time have not been able to diminish. True, and of necessity, his pristine vigor and physical abilities must be affected, but the mind and the magic still remain, and during the last eight or ten years, whenever we have seen him perform, *Richard* was still himself.[63]

Booth opened on 14 November 1852 as Richard III. Because Booth had not attended rehearsal, Ludlow had Henry Lynne ready to take the role. But Booth appeared, and Ludlow noted he played "very well," however, the "perfect jam" prevented the manager from seeing the performance. The total house was $950.75; Booth's share came to $350.75. The *Picayune* noted the next day that, though time had eroded Booth's voice and physique, "the beautiful elocution and correct reading for which he has ever been famous told powerfully upon the audience."

On the fifteenth he played Sir Giles to total receipts of only $437.75, netting him a paltry $93.87 and a review stating, "In the last, terrific scene, the striking play of countenance, the truth, energy and severity of gesture and attitude, the passions of the bad man overcome, were master pieces of acting that no other performer now on the English stage can pretend to equal."[64] He performed Pescara on the sixteenth during extremely inclement weather, drawing a mere $305.75 and a net to Booth of only $27.87. The *Picayune* reported, "never, even in his palmiest days, did the great tragedian look and act the part better than last night." Nor could the critic find fault with Booth's Shylock on the seventeenth, saying that in the role Booth "stands acknowledgedly without an equal." A $547 house yielded $148.50 for Booth. Booth's Bertram the next night was "fearfully grand" and "enchained the attention of the audience" and netted him $59.37 from a house of $368.75.

Booth appeared for his benefit on Friday, 19 November, as Sir Edward Mortimer and John Lump. This was his clear half, and he must have been gratified to see a house worth $809.00 appear, netting him $404.50, bringing his total for the engagement to $1,053.38, slightly better than the thousand dollars for ten nights he had offered Ludlow and Smith. Ludlow entered the figures in his diary after the show, commenting: "Booth gets ½ this house—He has played well this engt. and kept himself perfectly sober & right."[65]

The next day a long review appeared in the *Picayune*. It would be Booth's last, and the anonymous reviewer—did he sense an aura of finality about that engagement?—harkened back to Booth's early days in England.

> MR. BOOTH—The St. Charles Theatre was crowded last evening for the benefit of this veteran performer. Many ladies graced the dress circle with their presence. The play of the "Iron Chest," written for John Kemble, but in which he did not succeed, and which Elliston, a far inferior performer, achieved great success, was played on this occasion, Mr. Booth appearing in his favorite character of *Sir Edward Mortimer*. To say that he enacted it in a style that delighted every one would be speaking without exaggeration. Indeed, every successful performance during his too brief engagement, appeared to show Mr. Booth's powers to better advantage and the regret is general that he should stay so short a time with us. Talent like that he possesses is so rare now-a-days, when respectable mediocrity is the chief qualification of the American stage, that we cannot make up our minds to part with Mr. Booth until, at least, we have seen all the faces of the jewel of dramatic genius whose brilliancy has illumined his name not only for the present generation, but for posterity.
>
> Mr. Booth was called out after the play and again after the farce—the famous one of the "Review." Public curiosity was much excited to see him in a part so opposite to the tragic character he had represented in the early part of the evening, and it was difficult to recognize in the stupid, awkward Yorkshire clown, *John Lump,* the form and face and voice that moved the audience in *Shylock, Bertram,* and such powerful characters. The farce had evidently been prepared in haste, and the least said about it the better.

The reviewer might regret the roles Booth had not played in the Crescent City, but he would soon rejoice in the ones that he did.

But Booth had a rendezvous upriver, and the next day he boarded a steamboat, the *J. S. Chenoweth,* bound for Cincinnati. A fellow passenger, James H. Simpson, left an eyewitness account of the events of the next few days.

On the first day out of New Orleans, Simpson noted Booth walking back and forth in the saloon, his hands behind him and his head bowed in deep thought. Simpson thought he recognized Booth but could not recall his name. When a fellow passenger noted, "That is the tragedian, Booth," Simpson remembered that he had seen Booth's last performances in New Orleans.

On the second day out, Simpson noted Booth's absence from the saloon, inquired as to his whereabouts, and learned the actor was confined to his cabin with severe diarrhea. Simpson immediately went to Booth's quarters, apologized for his intrusion, and offered his services. After carefully inspecting Simpson, Booth accepted the offer. Simpson found Booth had been neglected, so he called the porter, had the room cleared out, fresh linen put on the bed, and some gruel made for the ailing actor. No medical assistance was available, and Booth began to waste away.

By the third day out, Booth could not turn over without Simpson's help. Furthermore, his jaws had locked, making speech difficult. Simpson, hoping to stimulate Booth's energies, soaked a rag in brandy and water and applied it to Booth lips. Upon tasting it, Booth tore it from his lips and with difficulty exclaimed, "No more in this world!" Simpson realized Booth's illness was fatal and sought to ease his mind. He asked the dying man if he had a wife; Booth replied, "Certainly I have." Simpson offered to relay any message to her, but Booth could no longer make himself understood. He tried, however, to tell Simpson of his travels in California, but that Good Samaritan understood only that Booth had suffered a great deal and had "been exposed very much."

On the fourth day Simpson read to Booth from the New Testament while the tragedian paid the deepest attention. When Simpson asked if he might pray for him, Booth's eyes grew dim with moisture, and he tried to embrace Simpson when he smoothed his pillow.

On the fifth day, about one o'clock, Junius Brutus Booth died, his last words to Simpson being "Pray! pray! pray!" accompanied by a beseeching look. No curtain fell, no footlights dimmed, as Booth left one stage for another.

The *J. S. Chenoweth* was just below Louisville, where the captain procured a metal coffin and wired Mary Ann to meet the ship in Cincinnati. Simpson left the boat in Cincinnati and did not meet Mary Ann.[66]

Mary Ann took her husband back to their home on North Exeter Street, arriving the ninth of December. The body lay in state for three days under the gaze of a marble figure of Shakespeare in a parlor draped in white, from which all decorations had been removed. So lifelike did Booth's body seem that the family sent for physicians to make certain he was not merely in a trance.

Asia recalled "people of every class" thronging the house to view the body and express sympathy to the family. On Saturday afternoon, the eleventh, Reverend Atkinson of Christ Church conducted funeral services at the North Exeter Street house, attended by the family, the Baltimore Dramatic Association, various members of Baltimore orchestras, and many personal friends. After the service they walked through the snowy streets to Baltimore Cemetery, where, following Mary Ann's wishes, John M. Vollandt's band played a dirge composed for the occasion. A large assemblage of black people watched from a distance.[67] The coffin was stored in a mausoleum, then buried the next spring.

Later the body was removed to a larger plot in Green Mount Cemetery in Baltimore, and on 1 May 1858—his father's birthday—Edwin had erected a marble shaft over his father's grave. Most of the Booths remain there today, in Dogwood Lot Number Nine, not far from the main entrance.

Typical of the expressions of sympathy that came to Mary Ann was a letter from Noah Ludlow, Booth's last manager in New Orleans.

> It was with deep regret and sorrow that we read here a telegraphic paragraph on the morning of the 2d inst. announcing the decease of your late worthy husband. It was the more startling because the least expected. During his engagement with us in the St. Charles Theatre, it was generally remarked how well he looked, and how well he performed. For myself, who remember him, since his first week's performance in the United States—and have been well acquainted with his professional career—I was agreeably astonished at the vigour, and correctness in delineation of character, evinced by him during the six nights he performed with us, and the conclusion of his engagement seemed a cause of regret to the public generally, who had witnessed his performance. As a matter of information to you, I would state that we paid him Ten hundred and Eighty-four dollars for his engt. of the six nights. Five hundred of which was turned into a draft on the Western Bank of Baltimore, and made payable to your order and is presumed was mailed to you from this City by Mr. Booth prior to his departure. He complained a little of illness the morning of the day he left here, but it was deemed

> nothing of consequence. He must have had some where near three hundred dollárs with him when he left here. Our clerk says he spoke of having to pay $25 that he had borrowed, then there were his expenses while here, and I believe some articles of clothing which he purchased in this city. He spoke of having been robbed on his route through Mexico, but I do not recollect of what amount. Trusting, Madam, that you will find consolation in the reflection that the dispensation of Providence are always for wise and merciful purpose and wishing you health and the enjoyment of life for many years, I am your obt. Serv & well wisher
>
> NML[68]

Many members of the theatrical profession wore black crepe bands on their arms for thirty days in tribute to their fallen fellow.

And so the long road ended in Baltimore, that road that had begun in Queen Street, London, just outside the British Museum. It had taken Booth through two marriages and twelve children, five of whom died young; through stardom in two hemispheres, from Amsterdam to San Francisco, from New Orleans to New Brunswick. On hearing the news of Booth's death, Rufus Choate, the former Whig senator, cried, "Booth dead! There are no more actors!"

But there were other actors, even actors named Booth.

8

Coda

I know not where is that Promethean heat
  That can thy light relume.

—*Othello,* V, ii, 12–13

Booth died without a will; Mary Ann had to settle the estate before getting on with her own life. The Orphan's Court of Baltimore granted letters of administration to the widow on 23 December 1852. With Tudor Hall and the Harford County property not included, Booth's estate, after thirty-one years of starring in America, came to $4,728.99.

Richard Junius Booth immediately filed exceptions, alleging that Mary Ann had not accounted for certain property, including Booth's professional wardrobe, a piano, and cash in hand. Mary Ann countered by claiming the wardrobe was of no great value, having been made by hand by Mary Ann for her husband. Booth had taken an extensive costume collection with him to California, but Mary Ann only recovered two trunks after his death. Appraisers considered them personal apparel, not counted as part of the deceased's estate.

Mary Ann then added that, insofar as cash went, Booth had been robbed crossing the Isthmus of Panama, leaving him funds insufficient to reach New Orleans. Apparently a stranger, a Texan named Reid, loaned Booth the necessary money. The piano and Booth's library had been included in the account. Faced with this information, Richard Junius Booth withdrew his exceptions, and the estate cleared.[1] That matter settled, the Booths from both sides of the Atlantic could continue with their own concerns.

Jane Booth Mitchell, aged fifty, was buried 4 May 1853 in the Baltimore Cemetery. Her husband moved into single quarters and continued his shiftless, literary life. Apparently the children dispersed to make their way as best they could. One daughter, Eliza, became an actress of no great distinction, eventually marrying a second-rate actor named William Ward.[2] She received some encouragement from her cousin Edwin Booth, but she never achieved eminence.

Adelaide Delannoy Booth remained in Baltimore, eventually applying for and receiving naturalization.[3] She lived at 535 West Baltimore Street on the second floor, renting a ten-by-twelve-foot room from Charles Zell, who operated a cigar store at street level. Richard eked out an existence from his earnings as a teacher of French at St. Mary's Catholic Academy and no doubt assisted his mother. But on 31 December 1849 Richard married Sarah P. Ware. The next year's census listed them as both having been born in England and Richard's occupation as teacher. The census recorded them as having four children, ranging in age from ten years to two months; apparently Sarah had children from a previous marriage. They lived, according to city directories, at 54 Hoffman Street in 1855–56, the next two years on Mosher Street near Pennsylvania Avenue, and in 1860 at 63 South High Street.[4]

On 9 March 1858 Baltimore physician E. Ridley Baer received an urgent call from West Baltimore Street. He found the aged Adelaide abed, attended by Zell's wife. Baer felt for a pulse but found none. As the landlady and physician gazed down at the corpse, a shudder passed through the body, the features became distorted, and the lungs emptied with a hoarse, gurgling rattle from her ashen lips. The landlady fainted as Adelaide Delannoy Booth died. Dr. Baer prepared Adelaide's body for the undertaker, who laid her to rest in the Cathedral Cemetery. It was reported that Richard Junius Booth took charge of his mother's remains and the inscription on her gravestone. The body was moved on 17 October 1887 to the New Cathedral Cemetery.[5]

Booth's oldest son then disappeared from the Baltimore records. He returned to England sometime during our Civil War; the 1860 entry was the last listing for him in Baltimore. He died in Clerkenwell, London, the old Booth neighborhood, in 1868 with an unidentified J. B. Booth in attendance.[6] He was buried with his wife, who died only a month earlier, in Highgate Cemetery, London. No stone marks their grave.

John Wilkes Booth became an actor and was the next of the Booth circle to die: 26 April 1865. The story of his assassination of President Abraham Lincoln, his flight, the pursuit, and his death needs no repetition; the tale has been told often, if not definitively. John Wilkes Booth is buried in an unmarked grave in the family plot in Green Mount Cemetery in Baltimore (although various theories hold that he escaped after the assassination). No definite proof exists as to whether Boston Corbett shot the assassin or whether John Wilkes Booth ended his wretched life with his own hand.

Lincoln's murder devastated the family. Edwin, who had by then risen to star status, retired from the stage but returned to what he called "the only profession for which God suited" him, achieving even greater acclaim. Most of the rest of the family went into seclusion, Mary Ann giving thanks that her son was killed at Garrett's farm rather than being hanged. Slowly they endured their burden, but scarred, terribly scarred.

The horror of the assassination triggered off an avalanche of persecution of actors in general and of Booths in particular. Preachers damned the theatre as the Devil's temple, lamenting that the president had been shot in one. Details of the Booth family's life were dragged out and examined; if the strain of madness was detected, it was trumpeted forth in every direction. If not found, no matter, it could be created. The more reasonable writers, while decrying murder most foul, held Edwin and his father of a nobler stripe. For example, the *National Intelligencer,* still running black-bordered stories of the assassination, even before John Wilkes Booth was captured, ran a long column about the Booths. The author, "Erasmus," extolled the elder Booth.

> No kindlier heart ever beat. He was a true friend, an accomplished gentleman, a benevolent nature, and his mind was

> keen and bright as a polished sword; and within were galleries adorned with all that art and literature have made highest, dearest, and most enduring. . . . If there was madness in the elder Booth, it was no vulgar fire, but the genuine Promethean heat. It was no swaggering affectation, no stupid wooing of coarse notoriety, that swayed him to and fro, and now and then dashed him, all wild and reckless, hither and yon, at the mercy of his resistless passions and impulses.

This in contrast to his assessment of John Wilkes Booth: "The monster wretch, compared with whose foul deed (the time, the place, the man murdered considered) the records of all other assassins pale; a deed without a single manly motive, engendered of cowardice, cruelty, and loathsome egotism—else the execrable offspring of hire and pay."[7]

The harangues continued against all Booths and all actors till the country pulled itself together and faced Reconstruction in the aftermath of the rebellion. Ironically, John Wilkes Booth, an ardent supporter of the Confederacy, had murdered the one man who could have led the South most successfully through Reconstruction.

The 1850 Baltimore census included a James Mitchell, "pedler," age fifty-four. On 27 April 1870 a Jas. Mitchell, aged seventy-five, was buried in the same lot in the Baltimore Cemetery as Jane Booth Mitchell; chronology would indicate the bootblack from Bloomsbury had come to rest. One other Mitchell, Col. Robert G., lies in the same lot, being interred there on 20 August 1904, aged seventy.[8]

Junius Brutus Booth, Jr., married Agnes Land Perry in 1867; they produced four children. After retiring from the stage, he owned and operated a large resort hotel, Masconomo House, which he built in Manchester, Massachusetts. He died there 16 September 1883. When his will was read, he left all his property to his third wife, Agnes Perry Booth, whereupon Marion Booth, his daughter by Harriet Mace (who had died in California in 1859), filed to set aside the will. They presumably settled out of court.[9]

Mary Ann Holmes Booth, the mother of the Maryland Booths, lived with her children for the rest of her life. After breaking a leg on an icy street in 1883, she was incapacitated till her death on 22 October 1885; her death certificate listed her age as eighty-three years, four months. She is buried beside her husband in Green Mount Cemetery, Baltimore.

Asia Booth married a childhood friend of the family, John Sleeper Clarke, actor, on 28 April 1859 at St. Paul's Church, Baltimore. Some suspected Clarke of marrying Asia only to attach himself to the Booth name and fame. Shortly after the assassination they moved to England, where Asia died 18 May 1888 at her home in Bournemouth.[10] Her body was returned to Green Mount Cemetery and buried 1 June 1888; Clarke's grave is in Teddington, a London suburb.

The reclusive Rosalie Booth devoted her life to caring for her mother and died 15 January 1889, having never married. She, too, lies in Green Mount Cemetery.

Edwin Booth, the "Prince of Players," rose to far greater heights than did his father; modern scholars account him the greatest of American Shakespearean actors. After 1865 he never—ever—again played Washington, D.C., even when invited. Eventually he built his own theatre in New York, but he had no more business sense than his father; the venture bankrupted him. He had married on 7 July 1860 Mary Devlin, an actress who retired from the stage at his request. She bore him a daughter, Edwina, born 9 December 1861 in England during Edwin Booth's first tour there. At some time during this tour, Edwin attended the funeral of the mother of Mary Ann Holmes Booth, thus Edwin's grandmother, who was apparently living in Reading at the time.

Mary Devlin Booth died on 21 February 1863, while Edwin lay in a drunken stupor in Boston; he thereafter forswore drinking. He married again, Mary McVicker, on 7 June 1869. Their only child, Edgar, died during his birth on 4 July 1870; his skull had to be crushed to save the mother's life. Mary McVicker Booth then descended into a virtual insanity, dying in 1881.

In 1891 the *New York Herald* reported Edwin had been the victim of a blackmail attempt by "a disreputable newspaper man and a person connected with the stage."[11] Actor Stuart Robson, a childhood friend of Edwin's, appeared also to have been involved but claimed total innocence of the matter.

In 1888 Edwin Booth founded a men's club, the Players, at 16 Gramercy Park, New York City, for actors and supporters of the theatre. The Players still operates and annually celebrates Founder's Night in honor of Edwin Booth. Edwin's two-room apartment at the Players remains as it was the night he died, 7 June 1893. As tributes poured in from all over the world, his funeral was held at the Little Church Around the Corner in New York City. While his coffin was being carried out of the church, three floors of the remodeled Ford's Theatre in Washington, D.C., collapsed, killing more than twenty workers. Edwin Booth was buried beside his first wife, Mary Devlin Booth, in Mount Auburn Cemetery in Cambridge, Massachusetts.

The last of the Maryland Booths, Joseph Adrian, became a physician and died in 1902.[12] The old Booth propensity for litigation arose once more: Junius III and Sydney Booth, sons of Junius Brutus Booth, Jr., contested Joseph's will on the grounds of mental incompetence but later withdrew their objections. Joseph's estate was estimated at thirty-five thousand dollars, plus "considerable" property in Virginia and New Jersey.[13] He is also buried in Green Mount, with his wife, Cora, and their son, Edwin T. Booth, who died in infancy.

Although Joseph Adrian was the only Maryland Booth to survive into the twentieth century, the strain of madness surfaced again in 1912. Junius Brutus Booth III, then operating a "cinematograph theatre" in Brightlingsea, England, suffered financial setbacks from low attendance. On 6 December he put a bullet through his wife's head, then inserted a revolver barrel into his mouth and fired. He was forty-four years old.[14]

But the land, as always, survived mere mortals. In this case, so did some of Booth's property and his intended retirement home, Tudor Hall. By the time of the assassination, Mary Ann had rented the farm to a family named Hall. The night of the Lincoln murder, federal troops allegedly surrounded and searched Tudor Hall, terrorizing the innocent family. The log house, which Booth had moved across the pastures, fell into ruin, was moved to a corner of the farm, and eventually became part of the substructure for a modern house which still exists.

The farm passed from the family in 1878 when Mary Ann sold the property to Samuel A. S. Kyle for thirty-five hundred dollars.[15] Kyle, a retired Baltimore business man, married a Harford County woman who had been raised near the farm. When Kyle died, his widow, Ella, married a blind musician, John F. Mahoney, whom she also outlived. In all, Mrs. Mahoney, who collected Booth ephemera and opened Tudor Hall as a museum, lived in the house some seventy years until her death in 1948.[16]

In 1949 John E. Clark, a Bel Air lawyer, purchased the property from Mrs. Mahoney's daughters and continued to open it to the public. Clark in turn sold the property to Richard and Betty Worthington, owners of the Bel Air newspaper, the *Aegis*, in 1954. Worthington subdivided part of the property, leaving only eight and one-half acres connected to Tudor Hall itself. Complaining that "people would not leave you alone," he also removed the historical marker on Route 22.

The Worthingtons left in 1961, selling the house and the surrounding eight acres to a Havre de Grace rubber company executive who "lived here with her chauffeur and always kept guns at the door and a big iron chain across the road."[17] The rubber baroness moved to Mexico and almost lost the property in a tax sale before the present owners, Howard and Dorothy Fox, took possession in 1968.

The Foxes found the old house in serious disrepair, but Howard Fox, a retired reconstruction expert and designer, set about bringing Tudor Hall to order. In 1984 they founded the Preservation Association of Tudor Hall (PATH), intending to operate the house as a living memorial to the Booths, as well as a bed and breakfast inn and a site for weddings, craft fairs, and various social functions. Shortly thereafter, they deeded the property to PATH, remaining as resident curators and overseeing the restoration. Booth's dream, Tudor Hall, has thus become a living memorial to the entire Booth family.

As one wanders about the remaining eight and one-half acres of the farm, the presence of the Booths is unmistakable. John Wilkes Booth's initials, carved with a diamond, remain in one of the front windows; one recalls that the future assassin tattooed himself with his initials on the back of his left hand. In a family of stars, identity seemed hard to come by. Some of the older trees date back to the days of the Maryland Booths; one can easily imagine Booth children (and Mitchell children, for that matter) clambering through the branches. Inside, one of the rooms is designated as John Wilkes Booth's, another as Asia's. But the elder Booth's presence dominates the site. He purchased the farm; he caused Tudor Hall to be built; the household was maintained by his labor, by his constant touring for more than a generation.

Professionally Booth was much admired; high compliments are scattered through the records of his career. Many of them are publicity puffery, ink spilled to ensure a good box office. Some, however, offer insights into the man and the actor.

One of the more thoughtful of the nineteenth-century critics was John Foster Kirk, a man highly educated, well traveled, facile with several languages, and of considerable literary accomplishment.[18] In the 1884 volume of *Lippincott's Magazine,* Kirk, who had just turned sixty, reminisced about Shakespearean actors he had seen over the years.

Kirk was a personal friend of Macready, who with Booth and Forrest he considered the only three actors worthy of the term, "eminent tragedians," pointing out that theatregoing in Kirk's youth was scarcely a reputable amusement. Other than at the Park and the Walnut Street Theatres, Kirk maintained, settings were "shabby beyond description" and the scripts mostly trash. Admitting Edmund Kean and David Garrick to have been the greatest English-speaking actors ever, Kirk assessed the three great stars of his youth.

Forrest, he felt, was very handsome with extraordinary physical advantages of which he took no advantage. Oddly enough, Kirk maintained that Forrest lacked fire, substituting power and rant, "thrusting his fist into the face of his audience," as it were. Adding that Forrest acted best when he acted least, Kirk deemed him deliberative and ponderous but with no real "electric current" passing through his nerves.

Kirk ranked Booth between Forrest and Macready. Suggesting it unlikely that Booth sought to imitate Kean (though Kirk had never seen Kean and observed Booth only in the 1840s), he nevertheless felt Booth lacked Kean's power of "moving the hearts and swaying the feelings" of his audiences. Kirk credited Booth for original inspirations, however, pointing out that a copyist could hardly fail to show "a deficiency of ease, energy, freedom, *abandon,*" adding that in Booth's acting these qualities were conspicuous.

As for Booth's voice, Kirk was aware of the injury to his nose, agreeing with James E. Murdoch that it had a more than usual nasal quality, but he hastened to add, "it was singular how little it detracted from the music of the voice, which was its special excellence." Compared to Forrest's or Macready's, Kirk found Booth's voice "more flexible and more sympathetic than either, better suited to the rhythmical expression of emotion, more capable of a sustained sweetness and an airy brilliancy." In general, Kirk credited Booth with "a 'complete harmony of physical and mental attributes," in which the "personality of the actor was forgotten, and all the details seemed the spontaneous workings and unconscious illustrations of the character he represented."

As to specific roles, Richard III naturally led the list. The critic considered Booth's moment in the scene that Colley Cibber had transferred from *Henry V, Part III* "far more distinct and vivid in my remembrance than anything I have witnessed at the theatre in recent years." So, too, the alternating sarcasm and mock humility in the scene with Lady Anne, the tent scene with its agony of fright, and, above all, the death struggle, based on Kean's rapid thrusts with a swordless hand, remained permanently etched in Kirk's memory.

For Kirk, however, Booth's best was Iago, which he called "the supple Italian nature passing from one guise to another with a Protean ease and grace." As Kirk reread the script, Booth's tone, looks, gestures, came back to him in every passage. Kirk had seen many Iagos before and after Booth's, but the role remained identified with that actor alone.

Although Kirk preferred Macready to Booth, he admitted no player he had ever seen displayed so well the actor's ability to transcend his own personality, seeming to become possessed and controlled by the character's distinct and complete individuality. The roles of Richard, Iago, and Sir Giles Overreach all are unscrupulous, malignant plotters, possessed of courage as their only virtue, but Booth, Kirk maintained, made each a particular character, with walk, gestures, attitudes, looks, and tones belonging to that personage and no other. Performers like Forrest were always Forrest; Booth perceived the art of acting far more deeply and effectively.

Kirk was in no way a slavering sycophant like Thomas R. Gould, at least about Booth. Admitting Booth's successes were never doubtful, he added, "nor were his failures." Shylock by Booth was, Kirk confessed, excellent without being first-rate; it did not, like Kean's, impress one "like a chapter of Genesis." But Booth's Othello Kirk was careful never to see, and the one time Kirk attended Booth's Macbeth he felt only shame for witnessing the exhibition. Booth's Hamlet the critic considered "singular," lacking the poetry, pathos, and intellectual excitement usually associated with the role. And his Lear Kirk considered not exactly Lear, but the very image of an old man who has lost his wits.

Kirk closed out his description of Booth with a most telling comment about the actor's entrance as Reuben Glenroy in *Town and Country*. Booth's character directs the attention of the cast to a cloud directly over his head; Kirk recalled that the entire audience would look up, expecting to see the cloud. Actors consider this sort of thing a mechanical trick, easily done, but Kirk shrewdly noted that the intention to produce the effect is often visible; he then added, "In Booth's method the intention was precisely what was not visible." Modern actors talk about playing an action as opposed to a result; Booth would have recognized the distinction.

But Kirk, in all fairness, considered Macready the best of the lot, the preeminent actor of the English stage. He lavished deserved praise upon the Englishman for his devotion to his profession, for restoring the Shakespearean texts to the originals, for striving to make every production a unified whole, the purity and dignity of his life, and by his "intimate relations with a host of distinguished persons." (Booth would have snorted at such propositions.) Kirk continued, "Not Booth in Richard nor Forrest in Metamora drew any such thunders of applause as accompanied and almost interrupted Macready's bursts of fiery passion," nor did either succeed in so "touching the heart and causing the eye to brim with tears."

Still, Kirk admitted, something was missing. He quoted a critic at Macready's Macbeth one evening as saying, "I see what it is: he has a grand conception of the character, but he cannot come up to it in the execution." Kirk denied that Macready loathed his profession, only the low social status it brought him, thus making acting not the profession for which Macready was best suited. Booth was never a citizen, but he was in most ways an American; elevated social standing he would leave to his family, and welcome.

A critic such as Kirk can possibly be more objective than can an actor's fellow players; actors are not prone to speak ill of their brothers, at least not in their memoirs. Most of the profession had only high praise for Booth. For example, one of the great gentlemen of the American stage, Joseph Jefferson III, who appeared with all the leading stars of his time, recalled of the elder Booth:

> He would saunter into the theatre just a few minutes before the play began; robe himself, sometimes quite carelessly; converse freely

> upon local matters in a plain, practical way, or perhaps give some reminiscences of bygone years,—his memory was wonderful,—ending with an amusing anecdote, and in the next moment walk upon the stage in the full assumption of his character, overawing the audience by the fire of his acting.

Jefferson then recalled Booth demonstrating a comic song to the young actor, interrupting it to play a powerful scene in *The Iron Chest,* then stepping into the wings to finish the song while the audience cheered him. But Jefferson hastened to add, "It must not be understood by this that Booth never became absorbed in his character; on the contrary, he sometimes carried his intensity in this respect to an extreme. It is only meant to show that he had also the power of dropping his character in the midst of his concentration, resuming it again at will. Macready had no such faculty whatever."[19] Jefferson also spoke fondly of the elder Booth's generosity to his fellows in the profession, a generosity carried on by Edwin.

So, too, James E. Murdoch (1811–93), an unusually intellectual actor of Booth's time, praised Booth as the man who most strongly impressed him.[20] Murdoch further complimented Booth for his literary tastes and abilities and for his remarkably clear mental qualities. Specifically, the younger actor recalled playing Wilford to Booth's Sir Edward Mortimer. In a confrontation scene, Murdoch claimed that for the first time he understood the reality of acting. "The fury of that passion-flamed face and the magnetism of the rigid clutch upon my arm paralyzed my muscles, while the scintillating gleam of the terrible eyes, like the green and red flashes of an enraged serpent, fascinated and fixed me spellbound on the spot."[21]

Murdoch also mentioned the incident in which Flynn broke Booth's nose, suggesting that for a time it affected his voice. Through discipline and practice, Murdoch claimed, Booth largely restored his resonance, although an unusual nasal quality remained.[22]

But of all actors, Booth's son Edwin knew him best. The loyal son sought for the rest of his life to describe his father, to explain him, even to excuse his undeniable eccentricities. Edwin freely admitted those "oddities" caused his father suffering, the suffering of those possessed by genius. "Great minds to Madness closely are allied," Edwin added, from his own greatest role, then:

> At the moment of intense emotion, when the spectators were enthralled by his magnetic influence, the tragedian's overwrought brain would take refuge from its own threatening storm beneath the jester's hood, and, while turned from the audience, he would whisper some silliness or "make a face"; but when he left the stage no allusion to such seeming levity was permitted. His fellow-actors, who perceived these trivialities, ignorantly attributed his conduct at such times to lack of feeling, whereas it was the very excess of feeling which thus forced his brain back from its utmost verge of reason. Only those who have known the torture of severe mental tension can appreciate the value of that one little step from the sublime to the ridiculous.[23]

Edwin described his father as reserved and diffident—almost bashful—when away from home but as gleeful as a child when behind his locked doors and bolted shutters. Contented with his family, Booth felt no need for others; Edwin claimed that Booth's wife and children thus became isolated and suffered from a sense of estrangement. Quirks of this sort still abound in the lives of artists and geniuses. Genius all too frequently emanates from oddities, traumas, frustrations, even neuroses.[24]

The elder Booth, Edwin recalled, could do justice to his work only when the spirit moved him; otherwise he might quit the theatre and be lost to the world for days. Irate managers he could pay off with free performances; Booth would hurt no one but himself.

Acting had caused such stress on Booth's nervous system that he insisted none of his children follow the stage. Three of them did, and a fourth, Joseph Adrian, dabbled in the business. Their father would have wished them in more healthful work, anything that was, as Edwin put it, *true,* rather than in that unreal world where "nothing is but what is not."

After Edwin had begun acting, Booth began to coddle his son, sharing his evening meal of gruel and insisting he wear his worsted nightcap to avoid taking cold. The elder Booth manifested an almost overly paternal solicitude for the heedless boy who had drifted into the theatre. Yet Booth gave Edwin almost no instruction, professional advice, or encouragement. The child was stung by his father's seeming indifference but later noted it made him exercise his callow wits and think, earning the son's eternal gratitude.

Although Jefferson recalled Booth dropping into the theatre just before curtain, Edwin recalled his father steeping himself in the role all day before the show, seeking to peak his powers at the time of the performance. If he was to play Othello, he would wear a crescent pin and mumble maxims from the Koran (no matter that Othello is a Christian in Shakespeare's play). If he was to present Shylock, he was a Jew all day, and, if in Baltimore, he would pass hours with a local learned Israelite, discussing Hebrew history.

As for Booth's overindulgence in spirits, Edwin claimed the charge was largely false. The son asserted that the fineness of his father's constitution was such that a bottle of porter's beer (his favorite beverage when fatigued) or a single glass of brandy and water would excite him five times as much as another. Edwin, like Asia, loved his father and forgave him, even as the American public did.

The same sensitivity—the ability to allow an emotion to fill the moment, essential to all great actors—empowered Booth with the ability to move even the extras to tears. Edwin recalled the supernumeraries in *Brutus* sniffing and rubbing their noses furtively, adding, "To affect seriously a stage mob denotes unusual if not extraordinary magnetism in the speaker." And in the same play, Edwin recalled the last scene in which the father (Booth) held the son (Edwin) at their final parting. Some senseless fellow in the audience made a rude remark, disturbing both auditors and actors. Edwin described the moment:

> Raising his head from off my breast, my father, without lapsing from the stern Roman character of the judge, with a lightning glance toward the fellow, said: "Beware! I am the headsman!" It was like a thunder-shock! all in front and on the stage seemed paralyzed for a few moments, but the applause that followed lasted many minutes; the scene thenceforward proceeded without interruption, and ended as it should end in tearful silence.

In our own time, some stage actors seem to have dominated an audience by sheer force of personality—Sir Laurence Olivier and Richard Burton come to mind. A small man, Junius Brutus Booth gained stature as he entered the sham world of the stage—his soul was big.

Scholars have correctly asserted that Booth had brought romantic acting to the United States far more effectively than had Edmund Kean. Charles Shattuck, for example, noted that Kean's first tour of

America began in triumph and ended in rioting against him. Booth's influence was more modest; Shattuck posits, "he put his roots down in America and practised his art in all parts of the country for over three decades. Eventually he was recognized as America's romantic actor *par éminence.* Thus, though Kean's impassioned playing would always be remembered, it was Booth rather than Kean who sustained the 'natural' style in America to the middle of the century."[25]

Thus, if Kean had been a theatrical Zeus, inventing the fiery passion of romantic acting, Booth functioned as a theatrical Prometheus, spreading the flame far and wide across North America.

And for this flame the emerging nation was more than ready. Booth and America freed themselves from the strictures of the past. Booth and America sought equality for all individuals and to the degree possible achieved it. Sympathy for the underdog marked both nation and man, as did a restless mobility, an itch to see over the next hill. Both the American people and Booth sought to fill their purses by incessant activity, both glorifying labor, almost for its own sake. And both shared open, casual, and candid relationships.

If today Booth is remembered first as the father of the assassin and second as the father of Edwin Booth, let it be noted that his profession has not forgotten him. On 5 April 1981 the elder Booth was elected to the Theatre Hall of Fame and his name added to the list in the lobby of the Uris (now the Ziegfeld) Theatre in New York.[26]

Looking back through the rainy windowpanes of history to an actor who died more than a century ago, we must recall a man's private life is lived in his head, not in the scraps of paper that survive him. It is his and his alone. But we must try.

Above all, Booth had intelligence. His ability with languages, for example, demonstrated his verbal aptitude. Jefferson spoke highly of Booth's memory; keeping all those roles in one's head is rarely demanded of modern actors, and one wonders how many of them could do it. Even his having moved his first American home, the log house, and his having used crushed bone as fertilizer on his farm bespeak his imagination and willingness to try a new way.

His intelligence no doubt led him to disillusionment with his profession; he was able to imagine what it could be, but he had to live with what it was. He had aspired to and reached the foothills of London stardom, which he equated with a permanent company in a theatre royal, touring only during the summers for inflated prices. Instead, he became an itinerant actor in America, performing for far less sophisticated audiences in ratty theatres with pickup companies of drunken ghosts or worse. He was surely discontented with his lot; the thinking person usually is. He worked in the theatre; the money was good; but he never perceived the essential jewel buried under the tinsel and the paste, the phony armor and the tin swords, the mock heroics. He lived in no golden age of playwrights; his was a pewter age of diluted and rewritten Shakespeare, of the drama as popular entertainment, titillation for the masses, not the bright intellectual exercise it can be—yet so rarely has been. Not even the London stage, which rejected him, cast him out, could claim in its smug complacency to have achieved anything like the lofty days of Shakespeare, Molière, or the Greek dramatists. Booth's personal library would indicate a more sophisticated taste, rare among actors of his time, but seemingly unrelated to his stage work.

The English then used the euphemism *strolling player* for actors who spent their careers on the road. Perhaps one could stroll on that little island on which one is never more than sixty-five miles from the sea, but Booth's new nation had some size to it. Riding harshly sprung stagecoaches over deep-rutted roads or braving ocean and river travel hardly constituted strolling, but the peripatetic Booth spent thirty-one years in such travel, including his humiliating English engagements. All in all, from February 1817 onward, he played almost three thousand performances during more than five hundred engagements in some sixty-eight cities. His quick mind attracted him to new sights, as attested by his notes and his journey to California, but the grinding monotony of endless travel might well have driven him to reach for the bottle.

So, too, might the monotony of his repertoire, typical of leading tragedians of the day. Numeric analysis of his engagements shows Booth's career in something of a new light. From the London engagement during which he rose to stardom in February 1817 through his last appearance in New Orleans, he played seventy-three roles, including five in afterpieces. His recorded appearances in the theatre amount to 2,801 bills; on 2,567 occasions he performed in the main bill only; 223 times he played in both the main bill and the afterpiece, and on eleven evenings he performed in the afterpiece only.

Comparing the number of times he played specific roles (2,042) to his total number of appearances on the main bill (2,790) reveals that the bulk of Booth's career involved acting only a few roles.

Role	Number of Performances	Percentage of Main Bills
Richard III	579	20.75
Sir Giles Overreach	328	11.75
Sir Edward Mortimer	190	6.81
King Lear	182	6.52
Hamlet	173	6.20
Iago	148	5.30
Pescara	146	5.23
Othello	106	3.79
Shylock	95	3.40
Bertram	95	3.40
Total	2,042	73.15

Ten roles, then, most of them quite demanding, made up nearly three-quarters of Booth's professional life. His 234 appearances in afterpieces represented only six roles, and two of those (The Stranger and Sam Johnson) he played only once in the afterpiece, another (Luke) only three times. While many of the leading actors of the time had similar demands made upon them, most modern actors have more variety in their roles, excepting the occasional long run. The effects of these demands go a long way toward explaining Booth's quirks.

We cannot deny Booth's disease, alcoholism. He was raised in a hard-drinking city during hard-drinking times by a hard-drinking father, but he must bear responsibility for his own actions. That this vegetarian, this lover of all life, displayed a propensity for violence while under the influence, even to self-destruction, only indicates the potency of the addiction.

We have only Dr. Rush's descriptions of Booth's symptoms, but Booth's health problems possibly contributed to his frequent intoxication. In an undated letter to Wemyss, Booth once complained, "The pain in my head is really so stupefying that until it ceases I am unfit for any human employ." The infected antrum seems suspect, but

Booth called it rheumatism, treating the pain with diet, tonics, and leeches. Time, however, he considered the only cure.[27]

How much Adelaide and his first son preyed on his mind we can only surmise; no record of his thoughts on that situation survive. His treatment of Adelaide was at best inept, at worst shabby. He was obviously married to the wrong woman when he met the right one, and nineteenth-century London did little to foster sexual equality. Booth had the example of the British royalty and their marital capers, if he needed one. Still, he maintained to the end that he had entered into a separate maintenance with Adelaide, and records show he regularly sent funds to her. Perhaps he tried to buy off a troubled conscience or felt nothing more was necessary. Certainly his father, the Bloomsbury lawyer, could have advised him with a full knowledge of the situation.

That this man, the father of an assassin, held all life to be sacred, carrying the doctrine to extremes, may strike us now as ironic. Whatever his motives, his religiosity took the highest form of spiritual theory, that of daily action. He lived his philosophy and preached only to his family. Not for him the gilded and marble-shod churches and sanctimonious piety, nor the infliction of dogma into others' lives. Booth was a man of peace till the horrors came out at night. If he had demons, they kept him from self-righteousness. He earned his demons and thereby his basic honesty. He was not always graceful under pressure. He acted heroes, but he was not one himself. He could act life because he knew it—knew the hollowness of guilt, the pangs of shame, the seduction of adulation, the ache of rejection, the cushion of friendship, the selflessness of an enduring love, the perspective of the soil, the obscenity of burying children, and the blighted aspirations of the artist.

Sometimes there was just not enough Booth to go around; then would he crumble, then would he fall into the insane freaks to which his flesh was heir, the savage quirks that branded him, then and forever, the mad tragedian. They spoke of his drinking, but never his thirst.

Let us only say in conclusion he was filled with imperfect virtues, and let those without sin step forward. May his perturbed spirit rest.

Appendix: Recorded Engagements

Notes

Works Cited

Index

Appendix

Recorded Engagements

Booth enacted seventy-three different roles during the major part of his career, from his first starring engagement in London in 1817 till his death in 1852. For this appendix, the roles are abbreviated (see below), with the number of recorded performances in parentheses. On thirty-four occasions, records indicate that Booth performed, but the specific role remains unknown (abbreviation UK).

A2 = Second Actor in Shakespeare's *Hamlet* (1)
AM = Amurath in Richard Sheil's *Bellamira; or, The Fall of Tunis* (4)
BA = Barabas, presumably in Christopher Marlowe's *Jew of Malta* (1)
BE = Bertram in Charles Robert Maturin's *Bertram* (95)
BR = Brutus in John Howard Payne's *Brutus; or, The Fall of Tarquin* (87)
BU = Brutus in *The Judgement of Brutus; or, Tarquin and Lucretia* (5)
CA = Cassius in Shakespeare's *Julius Caesar* (57)
CG = Caius Gracchus in J. S. Knowles' *Caius Gracchus* (1)
CO = Colonna in Richard Sheil's *Evadne, or, The Statue* (1)
DM = Dumont in Nicholas Rowe's *Tragedy of Jane Shore* (1)
DR = Darlemont in Thomas Holcroft's *Deaf and Dumb; Or, The Orphan Protected* (1)
DU = Ducas in Matthew Gregory "Monk" Lewis' *Adelgitha* (2)
DZ = Durazzo in William A. Court's *Montaldo* (4)
ED = Edgar in Shakespeare's *King Lear* (4)
EM = Sir Edward Mortimer in George Colman's (the younger) *The Iron Chest* (188)
EU = Eustache de St. Pierre in George Colman's (the younger) *The Surrender of Calais* (1)
FA = Fitzarden in William Thomas Moncrieff's *Lear of Private Life* (21)
FO = Fontaine in John Howard Payne's *Therese, The Orphan of Geneva* (2)
FZ = Fitzharding in John Tobin's *Curfew* (2)

FZ2 = Fitzharding in Mrs. Marie Therese Kemble's *Smiles and Tears; or, The Widow's Stratagem* (1)

GI = Sir Giles Overreach in Philip Massinger's *A New Way to Pay Old Debts* (328)

GL = Gloster in Nicholas Rowe's *Tragedy of Jane Shore* (13)

HA = Hamlet in Shakespeare's *Hamlet* (173)

HO = Hotspur in Shakespeare's *Henry IV, Part One* (6)

HR = Horatius in George MacFarren's *Horatii and Curatii* (15)

IG = Iago in Shakespeare's *Othello* (148)

JA = Jaffier in Thomas Otway's *Venice Preserved* (15)

JF = Jacob Foscari in Lord Byron's *Two Foscari* (1)

JL = John Lump in James Bland Burges' *The Review; or, Wags of Windsor*, afterpiece (53)

KH = King Henry in Shakespeare's *Richard the Third*, Colley Cibber's version (1)

KJ = King John in Shakespeare's *King John* (24)

LD = Ludovico in Richard Sheil's *Evadne; or, The Statue* (2)

LE = King Lear in Shakespeare's *King Lear* (182)

LU = Luke in James Bland Burges' *Riches* (12, also 3 times as an afterpiece)

MA = Malcour in H. M. Milner's *Gambler's Fate* (4)

MC = Macbeth in Shakespeare's *Macbeth* (59)

MU = Geoffrey Muffincap in Richard Brinsley Peake's *Amateurs and Actors*, afterpiece (20)

MW = Mawworm in Isaac Bickerstaffe's *Hypocrite* (1)

OC = Octavian in George Colman's (the younger) *The Mountaineers* (77)

OK = Oroonoko in Thomas Southerne's *Oroonoko* (5)

ON = Old Norval in John Home's *Douglas* (9)

OP = Opechan in *Pocohontas; or, The Indian Princess* (4)

OR = Orezembo in Richard Brinsley Sheridan's adaptation of August von Kotzebue's *Pizarro* (6)

OS = Orestes in Ambrose Philips' *Distrest Mother* (15)

OSf = Oreste in Jean Racine's *Andromaque* (2)

OT = Othello in Shakespeare's *Othello* (106)

PE = Pescara in Richard Sheil's *Apostate* (146)

PI = Pierre in Thomas Otway's *Venice Preserved* (38)

PN = Penruddock in Richard Cumberland's *Wheel of Fortune* (4)

PO = Posthumus in Shakespeare's *Cymbeline* (8)

PW = Prince of Wales in Shakespeare's *Henry IV, Part One* (1)

PZ = Pizarro in Richard Brinsley Sheridan's adaptation of August von Kotzebue's *Pizarro* (2)

R2 = Richard II in Shakespeare's *Richard II* (3)

R3 = Richard III in Shakespeare's *Richard the Third*, Colley Cibber's version (579)

RC = Richmond in Shakespeare's *Richard the Third*, Colley Cibber's version (2)

RD = Roderick Dhu in Sir Walter Scott's *Lady of the Lake* (10)

RG = Reuben Glenroy in Thomas Morton's *Town and Country* (76)

RI = Rinaldo in William Dimond's *Conquest of Taranto; or, The Eve of St. Clara* (6)

RL = Richelieu in Edward Bulwer Lytton's *Richelieu* (1)
RO = Romeo in Shakespeare's *Romeo and Juliet* (2)
RR = Rob Roy M'Gregor in Isaak Pocock's *Rob Roy M'Gregor* (4)
SE = Selim in Lord Byron's *Bride of Abydos* (10)
SH = Shylock in Shakespeare's *Merchant of Venice* (95)
SJ = Sam Johnson in *Oh, Hush; or, The Virginny Cupids,* afterpiece (1)
SN = Jeremy Sneak in Samuel Foote's *Mayor of Garratt,* afterpiece (136)
SR = Sertorius in David P. Brown's *Sertorius* (6)
ST = The Stranger in August von Kotzebue's *Stranger* (43, plus once as an afterpiece)
SY = Sylla in John Howard Payne's *Sylla,* adapted from the French original by Etienne de Jouy (7)
UK = unknown role (34)
YN = Young Norval in John Home's *Douglas* (3)
ZA = Zanga in Edward Young's *Revenge* (2)

Each of Booth's recorded performances appears below, grouped by engagement and enclosed in parentheses. For each evening's appearance, the day of the month in Arabic numerals is listed first, the month follows in lowercase Roman numerals, and the role performed is given by abbreviation. Thus the entry (12iiR3) would indicate that on the twelfth day of the second month (February) Booth played Richard III. The entries are in chronological order, divided by year, and headed by city and theatre (when the theatre is known). An asterisk (*) alone after the role abbreviation indicates a Booth benefit; an asterisk followed by a name or a title indicates Booth played in a benefit for someone else. In a few cases, Booth played a single role for several nights; those dates that include a dash (e.g., 13–17) indicate that he played the same role each evening. Sources follow each engagement, using some newspaper titles and collection names as abbreviated below.

From 31 March 1817 to 1822, most entries are recorded using Booth's account book and confirmed where possible by bills and newspapers. In his account book, Booth usually entered the gross box-office take for the performance, his terms, and his personal share from the performance. These figures are included after each performance in brackets [g = the gross; b = Booth's share]. The same shorthand is used for other periods when gross or shares or both are known. British monies are given in pounds, shillings, and pence, separated by a solidus(/); twenty shillings equaled a pound, and twelve pence equaled a shilling. U.S. monies are given in dollars and cents; one hundred cents equaled a dollar. Other abbreviations used include the following:

A&CA = Baltimore *American and Commercial Daily Advertiser*
ACCTBK = Booth's account book from 1817 to 1822, now in the New York Public Library Manuscripts Division
Ball = Robert Hamilton Ball, *The Amazing Career of Sir Giles Overreach*
BL = British Library, formerly a part of the British Museum, London
BPL = Boston Public Library, Booth Scrapbook, Rare Book Room

DA = Did not appear as advertised
DNI = *Daily National Intelligencer,* Washington, D.C.
EB = Edwin Booth
FSL = Folger Shakespeare Library, Washington, D.C.
GC = Garrick Club, London
Hoole = Stanley Hoole, *The Ante-Bellum Charleston Stage*
HTC = Harvard Theatre Collection, Cambridge, Massachusetts
Ireland = Joseph Norton Ireland, *A Memoir of . . . Thomas Abthorpe Cooper*
James = Reese James, *Old Drury of Philadelphia*
JBB2 = Junius Brutus Booth, Jr.
KC = Stanley Kimmel Collection, Merl Kelce Library, University of Tampa, Tampa, Florida
MC = Menken Collection (private)
McCain = William D. McCain, *"The Story of Jackson"*
McGlinchee = Claire McGlinchee, *The First Decade of the Boston Museum*
Mudd = Aloysius L. Mudd, "Theatres of Washington from 1835 to 1850"
NGLR = *National Gazette & Literary Register,* Philadelphia
Odell = George C. D. Odell, *Annals of the New York Stage*
PADA = *Poulson's American Daily Advertiser,* Philadelphia
PC = Players, New York
RE = Reengaged
TX = The Harry Ransom Humanities Research Center, University of Texas, Austin, Texas
USG = *United States Gazette,* Philadelphia
V&A = Victoria and Albert Museum, London
Warren = William Warren, *Life and Memoirs of William Warren*
Weisert = John Jacob Weisert, *The Curtain Rose*
Willard = George O. Willard, *History of the Providence Stage*

1815

From 24 July 1815 through 4 February 1817 Booth alternated between the theatres royal in Brighton and Worthing, both under Thomas Trotter's management, as well as performing occasionally at Covent Garden. For that period, each recorded performance is preceded by a B: for Brighton, a W: for Worthing, a CG: for Covent Garden, or a question mark when the theatre is unknown.

(W:24viiFrancis in *The Stranger,* Lothair in *The Miller and His Men*), (W:5viiiDon Antonio in *The Duenna,* *Miss Stephens), (W:9viiiClaudio in *Much Ado about Nothing,* Lothair), (W:10viiiSaville in *The Belles' Stratagem,* Lord Rivers in *The Day After the Wedding*), (W:12viiiDon Garcia in *A Bold Stroke for a Husband*), (W:14viiiDon Garcia and Lothair), (W:17viiiCapt. Bygrove in *Know Your Own Mind,* *Mrs. Glover), (W:26viiiCharles in *Busy Body*), (B:1ixHortensio in *Catherine and Petruchio*), (W:7ixCol. Epaulette in *Fontainbleu; or, Our Way in France!*), (W:9ixCol. Epaulette), (CG:18xSilvius in

As You Like It), (CG:20xSilvius), (CG25xSilvius), (CG:11xiHarcourt in *Percy*), (CG:14xHarcourt), (CG:18xHarcourt), (CG:23xHarcourt).

1816

(CG:8iDavila in *Pizarro*), (B:24iGlenalcon in *Douglas*), (B:27iScruple in *Ways and Means; or, A Trip to Dover*), (CG:19iiDavila), (B:24iiGlenalcon), (CG:6vPindarus in *Julius Caesar*), (CG:13vPindarus), (CG:31vLovel in *Henry VIII*, *Mr. and Mrs. C. Kemble), (CG:17viDavila), (CG:24viDavila), (CG:28viSilvius), (CG:29viLovel, *Theatrical Fund), (CG:5viiHenry in *The Magpie or the Maid*), (CG:9viiCadwall in *Cymbeline*), (W:20viiDowlas in *The Heir at Law*), (W:22viiBertrand in *Foundling of the Forest*), (W:27viiIsaac in *The Maid and the Magpie*), (W:29viiIsaac), (W:1viiiIsaac), (W:5viiiGibby in *The Wonder: A Woman Keeps a Secret*, and Isaac), (W:8viiiFitzharding in *Smiles and Tears*), (W:10viiiOrlando in *As You Like It*), (W:12viiiFitzharding in *The Curfew* and Isaac), (W:15viiiKalig in *The Blind Boy*), (W:19viiiOctavian in *The Mountaineers* and Kalig), (W:24viiiJack Bustle in *Where to Find a Friend*), (W:28viiiSir George Airy in *Busy Body*), (W:29viiiCostly in *Laugh When You Can; or, The Faithful Black*), (W:31viiiDurimel in *Point of Honor*), (W:2ixShadrack in *The Young Quaker*), (W:4ixJack Bustle), (W:7ixCharles in *The Jew*), (W:9ixKalig), (Windsor Theatre, 14ixHenry in *Who Wants a Guinea?*), (W:19ixOctavian), (B:25ixSir Giles Mortimer), (Windsor, 26ix-Fitzharding), (W:5xAlme in *Deaf and Dumb; or, The Orphan Protected*, and Kalig), (W:7xSir Giles), (W:8xBertram in *Bertram*), (W:9xOthello), (W:12x Lord Hastings in *The Tragedy of Jane Shore*), (W:14xHenry in *Speed the Plough*), (W:17xWyndham in *Royal Oak*), (B:22xRichard III), (W:26x Richard III), (W:31xBertram), (B:5xiHenry Bertam in *Guy Mannering*), (B:8xiBertram), (B:9xiOthello), (?:20xiUK in *Belles' Stratagem*), (B:22xi Fitzharding), (B:27xiGeorge Barnwell in *George Barnwell* and Oscar in *Oscar and Malvina*), (B:30xiHarry in *Valentine and Orson; or, The Wild Man in the Woods*), (?:3xiiSir Giles), (B:4xiiFaulkland in *The Rivals*), (?:6xii Richard in *The Magpie; or, The Maid of Palaiseau)*, (?:13xiiMacduff in *Macbeth* and Enrico Altieri in *For England Ho!*), (?:14xiiJaffier in *Venice Preserved*), (B:15xiiJaffier), (?:21xiiFoss in *The Poor Gentleman* and Ferdinand in *The Woodman's Hut*), (?:24xiiIago to Kean's Othello).

1817

(B:9iRigolio in *The Broken Sword*), (B:18iBertram and Sneak*), (B:25i Rigolio), (B:4iiZembuca in *Zembuca; or, The Net Maker and His Wife*, *Trotter). BL bills, MC.

Covent Garden: (12–13iiR3). GC bills, *London Times*.

Drury Lane: (20iiIG to Kean's Othello). GC bills, *London Times.*

Covent Garden: (25iiR3), (1iiiR3), (3iiiR3), (6iiiR3), (8iiiGI), (10iiiR3), (13iiiGI), (15iiiPO), (17iiiGI), (20iiiPO), (22iiiPO), (24iiiR3), (27iiiFZ), (29iiiPO). GC bills.
Woolwich: Terms of one-half. (31iiiR3) [g=23/12/6; b=11/16/3], (1ivBE) [g=20/10/0; b=10/5/0], (3ivOT) [g=14/14/7; b=7/7/0], (5ivGI, SN*) [g=21/4/6; b=10/2/3]. ACCTBK.
Covent Garden: (7ivPO), (8ivR3), (11ivEM), (15–16ivRI), (18ivRI). GC bills, *London Times.*
Cirencester: (19ivEM) [g=5/19/0; b=2/19/6], Gloucester [g=10/17/6; b=5/8/9], Cheltenham [g=39/19/6; b=19/19/9]. (Three performances in three cities in one day). ACCTBK.
Covent Garden: (21ivRI), (23ivRI), (25ivRI). GC bills.
Croyden: (29ivGI) [g=26/13/0; b=13/6/6]. ACCTBK.
Covent Garden: (30ivPO). GC bills.
Croyden: (8vEM) [g=19/11/0; b=9/15/0]. ACCTBK.
Bristol: (12vR3) [g=110/0/6; b=25/0/3]. ACCTBK.
Bath: (13vR3) [g=95/2/6; b=17/11/3], (15vGI) [g=83/5/6; b=11/12/9], (17vEM, SN*) [g=164/12/6; b=82/6/3]. ACCTBK.
Gloucester: (19vR3) [g=20/13/0; b=10/6/6]. ACCTBK.
Cheltenham: (20vR3) [g=31/3/0; b=15/11/6], (21vBE) [g=27/0/0; b=13/10/0]. ACCTBK.
Liverpool: Sharing after £65 and half the benefit. (24vGI) [g=80/19/6; b=7/19/9], (26vR3) [g=136/18/0; b=35/19/0], (27vBE) [g=60/12/0; b=0/0/0], (28vOT) [g=67/2/0; b=1/1/0], (30vJA) [g=102/7/6; b=18/13/9], (2viFZ) [g=88/15/0; b=11/17/6], (3viOC) [g=56/19/0; b=0/0/0]; (4viGI) [g=77/14/0; b=6/7/0], (5viHA, SN*) [g=153/19/6; b=76/19/9]. ACCTBK.
Manchester: Sharing after £70. (6viR3) [g=199/14/0; b=64/17/0]. ACCTBK.
Croyden: (14viR3, *"the actors") [g=22/6/0; b="ingratitude"]. ACCTBK.
Guildford: Half the receipts. (16viR3) [g=16/18/0; b=8/9/0]. ACCTBK.
Covent Garden: (25viR3, SN*). BL bills. ACCTBK says at Bristol for Pearman's benefit, an error of entry.
Bath: (26viR3) [g=56/8/6; b=0/0/0]. ACCTBK.
Bristol: (27viGI, *Pearman) [b="ingratitude"], (28viEM) [g=75/8/0; b=7/14/0], (30viEM). ACCTBK, BL bills.
Cheltenham: Taking one-third. (2viiHA) [g=27/17/0; b=9/5/8], (3viiGI, SN*) [g=18/0/6; b=6/0/2]. ACCTBK.
Covent Garden: (7viiIG, *Miss O'Neill), (14viiIG). BL bills, GC.
Chelmsford: Half after five pounds. (15viiR3) [g=13/19/0; b=4/9/6], (16viiSH) [g=13/6/0; b=4/3/0]. ACCTBK.
Covent Garden: (17viiIG). End of season. CG, V&A bills.
Cheltenham: (19viiRG, *"Mr. W.") [b="gratis"]. ACCTBK.
Birmingham: Sharing after £30 and taking half the last two nights. (21vii

R3) [g=70/16/0; b=20/8/0], (22viiR3) [g=34/0/0; b=2/0/0], (23 viiBE) [g=30/0/0; b=0/0/0], (24viiJA) [g=32/1/0; b=1/0/6], (25 viiIG) [g=40/8/6; b=5/4/3]. ACCTBK.

Gloucester: Half the receipts. (28viiUK) [g=12/6/6; b=6/3/3]. ACCTBK.

Birmingham: (29viiBE) [g=28/9/6; b=0/0/0], (30viiGI) [g=24/6/0; b=12/3/0], (31viiLE, SN*) [g=31/9/0; b=15/9/6]. ACCTBK.

Newcastle-on-Tyne: Half the receipts. (4viiiGI) [g=40/10/0; b=20/5/0], (5viiiR3) [g=29/10/0; b=14/15/0], (6viiiBE) [g=22/5/6; b=11/2/9], (7viiiHA, SN) [g=48/0/6; b=24/0/3]. ACCTBK.

Carlisle: Half the receipts. (8viiiR3) [g=16/16/0; b=8/8/0], (9viiiGI) [g=15/13/0; b=7/16/6]. ACCTBK.

Scarborough: Half the receipts. (18viiiBE) [g=28/10/6; b=14/5/3], (19viii R3) [g=41/19/0; b=20/19/6], (20viiiHA) [g=15/15/0; b=7/17/6], (21viiiLE) [g=25/7/6; b=12/18/9], (22viiiGI) [g=26/6/6; b=13/3/3]. ACCTBK.

Harrogate: Half the receipts. (26viiiBE) [g=18/16/0; b=9/8/0], (28viii EM) [g=28/9/0; b=14/4/6]. ACCTBK.

Lancaster: Half the receipts. (1ixGI) [g=34/16/0; b=17/8/0], (2ixEM) [g=32/9/0; b=16/4/6], (3ixR3) [g=56/14/0; b=28/7/0]. ACCTBK.

Preston: Half the receipts. (4ixGI) [g=26/0/6; b=13/0/3], (5ixOT) [g=8/12/0; b=4/6/0]. ACCTBK.

Rochdale: Half the receipts. (8ixBE) [g=8/5/6; b=4/2/9], (9ixOT) [g=9/12/0; b=4/11/0]. ACCTBK.

Newcastle-under-Tyne: Half the receipts. (12ixR3) [g=35/16/0; b=17/18/0], (13ixEM) [g=34/13/6; b=17/6/9]. ACCTBK.

Bristol: Half after £30 and half a benefit. (16ixOT) [g=30/5/6; b=0/2/9], (17ixSH) [g=52/1/0; b=11/0/6], (19ixHA, SN*) [g=46/16/0; b=23/8/0]. ACCTBK.

Margate: One-third for two nights; half for two nights. (29ixEM) [g=14/0/0; b=4/13/4], (30ixR3) [g=17/0/0; b=5/16/8], (3xGI) [g=22/1/6; b=11/0/9], (4xOT) [g=23/14/6; b=11/17/3]. ACCTBK.

Nottingham: Half the receipts. (8xEM) [g=36/7/6; b=18/3/9], (9xOT) [g=19/18/6; b=9/19/3], (10xSH, SN) [g=33/11/0; b=16/15/6], (11x GI) [g=31/16/0; b=15/18/0]. ACCTBK.

Derby: Half the receipts. (15xEM) [g=44/17/6; b=22/8/6], (16xGI) [g=26/10/0; b=13/5/0], (17xIG) [g=36/12/6; b=18/6/3], (18xBE) [g=10/9/6; b=5/4/9], (20xGI) [g=21/14/0; b=10/17/0]. ACCTBK.

Chesterfield: Half the receipts. (22xEM) [g=10/14/0; b=5/7/0], (23xGI) [g=22/16/0; b=11/8/0]. ACCTBK.

Covent Garden: (3xiIG). First night of season. V&A bills.

Lewes: (8xiiMC) [g=14/17/6; b=7/8/9], (11xiiEM) [g=12/6/0; b=6/3/0]. ACCTBK.

Windsor: (13xiiGI, *Penley) [b="meanness"]. ACCTBK.

Total Provincial Shares Year 1817—1,124/16/1.

1818

St. Albans: Half the receipts. (11iiSH) [g=7/2/0; b=3/11/0]. ACCTBK.

Wolverhampton: (6ivUK, *J. Vining) [g=23/0/0; b=0/0/0]. ACCTBK.

Stratford-upon-Avon: One-third the first night; half the second. (7ivSH) [g=6/12/0; b=2/4/0], (8ivR3) [g=16/16/0; b=8/8/0]. ACCTBK.

Worcester: One-third of the receipts. (9ivEM) [g=10/7/0; b=3/9/0], (10ivR3) [g=10/0/0; b=3/6/8], (11ivGI) [g=15/17/0; b=5/5/8], (13iv OC) [g=17/18/0; b=5/19/4]. ACCTBK.

Newcastle-on-Tyne: Ten pounds per night and half the benefit. (11vR3) [g=38/0/0; b=10/0/0], (12vGI) [g=29/0/0; b=10/0/0], (13vAM) [g =42/3/0; b=10/0/0], (14vAM) [g=18/6/6; b=10/0/0], (15vBA, SN*) [g=54/2/0; b=27/1/0]. ACCTBK.

Bolton: Half the receipts. (18vR3) [g=12/5/0; b=6/2/6], (19vBE) [g= 9/2/0; b=4/11/0], (20vGI) [g=11/18/0; b=5/19/0], (21vAM) [g= 20/6/6; b=10/3/3]. ACCTBK. Booth did not record dates for his last three roles.

Guildford: (3–5viUK). Booth entered "three nights at Guildford during the election," and entered 8/9/0, half the receipts. ACCTBK.

Ipswich: (16viR3), (17viGI), (18viEM), (19viAM, SN*). BL bills. The ACCTBK records only "4 at Ipswich" and "Lost 5/5/0."

Glasgow: Sharing four nights after £30 and second-best night clear. (29vi R3) [g=33/13/0; b=33/13/0], (30viMC) [g=26/5/0; b=0/0/0], (1viiIG) [g=15/10/6; b=0/0/0], (2viiHO) [g=23/12/6; b=0/0/0], (3viiGI) [g =16/15/6; b=0/0/0], (4viiHA, SN*) [g=36/1/0; b=0/0/0]. Booth's total income=47/7/0. ACCTBK, BL bills, *Glasgow Herald*.

Edinburgh: Seven nights half after £50 and best night clear. (6viiR3) [g=60/5/0; b=0/0/0], (7viiGI) [g=41/0/0; b=0/0/0], (8viiMC) [g= 45/10/0; b=0/0/0], (9viiHO) [g=65/6/0; b=65/6/0], (11viiGI) [g= 52/14/0; b=1/7/0], (13viiIG) [g=50/3/0; b=0/1/6], (14viiOT) [g= 19/7/0; b=0/0/0], (15viiHO) [g=27/16/0; b=0/0/0], (16viiR3) [g =20/3/0; b=0/0/0], (18viiHA, SN*) [g=44/4/0; b=0/0/0]. ACCTBK, BL bills, HTC bills, *Edinburgh Evening Courant*.

Perth: Half after £5. (27viiR3) [g=19/6/0; b=7/3/0], (28viiSH) [g= 8/8/6; b=1/16/6], (29viiHA) [g=12/10/0; b=3/15/0], (30viiOT) [g= 21/3/0; b=8/1/6]. BL bills. Booth entered the wrong dates for this engagement in the ACCTBK.

Hull: Half the first and last nights, and sharing seven nights after £30. (3viiiR3) [g=27/19/0; b=13/14/6], (4viiiBE) [g=35/18/0; b=2/19/0], (5viiiGI) [g=24/12/6; b=0/0/0], (6viiiOT) [g=20/19/0; b=0/0/0], (7viiiSH) [g=39/6/0; b=4/13/0]. RE. (10viiiMC) [g=30/2/0; b= 0/1/0], (11viiiOC) [g=33/0/0; b=0/0/0], (12viiiRG), (13viiiEM) [g= 23/1/6; b=0/0/0], (14viiiHA, SN) [g=78/8/0; b=39/4/0]. BL bills; Booth again entered incorrect dates in ACCTBK.

Lancaster: (24viiiR3) [g=25/19/0; b=0/0/0], (25viiiBE) [g=14/19/0; b=7/9/6], (26viiiGI) [g=18/19/0; b=9/9/6], (27viiiPE) [g=7/8/0; b=3/14/0], (29viiiHA) [g=3/15/0; b=1/17/6]. ACCTBK.

Namptwich: Half the receipts. (31viiiR3) [g=12/2/0; b=6/1/0], (1ixHA) [g=14/1/0; b=7/0/6]. ACCTBK.

Leamington: (4ixSH), (5ixR3) [b=16/0/0]. ACCTBK. Booth did not list the grosses.

Covent Garden: (9xiGL). GC bills.

NOTE: Two pages are cut from the ACCTBK at this point, but no engagements seem to be missing.

Whitehaven: Half the receipts. (28xiiR3) [g & b not entered], (29xiiGI) [g=8/19/6; b=4/9/9], (30xiiMC) [g=11/18/6; b=5/19/3]. ACCTBK. Total Provincial Shares Year 1818—383/10/5.

1819

Whitehaven (con't.): (1iSH), (4iLE), (5iRG), (6iR3), (8iEM, SN*) [g=42/9/6; b=21/4/9]. ACCTBK.

North & South Shields: One-third of receipts. (11iR3) [g=15/13/0; b=5/4/4], (12iGI) [g=9/7/0; b=3/2/4], (13iBE) [g=25/1/0; b=8/7/0], (14iR3) [g=38/1/0; b=12/13/8], (15iGI) [g=50/4/0; b=16/14/8], (16iBE) [g=24/17/6; b=8/5/10]. ACCTBK.

Sunderland: One-third of the receipts. (18iR3) [g=28/19/0; b=9/13/0], (19iGI) [g=7/19/0; b=2/13/0], (20iBE) [g=18/12/6; b=6/4/2], (21iMC) [g=11/7/0; b=3/15/8], (22iSH, SN*) [g=43/18/0; b=14/12/8]. ACCTBK.

Durham: One-third of the receipts. (23iR3) [g=37/2/0; b=12/7/4]. ACCTBK.

Sunderland: One-third of the receipts. (25iLE) [g=24/5/0; b=8/1/8]. ACCTBK.

Whitby: One-third three nights; half the fourth. (27iR3) [g=18/13/0; b=6/4/4], (29iRG) [g=25/0/6; b=8/6/10], (30iOC) [g=18/1/0; b=6/0/4], (1iiGI) [g=33/4/0; b=16/12/0]. ACCTBK.

Dublin: Five pounds per week; grosses not entered. (12iiR3), (16iiR3), (18iiBE), (19iiGI), (25iiBE), (1iiiOT), (5iiiR3), (8iiiOT), (9iiiBE), (10iiiGI), (13iiiZA), (16iiiPE), (22iiiRG), (24iiiRD), (27iiiRD), (29iiiOT), (30iiiRD), (31iiiHA, SN, and R3 soliloquy*), (3ivRD). BL bills, *Dublin Weekly Register*. Booth did not record specific performances in the ACCTBK.

Bridgnorth: One-third of the receipts, half for Reuben. (R3) [g=22/10/0; b=7/10/0], (SH) [g=25/6/0; b=8/8/8], (19ivGI) [g=16/8/0; b=5/9/4], (RG) [g=36/9/0; b=18/4/6], (R3) [g=32/11/0; b=10/17/0]. ACCTBK, *Shrewsbury Chronicle*. Booth did not record dates for this engagement.

Chester: (3vR3), (4vOC), (5vGI), (6vSH), (7vOT), (8vRG), (10vHO), (11vEM, SN*) [g=14/14/0; b=7/7/0]. ACCTBK. For the first seven performances, Booth listed only a total gross of £528, his share being 21/0/0.

Newport: One-third for three nights; half the fourth. (12vR3) [g=17/14/0; b=5/18/0], (13vGI) [g=15/18/0; b=5/6/0], (14vBE) [g=9/0/0; b=3/0/0], (15vRG, SN*) [g=19/19/0; b=9/9/6]. ACCTBK.

Bristol: (17vR3), (19vGI), (21vRR), (24vBR), (25vRR), (27vMC). ACCTBK, BL bills, *Bristol Mirror*. Booth listed only £18 as his share.

Bath: (29vR3) [g=105/7/6; b=10/10/?]. ACCTBK.

Bristol: (31vBR), (1viYN), (4viRR), (7viSH), (8viBR), (9viEU, *Mrs. H. Cummins), (11viOC), (14viBR), (15viCO, *M'Cready; DA), (25viR3, *Antonio), (28viRG, SN*) [g=52/9/0; b=26/4/6]. ACCTBK, *Bristol Mirror, Mercury, Gazette & Public Advertiser,* Barker. Booth did not list specific performances in ACCTBK.

Beverly: One-third of the receipts. (5viiR3) [g=11/12/0], (6viiGI) [g=5/16/0], (7viiBE) [g=14/12/0], (8viiSH, SN*) [g=14/16/0]. ACCTBK. Booth did not list his shares, but see Stockton, below.

Scarborough: (10viiR3) [g=8/0/0], (12viiBE) [g=8/9/0], (13viiGI) [g=10/11/6], (14viiRG) [g=8/14/0]. ACCTBK. Booth did not list his shares, but see Stockton, below.

Stockton: (21viiOC) [g=7/3/6], (22viiSH) [g=4/8/6], (23viiOT) [g=10/13/6], (24viiGI) [g=10/3/0]. ACCTBK. Booth did not list his shares, but he listed his total income for July as one-third of 112/19/0, or 37/13/0.

Durham: One-third of the receipts. (26viiOC) [g=2/0/0; b=0/13/4], (27viiSH) [g=1/7/6; b=0/9/2], (28viiOT) [g=2/14/0; b=0/17/4], (30viiGI) [g=2/16/6; b=0/18/2], (31viiR3) [g=8/1/0; b=2/13/8]. ACCTBK.

Harrowgate: One-third the first night; half the second. (5viiiOC) [g=13/13/0; b=4/13/8], (7viiiGI) [g=5/3/0; b=2/11/6]. ACCTBK.

Scarborough: One-third for four nights, half the fifth. (9viiiEM) [g=5/15/0; b=1/18/4], (10viiiOC) [g=3/3/6; b=1/1/2], (11viiiSH) [g=2/19/0; b=0/19/8], (12viiiR3) [g=10/9/6; b=3/9/10], (14viiiRG, SN*) [g=33/10/6; b=11/3/6]. ACCTBK.

Newcastle-upon Tyne: (16viiiHA), (17viiiOC), (18viiiR3), (19viiiRG), (20 viiiBE). ACCTBK. Booth listed only a total share of £30.

Newcastle-under-Lyme: One-third for three nights; half the fourth; the fifth "gratis." (17ixR3) [g=27/6/0; b=9/2/0], (18ixGI) [g=15/1/6; b=5/0/6], (20ixBE) [g=15/3/0; b=5/1/0], (21ixOC, SN*) [g=25/0/6; b=12/10/6], (22ixBR) [g=35/7/0; b="gratis"]. ACCTBK, BL bills. Close of season.

Oswestry: (30ixR3), (1xGI), (2xOC). ACCTBK. Booth listed only his total shares as 15/0/0.

Shrewsbury: (6xR3) [g=15/15/0], (7xBR) [g=16/18/0], (8xGI) [g=15/

14/0], (9xSH) [g=27/12/0]. ACCTBK. Booth listed only his total shares, 18/18/0.

Buxton: (12xR3) [g=7/4/0; b=0/0/0]. ACCTBK.

Stafford: (15xR3) [g=23/14/0], (16xGI) [b=12/0/0]. ACCTBK.

Brighton: (25xBR, *Hooper) [g=59/11/0; b="gratis"], (2xiRG, *E. Blanchard) [g=60/2/0; b="gratis"]. ACCTBK.

Croyden: (8xiBE) [g=14/9/0; b=0/0/0], (9xiR3) [g=10/4/0; b=2/9/6], (10xiGI) [g=8/2/0; b=4/1/0]. ACCTBK.

Newbury: Terms unclear; half the fourth night. (22xiEM) [g=2/18/6; b=illegible], (23xiR3) [g=10/6/0; b=1/18/0], (25xiBE) [g=8/2/0; b=1/1/0], (27xiOC, SN) [g=12/6/6; b=6/3/3]. ACCTBK.

Portsmouth: Half after £15; half the last night. (6xiiGI) [g=17/0/0; b=1/0/0], (7xiiRG) [g=9/12/0; b=0/0/0], (8xiiBR) [g=16/19/0; b=0/9/6], (10xiiOC, SN) [g=20/9/6; b=10/4/6]. ACCTBK.

Chichester: Half the receipts. (9xiiGI) [g=4/11/0; b=2/5/6], (11xiiEM) [g=7/0/6; b=3/10/3], (13xiiOC, SN) [g=13/8/0; b=6/14/0]. ACCTBK.

London, Royal Coburg: One hundred pounds for two weeks, plus one-third a benefit. (27–31xiiR3). ACCTBK, V&A bills.

1820

London, Royal Coburg (con't.): (1iR3), (3–8iHR), (10iHR, SN*) [g=139/11/6; b=46/10/0]. ACCTBK, V&A bills.

Dover: (17iGI) [g=5/17/0; b=1/12/4], (19iOT) [g=3/18/0; b=1/6/0], (21iHA) [g=4/8/0; b=1/8/4], (22iOC) [g=5/6/8; b=2/13/4]. ACCTBK.

Royal Coburg: (25–29iBU). Booth listed his share as £40. ACCTBK, V&A bills.

NOTE: A page is torn out of the ACCTBK at this point, but no engagements seem to be missing.

Aberdeen: Ten pounds per performance. (8iiiR3) [g=39/6/0], (9iiiHA) [g=26/18/0], (10iiiGI) [g=49/2/6], (12iiiBR) [g=32/0/0], (13iiiOT) [g=20/9/0], (15iiiRG) [g=46/12/0], (17iiiMC) [g=30/16/6], (18iiiOC, SN) [g=54/10/0]. ACCTBK.

Royal Coburg: (3–8ivUK in *The Crusaders*). Booth listed his share for five nights as 8/6/0. ACCTBK.

Covent Garden: Terms of £20 per night. (13ivLE), (17ivLE), (19ivLE). ACCTBK, BL, GC bills, *London Times*.

Royal Coburg: Ten pounds per night, plus a benefit. (24–29ivFA), (1–6vFA), (8–10vFA), (11–13vHR), (16vFA), (17vHR), (18vFA), (19–20vHR), (22–23vHR), (29vFA, one scene only*) [g=82/15/0; b=29/15/0]. ACCTBK, V&A bills.

Norwich: Sharing after £20 and half a benefit. (19viR3) [g=22/15/0;

b=1/7/6], (20viLE) [g=21/1/6; b=0/10/9], (21viGI) [g=13/0/0; b=0/0/0], (22viOC) [g=12/16/0; b=0/0/0], (24viFA, SN*) [g=32/15/0; b=16/7/6]. ACCTBK.

Rochester: Sharing after £15, plus half a benefit. (6viiR3), (8viiOC), (10viiGI), (11viiLE*) [g=21/7/0; b=10/13/6]. ACCTBK.

Maidstone: One-third of the receipts. (12viiLE) [g=17/6/0; b=5/15/10]. ACCTBK.

Cheltenham: (25viiRG), (26viiR3), (27viiGI), (28viiOC). ACCTBK. Booth listed neither grosses nor shares.

Gloucester: (31viiR3). ACCTBK. Booth listed no figures.

Cheltenham: (1viiiRG) [b=20/0/0]. ACCTBK.

Ludlow: (2viiiOC) [g=6/12/0; b=1/13/0], (3viiiBE) [g=5/12/0; b=1/10/4], (4viiiR3) [g=8/14/5; b=2/3/4], (5viiiGI, SN*) [g=10/12/6; b=5/6/3]. ACCTBK.

Drury Lane: Twenty pounds per night (with Kean). (15viiiRC) [g=392/10/0], (16viiiPI) [g=261/17/6], (19viiiIG) [g=368/10/6], (21viiiED) [g=260/4/6], (22viiiRC) [g=236/11/0], (28viiiIG) [g=352/16/6], (30viiiED) [g=215/4/0], (6ixIG) [g=281/16/5]. ACCTBK, BL bills, *London Times*.

Reading: (5xR3) [g=12/0/0], (6xOC) [g=8/17/0], (7xGI), (9xLE, SN) [g=23/0/0]. ACCTBK.

Surrey: (10xYN) [b=12/0/0]. ACCTBK.

Weymouth: Sharing after £10; half a benefit. (12xR3) [g=14/3/6; b=2/1/9], (13xHA) [g=8/16/0; b=0/0/0], (14xOC, SN*) [g=20/0/0; b=10/0/0]. ACCTBK, BL bills.

Plymouth: Terms not recorded; half a benefit. (16xR3) [g=23/16/6; b=0/0/0], (17xHA) [g=17/19/0; b=0/0/0], (18xOC) [g=12/1/0; b=20/0/0, "insured"], (20xLE, SN*) [g=53/16/0; b=26/18/0]. ACCTBK.

Dock: (21xGI) [g=17/17/0; b=0/0/0]. ACCTBK.

Drury Lane: (8xiIG) [g=175/13/6], (13xiIG) [g=145/2/6], (15xiLE) [g=126/1/6], (16xiDU) [g=85/17/0], (17xiLE) [g=53/13/6], (27xiPZ) [g=258/12/6], (4xiiOR) [g=239/9/0], (6xiiOR) [g=84/1/8], (12xiiCA) [g=69/9/6], (15xiiOP) [g=101/1/6], (16xiiOP) [g=100/4/0], (18xiiOR) [g=254/0/0], (19xiiOP) [g=101/1/7], (21xiiOR) [g=161/4/0], (26xiiDM) [g=245/19/0], (27xiiOR) [g=188/1/2]. Booth listed only his salary as follows: 4 Nov. (for three nights) 6/0/0; 11 Nov. (for three nights) 10/0/0; 18 Nov. (for six nights) 12/0/0; 25 Nov. (for six nights) 12/0/0; 2 Dec. (for six nights) 12/0/0; 9 Dec. 12/0/0; 16 Dec. 12/0/0; 23 Dec. 12/0/0; 30 Dec. 10/0/0.

1821

Drury Lane (con't.): (8–9iDZ), (11–12iDZ), (15iOR). GC bills. Booth again listed his salary as follows: 6 Jan. 12/0/0; 13 Jan. 12/0/0; then he inserted "Closed with Elliston by Agreem[en]t on above Date. Engt. pending with Glossop from Easter Monday till 'I don't know when' nor does he. Penalty £200." ACCTBK.

Richmond, Virginia: (6viiR3) [g=$242.25; b=0], (7viiEM) [g=343.00; b=46.50], (11viiLE*) [g=581.00; b=290.50], (13viiR3) [g=286.50; b=0], (14viiOC) [g=102.25; b=0], (16viiBR) [g=191.75; b=0], (18viiGI) [g=386.75; b=33.62], (20viiBE, SN) [g=437.25; b=252.62]. ACCTBK, Ball, Shockley.

Petersburg, Virginia: (23viiR3) [g=303.00; b=101.00], (8viiiGI) [g=170.00; b=100.00], (10viiiOC, SN*) [g=115.00; b=0], (13viiiOT) [g=390.00; b=100.00]. ACCTBK.

Richmond: Ninety dollars per night. (10ixR3) [g=420.00], (12ixMC) [g=361.00], (24ixRG) [g=350.00]. ACCTBK.

New York City: Ninety dollars per night. (5xR3) [g=1,150.00], (6xOC) [g=560.00], (8xBR) [g=760.00], (10xLE) [g=780.00], (12xR3) [g=560.00], (13xOT) [g=600.00], (15xHA) [g=1,123.00]. ACCTBK, Odell.

Baltimore, Maryland: (1xiR3) [g=383.00; b=66.50], (2xiEM) [g=315.25; b=32.57], (3xiOT) [g=303.50; b=26.50], (5xiLE) [g=360.25; b=55.12], (6xiRG) [g=194.00; b=0], (7xiOC) [g=525.25; b=225.25]. ACCTBK, *Baltimore American,* James.

Norfolk, Virginia: (10xiR3) [g=217.00; b=67.00], (12xiGI) [g=153.00; b=67.00], (13xiEM) [g=118.00; b=66.00]. ACCTBK.

Charleston, South Carolina: Ninety dollars per night. (29xiR3) [g=469.00], (30xiOC) [g=202.00], (3xiiLE) [g=550.00], (5xiiGI) [g=660.00], (7xiiHA) [g=869.00], (10xiiR3) [g=200.00], (11xiiRG, SN) [g=700.00]. ACCTBK, *Charleston Courier,* Hoole.

1822

New Orleans, Louisiana: Ninety dollars per night. (11iR3) [g=685.00], (12iGI) [g=276.50], (14iBR) [g=265.00], (16iLE) [g=200.00], (18iGI) [g=964?], (19iSH) [g=308.00], (21iRO) [g=256.50], (23iEM) [g=350.25], (25iOS, SN) [g=700.75]. ACCTBK, Kendall, Ludlow, Morrow.

Charleston: Ninety dollars per night. (22iiR3) [g=200.00], (23iiEM) [g=160.00], (27iiSH) [g=380.00], (28iiOS) [g=650.00], (1iiiOT) [g=565.00]. ACCTBK, *Charleston Courier.*

Savannah, Georgia: Ninety dollars per night. (7iiiR3) [g=250.00], (9iiiGI) [g=160.00], (11iiiRG) [g=220.00], (13iiiLE, SN*) [g=485.00], (15iiiOT) [g=325.00], (19iiiBE) [g=200.00], (20iiiOC) [g=160.00]. ACCTBK, *Savannah Daily Republican.*

Augusta, Georgia: One-third of the receipts; half 2 and 3 April. (25iiiR3) [g=400.00; b=133.00], (26iiiEM) [g=196.00; b=65.00], (27iiiOT) [g=167.00; b=55.50], (28iiiRG) [g=199.00; b=66.00], (29iiiLE) [g=508.00; b=169.30], (1ivBE) [g=402.00; b=134.00], (2ivOC) [g=110.00; b=55.00], (3ivR3) [g=118.00; b=59.00], (4ivHA) [g=296.00; b=108.00]. ACCTBK.

Boston, Massachusetts: (6vR3) [g=454.00], (8vEM) [g=250.00], (9vLE) [g=280.00], (10vGI) [g=202.00], (13vOT) [g=296.00], (15vBR) [g=190.00], (16vRG) [g=231.00], (17vOC) [g=183.00], (20vHA, SN*) [g=illegible]. ACCTBK, *Boston Daily Advertiser,* Ireland, Odell.

Providence, Rhode Island: (22vR3) [g=180.00], (24vEM) [g=96.00], (27vBR) [g=124.00], (31vOT) [g=194.00], (3viHA, SN*) [g=350.00]. ACCTBK, *Providence Gazette*. Booth's account book ends with this engagement.

Washington, D.C.: (1viiiR3), (3viiiEM), (6viiiLE), (10viiiOC), (13viiiHA, SN*). DNI, *Washington Gazette,* James.

Baltimore: (21xR3) [g=237.00], (23xBE) [g=188.00], (25xLE) [g=123.00], (26xEM) [g=207.00], (28xOT) [g=147.00], (30xGI) [g=222.00], (1xiMC) [g=124.00], (2xiOC) [g=237.00], (4xiHA, SN*) [g=269.00]. A&CA, James.

Richmond: (15xiEM), (16xiR3), (18xiOT), (20xiHA), (22xiLE*). RE. (25xiRG), (26xiOC), (27xiPI), (28xiGI), (29xiBE), (30xiMC, SN), (2xii PN, MU), (4xiiLE), (6xiiJF, *Miss Tilden), (7xiiR3). *Richmond Daily Mercantile Advertiser,* Shockley.

1823

Philadelphia, Pennsylvania: Chestnut Street Theatre: (17iiR3), (19iiEM), (21iiGI). USG, James, Wemyss.

Philadelphia: Chestnut Street Theatre: (2ivLE), (4ivRG), (5ivOC), (7ivOS, SN*). HTC bills, USG, Ireland, James.

Washington, D.C.: Washington Theatre: (17viiR3), (19viiOT), (22viiRG), (24viiLE), (26viiGI*). DNI, HTC bills.

New York: Park Theatre: (3ixR3), (4ixEM), (5ixOS), (10ixRG), (11ixR3), (12ixGI), (17ixLE), (19ixPO, MU*). *New York Mirror,* Odell.

Boston: Boston Theatre: (24xiR3), (26xiEM), (27xiRG), (29xiOC), (1xiiLE, SN, R3 soliloquy*). *Boston Daily Advertiser,* Clapp.

New York: Park Theatre: (5xiiOS). Ireland.

Philadelphia: Chestnut Street Theatre: (17xiiR3), (19xiiEM), (20xiiGI), (22xiiLE), (24xiiOS), (26xiiBE), (29xiiRG*). HTC bills, NGLR, USG, PADA, Ball, Landau.

1824

Philadelphia: Chestnut Street Theatre: (7iHA, *Aid for the Greeks). FSL bills, PADA, Ireland.

Baltimore: New Theatre: (28iR3), (30iEM), (31iOC, SN), (2iiOT), (4iiRG), (6iiLE), (7iiR3), (9iiGI, MU*). A&CA.

Philadelphia: Chestnut Street Theatre: (16iiR3), (17iiOC, SN), (18iiSH), (19iiRG), (20iiZA), (24iiBR*). PADA.

New York: (24iiiR3), (26iiiGI), (29iiiPO), (30iiiBE), (31iiiRG), (1ivSE, SN*). BPL, *New York Evening Post,* Ball.

Philadelphia: Arch Street Theatre: (6ivSE), (7ivGI, *Burke). PADA, Ball.

Baltimore: Holliday Street Theatre: (30ivBE, postponed), (3vBE), (5vOS), (7vR3), (8vEM), (10vSN), (13vRG), (14vPE, MU*), (15vR3), (17vPE, *Mrs. Duff). A&CA.

New York: Park Theatre: (26vR3), (28vGI), (29vSE), (2viLE), (4viOT), (9viPE). *New York Evening Post,* Ball.

Baltimore: (22xPE, *Conway). A&CA.

Baltimore: (28xiLE, *Mrs. Duff). A&CA.

1825

Charleston: Charleston Theatre: (18iiiR3), (19iiiEM), (21iiiGI), (23iiiRG), (25iiiLE), (26iiiOT), (28iiiLE), (29iiiSH), (30iiiCG, MU*). *Charleston Courier,* Hoole.

Baltimore: (11ivOT, *Cooper), (15ivHA), (16ivGI), (18ivLE), (20ivEM), (22ivBR), (25iv: Act IV of PE, Act II of EM, Act V of BR, SN*). A&CA.

Albany, New York: Pearl Street Theatre: (21vR3), (23vGI), (24vRG), (28vEM), (1viHA), (3viPE), (6viMC), (8viST*), (15viLE), (17viSH), (20viOT), (24viBR). *Albany Argus,* Ball, Phelps.

London: Drury Lane Theatre: (8xBR), (13xR3), (17xOT). GC bills, *London Times.*

Liverpool: Theatre Royal: (19xEM), (20xOT), (21xGI), (24xR3), (25xLE), (26xRG, MU*). BL bills, Ball.

Brighton: (3xiR3), (4xiOT), (5xiLE*), (7xiGI, SN). *Brighton Herald, London Morning Post.*

Manchester: (26xiiGI), (27xiiOT), (28xiiUK in *Venice Preserved*), (29xii MC), (30xiiR3). BL bills, *Manchester Courier.*

Sheffield: (31xiiLE). HTC bills.

1826

Manchester: (4iUK). Either BE as advertised in the *Manchester Courier* or LE as listed in BL bills.

Sheffield: (9iR3), (10iUK), (11iOC, SN*). BL bills, *Sheffield Mercury.*

Exeter: (16iR3), (17iGI), (20iRG), (23iBE), (25iLE, SN*). RE. (27iEM), (28iPE). *Exeter Flying Post.*

Bristol: Theatre Royal: (6iiR3), (7iiGI), (9iiR3), (10iiBR, SN*). BL bills, *Bristol Gazette & Mercury.*

Dublin: Theatre Royal: (10iiiR3), (13iiiR3), (14iiiOT), (15iiiEM), (16 iiiGI), (18iiiRG, RD*). HTC bills, *Fremman's Journal.*

London: Royalty Theatre: (10ivR3). BL bills.

Amsterdam: German Theatre, Amstel Street: (11vHA), (18vOT), (22vSH), (29vMC*). Coffing mss., Amsterdam Theatre Museum.

London: Royal Coburg: (7viBE), (8viFA), (9viFA, SN*). HTC bills, *London Morning Chronicle.*

New York: Chatham Gardens: (16xR3), (18xHA), (20xEM), (23xMC), (25xOT), (27xBR), (30xR3), (1xiOC), (3xiRG), (6xiGI, SN*), (7xiRD unconfirmed), (8xiIG), (9xiRD), (10xiOR), (16–17xiRD), (20xiJL), (30 xiOC), (2xiiOT), (4xiiRD), (5xiiFZ2), (6xiiSN, *Maywood), (11xiiON), (12xiiBR), (14xiiRR), (16xiiJL), (19xiiRD), (20xiiLE*), (23xiiSN). *New York Evening Post,* Ball, Odell.

Albany: South Pearl Street Theatre: (26xiiGI), (28xiiR3), (30xiiSH). *Albany Argus,* Ball.

1827

Albany (con't.): (2iUK), (4iEM), (6iOT), (9iBR*). *Albany Argus,* Ball.

New York: Chatham Garden Theatre: (15–16iSY), (17iSY, *the author). BPL, *New York American,* Odell.

Philadelphia: Philadelphia (Chestnut Street) Theatre: (26iR3), (27iEM), (30iSH), (1iiOT), (6iiRG), (8iiPE), (14iiGI), (15iiHA), (16iiLE, DA), (17iiJA), (19iiHA). RE. (21iiOC), (23iiLE), (24iiR3), (26iiBR), (28 iiSY), (5iiiSY). HTC bills, PADA, Ball, Ireland.

Baltimore: Baltimore Theatre: (16vRG), (18vR3), (21vHA), (23vEM), (25vSH), (26vBR), (28vLE*). A&CA, May mss.

Philadelphia: Walnut Street Theatre: (6ixR3), (8ixEM), (19ixHA), (21 ixGI), (24ixLE), (26ixR3), (28ixSH), (1xPE), (3xRG, MU*), (5xON), (8xIG, *Hamblin). USG.

Nashville, Tennessee: New Theatre: (28xiBE), (29xiIG), (30xiRG, *Caldwell), (1xiiEM, *Caldwell). HTC bills.

Cincinnati, Ohio: (11xiiR3), (?xiiBE), (?xiiEM), (17xiiOT). Ophia Smith.

1828

New Orleans: American Theatre, Camp Street: (14iR3), (16iHA), (18iGI), (19iOT), (21iOS), (23iLE), (25iRG), (26iGI), (28iSY), (30iSH, SN*), (1iiEM, *asylum for orphaned boys). RE. (2iiR3), (4iiBE), (6iiBR), (8iiPE), (9iiMC*), (13iiEM: Acts III–V of LE, *Still), (19iiOSf), (21 iiOSf). FSL bills, HTC bills, Kendall, Morrow, Smither.

New York: Park Theatre: (13vOT, DA). *New York Evening Post.*

New York: Park Theatre: (5viSH, *Mrs. Hill), (17viR3), (19viRG), (20viJA: IV of *Venice Preserved,* *Simpson), (21viGI), (23viSN, *Miss Kelly), (24viGI), (26viR3), (28viPE), (1viiJA, *Mrs. Duff), (2viiMC, MU*),

(3viiGI), (4viiRG, *Rees). BPL, HTC bills, *New York Evening Post,* Ireland, Odell.

Boston: Tremont Theatre as manager: (15ixR3), (23ixGI), (1xR3), (3xBR), (7xLE*), (13xIG). *Boston Daily Advertiser,* Ball.

New York: Bowery Theatre: (15xR3), (16xIG), (17xOT*). HTC bills, *New York Evening Post,* Odell, Shank.

Boston: Tremont Theatre as manager: (20xJA), (22xEM), (24xBE), (27 xCA, *Hamblin), (28xGI), (29xPE), (30xR3, *Clarke), (31xOS). *Boston Daily Advertiser,* Ball, Ireland, Landau.

New York: Bowery Theatre: (3xiGI), (5xiLE), (7xiR3). *New York Evening Post,* Odell, Shank.

Cincinnati: Cincinnati Theatre: (13xiiR3), (15xiiEM), (17xiiLE), (20xii GI*). *Cincinnati Gazette.*

1829

New Orleans: American Theatre, Camp Street: (7iR3), (9iHA), (10iGI), (12iSH), (14iMC), (16iST), (17iLE), (19iOT*), (20iRG), (22iPI), (24 iOC, *Catholic Association of Ireland). *L'Abeille,* Kendall, Morrow, Smither.

Natchez, Mississippi: (29iR3), (30iEM), (31iSH), (2iiOT), (3iiST), (5 iiRG), (7iiGI), (9iiHA), (12iiUK), (13iiR3*). Free.

New Orleans: American Theatre, Camp Street: (19iiR3), (21iiEM), (23 iiBR), (25iiBE), (26–28iiMA), (3iiiOS, SN*), (6iiiIG), (7iiiST), (9iiiJA), (12iiiUK in *Pizarro*), (14iiiOT, DA), (17iiiOT), (18iiiGL, *Mrs. Sloman), (24iiiGL), (26iiiON), (27iiiUK in *The Gamester*), (30iiiCA, *Cooper), (4ivLD, *Mrs. Sloman), (7ivFO: Acts IV–V of RC), (11ivFO), (14 ivEM), (15ivIG), (16ivST), (20ivED), (27ivPZ), (1vPI*), (4vKH), (5 vMA), (7vDR), (9vBE), (12vPN). HTC bills, *L'Abeille,* Dorman, Kendall, Smither.

New York: American Opera House, Chatham Street: (15viR3, *Mrs. Cowell). *New York Evening Post,* Odell.

Boston: Tremont Theatre: (22viR3), (24viPE), (25viST, *Mrs. Duff), (26 viGI), (29viOS*). *Boston Daily Advertiser,* Ball, Ireland.

Albany: Albany Theatre, South Pearl Street: (2viiR3), (6viiGI). *Albany Argus*, Phelps.

Philadelphia: Walnut Street Theatre: (23ixR3), (24ixEM), (25ixGI*), (26 ixPI), (29ixHA), (1xRG*). USG, Ball.

Boston: Tremont Theatre: (23xiR3), (26xiHA*), (30xiLE), (2xiiPE), (4 xiiR2), (7xiiLD, MU, broke down in Act III of LD). HTC bills, *Boston Daily Advertiser,* Ireland, Willard.

Philadelphia: Chestnut Street Theatre: (29xiiUK), (31xiiEM). HTC bills, USG, Ball.

1830

Philadelphia (con't.): (1iLE), (2iRG), (4iGI, DA), (13iR2), (15–16iST), (18iR3), (19iSH), (20iJA, SN*). HTC bills, USG, Ball.

Boston: Tremont Theatre: (25iHA), (27iMC), (29iR3), (1iiIG), (2iiST), (3iiKJ), (4iiRG), (5iiPI). *Boston Daily Advertiser, Providence Journal,* Ireland.

New York: Park Theatre: (9iiKJ, *Mme Celeste). *New York Post,* Odell.

Philadelphia: Chestnut Street Theatre: (10iiIG). USG.

Philadelphia: Washington Amphitheatre: (12iiR3), (13iiST), (15iiYN), (17 iiIG), (18iiJA). USG.

Philadelphia: Chestnut Street Theatre: (20iiGI), (23iiCA), (25iiPE), (27 iiCA), (1iiiOT*), (3iii: Act III of HA, Act V of BR, Act IV of *Damon and Pythias*), USG.

Philadelphia: Arch Street Theatre: (5iiiR3). USG.

Philadelphia: Walnut Street Theatre: (22iiiKJ). USG.

Washington, D.C.: Brown's Amphitheatre: (5ivR3), (7ivPE), (9ivSH*), (10ivST, *Mrs. Barnes). DNI.

Baltimore: Holliday Street Theatre: (21ivKJ), (23ivR3), (24ivGI), (26 ivBR), (28ivGI, RD*). A&CA, HTC bills. May mss.

Philadelphia: Walnut Street Theatre: (22vLE, JL, *Mrs. Flynn). HTC bills, USG.

New York: Park Theatre: (24vR3), (26vPI), (28vGI). *New York Post,* Odell.

Philadelphia: Walnut Street Theatre: (29vBE). HTC bills, USG.

New York: Park Theatre: (31vIG). *New York Post,* Hone, Odell.

Philadelphia: Walnut Street Theatre: (1viGI), (4viOC*), (23viLE, *Mrs. Duff), (26viR3), (28viEM), (30viPE), (2viiSE), (7viiPI, *Flynn). HTC bills, USG, Ireland.

New York: Bowery Theatre: (31viiiR3), (2ixGI), (4ixLE*). *New York Post,* Odell.

Baltimore: Holliday Street Theatre as manager: (11ixRG), (15ixR3), (17 ixBE), (20ixOS), (21ixOC), (22ixGI), (30ixR3), (2xR3), (5xIG), (6xOS, JL), (7xLU*). A&CA, HTC bills.

Philadelphia: Arch Street Theatre: (8xR3), (9xGI), (11xBR). USG, Webb.

Baltimore: Adelphi Theatre: (12xEM). A&CA.

Philadelphia: Arch Street Theatre: (13xHA), (15xKJ), (18xCA), (20xOT, SN*). USG, Webb.

Baltimore: Adelphi Theatre: (22xSN), (23xJA), (29xA2), (9xiLE, *Mrs. Flynn), (16xiJA), (17xiOT), (18xiSN, *Warren), (20xiSH), (22xi: Act III of OT, Act III of R3*). A&CA.

Philadelphia: Chestnut Street Theatre: (3xiiR3), (4xiiHA), (7xiiOS), (9 xiiSH), (11xiiEM*). RE. (14xiiSR), (16xiiSR) (18xiiSR), (20xiiIG), (21 xiiBE*), (23xiiLE, *Mrs. Flynn). HTC bills, USG, James.

1831

Richmond: Richmond Theatre: (3iR3), (5iGI), (7iSH), (10iHA), (11iBR), (12iRG), (13iR3), (14iEM), (15iST), (17iEM, SN*). Shockley.

Richmond: Richmond Theatre: (31iR3), (2iiST), (3iiPE), (4iiLE). Shockley.

Washington, D.C.: Washington Theatre: (15iiR3), (16iiGI), (17iiHA), (18 iiEM), (19iiIG). DNI.

Boston: Tremont Theatre: (13ivR3), (15ivGI), (18ivHA), (20ivPN), (22 ivLU), (25ivSR*). *Boston Daily Advertiser,* Ball.

New York: Bowery Theatre: (27ivR3), (28ivIG), (30ivR3), (2vJA*), (4 vKJ), (5vIG), (7vGI), (9v: Act IV of SH, Act III of HA*). *New York Evening Post.*

Philadelphia: Walnut Street Theatre: (11vGI), (12vHA), (13vEM), (14vR3), (16vOT*). RE. (17vOC), (18vSH). RE. (19vKJ), (20vJA), (21v: Act III of HA, Act IV of CA, JL, *Hamblin). HTC bills, NGLR, PADA.

New York: Bowery Theatre: (13viR3), (14viHA), (16viCA), (18viR3), (20viPW, SN), (22viGL), (24vi: Acts III & IV of ON, Act III of OT, scenes from MW*), (25viGL), (27vi: Act V of GI, Acts IV & V of JA, *Cooper), (29viPE), (30viST), (2viiGL), (6viiKJ, *Mrs. Duff), (7vii: Act III of LE, JL, *Mrs. Hamblin). *New York Evening Post,* Odell.

Philadelphia: Walnut Street Theatre: (8viiHO), (11viiCA), (13viiGL), (15 viiHO), (18viiOT), (19viiR3), (22vii: Act V of GI, MU, *Cooper), (26viiCA, *Hamblin), (28viiGL, *Pratt), (29viiOT, *Rowbotham), (30 viiJL, *Maywood). HTC bills, NGLR, PADA, *Philadelphia Daily Chronicle,* Ireland.

New York: Bowery Theatre: (18viiiCA), (19viiiOT), (22viiiGL), (24viii ON), (26viii: Act IV of SH, SN), (27viiiGI), (29viiiR3), (31viiiGI), (2ixKJ), (3ix: Act III of LE*). *New York Evening Post,* Odell.

Philadelphia: Walnut Street Theatre: (24ixR3), (27ixOT), (29ixHA), (30 ixGI), (1xMC*), (3xR3, *Young at the Arch Street Theatre), (4xLE), (5xRO), (6xR3). PADA, James.

Baltimore: Holliday Street Theatre: (28xiR3), (1xiiGI), (3xiiKJ, SN*), (8xiiIG). A&CA, May mss.

1832

Philadelphia: Arch Street Theatre: (25iR2), (30iOK), (31iGI), (1iiPE), (3iiLU), (6iiSR*). RE. (8iiHA), (10iiEM), (13iiSY), (15iiSR), (17iiLE), (18iiJL), (20iiKJ, SN*). PADA, *Philadelphia Daily Chronicle,* Webb, Wemyss.

New York: American Theatre, Bowery: (22iiPE, Act V of R3). *New York Post,* Odell.

Philadelphia: Arch Street Theatre: (25iiCA, *Mrs. Rowbotham). PADA, *Philadelphia Daily Chronicle, Spirit of the Times.*

Philadelphia: Chestnut Street Theatre: (27iiHA). PADA.

Philadelphia: Arch Street Theater: (14iiiIG, *Wilson). PADA, Webb.

Philadelphia: Chestnut Street Theatre: (19iiiR3), (21iiiGI), (23iiiOT), (26 iiiR3, MU*). PADA, *Philadelphia Daily Chronicle,* Ball.

Washington, D.C.: Washington Theatre: (9ivGI), (11ivEM), (13ivMC), (14ivR3), (16ivLE*). DNI, HTC bills.

Philadelphia: Walnut Street Theatre: (26ivGI), (28ivR3), (30ivHA), (3 vOT), (5vMC*), (7vKJ), (8vGI), (9vBR, LU*). PADA, TX, *Philadelphia Daily Chronicle,* Ball.

Philadelphia: Walnut Street Theatre: (29viGI), (30viR3), (3viiLE), (5 viiLU), (6viiCA, LU*). PADA, TX, *Philadelphia Daily Chronicle.*

Philadelphia: Arch Street Theatre: (18xHA), (20xR3), (22xST), (24xKJ), (26xGI*), (27xON, *Mrs. Warren). PADA, *Philadelphia Daily Chronicle,* Odell, Warren, Webb.

New York: American Theatre, Bowery: (14xiON, *Miss Vincent), (15xiIG, *Stevenson), (19xiR3), (21xiGI), (23xiLE), (26xiR3), (29xiOK), (1xii GI), (3xiiR3), (5xiiOK, SN*), (6xiiMW, *Wilson), (7xiiLE). *New York Evening Post,* Odell.

Boston: Tremont Theatre: (10xiiR3), (12xiiGI, DA), (14xiiLE), (17xiiGI), (19xiiRG), (21xiiKJ). *Boston Morning Post.*

New York: Bowery Theatre: Terms of $120 per week. (24xiiJA), (25xiiUK), (27xiiJA), (31xii: Acts I–III of RO, Act V of GI, *Miss Vincent). *New York Evening Post,* Odell.

1833

New York (con't.): (4iHA), (5iCA), (7iPE, LU*), (8i: Act II of EM, Act III of R3), (10iR3 with Bowery Company at Richmond Hill Theatre), (12iGI), (14iPE). *New York Evening Post,* Odell.

Baltimore: Holliday Street Theatre: (21iR3), (23iPE), (25iR3, *Miss Vincent), (28iMC), (30iLE*). A&CA, May mss.

Philadelphia: Walnut Street Theatre: (28iiiR3), (30iiiPE), (1ivIG), (4iv HA), (6ivLE), (8ivCA, *Hamblin), (11ivGL), (13ivPE, *Miss Vincent). USG, James.

New York: Bowery Theatre: (15ivR3). *New York Evening Post.*

New York: Bowery Theatre: (13xiR3), (15xiIG, DA, according to Kimmel), (18xiR3), (21xiCA), (23xiIG*), (25xiR3). *New York Post,* Odell.

NOTE: Booth alternated between New York and Philadelphia in mid-November 1833; the previous engagement and the next overlap.

Philadelphia: Arch Street Theatre: (16xiBR), (19xiSH), (20xiHA), (22 xiRG). USG, Webb.

Pittsburgh, Pennsylvania: (9xiiR3), (10xiiRG), (11xiiGI), (12xiiHA), (13 xiiCA), (14xiiPE), (15xiiCA, JL*). *Pittsburgh Advocate & Adviser.*

Cincinnati: Third Street Theatre: (25xiiHA), (26xiiUK), (27xiiEM), (28 xiiPE), (30xiiLE), (31xiiRG, *Joe Cowell). *Cincinnati Gazette,* Langworthy.

1834

Cincinnati (con't.): (2iUK*), (4iR3, *Joe Cowell). *Cincinnati Gazette,* Langworthy.

Louisville, Kentucky: (16iOT), (17iRG), (18iBR), (20iEM), (21iLE), (25 iHA, *Mrs. Cowell), (29iPE, *Old). *Louisville Herald,* Weisert.

Pittsburgh: (27iiPE). HTC bills.

Philadelphia: Walnut Street Theatre: (5ivR3, *Duffy), (7ivR3), (9ivGI), (11ivHA), (14ivLE), (16ivEM), (18ivR3*). USG, James, Webb.

New York: Bowery Theatre: (21ivR3), (23ivGI), (25ivR3), (28ivCA), (30 ivKJ), (2vLE), (6vCA), (8vGI), (10vR3), (13vMC), (15vOK, SN*). *New York Evening Post,* Shank.

Albany: Albany Theatre: (19vR3), (22vIG), (23vBE), (24vPE, JL*). *Albany Argus.*

New York: Bowery Theatre: (28vPE, JL). *New York Post,* Shank.

New York: Bowery Theatre: (8xR3), (9xIG), (10xR3), (13xCA), (15xGI*), (17xCA). *New York Post,* Odell, Shank.

Boston: Tremont Street Theatre: (21xR3), (23xGI), (24xBR), (25xPE), (27xPE), (28xR3), (30xEM), (3xiLE, MU*). *Boston Daily Evening Transcript.*

Boston: Warren Theatre: (7xiR3), (10xiCA), (11xiST), (12xiBE), (13xiCA), (14xiIG), (17xiSH, JL*), (18xiR3). *Boston Daily Evening Transcript.*

Richmond: Richmond Theatre: (5xiiEM). Shockley.

1835

Baltimore: (13iiMC). A&CA.

Philadelphia: Walnut Street Theatre: (19iiGI), (20iiPE), (21iiR3), (23iiST), (24iiHA*). HTC bills, USG.

Baltimore: Holliday Street Theatre: (27iiHA). A&CA.

Philadelphia: Walnut Street Theatre: (17iiiJA), (18iiiCA), (19iiiKJ*), (20 iiiPE, *Miss Meadow), (21iiiR3). USG, Ireland, Wilson.

Baltimore: Holliday Street Theatre: (7ivOC), (8ivEM), (9ivST), (10ivSH*), (11ivOT, *Mrs. Hamblin). A&CA.

Philadelphia: Walnut Street Theatre: (26viR3, *Jackson), (27viEM, *Rowbotham), (2viiRG*), (3viiOT, *Pratt). USG.

NOTE: Booth played both the Walnut Street and the Chestnut Street theatres during this engagement.

Philadelphia: Chestnut Street Theatre: (29viGI), (30viHA), (1viiLE), (4 viiR3). USG, Wilson.
New York: Bowery Theatre: (9viiR3), (11viiGI), (13viiR3*). *New York Evening Post,* Ball, Odell.
Philadelphia: Walnut Street Theatre: (22viiiR3), (24viiiGI), (25viiiHA), (26viiiBR*), (27viiiR3), (29viiiIG), (31viiiED), (1ixCA, SN*). USG, Ball, Wilson.
New York: Bowery Theatre: (3xiR3), (5xiGI), (7xiR3), (9xiIG), (14xiGI), (18xiOC), (21xiR3), (23xiIG, SN*), (24xiCA), (25xiGI). *New York Evening Post,* Hone, Odell.
Philadelphia: Walnut Street Theatre: (26xiGI*), (28xiGI). USG, *New York Mirror,* Ball.
New York: Bowery Theatre: (14xiiR3), (16xiiPE), (19xiiR3), (21xiiLE*), (23xiiCA, *Willard). *New York Evening Post,* Shank.
Washington, D.C.: American Theatre: (28xiiHA), (29xiiOT), (30xiiGI), (31xiiEM). DNI, *Washington Globe,* Wemyss.

1836

Washington, D.C. (con't.): (1iR3), (2iPE*). DNI, *Washington Globe,* Wemyss.
Philadelphia: Walnut Street Theatre: (11iR3), (12iHA), (13iGI), (14iEM), (15iPE), (16iR3), (18iR3), (19iOC), (20iIG). USG, Ball, Wemyss.
Washington, D.C.: National Theatre: (12iiR3), (13iiIG), (15iiGI*), (25 iiR3), (26iiSH), (27iiEM), (29iiLE), (2iiiRG, JL*). DNI, *Spirit of the Times, Washington Globe,* Wemyss.
Providence: Lion Theatre: (12vIG), (13vUK). *Providence Journal.*
Boston: Lion Theatre: (16vGI), (17vOT), (18vR3), (19vEM), (20vR3), (23vPE, MU*). *Boston Daily Evening Transcript,* Ball.
Providence: Lion Theatre: (25vR3), (26vGI). *Providence Journal.*
Philadelphia: Walnut Street Theatre: (30vHA), (31vGI), (1viPE), (2viLE), (3viR3), (4viOT, SN*). RE. (6viEM), (7viHA), (8viCA), (9viR3, *Deaf Burke), (10viSH), (11viIG, SN*). USG, *Pennsylvania Inquirer,* Wilson.
New York: National Theatre: (29viiiSH), (30viiiR3), (31viiiPI), (3ixR3). *New York Herald,* Odell.
Philadelphia: Walnut Street Theatre: (6ixST), (7ixHA), (9ixR3), (10ixMC), (12ixGI*), (13ixR3), (14ixPE), (15ixMC*). USG, Wemyss.
Boston: National Theatre: (19ixR3), (20ixPE), (21ixGI), (22ixSH), (23 ixMC). RE. (26ixIG), (28ixCA), (29ixHA), (3xLE, MU*). *Boston Daily Evening Transcript.*
Albany: (10xR3), (11xMC), (12xGI*). *Albany Argus,* Leech.
New York: Franklin Theatre, Chatham Square: (13xGI), (14xIG), (15xR3). *New York Herald,* Ball, Odell.
Philadelphia: American Theatre, Walnut Street: (18xIG), (19xPI). USG.

London: Drury Lane: (21xiR3), (25xiIG). GC bills, *London Sun, London Times.*

London: Royal Surrey Theatre: (5xiiR3), (6xiiEM, *Davidge), (7xiiHA), (8xiiR3), (12xiiMC), (13xiiST, *Mrs. R. Honner), (16xiiEM), (21xiiST), (22xiiR3). BL bills, *London Morning Herald.*

Birmingham, England: Theatre Royal: (26xiiR3, DA), (27xiiOT), (29 xiiHA), (30xiiGI), (31xiiR3). BL bills.

1837

Birmingham (con't.): (2iEM), (3iLE*). BL bills.

London: Royal Surrey Theatre: (13iiPI), (13iiiIG), (14iiiPI), (16iiiBE), (17iiiOT). BL, HTC bills.

New York: Bowery Theatre: (4viiR3) [g=200.00]. *New York Herald,* Odell.

Philadelphia: Walnut Street Theatre: (19viiIG), (20viiPI), (21viiCA), (22 viiLE, JL*). USG.

Boston: Tremont Theatre: (21viiiR3), (22viiiIG), (23viiiPE), (24viiiCA), (25viiiLE). *Boston Transcript.*

New York: Bowery Theatre: (28viiiR3), (29viiiMC), (30viiiGI), (31viiiLE), (1ixIG*), (2ixR3, *Hield). *New York Herald,* Odell.

New York: Bowery Theatre: (11xR3), (12xPE), (13xLE), (14xIG, JL). *New York Morning Herald, Spirit of the Times.*

Philadelphia: Walnut Street Theatre: (15xiHA), (16xiR3), (17xiGI), (18 xiMC). USG, Wemyss, Wood.

New York: Olympic Theatre: (22xiST), (23xiPI), (24–25xiR3), (27xiGI*). *New York Herald,* Odell.

Philadelphia: American Theatre, Walnut Street: (11xiiR3), (12xiiPE), (13 xiiOT), (14xiiLE), (15xiiR3), (16xiiLU, JL*). USG, Wemyss.

Baltimore: Holliday Street Theatre: (27xiiIG), (28xiiCA), (29xiiEM, *Vandenhoff), (30xiiR3, JL*). A&CA, May mss., *Baltimore Sun.*

1838

Washington, D.C.: National Theatre: (16iR3), (17iEM), (18iGI), (19iR3), (20:LE*). DNI, *Baltimore Sun,* Ball.

Richmond: Richmond Theatre: (23iR3), (24iGI), (25iEM), (26iLE, SN), (27iIG), (29iPI, LU), (30iPE, *Taylor). *Richmond Whig,* Shockley.

Washington, D.C.: (6iiBR, *Ward). DNI, Mudd.

Baltimore: Holliday Street Theatre: (7iiGI), (8iiBR), (9iiHA), (10iiKJ*). A&CA, May mss., *Baltimore Sun.*

Philadelphia: American Theatre, Walnut Street: (15iiR3), (16iiLU), (17 iiPE, SN*). *Philadelphia Pennsylvanian, Philadelphia Public Ledger.*

New York: National Theatre: (20iiR3), (22iiGI), (23iiOT), (24iiR3*), (2iiiIG). *New York Herald,* Odell.

Charleston: New Theatre: (19iiiGI), (20iiiR3), (21iiiIG), (22iiiLE), (23 iiiEM, JL, *Flynn), (24iiiSH), (27iiiLE), (28iiiR3), (29iiiCA, JL). *Charleston Courier, Spirit of the Times,* Hoole.

Richmond: (23ivOC, JL*). *Richmond Whig,* Shockley.

Baltimore: Holliday Street Theatre: (1vPE, DA, *Ward), (15vBE), (16vST), (17vR3*), (24vMC, *Lewellen), (12viPE, *Miss Monier). A&CA, *Baltimore Sun*.

Philadelphia: Walnut Street Theatre: (7viiIG), (9viiLE), (10viiGI), (11 viiPE), (12viiCA), (13viiPI), (14viiR3, SN*) [g=475.75]. *Philadelphia Public Ledger,* Wemyss.

New York: Franklin Theatre on 25 Aug., as R3, thereafter the Olympic Theatre: (27viiiR3), (29viiiGI), (30viiiOT), (1ixHA), (3ixSH), (6ixOT), (7ixBR), (8ixPE, *Flynn). *New York Herald,* Odell.

Philadelphia: Chestnut Street Theatre: (10ixR3), (11ixGI), (12ixOT), (13 ixLE), (14ixHA*). HTC bills, PC bills, USG.

Albany: Albany Theatre: (18ixR3), (19ixHA), (20ixIG*). *Albany Argus.*

New York: Olympic Theatre: (6xEM). *New York Courier and Enquirer.*

Pittsburgh: (22xR3), (23xHA), (24xLE), (25xGI), (26xRG). *Pittsburgh Advocate and Advertiser.*

Louisville: (19xiUK for the week, according to Weisert), (30xiKJ), (1xiiUK in *Venice Preserved*), (17xiiMC*). Weisert.

Nashville: (22xiiGI), (24xiiHA), (25xiiEM), (26xiiR3), (27xiiOC), (28 xiiPI), (31xiiGI). *Republican Banner,* Carson, Hunt, Langworthy.

1839

Nashville (con't.): (1iR3). *Republican Banner,* Carson, Hunt, Langworthy.

Vicksburg, Mississippi: (17iR3) [g=658.00], (18iGI), (21iPE*) [g=611.00], (22iEM) [g=268.00], (23iST), (24iMC*) [g=2,112.00]. HTC bills, *Vicksburg Daily Whig,* Free, Orange.

Natchez: (26iHA), (28iR3) [b=137.50], (29iGI), (30iLE). *Mississippi Free Trader and Natchez Gazette,* Free, Gates.

New Orleans: Saint Charles Theatre: (5iiR3), (6iiGI), (7iiSH), (8iiOT), (9iiR3), (11iiLE*), (12iiHA), (14iiR3), (16iiBR, SN*). *New Orleans Picayune,* Gafford, Smither.

New Orleans: Camp Street Theatre: (20iiR3), (22iiGI), (25iiLE), (27iiR3), (28iiPE). *New Orleans Picayune.*

Mobile, Alabama: Government Street Theatre: Terms of $100 per night. (7iiiGI), (8iiiEM), (9iiiR3), (11iiiPE), (12iiiLE), (13iiiHA*), (14iiiPI), (15iiiPE), (16iiiEM). *Mobile Register,* Bailey, Dorman, Ludlow.

New Orleans: American Theatre, Camp Street: (20iiiR3), (22iiiGI), (25 iiiLE), (27iiiR3), (28iiiPE, MU*). HTC bills, *New Orleans Picayune,* Smither.

Natchez: (11ivR3), (13ivLE), (18ivEM). *Mississippi Free Trader and Natchez Gazette,* Gates.

Jackson, Mississippi: (17ivR3), (19ivPE). Gates, McCain, McKee.

Louisville: City Theatre: (3vGI), (4vBE), (6v, scenes from HA, PE, ST, R3). Weisert.

New York: Franklin Theatre, Chatham Square: (19viGI), (20viR3), (21 viHA*). *New York Herald.*

Philadelphia: American Theatre, Walnut Street: (21viEM, *Kensington Fire Company), (22viR3), (24viR3, SN), (25viLE), (26viIG), (27viSH), (28viHA), (29viGI, MU*). RE. (1viiHA), (2viiIG), (3viiPE), (4viiR3), (5viiEM), (6viiBR, JL*). *Philadelphia Public Ledger.*

Baltimore: Holliday Street Theatre: (15viiHA), (16viiR3), (17viiLE), (18 viiBR*). RE. (19viiHA), (20viiR3), (22viiPE), (23viiR3, SN*). A&CA, *Baltimore Sun.*

Baltimore: Holliday Street Theatre: (22xR3), (23xIG, *Jackson), (24xGI), (25xHA*), (26xOC, *JBB2, who appeared as Diggory). *Baltimore Sun.*

1840

New York: New Chatham Theatre: (1iR3). *New York Morning Herald,* Ireland, Odell.

Baltimore: American Amphitheatre, Front Street: (24iOC), (25iGI), (27 iR3), (28iEM*), (29–30i: Act V, Scene vii, of R3), (31iOC, *the poor), (1iiIG), (3iiIG), (4iiBR), (5iiOC, SN*). *Baltimore Sun.*

Washington, D.C.: National Theatre: (10iiR3), (11iiIG), (12iiR3), (13iiLE, SN*). DNI, Mudd.

Baltimore: Baltimore Museum: (2iiiHA), (3iiiOC), (4iiiBR). *Baltimore Sun.*

Philadelphia: Walnut Street Theatre: (12iiiR3), (13iiiHA), (16iiiR3, DA), (17iiiIG). DNI, Wemyss.

New York: Chatham Theatre: (24iiiR3), (25iiiGI), (26iiiR3), (27iiiGI), (30iiiIG, SN), (31iiiPE, MU). *New York Herald,* Odell.

Providence: Providence Theatre: (2ivR3), (3ivIG), (6ivGI), (7ivEM), (8 ivGI*), (9ivR3), (19ivLE). *Providence Journal.*

Boston: National Theatre: (13ivR3), (14ivHA), (15ivGI, JL), (16ivIG), (17ivEM), (20ivLE), (21ivGI), (22ivPE), (23ivR3), (24ivRG, SN*). HTC bills, *Boston Post.*

Providence: Providence Theatre: (27ivLE), (28ivEM), (29ivGI), (30ivIG), (1vGI*). *Providence Journal.*

New York: New Chatham Theatre: (4vR3), (6vR3), (7vIG), (8vHA), (9v: scenes from LE, SH, R3, EM; JL*). *New York Herald.* Odell placed this engagement in the Olympic.

Philadelphia: Walnut Street Theatre: (15viHA), (16viGI), (17viR3), (18 viST), (19viPE), (20viOT, SN*). RE. (22viLE), (23viOS), (24viOK),

(25viR3), (26viON), (27vi: Act I of SH, Cavern Scene of PE, Act I of RL, JL*). USG, Wemyss.

New York: Chatham Theatre: (29viR3), (6viiEM), (7viiLE), (9viiGI), (19viiHA), (11viiR3, SN*), (13viiCA), (14viiOT), (15viiMC), (16vii OC), (17viiPI), (18vii: Act III of LE, Act II of EM, Act III of ON, JL*). *New York Herald,* Odell.

Baltimore: American Theatre, Front Street: (21ixGI), (22ixR3), (23ixPE), (24ixOC), (25ixHA), (26ixIG, SN*). *Baltimore Sun.*

New York: Chatham Theatre: (2xiGI), (3xiLE), (4xiEM), (5xiHA), (6 xiSH), (7xiR3, SN*), (9xiCA), (10xiR3, SN), (11xiOC), (12xiGI), (13xi: EM, Act II of OT, BE, and Act IV of ON*). *New York Herald,* Odell.

Philadelphia: Arch Street Theatre: (12xiiR3), (14xiiR3), (15xiiHA), (16 xiiGI), (17xiiRL), (18xiiHA), (19xiiR3, SN*), (25xiiR3). USG, Wilson.

NOTE: Booth played both the Arch Street and Walnut Street Theatres during this engagement.

Philadelphia: Walnut Street Theatre: (23xiiGI), (24xiiHA). USG.

1841

Washington, D.C.: National Theatre: (25iR3), (26iHA), (27iBE), (28 iLE*). DNI.

Philadelphia: Walnut Street Theatre: (3iiiGI), (4iiiHA), (5iiiOC), (6iii R3*). USG.

Baltimore: Front Street Theatre: (8iiiGI), (9iiiEM), (10iiiR3), (11iiiPE, *Sweeny), (12iiiR3), (13iiiBR*). *Baltimore Sun.*

Baltimore: Front Street Theatre: (1ivR3), (2ivOT, *William Wood, Jr.), (3ivSH). *Baltimore Sun, Spirit of the Times.*

Norfolk: Avon Theater: (12ivR3), (13ivSH), (14ivGI), (15ivEM), (17iv HA), (19ivPE, SN*), (20ivLE), (21ivBE), (22ivLE, SN, *Monier, postponed), (26ivPE, SN, *Monier). *American Beacon.*

New York: National Theatre: (11vHA), (12vR3). *New York Herald, Spirit of the Times,* Odell, Wemyss.

Boston: National Theatre: (18vGI), (19vR3, *Mrs. JBB2), (20vIG), (21 vR3, SN*). *Boston Post, Spirit of the Times.*

Boston: National Theatre: (8viLE, *JBB2). *Boston Post.*

St. John, New Brunswick: (17viHA). *St. John Evening News,* Leavitt.

New York: Chatham Theatre: (8viiGI), (9viiEM), (10viiR3), (12viiLE, SN*). *New York Herald.*

Baltimore: National Theatre: (26viiEM), (27viiR3), (28viiBE*). *Baltimore Sun.*

Philadelphia: Walnut Street Theatre: (11ixR3), (12ixLE), (14ixEM), (15 ixR3), (16ixIG). *Philadelphia Inquirer,* Wilson.

Baltimore: Front Street Theatre: (9xIG), (11xR3), (12xPI), (13xGL), (14xOC, SJ), (15xPE, JL), (16xON), (21xEM). *Baltimore Sun,* Wemyss.

1842

Philadelphia: Walnut Street Theatre: (30iiiR3), (1ivIG), (2ivHA), (4ivGI), (5ivLE), (6ivR3, JL*). *Dramatic Mirror, Philadelphia Public Ledger.*

Baltimore: American Theatre, Front Street: (12ivSH, *Texas Rangers), (14ivIG). *Baltimore Sun.*

Philadelphia: American Theatre, Walnut Street: (18ivR3), (19ivBE), (20ivMC), (21ivPE, *Master Marsden), (22ivSH, Act II of PE*), (23ivBE). *Philadelphia Public Ledger.*

Baltimore: Front Street Theatre: (13viLE), (14viBE), (15viIG), (16viR3), (18viHA, BR, SN*), (22viCA, *Weaver). *Baltimore Sun.*

New York: Bowery Theatre: (15viiiR3), (16viiiGI), (17viiiBE), (18viiiLE), (20viiiEM), (22viiiOC), (23viiiIG). *New York Herald,* Ball, Odell.

Baltimore: Front Street Theatre: (5ixEM, *Lennox), (12ixBE), (13ixR3), (14ixGI), (15ixOT), (16ixPE, JL*). *Baltimore Sun.*

New York: Chatham Theatre: (20ixGI), (21ixEM), (22ixR3), (24ixPE, SN, two acts of BE*). *New York Herald,* Odell.

Baltimore: Front Street Theatre: (10xR3, *Rice), (11xCA, *Ward). *Baltimore Sun.*

Philadelphia: Chestnut Street Theatre: (14xiR3), (15xiGI), (16xiLE), (17xiHA), (19xiR3, SN*). *Philadelphia Pennsylvanian,* Wilson.

Pittsburgh: (7xiiGI), (10xiiLE, JL*). *Pittsburgh Post,* Ball.

New York: Bowery Theatre: (22xiiR3), (23xiiIG). *New York Post,* Odell.

1843

Philadelphia: Walnut Street Theatre: (10iR3), (12iGI), (13iRG), (14iOC), (16iHA), (17iEM). *Philadelphia Pennsylvanian,* Wilson.

Boston: Marshall's Eagle Theatre: (23iGI), (24iIG), (25iBR), (26iHA), (27iR3*), (30iLE), (31iR3), (1iiBR), (2iiRG), (3iiEM, OC*). *Boston Post.*

Baltimore: Holliday Street Theatre: (16iiiR3), (20iiiHA), (21iiiBE, SN*). *Baltimore Sun.*

New York: Park Theatre: (3ivR3), (4ivLE), (5ivR3), (6ivBR, JL*), (8ivHA), (10ivR3), (11ivGI). *New York Herald,* Odell.

Philadelphia: Walnut Street Theatre: (12ivBR), (13ivMC), (14–15ivSE), (17ivSE), (18ivR3), (19ivLE, SN*), (20ivCA, *Wheatley). *New York Herald, Philadelphia Pennsylvanian.*

Boston: Tremont Street Theatre: Terms of one-third of five nights; half the sixth. (8vR3), (9vGI), (10vBR), (11vLE), (12vR3), (15vHA, JL*). RE. (16vMC), (17vPE), (18vR3), (19vEM, Trial Scene from SH*). *Boston Transcript.*

New York: Park Theatre: (24vR3), (25vGI), (26vR3), (27vEM), (29vPE), (30vR3), (31vPE), (1viPE, EM). HTC bills, *New York Herald,* Odell.
New York: Park Theatre: (16viR3), (17viGI), (19viPE), (20viR3), (21viRG, SH*). BPL, *New York Herald, Spirit of the Times,* Odell.
Philadelphia: American Theatre, Walnut Street: (12viiiBR), (13viiiMC), (14–15viiiSE), (17viiiSE), (18viiiR3), (19viiiLE, SN*), (20viiiCA, *Mr. Whatley). *Philadelphia Pennsylvanian.*
Philadelphia: Arch Street Theatre: (6ixR3), (7ixGI), (9ixEM), (13ixIG), (14ixCA), (15ixLE, *Miss Leforest), (18ixBR, SN*). *Philadelphia Public Ledger,* Wilson.
Baltimore: People's Theatre, Front Street: (29ixOC, *Mrs. Leforest), (30 ixPI), (2xR3), (4xR3), (25xBE). *Baltimore Sun.*
Baltimore: Holliday Street Theatre: (9xiCA). *Baltimore Sun.*
New York: Park Theatre: (11xiR3), (13xiCA), (14xiIG), (15xiR3), (16xiON), (17xiGI), (18xiIG), (20xiCA). *New York Herald,* Odell.
Philadelphia: Chestnut Street Theatre: (24xiR3). USG, Wilson.
Boston: National Theatre: (11xiiR3, broke down), (12xiiR3), (13xiiHA), (14xiiGI), (15xiiLE, SN*). RE. (18xiiR3), (19xiiRG, MU), (20xiiPE, JL), (21xiiST, one act of SH), (22xiiEM, OC*). HTC bills, *Boston Post.*

1844

New York: Park Theatre: (1iGI). *New York Herald,* Ball.
Philadelphia: Walnut Street Theatre: (17iGI), (18iHA), (19iST), (20iR3), (22iCA), (23iMC), (24iLE, JL*). RE. (25iR3), (26iOC), (27iPE), (29 iBR), (30iPE), (31iIG, SN*). RE. (1iiSH), (2iiEM), (3iiKJ, SN). USG, Princeton bills.
Charleston: New Charleston Theatre: (19iiGI), (20iiEM), (21iiR3), (22 iiPE), (23iiLE), (24iiHA, SN*). *Charleston Courier,* Hoole, Ketchum.
New York: Park Theatre: (11iiiR3), (12iiiGI), (13iiiPE), (14iiiRG), (15 iiiR3), (16iiiBE, SN*). *New York Herald, Spirit of the Times.*
New York: Olympic Theatre: (5iv: Act V of R3, *Mrs. JBB2). *New York Herald,* Odell.
Boston: National Theatre: (8ivR3), (9ivPE), (10ivGI), (11ivLU), (12ivLE, SN*). HTC bills, *Boston Transcript.*
New York: Park Theatre: (15ivR3), (16ivGI), (17ivPE), (18ivBR), (19ivR3), (20ivLU, SN*). *New York Herald, Spirit of the Times,* Odell.
Baltimore: Holliday Street Theatre: (29ivR3), (30ivGI), (1vEM), (2vR3*). *Baltimore Sun.*
Boston: National Theatre: (13vLU), (14vR3, *Pelby), (15vGI), (16vPE), (17vBR, EM*). RE. (20vMC), (21vIG, Act IV of SH, *Thorne), (22 vLE), (23vGI, MU), (24vR3*). HTC bills, *Boston Transcript.*
New York: Park Theatre: (8viR3), (10viGI), (11viR3), (12vi: scenes from

CA, *Simpson), (13viHA), (14viBE, SN*). *New York Herald, Spirit of the Times,* Odell.

Pittsburgh: (25ixGI), (26ixR3), (27ixEM), (28ixR3), (30ixHA), (1xLE), (2xOT, SN*). *Pittsburgh Post,* Fletcher.

Philadelphia: Walnut Street Theatre: (16xSH), (17xEM), (18xDU), (19 xR3), (21xIG), (22xGI), (23xBE), (24xR3), (25xRG), (26xBR). TX, *Philadelphia Public Inquirer,* Wilson.

Augusta: (7xiiPE), (9xiiR3), (10xiiEM), (11xiiHA), (12xiiIG, JL), (14 xiiR3*). *Georgia Constitutionalist.*

Charleston: New Theatre: (23xiiR3), (24xiiGI), (25xiiBR), (26xiiLE), (27xiiIG), (28xiiBE), (30xiiLU, MU*), (31xiiR3). *Charleston Courier,* Ketchum.

1845

New Orleans: American Theatre: (15iR3), (16iGI), (17iCA), (18iIG), (19 iR3), (20iLE*). RE. (21iIG), (22iPE), (23iBR), (24iHA), (25iPI), (26 iBE, JL*), (27iEM), (28iCA), (29iR3), (30iRG), (31iGI, SN*), (1iiMC, *Tuthill). *L'Abeille, New Orleans Picayune.*

Cincinnati: National Theatre: (15iiR3), (17iiGI), (18iiPE), (19iiIG), (20 iiHA), (21iiBE). RE. (22iiSH, SN* Mr. Sarzdar), (24iiR3), (25iiLE*), (26iiST, JL, *Mrs. A. Drake). *Cincinnati Enquirer,* Dunlap, Langworthy.

Baltimore: Egyptian Saloon, Odd Fellows Hall, Gay Street: (27iiiEM), (28iiiOC), (29iiiEM*). *Baltimore Sun.*

Philadelphia: Walnut Street Theatre: (31iiiR3), (1ivHA), (2ivGI), (3ivLE), (5ivR3), (7ivIG). *Philadelphia Public Inquirer,* Wilson.

New York: Palmo's Opera House: (15ivGI), (16–18ivUK), (19ivR3), (21 ivGI), (22ivIG), (23ivGI), (24–25ivPE). *New York Morning News, Spirit of the Times,* Odell.

Boston: National Theatre: (5vR3), (6vGI), (7vIG), (8vPE), (9vR3*). RE. (12vLE), (13vMC), (14vBR, JL), (15vHA), (16vBE, SN*). *Boston Transcript.*

New York: Chatham Theatre: (17vUK). *Albion, Spirit of the Times,* Odell.

Philadelphia: Walnut Street Theatre: (23vGI), (24vR3), (26vLE), (27vCA), (28vHA), (29vBE), (30vR3), (31vBR, SN*). *Philadelphia Public Ledger,* Wilson.

Richmond: Richmond Theatre: (16viR3), (17viPE), (18viGI), (19viEM), (20viBE), (21viIG, JL*). RE. (23viHA), (24viR3). *Richmond Enquirer.*

Baltimore: Front Street Theatre: (1viiRG), (2viiGI), (3viiEM*), (4viiR3). *Baltimore Sun.*

New York: Chatham Theatre: (22viiiLU, JBB2 as Hearwell), (27viiiLU), (28viiiGI), (30viiiR3), (1ixPE, SN*, JBB2 as Hemeya). *New York Courier-Enquirer, Spirit of the Times,* Odell.

Boston: National Theatre: (6xR3), (7xGI), (8xIG), (13xR3), (14xLE), (15xIG), (16xBR), (17xEM, OC*). *Boston Transcript.*

New Orleans: St. Charles Theatre: (18xiEM), (19xiIG), (20xiGI), (21xiLE, DA), (23xiR3), (24xiPE), (25xiSH). RE. (26xiLE), (27xiR3), (1xiiR3). HTC bills, *New Orleans Picayune,* Kendall.

Mobile: (4xiiEM), (5xiiIG), (6xiiGI), (8xiiR3), (9xiiBE), (10xiiLE), (11 xiiPE), (12xiiHA*). *Mobile Register & Journal,* Bailey.

New Orleans: St. Charles Theatre: (23xiiEM), (24xiiGI), (25xiiOC). HTC bills, *L'Abeille, New Orleans Picayune.*

1846

Cincinnati: National Theatre: (13iR3), (14iGI), (15iHA), (16iIG), (17iBR), (19iEM, SN*), (20iR3), (21iGI), (22iSH, JL*). *Cincinnati Gazette,* Dunlap.

Philadelphia: Walnut Street Theatre: (18iiR3), (19iiHA), (20iiGI), (21iiIG), (23iiKJ), (24iiLU), (25iiR3*), (26iiPI), (27iiCA). USG.

New York: Chatham Street Theatre: (28iiR3), (2iiiHA), (3iiiGI), (4iiiR3), (5iiiPE), (6iiiKJ, SN*). RE. (7iiiMC, JBB2 as Banquo), (9iiiR3, JBB2 as KH), (10iiiLE, JBB2 as Edmund), (11iiiKJ, JBB2 as Hubert), (12iiiR3, JBB2 as KH), (13iiiST, *Theodore Stuyvesant). *New York Courier and Enquirer,* Odell.

Philadelphia: Walnut Street Theatre: (11vIG), (12vR3), (13vPE), (14vSH), (15vR3*), (16vPI). USG, Wilson.

Pittsburgh: (25vR3), (26vGI), (27vPE), (28vLE), (29vIG), (30vR3*). *Pittsburgh Post,* Fletcher.

Louisville: (4viR3), (5viIG), (6viEM), (8viGI), (9viR3), (10viPE), (11 viST), (12viLE*). *Louisville Courier,* Dietz, Weisert.

St. Louis, Missouri: (22viEM). Fired, then RE. (24viGI), (25viR3), (26 viPE), (27viR3), (29viBE), (30viBR*). RE. (1viiLE), (2viiEM), (3vii PE). *Missouri Reporter, Missouri Republican,* Ludlow.

Boston: National Theatre: (6xR3), (7xGI), (8xIG), (13xR3), (14xLE), (15xIG), (16xBR), (17xEM, OC*). *Boston Transcript.*

New York: Bowery Theatre: (12xiHA), (13xiEM), (14xiR3), (16xiPI, SN*). RE. (18xiLE), (19xiGI), (20xiR3*). *New York Herald, Spirit of the Times,* Odell.

Boston: Howard Athenaeum: (23xiR3), (24xiGI), (25xiHA), (26xiEM), (27xiSH), (30xiLE), (1xiiR3), (2xiiPI), (3xiiR3), (4xiiPE, SN*). *Boston Transcript.*

1847

New Orleans: American Theatre: (9iEM), (10iR3), (12iPE), (13iIG), (14 iBR, SN*). RE. (15iBE), (16iMC), (17iR3), (19iBR), (20iR3, JL*). *New Orleans Picayune,* Skinner's *One Man.*

Vicksburg: (26iEM), (28iR3). *Vicksburg Daily Whig,* Gates.

Baltimore: Baltimore Museum: (8iiiEM), (9iiiST), (10iiiEM), (11iiiST), (12iiiPI), (13iiiR3*). RE. (15iiiOT), (16iiiST), (17iiiR3), (18iiiOC), (19iiiHA), (20iiiHA*). *Baltimore Sun.*

Richmond: Richmond Theatre: (29iiiGI), (30iiiPI), (31iiiR3*). *Richmond Whig.*

Baltimore: Baltimore Museum: (5ivGI), (6ivHA), (7ivGI), (8ivR3), (9 ivPE), (10ivPN), (16ivBE, *manager). *Baltimore Sun.*

Philadelphia: Walnut Street Theatre: (19ivGI), (20ivKJ), (21ivR3), (22 ivPE), (23ivPI, SN*), (24ivMC). USG.

Baltimore: Holliday Street Theatre: (17vR3), (18vGI), (19vPE, SN*). *Baltimore Sun.*

New York: Bowery Theatre: (24vHA), (25vGI), (26vLE), (27vR3*), (28 vMC), (29vPI, SN*). *New York Herald,* Odell.

Albany: Albany Museum: (2viR3), (3viEM), (4viHA), (5viST), (7viLE), (8viGI, SN*), (9viIG, *Mrs. Price). *Albany Argus.*

Baltimore: Baltimore Museum: (30viIG), (1viiBE), (2viiR3*), (3viiGI, *Kate Ludlow). *Baltimore Sun.*

Albany: Albany Museum: (1ixBE), (2ixIG), (3ixSH). *Albany Argus.*

Boston: Howard Athenaeum: (6ixHA), (7ixR3), (8ixPE), (9ixGI), (10 ixSH). RE. (13ixR3), (14ixOT), (15ixIG), (16ixOT), (17ixLE, SN*). HTC bills, *Boston Transcript,* Ball.

Boston: Federal Street Theatre: (1xOT to JBB2's IG). HTC bills, *Boston Post.*

Baltimore: Front Street Theatre: (20xOT), (21xEM), (22xPE), (23xR3), (25xLE), (26xR3*). *Baltimore Sun.*

Baltimore: Front Street Theatre: (5xiOC, *Mrs. Booth). *Baltimore Sun.*

Baltimore: Holliday Street Theatre: (10xiEM), (11xiGI), (12xiRG), (13 xiR3). *Baltimore Sun.*

Philadelphia: Arch Street Theatre: (20xiR3), (22xiGI), (23xiLE), (24xi EM), (25xiOT), (26xiRG), (27xiR3). *Philadelphia Inquirer, Philadelphia Public Ledger.*

Cincinnati: Athenaeum: (20xiiR3), (21xiiGI), (22xiiPE), (23xiiOT), (24 xiiLE), (27xiiSH, JL), (28xiiR3*). *Cincinnati Daily Enquirer,* Dunlap.

1848

New Orleans: American Theatre: (9iEM), (10iGI), (11iLE), (12iIG), (13 iBR), (14iOT), (15iPE*). RE. (16iR3), (17iUK), (18iBE), (19iGI), (20 iR3*). *New Orleans Picayune.*

Vicksburg: New Theatre: (26iR3), (27iGI), (28iEM), (29iIG billed, but theatre burned). *Vicksburg Whig,* Gates.

New York: Park Theatre: (1iiiR3), (2iiiGI), (3iiiOT), (4iiiR3), (6iiiPE), (7iiiGI), (8iiiLE, SN*), (9iiiBE). *New York Herald, New York Post, Spirit of the Times,* Odell.

New York: Chatham Theatre: (10iiiEM). *New York Herald, Spirit of the Times,* Odell.

Philadelphia: Arch Street Theatre: (11iiiR3), (13iiiOT), (14iiiBR), (15 iiiLE), (16iiiPE, JL*). *Philadelphia Public Ledger,* Wilson.

New York: Chatham Theatre: (17iiiGI). *New York Herald.*

Boston: Federal Street Theatre: (20iiiR3), (21iiiPE), (22iiiOT), (23iiiHA), (24iiiBR). RE. (27iiiR3), (28iiiGI), (29iiiLE), (30iiiOC), (31iiiBE, SN*), (3ivEM, *Mrs. Mestayer). *Boston Post, Boston Transcript.*

Washington, D.C.: Adelphi Theatre: (26ivHA), (27ivOT), (28ivBE), (29 ivEM). RE. (1vR3). DNI.

Baltimore: Front Street Theatre: (29vHA, *Lyne), (2viBE*), (3vi: Act IV of SH, *Wallack). *Baltimore Sun.*

Baltimore: Baltimore Museum: (1viPI). *Baltimore Sun.*

Baltimore: Howard Athenaeum: (10viiGI), (11viiOT), (12viiEM), (13vii R3*). *Baltimore Sun.*

Philadelphia: Arch Street Theatre: (9viiiR3), (10viiiGI). *Philadelphia Public Ledger,* Ball, Wilson.

Albany: Albany Museum: (14viiiOT), (15viiiGI), (16viiiEM), (17viiiIG), (18viiiR3* billed, but fire destroyed the downtown area). *Albany Argus.*

Chicago, Illinois: Chicago Theatre: (22ixR3), (23ixGI), (25ixBR), (26 ixEM), (27ixPE), (28ixHA), (29ixR3), (30ixSH, JL*). *Chicago Daily Journal,* Bergfald, Wilt.

St. Louis: St. Louis Theatre: (9xGI), (10xOT), (11xEM), (12xR3), (13xBR), (14xHA*). RE. (16xR3), (17xPE), (18xSH, *Emily Coad), (19xIG), (20xST), (21xBE, *Fuller). HTC bills, Missouri Historical Society Scrapbook, *Missouri Republican.*

Cincinnati: National Theatre: (30xR3), (31xHA*). *Daily Cincinnati Gazette,* Dunlap.

Baltimore: Baltimore Museum: (25xiR3), (27xiGI), (28xiHA), (29xiBR*). RE. (30xiLE), (1xiiST), (2xiiPE, SN*). *Baltimore Sun.*

Pittsburgh: Pittsburgh Theatre: (8xiiEM), (9xiiGI). *Pittsburgh Daily Gazette,* Fletcher.

Cincinnati: National Theatre: (13xiiR3), (14xiiGI), (15xiiLE), (16xiiOT), (18xiiR3), (19xiiHA), (20xiiPE, SN*). *Daily Cincinnati Gazette,* Dunlap, Langworthy.

Louisville: Louisville Theatre: (23xiiR3), (25xiiGI), (26xiiPE), (27xiiHA), (28xiiBE), (29xiiOC, JL*), (30xiiEM, *J.W. Bates). *Louisville Daily Journal,* Dietz, Weisert.

1849

New Orleans: American Theatre: (9iEM), (10iGI), (11iBE), (12iMC), (13 iR3), (14iCA*), (15iOT). RE. (16iHA), (17iSH), (18iPE), (19iBR), (20iR3), (21iLE*). *New Orleans Picayune.*

Mobile: (24iEM), (25iGI), (26iR3), (27iBR), (29iLE), (30iR3), (31iOT*). RE. (1iiSH), (2iiGI), (3iiST, SN*). *Mobile Register & Journal,* Duggar.

New Orleans: American Theatre: (6iiPE), (7iiGI), (8iiR3), (9iiMC), (15 iiST), (16iiR3), (19iiUK), (20iiSH), (21iiEM), (22iiR3*). *New Orleans Picayune.*

Cincinnati: National Theatre: (21iiiR3), (22iiiGI), (23iiiPE), (24iiiBR), (26iiiHA*). *Daily Cincinnati Gazette,* Dunlap.

Pittsburgh: Pittsburgh Theatre: (3ivR3), (4ivEM), (5ivGI), (6ivLE*), (7ivR3). *Pittsburgh Daily Gazette.*

Baltimore: Front Street Theatre: (12viCA, *Barton). *Baltimore Sun.*

Boston: Boston Museum: (20viiiR3), (21viiiRG), (22viiiSH), (23viiiR3), (24viiiGI*). RE. (27viiiHA), (28viiiSH), (29viiiR3), (30viiiOC), (31 viiiPE*). RE. (3ixLE), (4ixPE), (5ixBR), (6ixEM), (7ixOT*). RE. (10 ixR3, EB as Tressel), (11ixIG), (12ixHA), (13ixLE), (14ixGI*). *Boston Transcript,* McGlinchee.

Providence: Providence Museum: (24ixGI), (25ixR3), (26ixSH), (27ixIG, EB as Cassio), (28ixLE*), (29ixEM, EB as Wilford). *Providence Journal,* Barton Hill.

Philadelphia: Chestnut Street Theatre: (5xGI), (6xR3), (8xHA), (9–10 xPE), (11xR3). *Pennsylvania Inquirer,* Wilson.

Norfolk: Avon Theatre: (12xiEM), (13xiHA), (14xiIG), (15xiR3, *Roberts), (16xiBE), (17xiEM*, EB as Wilford, JL). *Norfolk American Beacon, Southern Argus.*

Pittsburgh: (6xiiHA), (7xiiGI), (8xiiR3), (10xiiEM*, EB as Wilford). *Pittsburgh Daily Dispatch,* Fletcher, Barton Hill.

1850

Mobile: Mobile Theatre: (21iBE), (22iGI), (23iEM), (24iSH), (25iPE), (26iR3*). RE. (28iIG), (29iPI), (30iOT), (31iPE), (1iiR3), (2iiLE). *Mobile Daily Register.*

Charleston: Charleston Theatre: (12iiGI), (13iiR3), (14iiBE), (15iiIG), (16iiEM, SN*, EB as Wilford). *Charleston Courier,* Ketchum.

Savannah: (21iiGI), (22iiIG), (23iiR3). *Savannah Morning Daily News,* Green.

Richmond: Richmond Theatre: (1ivUK), (2ivPE), (3–4ivUK). HTC bills and letters, KC.

Philadelphia: Connor's Theatre (Arch Street): (17vGI), (18vR3), (20vIG), (21vPE), (22vEM, JL*, EB as Wilford). MC bills, *Philadelphia Public Ledger,* Wilson.

Baltimore: Holliday Street Theatre: (27vR3), (28vBE), (29vPI), (30vGI), (31vIG), (1viR3). May mss., *Baltimore Sun.*

Boston: Boston Museum: (12viiiGI), (13viiiBR), (14viiiSH), (15viiiPE), (16viiiR3), (19viiiHA), (20viiiRG), (21viiiR3, DA), (26viiiR3), (27 viiiPE), (28viiiHA), (29viiiGI), (30viiiEM*). RE. (2ixOT), (3ixSH), (4ixLE), (5ixIG), (6ixR3*). RE. (9ixLE), (10ixSH), (11ixR3), (12ixIG), (13ixHA*). *Boston Transcript,* McGlinchee.

Lowell, Massachusetts: (16ixEM), (17ixBE), (18ixR3), (19ixHA), (20ixSH, JL*). HTC bills.

New York: National Theatre: (23ixR3), (24ixIG), (25ixGI), (26ixLE), (27ixEM*, EB as Wilford), (28ixR3), (30ixHA), (1xR3, EB as Tressel), (2xRG), (3xMC), (4xPE, EB as Hemeya), (5xOC, SH*). PC bills, *New York Herald,* Odell.

Baltimore: Holliday Street Theatre: (31xR3), (1xiHA), (2xiBR, JL*, EB as Titus). May mss., *Baltimore Sun.*

Washington, D.C.: Adelphi Theatre: (4xiR3), (5xiGI), (6xiHA), (7xiST), (8xiPE, EB as Hemeya), (9xiR3). DNI, Mudd.

Brooklyn, New York: Brooklyn Museum: (2xiiGI), (3xiiIG, DA), (9xiiR3), (10xiiEM, EB as Wilford). *Brooklyn Eagle,* Harrison, Odell.

Providence: Providence Museum: (16xiiHA), (17xiiSH), (18xiiR3), (19 xiiGI), (20xiiLE), (21xiiBR*, EB as Titus). *Providence Journal.*

Boston: Boston Museum: (23xiiR3), (24xiiSH), (25xiiEM), (26xiiGI), (27xiiHA), (28xiiR3). RE. (30xiiR3), (31xiiPE). HTC bills, TX, *Boston Transcript, Spirit of the Times.*

1851

Boston (con't.): (1iLE), (2iIG), (3iR3*). HTC bills, TX, *Boston Transcript, Spirit of the Times.*

Lowell: Lowell Museum: (6iGI), (7iR3), (8iPE, EB as Hemeya), (9iIG), (10iSH*). RE. (13iPI), (14–15iUK), (16iBR, EB as Titus), (17iR3). Performing Arts Research Center (New York Public Library) bills, Princeton bills, *Lowell American.*

Washington, D.C.: Adelphi Theatre: (24iiR3), (25iiPE, EB as Hemeya), (27iiIG, EB as Cassio), (28iiHA*, EB as Laertes). DNI, MC.

Philadelphia: Barnum's Museum: (3iiiR3), (4iiiGI), (5iiiEM), (6iiiHA), (7iiiSH), (8iiiR3), (10iiiHA*), (11iiiIG), (12iiiOT), (13iiiPE), (14iiiSH), (15iiiR3), (17iiiLE), (18iiiST), (19iiiMC), (20iiiBR), (21iiiR3), (22iii SH), (24iiiMC), (25iiiIG). *Philadelphia Daily News, Public Ledger,* Wilson.

New York: National Theatre: (31iiiLE), (1ivR3), (2ivGI), (3ivMC), (4ivIG), (5ivR3, EB substituted). *New York Herald,* Clarke, Odell.

Richmond: (21ivPE, EB as Hemeya), (22ivR3, EB as RC), (23ivIG, EB as Cassio), (25ivEM*, EB as Wilford), (26ivBR*, EB as Titus), (28ivR3, EB as RC), (29ivLE, JL*). MC, *Richmond Enquirer, Richmond Whig,* Aronson.

Washington, D.C.: National Hall: (5–6vLE, EB as ED both nights), (7vR3, EB as RC), (8vST, JL*), (14vSH, EB as Gratiano), (15vGI), (16vMC, EB as Macduff, then Trial Scene from SH, EB as Gratiano, *Mrs. M. Jones), (17vEM, EB as Wilford, then ON, EB as YN). DNI, MC.

Philadelphia: Barnum's Museum: (16viHA). *Philadelphia Public Ledger,* Wilson.

New York: National Theatre: (11viiiGI), (12viiiR3), (13viiiIG), (14viiiLE), (15viiiR3). *New York Herald,* Odell.

Boston: Boston Museum: (20viiiR3), (21viiiSH), (22viiiEM), (25viiiGI), (26viiiPE), (27viiiBR), (28viiiSH), (29viiiR3*). RE. (1ixHA), (2ixST), (3ixLE), (4ixPE), (5ixR3), (8–9ixOT), (10ixGI), (11ixLE), (12ixR3*). HTC bills, *Boston Transcript.*

New York: National Theatre: (15ixIG), (16ixR3), (17ixPE), (18ixLE), (19ix: Act IV of SH, then EM). *New York Evening Post,* Odell.

Baltimore: Holliday Street Theatre: (3xOT), (4xR3*). May mss., *Baltimore Sun.*

Boston: Boston Museum: (22xR3), (23xSH), (24xOT), (27xHA), (28xIG), (29xGI), (30xSH), (31xR3*). *Boston Transcript.*

Providence: Providence Museum: (3xiR3), (4xiSH), (5xiIG), (6xiPE*). *Providence Journal.*

Philadelphia: Chestnut Street Theatre: (24xiR3, DA). *Philadelphia Pennsylvanian, Philadelphia Public Ledger.*

1852

Baltimore: Holliday Street Theatre: (1iR3), (2iGI), (3iCA*), (10iST, *Julia Dean). May mss., *Baltimore Sun.*

Philadelphia: Chestnut Street Theatre: (14iR3), (15iPI), (16iHA), (17iPE), (19iCA, *James Quinlan), (20iGI), (21iBE), (22iR3), (24iMC), (26iPI), (27iEM), (28iCA), (29iKJ), (30iBR*), (31iEM, ST, *Murdoch). *Philadelphia Public Ledger,* Wilson.

New York: National Theatre: (2iiIG), (3iiR3), (4iiGI), (5iiLE), (6iiPE*), (7iiR3). PC bills, *New York Herald,* Odell.

Baltimore: Holliday Street Theatre: (12iiBR, EB as Titus), (13iiR3), (24 iiPE, *Thaddeus J. Barton). A&CA, May mss., *Baltimore Sun.*

Baltimore: Holliday Street Theatre: (16iiiPI), (17iiiCA). HTC bills, *Baltimore Sun.*

Charleston: Charleston Theatre: (22ivR3), (23ivIG), (24ivGI), (25ivHA), (26ivEM, JL*, EB as Wilford), (29ivR3, *J.H. Allen), (30ivGI, *Mrs. Sandrue). *Charleston Courier,* Ketcham.

Augusta: Concert Hall: (31iiiGI), (1ivIG), (2ivR3), (3ivHA). *Georgia Constitutionalist.*

New York: National Theatre: (17vIG), (18vR3), (19vBE). *New York Herald,* Odell.

Baltimore: Holliday Street Theatre: (31vR3), (1viBR), (2viLE, EB as ED), (3viGI, SN*), (5viGI). May mss., *Baltimore Sun.*

San Francisco, California: Jenny Lind Theatre: (30viiEM, EB as Wilford), (31viiGI, EB as Allworth), (1viiiHA, EB as Laertes), (2viiiOC, EB as Virolet), (3viiiOT, JBB2 as IG, EB as Cassio), (4viiiSH, EB as Gratiano), (6viiiR3, EB as RC), (7viiiPE*, EB as Hemeya), (8viiiR3*), (9viiiST, EB as Francis, *San Francisco Orphans Asylum), (11viiiBR), (12viiiLE), (13viiiEM, EB as Wilford), (14viiiIG, EB as Cassio, JBB2 as OT), (15viiiMC). HTC bills, *Daily Alta,* Benoff, Fenton, Barton Hill.

Sacramento, California: American Theatre: (19viiiEM), (20viiiGI), (21 viiiSH), (23viiiHA), (24viiiPE), (25viiiLE), (26viiiBR*), (27viiiR3), (28viiiOC), (30viiiR3), (31viiiST), (1ixMC), (2ixPI, EB as JA, *EB), (3ixBR), (4ixST, DA), (6ixR3, SN*). Hume.

San Francisco: Adelphi Theatre: (27ixBE), (28ixR3), (29ixGI), (30ixSH). *Daily Alta,* Holmes.

New Orleans: St. Charles Theatre: Terms of half after $250 for five nights, then a clear half benefit. (14xiR3) [g=950.75; b=350.75], (15xiGI) [g=437.35; b=93.87], (16xiPE) [g=305.75; b=27.87], (17xiSH) [g=547.00; b=148.50], (18xiBE) [g=368.75; b=59.37], (19xiEM, JL*) [g=809.00; b=404.50]. *New Orleans Picayune,* Kendall, Ludlow diary, Turner.

Notes

Introduction

1. Asia Booth Clarke, *The Unlocked Book: A Memoir of John Wilkes Booth by His Sister Asia Booth Clarke* (New York: G. P. Putnam's Sons, 1938. Reprint. Benjamin Blom, 1971), 69–70. Asia later described the burning of Booth's records without specifying time or place. She recalled obtaining some additional records from "an old relative," possibly Booth's brother-in-law, James Mitchell. Adam Badeau, a friend of Edwin Booth's, recalled staying at Tudor Hall in 1858, there seeing "old books and letters, and journals, and pamphlets," according to his article, "A Night with the Booths," *New York Times,* 7 Aug. 1858.

1. A Gentleman of the Name of Booth

1. Drury Lane and Covent Garden still operate today. Both theatres originated from royal patents or licenses, awarded by Charles II shortly after the Restoration of the British monarchy in 1660. Until the revocation of the Licensing Act in 1843, Covent Garden and Drury Lane offered the only legitimate theatre (the origin of that term) in London, although other producing agencies attempted to overcome the monopoly. Booth became ensnarled in the controversies over this monopoly in 1820.

2. Gabriel Harrison, *John Howard Payne, Dramatist, Poet & Author of Home, Sweet Home! His Life and Writings* (Philadelphia: Lippincott, 1885. Reprint. New York: Benjamin Blom, 1969), 72. Payne (1791–1852), an American actor and playwright, emerged as a literary and theatrical child prodigy at age fourteen and had himself appeared at Drury Lane with great success. Among his scripts was *Brutus; or, The Fall of Tarquin,* later played by Booth.

3. Charles and Mary Cowden Clarke, *Recollections of Writers* (New York: Charles Scribner's Sons, 1878), 15. William Godwin (1756–1836), an English novelist and political writer, later became the father-in-law of Percy Bysshe Shelley.

4. Unidentified clipping, Harvard Theatre Collection, Cambridge, Massachusetts. Sally Booth (1794–1867) made her London debut in 1810.

5. Booth's newspaper reviews for 12 and 13 February 1817 were examined in the Colindale Newspaper Archives, a branch of the British Library, London. Reviews customarily appeared the day after the performance. The same archives provided provincial reviews when Booth later toured the United Kingdom.

6. Izola Forester, *This One Mad Act . . . The Unknown Story of John Wilkes Booth and His Family* (Boston: Hale, Cushman & Flint, 1937), 135–36. The Booth Spanish ancestry has stimulated considerable controversy, but attempts to corroborate or negate the legend by correspondence with the leading Spanish and Portuguese archives have proven fruitless. Searching the *Archivo Biografico de España* at the University of Rochester, Rochester, New York, for the names Ricardo Bethe or Bothe failed to locate either. As for the Booth genealogy, Stanley Kimmel, *The Mad Booths of Maryland,* 2d ed. (New York: Dover Publications, 1969), traced them no further than John Booth, the Clerkenwell silversmith. Late in his life, Edwin Booth (Junius Brutus Booth's son) sought to connect his family to Barton Booth, the early eighteenth-century Drury Lane actor-manager, and to that end subsidized research in the London archives. He accumulated a list of wills recorded in London of various people named Booth, some related, some not, many unidentified, but failed to determine any relationship with Barton Booth. The list is now in the Players, New York. Ernst Friedrich Kraentzler recorded some of the Booth genealogy in his article, "John Wilkes Booth—Ancestry and Family," *Genealogical Digest: Genealogy Club of America Magazine* 8(Aug. 1977): 163–70, in which he assumed the accuracy of Izola Forester's connection to the Booths but offered no further documentation.

7. Clerkenwell was then a London parish extending northwards from St. Andrew's, Holborn, and Smithfield to the Pentonville Road, bounded on the west by the Fleet River (the old River of Wells) and on the east Goswell Road, from the Charter House to the Angel at Islington. Clerkenwell had early become a favorite spot for Londoners. The area gained its name for its mineral wells, said to have medicinal qualities, near which local parish clerks performed religious plays annually. By the sixteenth century the area gained a tainted notoriety as a resort of thieves and prostitutes, as described by Elizabethan and Restoration playwrights. Shakespeare's Falstaff, speaking of Justice Shallow, says, "This same starv'd justice hath done nothing but prate to me of the wildness of his youth, and the feats he hath done about Turnbull Street, and every third word a lie" (*2 Henry IV,* III, ii, 304–7). By the eighteenth century, however, streets were rebuilt in the Georgian manner, and the quality began to displace the criminal element. By the time the Booths arrived, Clerkenwell flourished as a center for rising merchants. The silversmithing Booths no doubt chose Clerkenwell to avoid the City of London's trade-guild regulations. Asia Booth Clarke claimed that many of

the Clerkenwell Booths were born in the house of Bishop Burnet, a former bishop of Salisbury who died there in 1715. The Burnet house stood on the west side of St. John's Square, "a noble mansion of two storeys in height." The house was razed in the 1880s. Similarly, many of the Clerkenwell Booths were buried in the yard of the ancient church of St. John of Jerusalem. Of the church the Booths would have known, only the crypt remains today, and the gravestones of the Booth and Wilkes families have long since disappeared under modern urban improvements.

8. Elizabeth Wilkes claimed to be the cousin of John Wilkes, the Westminster republican, onetime mayor of the City of London and ardent supporter of the American colonies. Examination of various Wilkes biographies, family trees, and papers finds no mention of such a relationship, but the Wilkes and Booths of Clerkenwell were clearly well acquainted; surnames for both families are strikingly similar (e.g., Israel). *The Oxford English Dictionary* defines *cousin* as "a kinsman or kinswoman, a relative," as well as the modern meaning. According to the *International Genealogical Index* of the Church of Jesus Christ of Latter-Day Saints, Columbia, Missouri, an Elizabeth Wilkes was born 27 January 1705, the daughter of Benjamin and Ann Wilkes. The child was christened at St. James, Clerkenwell, 4 February of the same year. No relationship to John Wilkes has surfaced, but in Richard Booth's and John Brevitt's letter of 28 October 1777 (later in chapter 1) the young men refer to "being of the same family as yourself." On 5 November 1777, John Booth wrote to John Wilkes, mentioning "in the connection of Blood with which we stand," seeming to bear out the relationship.

9. Edwina Booth Grossman, *Edwin Booth: Recollections by His Daughter Edwina Booth Grossman and Letters to Her and to His Friends* (New York: The Century Co., 1894), 208.

10. The children of John and Elizabeth Booth were (1) John, baptized at St. Sepulchres' on 9 April 1750; (2) Israel Wilkes Booth, born 12 May, baptized 2 June 1751; (3) Wilkes Booth, born 1 February, baptized 19 February 1753; (4) Martha Booth, born 15 April, baptized 28 April 1754; (5) Benjamin Booth, baptized 11 July 1756; (6) Mary Booth, baptized 11 June 1758; and (7) Richard Booth, baptized 26 November 1759. All baptisms, except John in 1750, were at St. John of Clerkenwell, as recorded in the parish registers, examined at the Greater London Record Office. Some confusion arises concerning Richard Booth's birth date. His tombstone in Green Mount Cemetery in Baltimore reads "Sacred to the Memory of Richard Booth Who died Dec. 29th 1839, Aged 76 years & 43 days." This would establish his birthday as 16 November 1763, but the parish records of St. John the Baptist Church, Clerkenwell, record the baptism of Richard Booth, son of John and Elizabeth Booth, on 26 November 1759. I assume the latter date is correct and the year on the tombstone four years too late. Kraentzler, "John Wilkes Booth," listed Richard's birth date as 14 December

1755, citing an unspecified parish register printout, and Kimmel, *The Mad Booths,* listed it as 1763. Finally, Edwin Booth's genealogical notes on his family list Richard's baptism as 26 November 1759. The 1759 birth date would make Richard eighteen years old when he and Brevitt struck out for America, a likely age for such a venture.

11. According to records in the London Public Record Office, Richard Booth began his articles with John Harries, Gentleman, 25 March 1776 (Entry No. 3276). After two years (13 April 1778) he continued to the end of his seven-year term with Abraham Rhodes of Clerkenwell, Gentleman. The interval matches the dates of Richard's escapade with John Brevitt. Brevitt was born 29 November 1760 in Wolverhampton, Staffordshire, the son of Joseph and Ann Brevitt, according to his brother, Joseph, in genealogical notes now in the Maryland Historical Society, Baltimore. Brevitt later went to America, became a Lieutenant in the 4th Maryland on 20 September 1780, was retained in the Maryland Battalion in 1783, and served until November of that year. Following the war he married Miss Swope, a Baltimore Quaker, and settled in that city.

12. Arthur Lee (1740–92) had been sent to Europe to ascertain the views of European countries concerning a war between the colonies and England. A Virginian, he was a distant relative of Robert E. Lee.

13. Asia Booth Clarke, *The Elder and the Younger Booth* (Boston and New York: Houghton, Mifflin and Co., 1881), 4–8.

14. Asia Booth Clarke, *The Elder Booth,* 7–8.

15. John Booth dated his will 8 August 1783; it is filed as Probate #11/1157/437. Elizabeth Booth proved the will 4 October 1787. The will mentions only Wilkes Booth, silversmith, of Albermarle Street, Clerkenwell, and Richard Booth of Gray's Inn, Gent. Apparently John, Benjamin, and Israel were by that time deceased. Elizabeth Booth made her seventeen-page will on 28 May 1799, filed as Probate #11/1362/574. Wilkes and Richard Booth proved the will on 17 September 1801. A codicil provides for Richard's daughter, Jane; another for John Wilkes Booth, the son of Wilkes Booth; a third provides for Algernon Sidney Booth, Richard's son, who died 2 June 1803. Part of the will is unreadable, but according to Junius Brutus Booth's account book, he also received moneys from his grandmother.

16. Parish records of St. Mary's, Finchley, a borough seven miles north west of St. Paul's.

17. An entry in the parish register for St. John's of Clerkenwell recorded the burial of Algernon Sydney Booth, age five, on 2 June 1803. His birth in 1798 would thus agree with Junius Brutus Booth's later recollections of his brother; Algernon would have died when the future actor was seven.

18. Burial records, St. John's of Clerkenwell parish registers, Greater London Record Office.

19. Specifically, Bloomsbury extends from Euston Road on the north to New Oxford Street and High Holborn on the south, and from Gray's Inn Road

on the east to Tottenham Court Road on the west. Richard Booth's London addresses were recorded in the *Universal British Directory* (London: British Directory Office, 1790, 1793); *Browne's General Law List,* (London: John Browne and J. Butterworth, 1796); and various London city directories from the period, all examined in the British Library. In 1799 he lived at 125 Great Russell Street, Bloomsbury, and for the next two years at 27 John Street, Tottenham Court Road. From 1802 to 1805 Richard Booth resided at 145 Tottenham Court Road. After brief sojourns at 190, 145, and 211 Tottenham Court Road, he finally settled at 4 Queen Street, Bloomsbury, his last directory entry there being for 1817, the year his son challenged Edmund Kean on the Drury Lane stage. The last recorded depiction of Queen Street, Bloomsbury, was in 1819 on Holwood's map; in 1827 it appeared as Museum Street on Greenwood's map. Various guides to street names do not indicate when the renumbering took place. Susan Palmer of the Greater London Record Office verifies the location of Richard Booth's Queen Street home as the modern No. 38 Museum Street, adding that much of the original structure probably remains beneath the nineteenth-century alterations.

20. Extracted from a letter by Booth in the Menken Collection (private) dated 1 May 1839, from Louisville, Kentucky.

21. Letter from P. R. Quarrie, Eton College Librarian and Keeper of the College Collections, citing H. E. C. Stapelton's *The Eton School Lists, 1791–1884.* The surname Booth does appear in the Eton day-school rolls for this period; perhaps Booth attended, but no specific record remains.

22. Two early Booth biographers charge the youngster with these sexual indiscretions: William Oxberry in *Oxberry's Dramatic Biography and Histrionic Anecdotes* (London: G. Vertue, 1825) vol. 4; and "An Old Actor" in *Memoirs of Mr. Booth, Containing a True Statement of All the Circumstances Attending His Engagements at the Rival Theatres, With a Few Remarks upon His Conduct; By an Old Actor* (London: T. Keys, 1817). The latter suggested Booth, aged twelve, had rendered pregnant Molly, a neighbor's maidservant, who, being turned out of her position, sought assistance from a thunderstruck Richard Booth. The magistrate considered the maid, "poor Molly," the best judge of matters and found for the defendant. No court records of these two paternity suits have yet appeared.

23. Booth described Old Piggot in the *Literary Subaltern* (Providence) articles (see Works Cited). Old Piggot was no doubt George Piggot (fl. 1803–30), a master printer at 60 Old Street, opposite St. Luke's Hospital, according to William B. Todd, *A Directory of Printers and Others in Allied Trades, London and Vicinity, 1800–1840* (London: Printing Historical Society, 1972), 151.

24. According to Covent Garden playbills in the Garrick Club, London, and in the British Library, Booth could have seen *Othello* at Covent Garden during the autumn of 1813, either 7 or 13 October, with William Augustus Conway as the Moor and Daniel Egerton as Iago.

25. As an extreme example, Sarah Siddons, England's greatest actress, received between four and five thousand pounds a year as early as 1784–85. Eleven years later Siddons had saved ten thousand pounds from her income. By 1800 she was receiving thirty guineas a week.

26. Oxberry, *Dramatic Biography,* vol. 4, 181. Oxberry describes the "nursery of Booth" as under the direction of Mr. George, son of a pianoforte manufacturer in the vicinity of Tottenham Court Road. While the milkman had no theatrical career, his sister, Amelia Angelica George, who also appeared in the Pancras Street theatre in children's roles, later achieved a minor reputation as a singer-actress at Covent Garden and in the provinces.

27. Booth's Continental diary was partially published twice, once in the *Memoirs of Junius Brutus Booth, From his Birth to the Present Time; With an Appendix, Containing Original Letters, From Persons of Rank and Celebrity; and Copious Extracts from the Journal Kept by Mr. Booth, During His Theatrical Tour on the Continent* (London: Chapple, Miller, Rowden, and E. Wilson, 1817), and again by Asia Booth Clarke, *Booth Memorials: Passages, Incidents, and Anecdotes in the Life of Junius Brutus Booth, (The Elder.) By His Daughter* (New York: Carleton, 1866). Nine pages of the original manuscript survive at the Players.

28. The anonymous author of *Memoirs of Junius Brutus Booth* suggested that Booth sailed with a company of thirty-six. Examination of the extant bills from Booth's Continental tour, however, indicate only twenty-nine performers appeared. The men included J. B. Booth, Samson Penley, James Salter, Jonas, Montford, Seltzer, Franklin, Burton, Platt, Gutteridge (or Guttendy), James, J. Jonas, Cordell, and Brunton. The five actresses were Penley, Lucas, Watson, M. Jonas, and Beynon. While the company toured, such stars as Mr. and Mrs. Charles Kemble, Mrs. Dorothy Jordan, and Mrs. Rosemond Mountain made guest appearances.

29. Booth's diary, Players.

30. Professor Ben Albach, "A Dutch Actor's Experiences with English Theatres in Amsterdam, in May–July 1814," in *Western Popular Culture* (London: Methuen & Co., 1977), 75–90. Albach supplied information for Booth's first Continental engagement, taken from announcements in the *Amsterdamsche Courant* for 1814. No reviews appeared, and the advertisements did not list actors and roles, but Booth's own collection of playbills in the Menken Collection record a few of his performances:

18 May: *The Honey Moon* and *The Weather-Cock*
21 May: *John Bull, or, The Englishman's Fireside* and *The Bee-Hive*
23 May: *Hamlet* and *The Purse, or, The Benevolent Tar*
25 May: *Speed the Plough* and *Raising the Wind*
28 May: *The Jew* and *The Hunter of the Alps*
31 May: *The Soldier's Daughter* and *Fortune's Frolic*

2 June: *The Wonder: A Woman Keeps a Secret* and *Ways and Means of a Trip to Dover*
4 June: *Lovers' Vows* and *The Miller and His Men*
6 June: *Barbarossa, or, The Captive Queen* and *The Miller and His Men*
8 June: *The Mountaineers* and *The Jew and the Doctor*
13 June: *Romeo and Juliet*
15 June: *The Peasant Boy* and *High Life Below Stairs*
18 June: *The Stranger* and *Of Age Tomorrow*
20 June: *The Voice of Nature* and *The Forty Thieves*
22 June: *George Barnwell* and *The Forty Thieves*, Booth as Oreobrand
25 June: *The Stranger* and *Of Age Tomorrow*
27 June: *The Battle of Hexam* and *Don Juan*
1 July: *Alexander* and *Don Juan*
2 July: *She Stoops to Conquer* and *Inkle and Yarico*
4 July: Booth as Whisper in *Busy Body* and as Sandy in *Highland Reel; or, The Scotch Piper*
6 July: *Follies of a Day, or The Marriage of Figaro* and *Inkle and Yarico*
9 July: Booth as the Waiter in *Laugh When You Can; or, The Faithful Black* and as Zaphnor in *The Mogul Tale.*

31. Jelgerhuis (1770–1836) was a Dutch costumer, teacher, actor, and graphic artist. His manuscript description of the Jonas-Penley Company is held by the University of Amsterdam Library, Rare Book Room. Translation by Annamarie van Dyk.

32. John Astley was probably the son of Philip Astley (1742–1814), a retired cavalryman who specialized in equestrian dramas in London.

33. The poem Mrs. Benyon gave Booth, from Asia Booth Clarke's *Booth Memorials*, 25–26:

Oft have you seen a rash, adventurous boy,
Just taught to spurn his nurse and childish toy,
Of prosp'rous voyages having read at home,
Burn with desire through foreign climes to roam.
Without experience, and with fancy hot,
Paint pleasure every where, where he is not.
Maternal care he leaves without a sigh,
For the fond pleasure of variety.
His tender mother, finding precept vain,
With generous fondness, strives to hide her pain;
With care, his sea-habiliments provides,
Wipes from her cheek the tear that silent glides.
The infatuate youth, still stubborn to his plan,
Tries them, then struts, and thinks himself a man.
But when, at last, the day of parting's nigh,
He drops the tear, and heaves the tender sigh:
His flatten'd fancy now no sunshine shows,

But shivers at the storm, ere yet it blows;—
Oh! should it pour on this devoted head,
And drive me back, your vengeance I should dread;
Not your indulgence could I hope to prove—
You'd spurn the prodigal that slights your love.
Such is MY case, yet pity, though you blame,
Nor aggravate my sense of grief, of fear, and shame.

34. From the Menken Collection: 27 July, Booth as Tobias in *The Stranger*; 3 August, Booth as Trick in *How To Die for Love*; 8 August, Booth as Rochdale in *John Bull.*

35. Agatha Delannoy-Versluys was the widow of Samuel or Auguste Delannoy, a successful merchant who moved from Leyden (Leiden), Holland, to Brussels about 1798, dying shortly thereafter. Some Delannoys came to America as early as 1621, changing their name to Delano. Their most famous descendant was Franklin Delano Roosevelt, according to Daniel W. Delano, Jr., in a letter to Stanley Kimmel, 11 April 1946, now in the Kimmel Collection, University of Tampa, Florida. See also Major Joel Andrew Delano, *The Genealogy, History, and Alliances of the American House of Delano 1621 to 1890* (New York: n.p., 1899), 61. The Delannoy daughters included Marie Josepha Agatha, born 8 January 1790; Marie Christine Adelaide, born 4 January 1792; Therese Eleonore, born 12 July 1793; and Amelie Francoise Julienne, born 28 August 1795, according to the Brussels Municipal Archives.

36. The Jonas-Penley Company's performances in Brussels were recorded by Professor Willem Schrickx of Ghent. The Menken Collection bills supplied further documentation.

15 Aug.: Booth as Rochdale in *John Bull*; the afterpiece was *Of Age Tomorrow*
17 Aug.: *The Honey Moon* and *Raising the Wind*
19 Aug.: *The Soldier's Daughter* and *Lovers' Quarrels*
22 Aug.: *Ways and Means of a Trip to Dover* at the Théâtre du Parc
23 Aug.: *A Cure for the Heartache*, Booth as Bronze
26 Aug.: *The Stranger*
29 Aug.: *The Wonder*
30 Aug.: *She Stoops to Conquer*
1 Sept.: Booth as Tobias in *The Stranger*
6 Sept.: *The Wonder*, with Mrs. Jordan
8 Sept.: Booth as Malfort in *The Soldier's Daughter,* with Mrs. Jordan; as Joey in *The Bee-Hive*
10 Sept.: Booth as Snake in *School for Scandal*
13 Sept.: *Busy Body*
20 Sept.: Booth as Armstrong in *The Iron Chest* and as Charles in *Village Lawyer*
22 Sept.: Booth as Frederic in *The Wonder*, with Charles Kemble

24 Sept.: *The Honey Moon,* with Charles Kemble
26 Sept.: *Hamlet*, with Charles Kemble
1 Oct.: *Richard the Third*, with Charles Kemble
3 Oct.: *The Mountaineers*, with Charles Kemble
5 Oct.: *Romeo and Juliet*, with Charles Kemble
8 Oct.: *Hamlet*, with Charles Kemble
10 Oct.: *The Provoked Husband*, with Charles Kemble
12 Oct.: Booth as Malcolm in *Macbeth*, with Charles Kemble; and as Souffrance in *My Grandmother*
15 Oct.: Booth as Acres in *The Rivals,* with Charles Kemble; and as Philip in *High Life Below the Stairs*
18 Oct.: *Road to Ruin*, with Charles Kemble and wife, and *Don Juan*
20 Oct.: *Inkle and Yarico*, with Mrs. Mountain, and *Don Juan*
22 Oct.: Booth as Eustace in *Love in a Village*, and as William in *The Review; or, Wags of Windsor*
28 Oct.: *A Tale of Mystery,* with Mrs. Mountain
30 Oct.: *The Bee-Hive*, with Mrs. Mountain
1 Nov.: *Timon the Tartar*
4 Nov.: Booth as Rochdale in *John Bull*; the afterpiece was *Timon the Tartar*
5 Nov.: *Timon the Tartar*
8 Nov.: *The Castle Spectre* and *The Travellers Benighted*
12 Nov.: Booth as the Earl of Pembroke in *The Earl of Warwick;* the afterpiece was *The Romp*
16 Nov.: *The Weather-Cock* and Booth as Megrim in *The Blue Devils*
22 Nov.: *Othello* and *Tom Thumb*

37. This casual remark from Booth's diary is the only indication he had seen Kean in 1814, Kean's first year at Drury Lane. Kean had debuted as Shylock and repeated the role several times that season.

38. Oxberry, *Dramatic Biography*, vol. 4, 186.

39. Players.

40. *Literary Subaltern,* 15 Jan. 1830.

41. The bill for 30 November 1814 in Ghent is reproduced in Asia Booth Clarke's *Booth Memorials*, 165. Mr. Cordell acted the title role; Miss Watson appeared as Desdemona. Jonas and Penley listed themselves as directors from the theatres royal at Windsor and Brighton, "under the immediate Patronage of his Royal Highness the Hereditary Prince of Orange." Booth did not appear in the afterpiece, *Don Juan*. Booth's only Ghent playbill in the Menken Collection records his acting Stephano in *A Tale of Mystery* on 7 December 1814.

42. After the opening on 2 January, the only recorded Ostend performances, taken from bills in the Folger Shakespeare Library, Washington, D.C., and the Menken Collection, are

14 Jan.: Booth as Iago to Cordell's Othello
18 Feb.: Booth as Richard III and as Bagatelle in *The Poor Soldier*

7 Mar.: *The Mountaineers*, Booth as Virolet, Cordell as Octavian
13 Mar.: *Richard the Third*, Booth benefit in title role
25 Mar.: Booth as Sir Edward Mortimer in *The Iron Chest* and as Bagatelle in *The Poor Soldier*
28 Mar.: Booth as Old Norval in *Douglas,* benefit of Mr. Brunton; the afterpiece was *Hurry Skurry; or, All at Work*
30 Mar.: *The Prize*, Booth not appearing

43. A practice begun in the eighteenth century, the *afterpiece* was a short comedy or farce performed after the main production. On occasion, performers would appear in both the full-length play and the afterpiece. The custom fell out of favor in the late nineteenth century. *Benefit performances* began in the 1680s in London. A performer would select the script(s) for the evening and receive the box-office proceeds after the manager deducted expenses. Such benefits could substantially increase the performer's income and served as an index to his or her popularity. The practice disappeared in the 1880s.

44. Folger Shakespeare Library, dated 17 March 1815.

45. Quoted in Frank A. Burr, "Junius Brutus Booth's Wife Adelaide," *New York Press*, 9 Aug. 1891.

46. The last portion of Booth's diary appears only in Asia Booth Clarke's *Booth Memorials*. The French passage translates, "The most dangerous passions ferment when the intellect has not been well employed, resulting in a coterie of eccentric notions and disorderly cravings" (author's translation).

2. Showdown at Old Drury

1. *Memoirs of Junius Brutus Booth,* 68. Williams, who wrote under the pseudonym Anthony Pasquin, had lurked around the fringes of the London theatre as a sometime newspaper critic, the terror of performers good and bad. He later emigrated to America, started a paper called *The Federalist,* and died indigent in Brooklyn, New York, 23 November 1818.

2. Quoted in Asia Booth Clarke, *The Elder Booth,* 9–10.

3. St. George's of Bloomsbury Parish registers, examined in the Greater London Record Office.

4. The letters from Booth and Adelaide appeared in Burr, *New York Press*. Burr, about whom little is known, explained how he gained knowledge of these letters. He was wandering the streets of Baltimore, Maryland, about 1882 and chanced upon a Catholic cemetery. Entering the grounds, he found a tombstone for Mary Christine Adelaide Delannoy, its inscription reading: "Jesus—Mary—Joseph Pray for the soul of Mary Christine Adelaide Delannoy, Wife of Junius Brutus Booth, Tragedian. She died in Baltimore March the 9th, 1858, aged 66 years. It is a holy and wholesome thought to pray for the dead. May she rest in peace." Burr, who knew nothing of Adelaide at that point, queried the sexton, who told him, a man "who looked like a priest,"

probably Richard Junius Booth, Adelaide's son, used to come regularly to visit the grave, paying the sexton for the upkeep. The stranger's visits stopped during the Civil War. Burr wrote a brief newspaper article, "A Graveyard Secret," about the incident and thought no more about it. Some months later, Burr received a note, inviting him to learn more about this mystery by calling upon "a certain distinguished professor of literature at one of the prominent universities." Burr did so, and the professor showed him some hundred or more letters by or to Booth and Adelaide. In his *New York Press* article, Burr quoted several of the more important letters but failed to name the professor or to explain what became of the documents. Many of the earlier letters were apparently written in French; the only surviving original is by Booth to Mme Delannoy in Brussels, written in passable French. The rest of the letters have disappeared.

5. Forty francs was apparently the equivalent of two pounds, Booth's salary at Covent Garden in 1815–16, although the translation of the letter may have been by Burr. Exchange rates fluctuated wildly at this time.

6. Mary Theresa Odell chronicled the history of the Brighton and Worthing Theatres Royal under Trotter in four volumes, but for the 1815–16 season she recorded only a single performance by Booth in *The Theatre Royal, 1814–19: Mr. Trotter of Worthing and the Brighton Theatre* (Aylesbury: Aldridge Brothers, 1944), 49. Booth's personal collection of playbills, now in the Menken Collection, remains the only substantial source of information for this period of Booth's career.

7. Parish registers, St. George's of Bloomsbury, examined at the Greater London Record Office. No record of this child's death has yet surfaced; presumably she died in her infancy.

8. Records of Booth's performances at Covent Garden during 1815–16 were extracted from playbills in the Garrick Club and in the British Library.

9. Asia Booth Clarke, *The Elder Booth,* 12.

10. A single Windsor bill in the Menken Collection records Booth as Henry in *Who Wants a Guinea?* on 14 September 1816.

11. A nineteenth-century actor's repertory was also known as "possession of parts," meaning the sort of character in which he or she might specialize (e.g., old man, old lady, juvenile, walking gentleman, low comedian, pert chambermaid, etc.). Booth's line was that of leading tragedian, the top rank in the acting hierarchy.

12. John [Adams] Ellsler, *The Stage Memories of John A. Ellsler,* edited by Effie Ellsler Weston (Cleveland: The Rowfant Club, 1950), 82–83.

13. Letter, University of Pennsylvania Library, Rare Book Room. Jane Chambers was born Jane Rodney around 1857, the possibly illegitimate daughter of George Brydges Rodney (1719–92), a naval hero and the first Baron Rodney. On 12 September 1784 she married George Chambers, the only son of Royal Architect Sir William Chambers, designer of Somerset House. In 1804, however, after bearing nine children, she deserted her

husband for a Captain Caulfield, a military man and amateur actor. Chambers sued Caulfield for alienation of affections as described in the *London Times*, 4 Dec. 1804. Among Jane Chamber's nine children was a son, Montague Chambers, an aspiring playwright, with whom Booth corresponded before he left England for America.

14. Richard Booth's letter of 16 October 1816 to the Drury Lane Committee, now at the University of Texas, Harry Ransom Humanities Research Center, was published in the *Boston Evening Transcript,* 15 Feb. 1905.

15. Sir William Garrow (1760–1840), member of Parliament and a judge, was appointed baron of the Exchequer in 1817.

16. [John Ford], *The Actor; or, A Peep Behind the Curtain, Being Passages in the Lives of Booth and Some of His Contemporaries* (New York: Wm. H. Graham, 1846), 9.

17. Notes taken by James Winston during Booth's first engagement, Harvard Theatre Collection.

18. Drury Lane Theatre (the third theatre of that name on the site) burned on 24 February 1809. No funds were available for rebuilding until a brewer and member of Parliament, Samuel Whitbread, raised four hundred thousand pounds. A committee, including Lord Holland, Lord Byron, and Douglas Kinnaird, formed to facilitate rebuilding. Construction started on 29 October 1811; the new Drury Lane opened 10 October 1812. Because the previous manager, Richard Brinsley Sheridan, had run the theatre into enormous debt, the new manager, Samuel James Arnold, operated under the supervision of a committee, including the earls of Essex and Dudley, Lord Holland, Lord Byron, William Adam, Harvey Combe, John Dent, Richard Ironmonger, Douglas Kinnaird, Colonel John MacMahon, Peter Moore, Charles Ward, and Samuel Whitbread. Only Arnold had any previous theatrical experience. Walter Macqueen-Pope, *Theatre Royal, Drury Lane* (London: W. H. Allen and Co., 1944), 249, suggested that Madame Storace, then a star, had told Kinnaird of Booth's worth, but while the Drury Lane Committee debated whether to hire him, Covent Garden offered their engagement. Kinnaird then hired Booth when Covent Garden could not come to terms.

19. Winston's manuscript notes in the Harvard Theatre Collection state, "[Mr. R. Jones?] told Mathews saw him soon after and was convinced he had been made drunk for the purpose."

20. The most comprehensive treatment of the entire Booth-Kean episode appeared in the *Theatrical Inquisitor and Monthly Mirror,* February and March 1817, from which I have drawn the basic facts of the story, including texts of most of the placards, circulars, and bills with which both theatres saturated London. Several of the original documents are held by the British Library; by the Victoria and Albert Museum, London; and by the Players.

21. *Memoirs of Mr. Booth,* 23.

22. John Fawcett (1768–1837) was connected with Covent Garden from 1791 as stage manager, actor, playwright, and treasurer till his retirement in 1830. Winston described him as "like a pineapple, rough outside, but full of sweetness within." Whereas Henry Harris was overall manager of the theatre, Fawcett supervised productions. See Philip H. Highfill, Jr., Kalman A. Burnim, and Edward A. Langhans, *A Biographical Dictionary of Actors, Actresses, Musicians, Dancers, Managers & Other Stage Personnel in London, 1660–1800,* vol. 5 (Carbondale and Edwardsville: Southern Illinois University Press, 1978), 195–204.

23. Shakespeare's *Richard the Third* opens with the humpbacked monster's soliloquy, "Now is the winter of our discontent." Booth and Kean, however, both used Colley Cibber's melodramatic revision of the play, first published in 1700, in which Richard does not enter till Act I, scene ii.

24. The Lord Chamberlain was a court officer in complete charge of theatrical matters. All scripts had to be submitted for approval; if not, a script could not be performed. During Booth's confrontation with Kean in 1817, Lord Salisbury functioned as Lord Chamberlain. His Examiner of Plays, John Larpent, served from 1778 to 1824, when George Colman (the younger) took the position, inspiring one scholar to comment, "Rake followed bigot." Overall, the situation and personalities contributed substantially to the puerility of English drama during this period.

25. The remainder of the Booth-Kean street ballad, from a copy in the Harvard Theatre Collection (also published in J. W. Robinson's *Theatrical Street Ballads: Some Nineteenth-Century Street Ballads about the Theatre* [London: The Society for Theatre Research, 1971], 44–47), ran:

-2-

When Booth perform'd King Dick,
All declar'd he'd done the trick:
Tho' Kean is reckon'd clever,
'Twill now be "Booth for ever!"
Such a strut and such a stare
Were never seen I swear:
  His equal was never seen, O!
  In a trice ask'd his price,
  Strange to say, they said nay,
  'We'll give two pounds'—'No no zounds'
  In a fury off to Drury,
  Come out there, make 'em stare,
  Play the scene, be mighty Kean!
    Hey down, &c.

-3-

When Covent Garden found
That so firm he stood his ground,
They offer'd terms so grand,
That he could not them withstand;

He a letter wrote to Rae,
And swore he couldn't play,
Thinks he this act as a screen O!
Print a bill—say I'm ill—
Got the gout—can't come out,
I will play another day!
Gammon bold—sack the gold,
Hey down, &c.

-4-

When in Dick he next appear'd
A row was greatly fear'd
Then came forward little Booth,
"Pray take pity on my youth
"I should not have made you fools
"But I was twixt two stools
"And I fear'd I should slip between O
"Hear my story—I implore ye,
"Pardon pray—let me play,
"Grateful ever forget it never,
"If you'll hear me I'll revere ye,
"Sign my peace discord cease."
Hey down, &c.

-5-

Now the audience were not proof
Against the plea of youth,
They listen'd to his tale,
And let harmony prevail,
Said they "We are content."
And the Olive Branch they bent,
For Britons will to mercy ever lean O
His appeal made them feel,
They relented—were contented—
Heard him through—stopp'd the row
(Spoken.) And home went King Dick as happy as a prince soliloquizing thus: "Now is the winter of our discontent made glorious summer by the smiles of peace, and all the clouds that lour'd upon my head—in the deep bosom of oblivion buried, Richard's himself again!" with his
Hey down, &c.
Thus ended the farcical scene, O!
Printed and sold by Jno. GREEN, 14 Crown Street, Soho.

26. Asia Booth Clarke, *Booth Memorials,* 44.

27. *Theatrical Inquisitor,* Apr. 1817, 279.

28. The text of the 1817 *Memoirs of Junius Brutus Booth* offers few clues to the author's identity. One of Booth's paternity suits is described on page 12 ("He was charged by a frail nymph with a deed—of which she could no longer conceal the evidence") in words very similar to Oxberry's in 1825

("He was charged by a frail nymph with that 'deed of darkness' which her situation could no longer conceal") on page 445 of his *Dramatic Biography.* Oxberry (or his widow, who completed the text) apparently drew upon the 1817 *Memoirs of Junius Brutus Booth* for the Booth essay. On page 14 of the *Memoirs of Junius Brutus Booth,* the author noted he first met Booth on the voyage to the Continent in 1814 and seems to have observed Booth at close range during the tour. On page 43 the author refers to Salter as Booth's friend and seems familiar with the events of the Booth-Kean controversy.

29. William Charles Macready (1793–1873) made his London debut at Covent Garden on 16 September 1816, beginning a slow but steady rise to the top of his profession, with which he was never comfortable. By 1819 he rivaled Kean and until his retirement in 1851 dominated and greatly reformed the London stage.

30. William Charles Macready, *Macready's Reminiscences, and Selections from His Diaries and Letters,* edited by Frederick Pollock (New York: Macmillan, 1875), 107.

31. *Literary Subaltern,* 19 Feb. 1830.

3. This England

1. Quoted by Burr, *New York Press.*
2. *Theatrical Inquisitor,* June 1818, 414–16.
3. Quoted in the *Theatrical Inquisitor,* Nov. 1818, 397.
4. *Theatrical Inquisitor,* Nov. 1818, 399–400.
5. *Theatrical Inquisitor,* 400.
6. Macready, *Reminiscences,* 131.
7. *Theatrical Inquisitor,* Mar. 1819, 237.
8. *International Genealogical Index.*
9. Eleanor Ruggles, *Prince of Players: Edwin Booth* (New York: W.W. Norton & Co., 1953), 22.
10. *Detroit Free Press,* 21 July 1893, quoting the *Oswestry Advertiser,* confirmed by correspondence with the County Library of Bridgnorth. Booth would have been able to vote in parliamentary elections, but a common phrase of the day was "as one-sided as a Bridgnorth election," due to extreme local corruption.
11. Kathleen Barker, "Better than Fiction?" *Theatre Research/Recherches Théâtrales* 10(1969): 86–88. Booth's own version of the event appeared in the *Literary Subaltern,* 22 Jan. 1830. R. J. Broadbent, *Annals of the Liverpool Stage* (Liverpool: Edward Howell, 1908. Reprint. New York: Benjamin Blom, 1969), 185, inexplicably placed the incident in that city in 1821, positing that Booth fled to America to escape prosecution. Similarly, F. W. Hawkins, *The Life of Edmund Kean from Published and Original Sources* (London: Tinsley Brothers, 1869. Reprint. Benjamin Blom, 1969), vol. 2, 123, stated Booth left England to "avoid the consequences of having killed

Diavolo Antonio, a celebrated Portuguese slack-wire dancer, in a duel." The Liverpool bills for 1821 make no mention of Booth. George Speaight quoted Broadbent in his brief article, "Il Diavolo Antonio," *Theatre History Studies* 4(1984), 116–17, suggesting Lincoln would not have been assassinated if the incident had not taken place. Il Diavolo Antonio, whose real name was Antonio Blitz, had first appeared in England at Astley's in 1816 and performed at the theatre royal in Glasgow as late as 1827. He primarily performed on the slack rope, but he also juggled, did "feats of strength," and presented trick puppets. The *Spirit of the Times,* 3 June 1837, referred to Antonio as giving extraordinary exhibitions on the rope, then reported "on good authority" that he and most of his family had been killed in Florida by Seminoles.

12. *Literary Subaltern,* 22 Jan. 1830.

13. Folger Shakespeare Library.

14. The Royal Coburg Theatre, now known as the Old Vic, continues as a producing theatre, having undergone much alteration and restoration. In 1816 the landlord of the nearby Surrey Theatre, Mr. Temple West, anticipating the completion of Waterloo Bridge, raised his rent from £226 to £4,200, inspiring Messrs. James Jones and James Dunn, the managers, to build their own theatre. They secured a patent for the production of musicals through John Thomas Serres, marine painter to the king at the time. When money ran short for construction, they solicited the assistance of John Joseph Glossop, the stagestruck son of a wealthy merchant. After many delays, the theatre opened to the public 9 May 1818.

15. Peter Roberts, *The Old Vic Story: A Nation's Theatre 1818–1976* (London: W. H. Allen, 1976), 42–43.

16. A detailed account of the trial was published by the *British Stage and Literary Cabinet* in 1820. The law, from 10th GEO. II. c. 28, read, in part: "every person who shall, for hire, gain, or reward, act, represent, or perform, or cause to be acted, represented, or performed, any interlude, tragedy, comedy, opera, play, farce, or other entertainment of the stage, or any part or parts therein, without authority, by virtue of letters patent from his Majesty, his heirs, successors, or predecessors, or without license from the Lord Chamberlain of his Majesty's household for the time being, for every such offence, forfeit the sum of £50." The case also appeared in *Reports of Cases Argued and Determined in the Court of King's Bench* (London: J. Butterworth and Son, 1821), vol. 4, 616–19.

17. James Winston, *Drury Lane Journal: Selections from James Winston's Diaries 1819–1827*, edited by Alfred L. Nelson and Gilbert B. Cross (London: The Society for Theatre Research, 1974), 3.

18. Nahum Tate (1652–1715), a poet and playwright devoid of talent, rewrote *King Lear*, omitting the Fool and allowing Cordelia to survive and marry Edgar. This version held the stage until Macready restored the original text in 1838.

19. *Theatrical Inquisitor,* Apr. 1820, 249.

20. Asia Booth Clarke, *Booth Memorials,* lavished praise upon her father's 1820 Lear, calling it "one of the proudest efforts of his genius," adding, "'Lear' was represented three nights a week for several successive weeks," contrary to the records.

21. William Thomas Moncrieff (1794–1857), the son of a London tradesman, wrote songs, managed various minor theatres, penned more than 170 dramatic pieces, and published various other works. He wrote his theatrical reminiscences, titled "Dramatic Feuilletons," for the *Sunday (London) Times* in 1851 but made no mention of Booth.

22. The Columbia University Theatre Collection, New York, holds Booth's letter, addressed to Montague Chambers, Esq.; Bryanstone Street, Portman Square 27. Montague Chambers was the fifth and last child of Jane Rodney Chambers, Booth's early patroness.

23. Victoria and Albert Museum.

24. The 1820–21 Booth diary was described in the *New York Times,* 12 June 1921, section IV, 4. Workmen had discovered the document during renovation of the Walnut Street Theatre in Philadelphia and turned it over to C. C. Wanamaker, the theatre's manager. Wanamaker said he refused a thousand dollars for it, preferring to keep it in the Walnut Street Theatre's "trophy room." The diary has since disappeared, but the *Times* article quoted sections from it, such as the shooting incident in Oakley Street discussed next in the text.

25. Letter dated 29 May 1820 from Booth to Charles Mathews, the elder, Victoria and Albert Museum. This letter listed a return address as 10 Pratt Street, Lambeth. Another letter in the Folger Shakespeare Library dated 14 August 1820 is signed by Booth from Croft Street, Lambeth, but no such street appears on the city maps of the time.

26. Letter from Elliston to Booth, Players.

27. John Cooper (fl. 1810–70) was a provincial star in 1820; Elliston cajoled him to take a reduced salary "for the good of the theatre," but Cooper demanded and received his own terms. A steady but mechanical actor, he retired about 1858. James William Wallack (1795–1864), the son of an English theatrical family, made his stage debut at age four. By 1812 he was at Drury Lane, which he left in 1818 for an American tour. After his return to Drury Lane in 1820, he returned to the United States in June 1821. He alternated between the two countries for the rest of his career.

28. The greenroom is a backstage room in which the cast members wait for entrances or chat with their friends before and after the performance. The practice began during the Restoration. During the Booth-Kean period, Drury Lane had two greenrooms, one for actors paid more than five pounds a week, and one for those paid less.

29. *John Bull,* 31 Dec. 1820.

30. Many accounts of the Booth family refer to Mary Ann Holmes as a flower girl, including Kimmel, *The Mad Booths,* and Ruggles, *Prince of*

Players, but none supplies documentation. The earliest reference to her as a flower girl (of which I am aware) is from the *Baltimore American and Commercial Advertiser,* 22 Apr. 1865, in "A Scandalous Story About the Booth Family." The unsigned story, reprinted from the *Cincinnati Commercial,* contains numerous errors of fact but refers to the mother of the Maryland Booths as "a flower girl named Rosalie, who regularly sold flowers to market customers in that quarter of London [the Haymarket]." The article continued: "She possessed rare personal attractions, and was, in fact, exceedingly beautiful." Asia Booth Clarke understandably glossed over her parents' lives in England.

31. The Holmeses' genealogical background is extracted from entries in the *International Genealogical Index,* which records Mary Ann's christening at St. Mary's, Lambeth, 29 August 1802, the daughter of Robert and Sarah Holmes (Batch P006281, Sec. Sh. 2019). Two apparent brothers are listed, as well: Robert Thomas Holmes, christened 22 September 1811 (Sec. Sh. 8530); and William George Holmes, christened 27 February 1807 (Sec. Sh. 4176). Kimmel, *The Mad Booths,* listed Mary Ann's birth date as 27 June 1802, making her nineteen when she encountered Booth, but he supplied no documentation. Edwin Booth wrote to his daughter Edwina on 2 June 1875 to remind her that that day was Mary Ann Holmes' seventy-first birthday (see Grossman, *Edwina Booth,* 43). The Mormon records seem more trustworthy than the Booth family's memories in this case. Most of these dates are confirmed by the registers for St. Mary's Church, Lambeth, which contains baptismal records for Mary Ann Holmes (29 August 1802); Thomas, son of Robert and Sarah Holmes (7 April 1805); William George, son of Robert and Sarah Holmes (27 February 1807, born 17 October 1806); and Thomas Frederick, son of Robert Holmes, seedsman, Bridge Road, Lambeth, and Sarah Holmes (1 January 1820). Clouding the issue, Mary Ann Holmes Booth's death certificate, dated 22 October 1885, listed her birthplace as London and her parents as Frederick (rather than Robert) and Sarah L. Holmes.

32. Winston, *Drury Lane Journal,* 28. In a set of notes at the Harvard Theatre Collection, Winston maintained that Booth married Adelaide in Brussels in 1814 and again at St. George's, Bloomsbury, then absented himself with the daughter of a corn chandler (dealer) of "West Row near Marsh Gate—leaving an infant child 3 years old totally destitute." No West Row appears on any map of the period. The burial registers for St. Mary's, Lambeth, record the burial of a Robert Holmes, aged forty-five, of Mount Street, as 23 December 1823; apparently he did not die of a broken heart in 1821 as Winston wrote.

33. In addition, *Robson's Improved London Directory, Street Guide, and Carrier's List, for 1820* (London: William Robson and Co., 1820), 287, listed Robert Holmes, nursery- and seedsman, at 3 Mount Street, Lambeth, as does the *Triennial Directory of London, Westminster, Southwark, and Ten*

Miles' Distant, for the Years 1817, 1818, 1819 (London: W. Flint, 1819). In 1822 and 1823 *The Post-Office Annual Directory* (London: T. Maiden, 1812, 1822, 1823), includes the same Robert Holmes at the same address. The parish registers of St. Martin-in-the-Fields indicate a Robert Holmes married a Sarah Lewis, by banns, 19 July 1801. Sarah Lewis, born 20 September 1776, was the daughter of William and Ann Lewis.

34. Kimmel, *The Mad Booths,* 27, presented a romantic, detailed, and undocumented story of Booth's assignations with Mary Ann. His notes and papers in the Kimmel Collection contained no confirmation for his version. Kimmel was unaware of the Winston diary and notes.

4. An Object of Interest

1. Letter by Edwin Booth, Folger Shakespeare Library.

2. *New York Clipper,* 4 Mar. 1861, 21.

3. Richmond productions had ceased after a disastrous theatre fire in 1811 which killed seventy-two persons. Charles Gilfert, however, opened "The Theatre" in 1819, sometimes exchanging productions with James H. Caldwell's company in Petersburg.

4. Thomas Abthorpe Cooper (1776–1849), a neoclassic actor in the tradition of Kemble and Siddons, remained in the United States, appearing in New York as Antony in 1835 at age sixty-one, continuing to act until 1849.

5. Noah Ludlow (1795–1886) was one of the first actors to play much of the frontier and Mississippi Valley. From 1835 to 1853 he managed with Sol Smith as a partner, operating several theatres in St. Louis, Missouri; New Orleans, Louisiana; and Mobile, Alabama, as described in his detailed autobiography, *Dramatic Life as I Found It: A Record of Personal Experience; With an Account of the Rise and Progress of the Drama in the West and South, with Anecdotes and Biographical Sketches of the Principal Actors and Actresses Who Have at Times Appeared upon the Stage in the Mississippi Valley* (St. Louis: G. I. Jones and Co., 1880. Reprint. New York: Benjamin Blom, 1966).

6. Ludlow, *Dramatic Life,* 223–24.

7. George Frederick Cooke (1756–1812) was the first English star to appear in North America. He made his English debut in 1776 and rose to stardom in 1800. His lack of dependability due to drink eroded his favor; in 1810 he came to the United States and died here two years later. Audiences especially admired his passionate Richard III.

8. Asia Booth Clarke, *Booth Memorials,* 67; also Ford, *The Actor,* 65.

9. Ludlow, *Dramatic Life,* 226.

10. *National Advocate,* 8 Oct. 1821, quoted in George C. D. Odell, *Annals of the New York Stage* (New York: Columbia University Press, 1928), vol. 3, 11.

11. Odell, *Annals of the New York Stage,* vol. 2, 582.

12. Quoted in Asia Booth Clarke, *The Elder Booth,* 63.

13. William B. Wood, *Personal Recollections of the Stage, Embracing Notices of Actors, Authors, and Auditors, During a Period of Forty Years* (Philadelphia: Henry Carey Baird, 1855), 271–72.

14. Over the Baltimore and Norfolk engagement entries in his account book, Booth wrote, "Not counted for Gilfert and Graham."

15. Booth's memorandum book, a small red-leather volume, was also an almanac. It is held by the Players. Tucked into the inside back cover is an unidentified lock of brown hair.

16. Considerable controversy surrounds the birthplace of Junius Brutus Booth, Jr. Kimmel, *The Mad Booths,* quoted the list of Free Inhabitants at the Census Bureau for the Fifth Ward in Baltimore, taken on 17 July 1850, when the Booths lived on North Exeter Street, as naming the birthplace of Junius Brutus Booth, Jr., as South Carolina. Kimmel also cited the War Department Archives, which quoted J. B. Booth, Jr., as saying he was born in Charleston. Kimmel further said that Booth was "announced to appear elsewhere on that date, [making] it unlikely that he was able to be present . . . at the birth of his namesake." Booth was in fact in passage from Charleston to New Orleans, according to his memorandum book, of which Kimmel was unaware.

17. James H. Caldwell (1793–1863), born in England, pioneered theatre in the Mississippi Valley and arrived in New Orleans in 1820. He was ruined by the 1837 American financial crisis.

18. Ludlow, *Dramatic Life,* 229–30.

19. Booth's performance of Orestes led to later accounts that he had played the role in French during this engagement. James Rees, *The Dramatic Authors of America* (Philadelphia: G. B. Zieber, 1845), 68, seems to have started this theatrical myth, and "Hamlets on the Stage," *Atlantic Monthly,* Aug. 1869, furthered it. Asia Booth Clarke, *Booth Memorials,* 88, contributed to the legend by citing advertisements printed in French in the New Orleans papers, as described in chapter 5. Ludlow, *Dramatic Life,* 231–32, found all this beyond belief and refuted it. He also tried to debunk it in a letter to Col. John Forsyth, dated 21 April 1876, examined at the Missouri Historical Society, St. Louis.

20. Theodosia Walton, "New Booth Diary," *New York Times,* 12 June 1921. This is the same diary in which Booth recounts being fired upon in Lambeth in chapter 2.

21. Baltimore suffered from an epidemic of yellow fever in 1820–21; Asia Booth Clarke, *Booth Memorials,* 77, and *The Elder Booth,* 65–66, implied that her father chose to site his new home in Harford County to avoid the fever. See Eugene Fauntleroy Cordell, *The Medical Annals of Maryland: 1799–1899* (Baltimore: Williams & Wilkins Co., 1903), 686.

22. John Brevitt, who had attempted to come to America with Richard Booth in 1777, later succeeded and became an officer in the 2nd Maryland. He eventually settled in Baltimore and on 4 May 1784 married a Quaker girl, Mary Swope, in Harford County (records in the Maryland Historical

Society). For many years, the Baltimore directories listed him as a "tobacco manufacturer" with a partner named Starr; by 1822 he was listed as a "gent.," living on the north side of Conway, west of Hanover Street. John Brevitt's brother, Joseph B., a physician and author of *A History of Anatomy,* had also come to America, had also married (2 November 1798) a Quaker (Cassandra Webster Woodland) from Harford County, and had settled in Baltimore by 1800. He died 15 April 1839, having sired at least three children: Cassandra Ann, Elizabeth Boraston, and George Fox Brevitt. Booth therefore had at least two relatives living in Baltimore when he first arrived there; they presumably informed him of Harford County as a potential residence.

23. Mrs. Elijah B. Rogers explained that she and her husband had rented out their farm for six years to a Mr. William Hanna while they lived in Bel Air. When Rogers wished to return to his farm, he built the log house to live in until Hanna's lease ran out, then the Rogers moved into their farmhouse, and Booth rented the log house. Mrs. Rogers lived on the farm adjacent to the Booths' property. In 1886 a Baltimore physician, William Stump Forwood, drafted a biography of the elder Booth, drawing heavily upon Asia Booth Clarke's already-published works. Forwood wrote to Mrs. Rogers, asking her for information about the Booths. She replied with six letters, now in the Manuscript Division of the Library of Congress. While her memory was suspect (she claimed that Junius, Jr., was born on the Bel Air farm), her letters remain a valuable source for this portion of Booth's Maryland life.

24. Asia Booth Clarke, *Booth Memorials,* 78–79.

25. Daniel J. Watermeier, ed., *Between Actor and Critic: Selected Letters of Edwin Booth and William Winter* (Princeton New Jersey: Princeton University Press, 1971), 274. Further evidence of Booth's purchase of a female slave includes a document in the Harford County, Maryland, Court House, supplied by David Reuwer of Bel Air. The document reads in part: "July 29th. 1824. . . . I John Monahan of Harford County and State of Maryland for and in consideration of the sum of ninety dollars to me in hand paid by Junius Brutus Booth of the county and state aforesaid . . . do bargain sell and deliver unto the said Junius Brutus Booth a negro woman name Harriett Eighteen years of age to serve five years from august [*sic*] 12th 1824 then to be free it is hereby understood and agreed upon by the parties that all the posterity of said negro woman shall serve unto the age of twenty-four years of age and then to be free and it is agreed by the aforesaid parties that the said negro woman nor any of her posterity shall not be removed out of the state of Maryland to have and to hold."

26. Kimmel, *The Mad Booths,* 38, described Joe Hall as a giant who boasted descent from a Madagascan prince, but he cited no documentation. Joe Hall's wife, Ann Hall, is buried near Bel Air.

27. William Warren, the elder (1767–1832), came to the United States from England in 1796, eventually to manage the Chestnut Street Theatre in Phila-

delphia with Wood. He retired in 1829. Charles Mathews, the elder (1776–1835), made his London debut in 1803, soon winning an enviable reputation as an eccentric comedian. He won his greatest success with his "At Homes," a unique form of entertainment which showcased his amazing ability as a mimic.

28. *Baltimore American and Commercial Daily Advertiser,* 23 Oct. 1822.

29. Francis Wemyss (1797–1859) was an English actor who came to the United States in 1821. A genial and cultured man, Wemyss managed theatres in several American cities but never reached distinction, either as an actor or as a manager.

30. Asia Booth Clarke, *Booth Memorials,* 82.

31. Charles Durang, "The Philadelphia Stage from the Year 1749 to the Year 1855, Partly Compiled from the Papers of His Father, the Late John Durang," *Philadelphia Sunday Dispatch* (1854), 179.

32. Mary Ann Dyke (1794–1857), born in London, married John Duff, an Irish actor, and made her first appearance in New York in 1823. Booth considered her the finest actress he had ever seen, but he advised her to avoid London.

33. Stephen Price (1783–1840), who began importing English stars to America with Cooke in 1810, was the first American theatre manager who was neither playwright nor actor. Most of his career was with the Park Theatre, but he managed Drury Lane in London from 1826 to 1830.

34. Wood, *Personal Recollections of the Stage,* 300.

35. *Baltimore American and Commercial Daily Advertiser,* 6 Feb. 1824.

36. Thomas Hilson (1784–1834?), another English-born actor, originally named Hill, first appeared in New York in 1811, where he became a great favorite. He won most favor as Shylock and as Iago.

37. *Baltimore American and Commercial Daily Advertiser,* 14 May 1824.

38. Transcript, Kimmel Collection.

39. Booth's deed to the Harford County farm, examined in the Harford County Court House in Bel Air (HD-7-407), recorded the price of the land as $733.20.

40. The actor with whom Booth was chatting would have been Jacob Woodhull (d. 1832), who acted at the Park for some fifteen years. The Wallack in this case, Henry John Wallack (1790–1870), was leading man in 1824 at the Chatham Theatre, a few blocks from the Park, and James William Wallack's brother.

41. William Augustus Conway (1789–1828) was born in Ireland and came to the United States in 1824 with considerable success. A moody type, Conway threw himself into the ocean near Charleston and drowned, an incident of importance to Booth later.

42. Harvard Theatre Collection.

43. Menken Collection.

44. One may wonder if Booth actually wrote *Ugolino*, given the case of *No!,* which appeared later over his name (see chapter 5). A search of script

libraries in the United States and England has failed to discover any similar work. Further credence to Booth's authorship is supplied by Joseph Norton Ireland in *Mrs. Duff* (Boston and New York: Houghton, Mifflin and Co., 1882), 48; Ireland posits that Booth wrote the role of Olympia in *Ugolino* specifically for Mrs. Duff, an actress Booth much admired. John Wilkes Booth revived *Ugolino* at the Boston Museum on 27 May 1864, starring in the title role.

45. Typed transcript, Kimmel Collection, dated 15 June 1825.

46. Harford County Business Records, Manuscript Division, Maryland Historical Society.

47. Harvard Theatre Collection.

48. Booth referred to Thomas Burke, who died in Baltimore on 6 June 1825. He had made his American debut in Charleston in 1802 and was the half-brother of Joseph Jefferson III.

49. Charles Mayne Young (1777–1856) was a sometime leading man who had played support for Kemble, Siddons, Macready, and Kean. Elliston had gone to Ramsgate to recuperate from a stroke, probably brought on by drink and debauchery. His son, William Gore, assisted him, and Elliston had appointed James William Wallack as stage manager. Harvard Theatre Collection.

50. *London Times,* 21 Jan. 1825.

51. One such ballad, reprinted in Robinson, *Theatrical Street Ballads,* 48–51, was titled, "Little Breeches, and the Cock of Drury Lane," "Little Breeches" being a nickname Kean used for Mrs. Cox in his letters. A typical pair of verses:

> Then into bed they softly crept, as happy as could be,
> And what befel, I cannot tell, I was not there to see;
> But in the middle of the night the cock began to crow,
> Which let the servants understand what game was on the go.
>
> O Little Breeches, you're the girl I ever shall adore,
> I feel more happy in your arms than e'er I was before;
> I'd slight the richest dame on earth, And take you in your smock,
> The sting well fits the towdy, exclaim'd the little cock.

A *towdy,* according to *The English Dialect Dictionary,* vol. 7, 209, was Scottish slang for "a young hen, one that has never been laid, also, a young unmarried woman." *The Scottish National Dictionary* concurs, adding alternate definitions of "the buttocks, the posterior."

52. Booth's family arrangements while in London in 1825 are hazy at best. Kimmel, *The Mad Booths,* 43, offering no documentation, maintained that Booth dropped off his family in Reading with Mary Ann's mother and went up to London alone. He said further that Adelaide was boarding not far

from Booth's former home, failing to indicate whether he meant Queen Street or Lambeth, and that Adelaide had lost her youthful appearance. Finally, Kimmel observed, "Adelaide meant nothing to him now, but for the sake of appearances and his fondness for little Richard, he permitted a family portrait to be painted and continued to act the part of faithful husband during his stay in England." Burr, *New York Press,* stated, "When he [Booth] returned to England in 1825 he met his wife as though nothing had happened, and Mr. Williams . . . painted the portrait of himself, wife and boy. This letter indicates a different purpose, but Mr. Booth did not desire to be painted in costume, and chose the family portrait instead." Burr's reference to Williams' 8 March letter to Booth introduced the following: "Sir—It gave me consolation in my distressed state to find that amid the whirl of popular applause you are not so elated as to shut your portals against the poor and needy. I will honor myself by waiting upon you, as permitted by Mrs. Booth, upon Monday between 9 and 10 in the morning; and should I experience a slender ray of your beneficence, as I am no parasite I shall endeavor to cherish the circumstance in my memory with becoming gratitude, so long as I possess the power of recollection. If I still retain a degree of emulation as an artist my greatest ambition would be to attempt your portrait in one of your favorite characters. But this I doubt I must contemplate as a chimera. Therefore, sincerely wishing your pre-eminence in your promising career, I am, sir, with due respect, your unfeigned, humble servant, T.W." This "T.W." may have been Thomas H. Williams (fl. 1801–30), listed in H. L. Mallalieu, *Dictionary of British Watercolour Artists up to 1920* (Woodbridge, England: Antique Collectors' Club, 1976), 280, as an illustrator, engraver, and watercolorist. In any event, the portrait has disappeared, as has the letter quoted by Burr.

53. *London Times,* 10 Oct. 1825.

54. *London Morning Chronicle,* 10 Oct. 1825.

55. This event was reported in most of the newspapers for 14 October. James William Wallack (1795–1864) was the brother of Henry John Wallack and Elliston's stage manager at Drury Lane in 1824.

56. Burr, *New York Press.* Burr then commented, "It is unnecessary to introduce into this narrative the correspondence which took place between husband and wife [Adelaide] after Mr. Booth left for his return to America, in 1826." The next letter Burr quoted was dated 1839.

57. *London Morning Post,* 14 Oct. 1825.

58. *London Morning Herald,* 17 Oct. 1825.

59. The rules by which Lewis caused the uproar in Manchester indicate the state of affairs between actors and managers at this time. As published, they were: "Any performer, engaged at this Theatre, refusing publicly to act, sing, and perform, *any* and *every* character, *part,* prologue, or epilogue, of all and in all tragedies, comedies, plays, *operas, choruses, farces, burlettas, masks, preludes, interludes, pantomimes, dances, processions,* and of and in all enter-

tainments or exhibitions whatsoever, which shall be exhibited at the Theatre Royal, when and as often as he or she shall be required or wanted so to practice, rehearse, publicly act, sing or perform, by the said lessees, or their successors, or by the managers for them, or by their prompter, or by any other person in their behalf, or by notice in the public newspapers, or in the posted playbills, shall forfeit, *for each refusal, five pounds.* If any performer, engaged at this Theatre, shall, by sickness, or other bodily indisposition, or infirmity, or by any restraint, accident, or cause whatsoever, be absent from or incapable of attending, practising, rehearsing, publicly acting, singing, or performing in the said Theatre Royal, in manner herein before-mentioned, then it shall and may be lawful for the aforesaid lessees, or their successors, to stop and retain, for their own use and benefit, the aforesaid weekly sums, or part thereof, according to the duration of such absence, payable weekly as aforesaid, for and during all the time or times of such absence, or incapacity, and the said performer shall not have any claim on them, or on either of them, for the same, or any part thereof, any thing therein contained to the contrary, notwithstanding. *For each night's absence, from sickness or any other cause, the penalty is five pounds;* but if a performer sends a doctor's certificate of illness, he only loses his salary during the period of such illness; and then must give notice when he is able to perform again."

60. The Royalty Theatre was built in 1787 with a license from the governor of the Tower of London, near which it stood. The patent houses objected, and the theatre had a checkered history as the East London Theatre for a time. After burning down during Booth's engagement, the theatre was rebuilt, and it reopened as the Royal Brunswick on 25 February 1828. Three days later it collapsed during a rehearsal, killing fifteen persons.

61. Asia Booth Clarke, *Booth Memorials,* 86, and *The Elder Booth,* 74, held that Booth performed for the Prince of Orange there, but the director of the City Archives of Amsterdam reports that the prince was nowhere near Amsterdam at that time. Kimmel, *The Mad Booths,* 44, still citing no sources, said Booth took Mary Ann and his American family with him, keeping them out of sight of Adelaide's relatives there.

62. Performance dates (see the Appendix) were taken from the Coffing manuscript from the Netherlands Theatre Institute, Amsterdam, courtesy of Wout Spies. Booth had appeared in Birmingham and Bristol with a young actress, Harriet Smithson, later named Harriet Berlioz. She had acted with him in *The Horatii and Curatii* at the Royal Coburg Theatre and at Drury Lane in 1820–21. She was also in the Drury Lane company in 1825. Her brother, Joseph, managed various fly-by-night companies on the Continent from time to time. His management in Amsterdam in 1826 was a financial and artistic disaster; Joseph Smithson abandoned the project shortly after Booth left. The rest of the company held two benefits to raise money to pay their expenses and return to England.

63. Harvard Theatre Collection.

5. The Fire Must Burn

1. Asia Booth Clarke, *Booth Memorials*, 86–87.

2. *Baltimore American and Commercial Daily Advertiser*, 16 Aug. 1826.

3. The Chatham Theatre was built in 1823 on the north side of Chatham Street between Pearl and Duane Streets. The 1827 season was the Chatham's only successful one, although it offered strong competition to the Park. In 1832 it was converted into a Presbyterian chapel.

4. Montrose J. Moses, *Famous Actor-Families in America* (New York: Thomas D. Crowell & Co., 1906), 263. George Holland (1791–1870) came to America but not to work for Booth; he appeared first in New York at the Bowery Theatre on 12 September 1827, by which time Booth had long since severed his relations with the Chatham.

5. By "Mr. D—," Booth surely refers to John Dwyer, then at the Chatham. He was born in Tipperary, Ireland, made his professional debut in Dublin and his London debut at Drury Lane on 1 March 1802. Drink eroded his powers until he became untrustworthy and obese; he died in retirement in New York in 1837. Mrs. Emma Romer (1814–68) was a dramatic singer. Mrs. Frances Alsop was the same actress who made her debut at Covent Garden as Rosalind on 18 October 1815, with Booth making his first appearance at that theatre as Sylvius. She came to the United States in 1820, debuted at the Park, and died the following spring. Mr. Entwistle was an English actor who debuted at the Park 23 October 1809 but never achieved eminence. Kirby the Clown, according to Wemyss, was James Kirby, who had appeared at the Royalty Theatre, London, in 1808, and first appeared in America at the Broadway Circus in New York. He drowned himself in Philadelphia in 1826.

6. Harvard Theatre Collection.

7. Sol Smith, *The Theatrical Journey-Work and Anecdotal Recollections of Sol Smith, Comedian, Attorney at Law, Etc.* (Philadelphia: T. B. Peterson, 1854), 17–18.

8. The question remains whether Booth ever played Oreste in French, as opposed to acting the role in the English *The Distrest Mother* in 1822. Asia Booth Clarke described the event in *The Elder Booth*, 76: "[Booth] played Richard III for sixteen nights to densely crowded houses. During his leisure hours he had perfected himself in several French dramas, playing, among other parts, *Faiel* in 'Gabrielle De Vergy,' *Tancred, Shakspere* in 'Shakspere Amoureux'; and being a proficient in the French language, he was solicited by Mr. Davis, of the Theatre d'Orleans, to play *Orestes,* in Racine's tragedy of 'Andromaque.' His accentuation was so perfect, and every peculiarity of French acting was so minutely observed by him, that the astonishment and delight were universal. At the close of the performance he was loudly called for, and cries of 'Talma! Talma!' saluted him, amid every sound of applause and approbation." Asia erred on several counts; examination of the bills and

newspaper accounts reveal no performances of Faiel, Tancred, or Shakespere, nor did Booth play Richard anything like sixteen nights. Noah Ludlow, as previously noted, suggests no such thing happened, but he was in Mobile, Alabama, with another company during the winter and spring of 1828 and so was not present for this performance. The most detailed history of the New Orleans theatre is John Kendall, *The Golden Age of the New Orleans Theatre* (Baton Rouge: Louisiana State University Press, 1952), 46–47, in which he posits: "It was during this visit . . . that Booth played Orestes in Racine's *Andromaque* at the Orleans theater. He spoke the part in French, and was supported by the French dramatic company then playing at this house. According to Booth's daughter, Asia, he was a phenomenal linguist, and spoke French fluently. In consenting to appear at the Orleans, he was deferring to the wishes of the French citizens, many of whom, unacquainted with the English language, were desirous of hearing the celebrated actor in one of the masterpieces of French literature. In 1822, at the request of the public, he had given the play in English at the Camp, availing himself of Phillips' version, known as *The Distressed Mother;* and apparently it was the repetition of this old play early in his current engagement which prompted the request that Racine's immortal verses should be rendered in their original form. This Booth did to the satisfaction of all concerned. Miss Placide, who had by this date returned to the city, took part in the two performances which Booth gave on February 19 and 21. By virtue of her French descent and long residence in New Orleans she spoke French as well as she did English, and shared the honors of the occasion." The Folger Shakespeare Library in Washington, D.C., holds two playbills for the production in question; both are in French. And the French-language newspaper of New Orleans, *L'Abeille*, contains advertisements for a performance of *Andromaque, Tragédie en cinq actes et en vers, de Racine, dans laquelle Mr. Booth jouera le rôle d'Oreste,* specifically naming Racine. Unfortunately, *L'Abeille* published no reviews of the event. Asia Booth Clarke cited an unidentified New Orleans newspaper's review in *The Elder Booth*, 77–78: "A spectacle of deep interest, one as novel as it was pleasing, was offered last Tuesday night in the Orleans Theatre, to the lovers of dramatic talents. Yielding to the solicitations of several gentlemen of this city, Mr. Booth consented to present himself before a French audience in the part of 'Orestes.' This effort, perilous in the extreme, and which nothing but a wish to give to Frenchmen an opportunity of judging fairly, of what is termed the *English style of tragic acting,* could have urged Mr. Booth to risk, has been crowned with the most flattering success. The ever-increasing interest excited by the warmth of his feelings, the earnestness of his manner, and the impetuous ardor of his delivery, and above all whenever passion rose high, when the furies goaded 'Orestes' to crimes, criticism was merged in admiration, and with one voice all wondered that a stranger should thus feel and express all the beauties of Racine." Asia had edited the review somewhat to flatter her father. Brander

Matthews and Laurence Hutton, eds., *Actors and Actresses of Great Britain and the United States from the Days of David Garrick to the Present Time* (New York: Cassell & Co., 1886), vol. 3, 114–15, quoted the review, taken from the *Louisiana Courier* (English edition), 21 Feb. 1828. It was also reprinted in *The Nation* 31(23 Sept. 1880): 223–24. Matthews and Hutton included the following excerpts. "He was aware that his pronunciation was far from being considered correct even by his most partial friends, but relying on the indulgence of a polite audience he determined to make the attempt, depending on his power of action to diminish, at least, the defect of his accent. . . . After the first scene the unpleasant effect of his English accent was lost. . . . There certainly were moments when the dialogue did not call for the enthusiastic vigor which carried away the hearers without giving them time to attend to mere sounds, when harsh and discordant words wounded the delicacy of French ears. . . . The spectators, after the curtain dropped, called for Mr. Booth and saluted him by long and reiterated applause." Asia continued: "Mr. Davis offered my father $300 per night for a period of twelve nights; but prior engagements would not allow him to remain for so long a term." Finally, Ford, *The Actor*, 75–76, described Booth as playing one night as Oreste in French to general acclamation.

9. Library of Congress, Manuscript Division.

10. *Boston Daily Advertiser*, 30 Aug. 1828.

11. Joe Leathley Cowell (1792–1863) was an English comedian who became extremely popular in the United States. He died in England.

12. By 1831 their children included Henry Byron Booth, Mary Ann Booth, Frederick Booth, and Elizabeth Booth, but birth dates remain uncertain. Mrs. Rogers stated that Mary Ann had a child about every two years, which was typical of those times. Kimmel, *The Mad Booths*, n.p., listed Henry Byron as being born in 1825, Mary Ann in 1827, Frederick in 1829, and Elizabeth in 1831. The Booth family Bible, now at the Museum of the City of New York, Theatre Collection, recorded no birth dates.

13. The *Theatrical Censor*, 4 Nov. 1828, 122–23. The remainder of the Tremont Association's tribute to Booth read, "The office of principal Director, is, they are aware, one of great labor and responsibility; and in performing its requisitions, they have been pleased to observe, your constant endeavours to provide for the improvement, as well as gratification of the patrons of the drama; and that those exertions have not only received the approbation of your immediate friends, but of the community at large. Nor have your histrionic efforts been attended with less success. Their merits are universally acknowledged, and will long continue to be appreciated. In token of their personal regard, they beg to present, through your friend and successor, J. Cowell, Esq. the accompanying plate and cup, as a slight but sincere testimony of that high respect which they, in common with their fellow citizens, entertain for a scholar and man of genius."

14. Miss Lane (1820–97) was the future Mrs. John Drew, the grand-

mother of John (1882–1942), Lionel (1878–1954), and Ethel Barrymore (1879–1959). Her first appearance in America had been 26 September 1827 at the Walnut Street Theatre as the Duke of York to Booth's Richard, according to the *New York Dramatic Mirror,* 19 Nov. 1902, and Mrs. John Drew, *Autobiographical Sketch of Mrs. John Drew* (New York: Charles Scribner's Sons, 1899), 21.

15. *Louisiana Courier,* 26 Feb. 1829.

16. Smith, *Theatrical Journey-Work,* 32.

17. Sol Smith, *Theatrical Management in the West and South for Thirty Years* (New York: Harper & Brothers, 1868), 229–30.

18. Henry Pitt Phelps, *Players of a Century: A Record of the Albany Stage* (Albany: Joseph McDonought, 1880), 182; and James Marshall Leonard, "The Letters of William Duffy, Albany Theatre Manager, 1830–1835," (Ph.D. dissertation, Cornell University, Ithaca, New York, 1971), 197.

19. An unidentified, undated clipping in Theatre Cuttings 75, British Library, quotes the *Boston Bulletin* describing the entire incident. The story implies that Booth on Saturday the fifth (*Evadne* was billed for Monday the seventh) made several attempts to strangle a gentleman with whom he was sharing a bed, forcing the man to seek another room. The rest of the story agrees with documented sources for the most part.

20. Except where noted, the entire account is taken from William W. Clapp, Jr., *A Record of the Boston Stage* (Boston and Cambridge: James Munroe and Co., 1853. Reprint. New York: Greenwood Press, 1969); and Charles Blake, *An Historical Account of the Providence Stage: Being a Paper Read before the Rhode Island Historical Society, October 25th, 1860 (With Additions)* (Providence: George H. Whitney, 1868. Reprint. New York: Benjamin Blom, 1971).

21. *Literary Subaltern,* 22 Jan. 1830.

22. *Providence Journal,* 24 Dec. 1829.

23. *United States Gazette,* 6 Jan. 1830.

24. Harvard Theatre Collection.

25. Harvard Theatre Collection. John Rowland Durrant (?–1853) was one of the founders of the Garrick Club in 1833.

26. Harvard Theatre Collection.

27. Philip Hone, *The Diary of Philip Hone 1828–1851,* edited by Allan Nevins (New York: Dodd, Mean and Co., 1927), 25. Hone, a successful businessman who retired at age forty, was an avid theatregoer, well acquainted with theatrical luminaries of his day. From 1828 to 1851 he kept a secret diary, which furnishes a detailed picture of New York life in that period. The diary is now at the New York Historical Society, New York City.

28. Asia Booth Clarke, *The Elder Booth,* beginning on p. 80; Baltimore newspaper reviews and advertisements; as well as Alonzo May's unpublished history of the Baltimore theatre, examined in the Maryland Historical Society.

29. Asia Booth Clarke, *Booth Memorials,* 96.

30. For partial lists, see J. P. Wearing, *American and British Theatrical Biography: A Directory* (Metuchen, New Jersey: Scarecrow Press, 1979), 122–23.

31. Francis Courtney Wemyss, *Twenty-six Years of the Life of an Actor and Manager* (New York: Burgess, Stringer and Co., 1847), 187.

32. Folger Shakespeare Library.

33. Folger Shakespeare Library.

34. From a transcript in the John T. Ford Papers in the Library of Congress, supplied by Gayle Harris. The location of the original is unknown.

35. Thomas Dartmouth Rice (1808–60) was a hugely popular imitator of Negroes, famous for a song-and-dance act, "Jump Jim Crow."

36. *New York Mirror,* 29 Dec. 1832, 206.

37. Players.

38. *Spirit of the Times,* 24 Nov. 1832.

39. Players.

40. Ford, *The Actor,* 92–95.

41. Booth file, Manuscript Division, Library of Congress.

42. According to newspaper advertisements, Booth was not in Baltimore, Washington, D.C., or Philadelphia. He suggests in his letter to Wemyss that he was performing in Richmond, but no newspaper advertisements from the time have survived.

43. Folger Shakespeare Library.

44. Harvard Theatre Collection.

45. Harvard Theatre Collection.

46. Harvard Theatre Collection.

47. Edwin Booth's birth coincided with one of the brightest meteor displays ever witnessed, being one of the Leonid meteor showers which used to bombard the earth about every thirty-three years. Our planet now misses the heaviest part of the shower. According to Adam Badeau ("Boyhood of Edwin Booth," in an unidentified Chicago newspaper clipping, 29 Jan. 1893, Howard University, Emma Marble Album, 134, Channing Pollock Collection), Edwin for most of his life considered his birthday 15 November 1834, to which his mother readily agreed. Junius Brutus Booth, Jr., insisted on 13 November 1833, recalling he rode a horse to fetch the doctor, accompanied by an elderly servant who was terrified by the falling stars. A similar shower had taken place in November 1834, so the matter remained unresolved till Edwin discovered a letter from his father dated November 1833, mentioning his birth. Edwin thus never had a fifty-eighth birthday, having by then discovered his and his mother's error.

48. Harvard Theatre Collection.

49. Wemyss, *Twenty-six Years,* 225–26.

50. From a transcript in the Kimmel Collection. Asia Booth Clarke described Booth's purchase in *Booth Memorials,* 110: "About this time my

father purchased two Egyptian mummies with a view of presenting them to General Jackson. They were to be sent to the Hermitage; but, finding that they were such rare specimens, it was suggested that they should be reserved for the Museum in Washington, for which Mr. Varden was then collecting curiosities. The mummies were priests of the god 'Apis'; and, on examination, the papyrus manuscripts, although in excellent and legible order, proved to be of such antiquity that it was impossible for the literati of that day to translate their meaning. Languages, like nations and religions, take their turns and seem to prove the mutability of nature. Mr. Varden's design being ineffectual, the mummies were subsequently deposited in the Patent Office, Washington, and removed thence to the Smithsonian Institute."

51. 20 January 1834, from a transcript in the Kimmel Collection.

52. Ludlow, *Dramatic Life,* 416.

53. A Booth letter fitting the following story and this chronology is held by the Harvard University Library, Cambridge, Massachusetts:

United States Hotel
Jan. 4. 1834

Sir

I hope you will excuse the liberty of a Stranger addressing you on a subject he feels great interest in. It is to require a place of Interment for his friend in the church-yard, and also the Expense attendant on the purchase of such place of temporary Repose.

Your communication on this matter will greatly oblige

Sir
Your respectful &
obedt. Servant
J.B. Booth

54. Harvard University Library, dated from Louisville, 13 January 1834. Also quoted in the *Spirit of the Times,* 12 Jan. 1884.

55. Ludlow, *Dramatic Life,* 417–18.

56. Quoted in Otis Skinner, *Mad Folk of the Theatre: Ten Studies in Temperament* (Indianapolis: Bobbs-Merrill Co., 1928), 281–82. Skinner claimed the letter was in the collection of Samuel H. Cowell, the son of the addressee, Theatre Royal, Edinburgh, and was a folded sheet, not an envelope. The letter was also published in the *Cincinnati Enquirer*, 20 Oct. 1935.

57. Wemyss, *Twenty-six Years*, 229–30.

58. Booth and Houston enjoyed a long friendship, as described in Marquis James, *The Raven: A Biography of Sam Houston* (Indianapolis: Bobbs-Merrill Co., 1929). They had met in Washington, D.C., when Houston served as senator, about 1823. See also George Sorenson, "Sam Houston in the Theatre," *Theatre Southwest* 12(Feb. 1985), 16–19.

59. Edwin Forrest's brother, William, had died in February 1834. Harvard Theatre Collection, dated 24 March 1834.

60. Booth doubtless referred to the racial riots described in note 62.

61. Harvard Theatre Collection.

62. Booth refers to George Percy Farren (1786–1861), who came to America and became the stage manager for Hamblin at the Bowery Theatre in New York City. He had a benefit billed for 9 July 1834, featuring Forrest as Metamora. The same night, however, an antislavery society planned a meeting at the Chatham Street Chapel, formerly the Chatham Theatre. A large mob of proslavery citizens gathered and broke into the chapel but discovered no meeting was to be held. They then recalled that Farren had been accused of cursing all Americans, calling them jackasses, and promising to gull them whenever he could. The mob broke into the Bowery and brought the performance to a halt. They ignored Hamblin when he tried to speak to them, but Forrest restored a measure of peace, followed by the arrival of one hundred watchmen who saw the mob out of the theatre. The mob then stormed the house of an abolitionist, Lewis Tappan (1788–1873) on Rose Street, broke all his windows, burned his furniture, and were finally dispersed about 2:00 A.M. Farren shortly afterwards joined Noah Ludlow and Sol Smith's company in the southern states. Booth also referred to Joshua R. Anderson, who rose to stardom at Drury Lane, married Josephine Bartolozzi, the sister of Mme Vestris, and came to America in 1831. He, like Farren, had made derogatory remarks about the United States, and his debut on 14 October 1831 sparked three days of rioting and forced his withdrawal from the stage. See Odell, *Annals of the New York Stage*, vol. 3, 548–60 and 387–88; also Hone, *Diary*, 49–50.

63. Folger Shakespeare Library. Booth played the title role, a slave character, in *Oroonoko*, at the Bowery for Farren, deviating from stage tradition by acting in bare feet.

64. James Rush Diary, 1830–42, Pennsylvania Historical Society, Philadelphia.

65. Library of Congress, Manuscript Division, Andrew Jackson Papers, Series 1, Reel 46.

66. Harvard Theatre Collection.

67. Harvard Theatre Collection.

68. James Rush Diary, 1830–42, Pennsylvania Historical Society, Philadelphia.

69. Quoted by Asia Booth Clarke, *The Elder Booth*, 95–96. The Northern Venus referred to Frigga, the Norse goddess of love.

70. Hone, *Diary*, 184.

71. Harvard Theatre Collection.

72. Wemyss, *Twenty-six Years*, 265.

73. Quoted in The *Spirit of the Times*, 28 June 1851, 220.

74. *Baltimore Sun*, 27 Dec. 1905.

75. Wemyss, *Twenty-six Years*, 265.

76. The *Georgetown Metropolitan* published the same story earlier, on 11

April 1836, adding the following comment: "The last time we saw Booth was in *King Lear*, and we never witnessed that terrible tragedy performed with more thrilling and impressive effect, though it was evident, as we mentioned at the time, that is was more from deep and saddened feeling than . . . from any high and sustained conception of the part. His delineation of the mad scene in particular—that scene which Lamb said never could, or should be acted—was more touching and harrowing in its effect than we had ever seen it, even by Kean or Macready. 'See,' said a distinguished lady beside us, who was altogether overpowered by the scene, 'See how the sword is wearing out the scabbard.' We mention this vivid recollection merely to show the giant power of his mind, even in decay."

77. Folger Shakespeare Library.

78. *Spirit of the Times,* 11 June 1836.

79. Information on the litigation supplied by Don Grose.

80. Clapp, *A Record,* 313.

81. Folger Shakespeare Library.

82. *United States Gazette,* 1 June 1836.

6. An Apparent Heir

1. Asia Booth Clarke apparently intended to add considerable material to *The Elder and the Younger Booth* for a new edition in England, but the revision was never published. Her proposed additions are inserted in a copy of the 1881 edition held by the University of Illinois, Rare Book Room. It includes some of Booth's travel notes: "We left Philadelphia, Oct. 20th, 1836, in ship 'Susquehanna,' Captain Cropper. Towed down by steam to Capes Henlopen and May, with a vessel bound to Laguira. Off the Capes, spoke ship 'John Causland,' from Batavia; about midnight, discharged the pilot. Next day, a large owl lighted on the spanker-boom. In the Gulf *Les Ames damnees* or Mother Cary's Chickens, following our wake, and the gulf-weed thick about our quarter. A man died on Sunday morning in a fit of delirium tremens, and after breakfast, all hands went on deck to see the ceremony of burial, which was brief in preparation and performance. Wednesday, caught a bird of the swallow genus, by its bill and claws. Fed it on soaked biscuit and corn-meal mush. Thursday becalmed. Friday, a strong breeze in the fore part of the day sent us at eleven miles an hour; toward night we only measured eight. We have now crossed the southernmost edge of the Grand Bank of Newfoundland. We are on deep soundings. Have left St. John's to the west of us. Rainy and cold; thermometer 45 degrees Fahrenheit. Caught a small red bird. We are now ten days out; have come about half way. Wednesday, about 10 A.M., saw a barque whose sails and boats had been removed; no signs of a human being about her; could read on her stern 'Louisa of Plymouth.' Our captain would not board her,—said she was water-logged. Saturday, Guy Fawkes' Day. Wind still ahead; all looks gloomy.

Eating and drinking and occasionally reading, with a game of draughts or chess to while away the monotonous hours. Read 'Memoirs of Crockett,' by himself. Saw him in Washington in 1834, introduced to him by Gov. Houston. Both singular geniuses. One is dead, the other now President of Alamo, Texas. Crockett was in Congress in 1834; not being re-elected, he adventured among the recruits for Texas, and fell at the assault of Alamo, by the hands of Mexican under Santa Anna. This ship keeps her steerage passengers forward, and the crew have a room in front of the mainmast, the length of which room to the stern being assigned for the twenty-dollar travelers. This plan keeps the steerage passengers from coming into altercation with the others by intervention of the crew. Just twenty-one days from Walnut-street wharf, Philadelphia. Land visible on our larboard side. Saw two vessels on horizon at 6 P.M.; were abreast of Waterford Lighthouse, bearing N.N.E.; fifteen miles off, passed Salter's and Tuskan revolving light. About ten, a heavy gale sprung up, accompanied by frequent lightning and rain. This was the only time, as yet, that there has been any appearance of danger, several seas shipping and washing right up to the wheels from the bows. Friday, saw an English ship to windward of us, and the coast Angelsea about noon. Weather foggy and wind ahead. At 2 P.M. fog disappeared and disclosed to our astonished eyes the Isle of Man, four miles ahead! We had overshot our port seventy or eighty miles; had to bout ship and return. Pilot came on board Saturday at daybreak. Read in paper of Forrest's success and rejoiced at it. Snow perceptible on hill-tops, towards [Mt.] Snowdon. Landed in Liverpool about noon." Booth frequently took copious notes as he traveled; presumably most of them were destroyed by his widow.

2. Richard Moody, *Edwin Forrest: First Star of the American Stage* (New York: Alfred A. Knopf, 1960), 149–50.

3. John Cooper (fl. 1810–70) debuted at Drury Lane in 1820 and on 8 November of the same year played Othello to Booth's Iago. He acted at Covent Garden and Drury Lane for the next twenty-five years.

4. Alfred Bunn (1798–1860) in 1833 undertook management of both Covent Garden and Drury Lane but failed. He had been stage manager for Elliston at Drury Lane in 1823.

5. Charles Kemble (1775–1854), the youngest brother of John Philip Kemble, appeared as a child star and made his London debut on 21 April 1794. For a time he managed Covent Garden but was saved from bankruptcy by the excellent acting of his daughter, Fanny. Kemble retired in 1832 to become Examiner of Plays, but he continued to give Shakespearean readings.

6. Booth apparently means Jane Booth Mitchell, his sister, who had had several children by James Mitchell but was suffering from poverty due to her husband's idleness.

7. Players.

8. Booth's son Henry Byron was buried at the Pentonville Chapel. The graveyard has been destroyed; the site is now the Grimaldi Park, named after

the clown with whom Booth had shared early bills in Brighton; Grimaldi was also buried in Pentonville. As a later letter indicated, Henry Byron Booth died 28 December 1836, not in 1837 as Kimmel stated. George Horton Barrett (1794–1860) became principal director at the Bowery in 1826, later at the Tremont in Boston, and at Burton's and the Broadway Theatre in New York. Thomas Ternan (1804–46) was an Irish actor of no particular significance. The letter is from the Menken Collection.

9. Harvard Theatre Collection. H. H. Rowbotham (d. 1837) was an actor with whom Booth had often appeared in Philadelphia.

10. Burr, *New York Press.*

11. The Mitchells departed England on 1 March 1838 on the packet *Ontario*, arriving in New York City on 26 March and going thence to Baltimore and Harford County. Neither the exact number nor the names of the Mitchell children have been clearly recorded. The Maryland Census for 1850 lists a Mitchell household in the Sixteenth Ward of Baltimore, consisting of (1) James Mitchell, age 54, occupation "Pedler"; (2) Jane Mitchell, age 51; (3) George Mitchell, age 25, laborer; (4) Robert Mitchell, age 19, collector; (5) Maria Mitchell, age 15; (6) Charlotte Mitchell, age 13; and (6) Richard Mitchell, age 11. All were born in England, except Richard, who was born in Maryland. The census also indicated that Charlotte and Richard had attended school that year.

12. Library of Congress, Booth File, Manuscript Division.

13. Wood, *Personal Recollections of the Stage,* 405.

14. Henry E. Willard and William R. Blake had modeled their new theatre on the London Olympic run by Madame Vestris and opened for business at 444 Broadway, between Howard and Grand Streets. They failed, but the theatre later became most successful under William Mitchell as Mitchell's Olympic. Samuel Woodworth (1785–1842), a poet and playwright, wrote *The Forest Rose,* one of the first American dramas to contain the Yankee character. He became paralyzed later in life; the successful benefit to which Booth referred marked the first appearance of William E. Burton. The letter is at the Pennsylvania Historical Society, Philadelphia.

15. Francis Courtney Wemyss, *Theatrical Biography: Or, The Life of an Actor and Manager* (Glasgow: R. Griffin & Co., 1840), 242.

16. *Spirit of the Times,* 3 Mar. 1838.

17. Asia Booth Clarke, *Booth Memorials,* 130.

18. *Spirit of the Times,* 24 Mar. 1838.

19. *Spirit of the Times,* 7 Apr. 1838. Charles H. Eaton debuted in Boston in 1833 and toured as a Shakespearean tragedian till his death in Pittsburgh in 1842.

20. Asia Booth Clarke, *The Elder Booth,* 97–98; Thomas Ridgeway Gould, *The Tragedian: An Essay on the Histrionic Genius of Junius Brutus Booth* (New York: Hurd and Houghton, 1868. Reprint. New York: Benjamin Blom, 1971), 35–36.

21. *Mercury,* 21 Mar. 1838.

22. *Charleston Courier,* 30 Mar. 1838.

23. Missouri Historical Society, St. Louis.

24. Kimmel, *The Mad Booths,* asserted that Richard Booth, the grandfather of John Wilkes Booth, named the new baby, the only time he was allowed this privilege.

25. *Baltimore Sun,* 15 May 1838.

26. *Baltimore Sun,* 21 May 1838.

27. Missouri Historical Society, St. Louis. Most of the correspondence between Booth and the managers was published by William G. B. Carson, "Sol Smith and Theatre Folk 1836–1865," *Glimpses of the Past* 5(1938): 99–136.

28. Ludlow, *Dramatic Life,* 509–10.

29. Drew, *Autobiographical Sketch,* 49–50.

30. *Baltimore Sun,* 18 July 1839.

31. Asia Booth Clarke, *Booth Memorials,* 133–34.

32. Asia Booth Clarke, *Personal Recollections of the Elder Booth* (London: Privately Printed, n.d.), 36–37. Kimmel, *The Mad Booths,* 58, claimed Richard Booth's first gravestone had a Hebrew inscription but supplies no documentation. Ella V. Mahoney, *Sketches of Tudor Hall and the Booth Family* (Bel Air, Maryland: Tudor Hall, 1925), 55, cited a Mr. Mears who claimed Richard's first stone had an inscription in Hebrew. When the grave was moved from Old Baltimore Cemetery to Green Mount, the original inscription was buried with Richard and replaced by the present Latin inscription, which reads, "Sacred to the memory of Richard Booth Who died Decr. 29d 1839, Aged 76 years & 43 days. *Ex vita, ita discedo iamquam ex hospitio in servum Regnuum inclytissimi Ducis; illinc ire ad Astra.*" The Maryland Historical Society records Richard Booth, age 77, died of old age and was buried during the week of 6 January 1840 in Christ Church Burying Ground, Baltimore, presumably where Weaver had a vault. This cemetery was disbanded between 1851 and 1856; the present Johns Hopkins Hospital is now on the site. Richard's body was reburied at Baltimore Cemetery 11 March 1851 and moved to Green Mount Cemetery in June 1869, according to information supplied by James O. Hall and Michael Kauffman.

33. Unidentified clipping, Folger Shakespeare Library, W.a. 67.

34. Wemyss, *Twenty six Years,* 323.

35. *New York Morning Herald,* 9 May 1840.

36. Harvard Theatre Collection.

37. Wemyss, *Twenty-six Years,* 324–25.

38. Described by Edwin Booth in his widely reprinted essay, "Edmund Kean and Junius Brutus Booth." The Folger Shakespeare Library holds a typed manuscript of the essay.

39. Menken Collection.

40. *New York Herald,* 7 July 1840. A Charles J. Houpt, dentist and manufacturer of mineral teeth, appeared in Archibald McElroy's *Philadelphia*

Directory (Philadelphia: A. McElroy, 1840), 119, at 246 Sassafras Street, also in 1844. Directories for the next two years listed him at 294 Chestnut Street, according to information supplied by John M. Whittock, Jr., Evans Museum and Dental Institute, Philadelphia.

41. James Rush Diary, 1830–42, Pennsylvania Historical Society, Philadelphia. Rush (1786–1869) was the seventh of thirteen children born to Benjamin Rush, one of the signers of the Declaration of Independence. Rush received his M.D. from the University of Pennsylvania in 1809, studied in Edinburgh for a time, and returned to Philadelphia in 1811. In 1819, however, he married a wealthy merchant's daughter who inherited something more than one million dollars. Rush devoted most of his energies not to medicine but to social and scientific interests. He published several books and kept several diaries and notebooks, now in the Pennsylvania Historical Society.

42. In one of his extant notebooks, Rush listed several reasons why an actor could not be a gentleman. He lists (1) their lack of feeling, (2) their usual lack of education, (3) their excessive vanity, (4) their greed, and (5) the despicable characters they regularly played. Rush considered John Philip Kemble marked by a dull formality of manner, Kean by fantastic affectation, and he wrote off Fanny Kemble as "that little humbug." Rush puzzled over the success of Kean and Fanny Kemble and the "absence of noise" about Booth, adding, "the two former being both pieces of miserable affectation, and the latter living nearer to nature than any actor I have ever heard." In another notebook, Rush in 1828 referred to Booth as "an actor of true and strong and delicate feeling—He always carries along with the part and himself all those who likewise are of strong and true and delicate feeling." Rush particularly admired Booth's vocal powers. Booth apparently socialized with the Rushes and sent them copies of books he especially admired, such as Edward Bulwer Lytton's *Paul Clifford.*

43. Charlotte Cushman (1816–76), the United States' first great actress, was born in Boston and made her New York debut in 1836. A plain woman, she was especially admired as Lady Macbeth, which she later played with Edwin Booth. The Charlotte Cushman Club in Philadelphia contains many of her records and much memorabilia.

44. Wemyss, *Twenty-six Years,* 354–55.

45. *Spirit of the Times,* 29 May 1841. Kimmel, *The Mad Booths,* 60, maintained that Junius Brutus Booth, Jr., married Clementine De Bar in 1844; this 1841 reference would indicate otherwise, although the union may not have been official.

46. *Dramatic Mirror,* 23 Apr. 1842.

47. *Spirit of the Times,* 8 Apr. 1843.

48. Quoted in the *New Orleans Picayune,* 15 Apr. 1843.

49. Burr, *New York Press.*

50. Burr, *New York Press,* included two relevant letters:

Tuesday, Nov. 22, 1841.

Mrs. Davidge presents compliments to Mrs. Booth, and begs to say her name will be left at the box door of the Surrey Theatre on Thursday next; and also an order left with the stage doorkeeper to admit Mrs. B.'s son and friend behind the scenes.

Davidge

Thursday morning

Mrs. G. Ward solicits the honor of Mrs. Booth's name as a subscriber to the inclosed work under the patronage of the most respectable ladies and gentlemen of the Theatres Royal, Covent Garden and Drury Lane, as also of the nobility. Mrs. Kean and Miss O'Neill are among the latest of the subscribers. The honor of Mrs. Booth's name will be highly flattering.

Thornton, Elliston, McCarthy, Criss, Sanford, N. Johnson, Macready, Watson.

51. Burr, *New York Press.*

52. Burr, *New York Press;* apparently he cited documents now lost.

53. Kimmel, *The Mad Booths,* 63, cited no documentation but claimed Richard Booth arrived in 1842. Such a date is unlikely; Burr, *New York Press,* cited Richard's will: "I, the undersigned, Richard J. Booth, nominate for my sole heir my mother, Marie Christine Adèlaide Delannoy, wife of Junius Brutus Booth, living at Brussels, to whom I leave all my property, real and personal, of which I may be possessed at the time of my decease. R.J. BOOTH. Done at Brussels the 24th day of September, 1843."

54. *Brother Jonathan,* 3 June 1843, 148.

55. *Brother Jonathan,* 24 June 1843, 234.

56. *Spirit of the Times,* 24 June 1843.

57. *Boston Post,* 12 Dec. 1843.

58. *Boston Daily Evening Transcript,* 8 Apr. 1844.

59. *Boston Daily Evening Transcript,* 10 Apr. 1844.

60. George Vandenhoff, *Dramatic Reminiscences; Or, Actors and Actresses in England and America* (London: Thomas W. Cooper & Co., John Camden Hotten, 1860), 218–19. Vandenhoff (1813–85), born in England, first appeared at Covent Garden in 1839. He debuted in New York in 1842 and remained in America until 1853, when he returned to England. His last appearance was in 1878.

61. *Spirit of the Times,* 6 Sept. 1845.

62. Information supplied from Baltimore, Maryland, Court House records (AWB 357-265) by James O. Hall. House number 62 represents the old numbering system; the house, typical of Baltimore row houses, was renumbered 220 North Exeter. The block was razed for construction of the Baltimore Post Office.

63. Descriptions of this house from Walter Edgar McCann, "The Booth Family in Maryland," *Our Newsman* (n.d.), 404–10, also quoted in the

Maryland Historical Society, Alonzo May manuscript. On 20 May 1847 Booth bought two lots adjoining for $180 on a ninety-eight-year lease with three dollars annual ground rent.

64. Missouri Historical Society, St. Louis.

65. Missouri Historical Society, St. Louis.

66. *Spirit of the Times,* 6 Dec. 1845.

67. Harvard Theatre Collection.

68. Folger Shakespeare Library. The remainder of the bill is glued to another sheet and unreadable.

69. Olive Logan, *Before the Footlights and Behind the Scenes: A Book about "The Show Business" in All Its Branches* (Philadelphia: Parmalee & Co., 1870), 499–501.

70. Ludlow, *Dramatic Life,* 644–45. See also the *St. Louis Reporter,* 23–29 June 1846.

71. Ford, *The Actor,* 1.

7. No More in This World

1. Burr reprinted Adelaide's letters in the *New York Press.*

2. Burr, *New York Press.*

3. *Spirit of the Times,* 21 Nov. 1846.

4. Maude Skinner and Otis Skinner, *One Man in His Time: The Adventures of H. Watkins, Strolling Player 1845–1863 from His Journal* (Philadelphia: University of Pennsylvania Press, 1938), 45–46.

5. Transcript, Kimmel Collection.

6. An undated clipping in the Maryland Historical Society further complicates the exact date and place of Adelaide's confrontation with Booth. It was written by a Professor John Hill Hewitt (1801–90), a journalist, musician, and poet who operated around the fringes of the theatre. In the article, written for the *Baltimore American,* Hewitt referred to Burr's article in the *Philadelphia Press* which in fact appeared in the *New York Press.* Hewitt claimed he referred to his diary to describe the meeting between Adelaide and Booth. The gist of the article: "In the year 1848 I entered into a speculation jointly with John K. Randell, George P. Kane and Charles Howard, and on the 12th of June opened a small summer theater on the northeast corner of Baltimore and Charles streets. It was called the Howard Athenaeum. The elder Booth was one of the many stars that gave lustre to its stage. Being business manager of this cosy little concern, I occupied my office on the second floor both day and a great deal of the night. One day, while at my desk, a lady dressed in black silk, accompanied by a good-looking lad, came to the door and asked if she could see Mr. Booth, who was at the moment on the stage rehearsing the play of 'A New Way to Pay Old Debts.' I requested her to enter and be seated, stating that the gentleman at the time was very busy, but would shortly be at leisure. I entered into

conversation with the stranger, and found her rather reticent, but still pleasant in her bearing and polished in her language, though a little marred by the German accent. I soon learned that she had just arrived in this country, and the lad was her son. As to the nature of her visit, I could learn nothing. The rehearsal came to an end, and I sent a messenger for Mr. Booth, requesting his presence at the office, as a lady wished to see him. He came promptly, and then a dramatic scene was enacted which I shall never forget. Booth started back when his glance fell on the lady, who encountered it boldly and with folded arms. They gazed on each other for some time without either uttering a word. The boy made a movement toward the actor, but was held back by the mother, while I stood perplexed, not knowing whether to remain or abandon my post, for I had not the slightest idea of the *denouement* of the drama. At length Booth exclaimed in a husky voice. 'You here!' and the lady answered scornfully, 'Yes, I have come, and this is your son,' presenting the lad. The truth flashed upon me, and I vacated the office instanter, thinking it best to let them settle their domestic troubles without a witness. In a short time a hack was ordered, and they departed from the building. The lady, as I subsequently learned, was the great actor's trans-atlantic wife, and the youth was Junius Brutus Booth, Jr. How they settled the affair I never learned." Hewitt opened the Howard Athenaeum on 12 June 1848, according to advertisements in the *Baltimore American* and *Sun*. Booth did indeed perform there, opening on 10 July 1848 in *A New Way to Pay Old Debts.* But between Adelaide's arrival in mid-November 1846 and Booth's 1848 engagement at the Howard Athenaeum, Booth had performed in Baltimore for some seven engagements. Adelaide would hardly have waited so long to confront Booth, and Hewitt's motives in writing such a story remain obscure. The son in question was not, of course, Junius Brutus Booth, Jr., but Richard Junius, who had been traveling with his father for a few years and so hardly needed to be "presented" to him.

7. *Maryland Acts,* 1841, Chapter 262, Section 5, specified: "*And be it enacted,* That no person shall be entitled to make application for a divorce under this act where the causes for divorce occurred in another State, unless such person so applying shall have resided within this State for two years next preceding his or her application." Abandonment and adultery were both listed as valid causes for which a divorce might be granted.

8. Burr, *New York Press.*

9. The Maryland Historical Society holds both documents. The first reads, "Whereas the undersigned Junius B. Booth in the year of 1826 entered into an agreement with his wife Marie C. A. Booth (formerly Delannoy) to pay her annually the sum of seventy-five pounds sterling by way of separate maintenance, during her life, which said sum has ever since been paid to her up to the 1st day of May 1847 inclusive: And whereas the undersigned have agreed to modify said agreement by the said Junius B. Booth paying to her the sum of One Thousand Dollars (the receipt of which is hereby acknowl-

edged) as ten years of advance of 20£ sterling of said annuity, and by giving an assignment of and an order for an annuity of 50£ sterling given to him by the will of his grandmother, the late Elizabeth Booth, payable out of and charged on the rents of certain lots in the city of London, devised to and held by John Wilkes Booth of said city, In Trust, among other objects to pay said annuity, which said annuity of 50£ stg. the said Mary C. A. Booth is to receive during her life, and after her death the same is to descend to, or be devised to Richard J. Booth, son of said Junius and Mary, in as large and beneficial estate as the said Junius can grant or devise, and the said Richard take in the same. In consideration whereof the undersigned Mary hereby agrees to accept the said advance and assignment in full of all claims and demands which she may have or ever has had against the undersigned Junius of every nature and kind whatsoever: And she further agrees that she will make no other claims against the said Junius for dower; or to administration on his estate, or to any part of his estate, provided the said 50£ stg. annuity be paid to her for life, and the said Junius, or his heirs or representatives shall on or before the first day of May 1857 pay to her, if then living, a further sum of one thousand dollars as another advance for ten years of said annuity of 20£ stg., for the period between the 1st of May 1857 and 1 May 1867, and shall thereafter pay her, during her life, the said 20£ stg. annually: And if from any cause the said 50£ stg. annuity should not be paid to the said Mary, the said Junius B. Booth agrees and binds himself, his heirs and representatives, to remit the equivalent amount to her during her life in half yearly payments of 25 £stg. This arrangement and agreement being made with the understanding, and on condition that the said 50£ stg. annuity shall be paid to the said Mary C. A. Booth during her life, and from and after her death, the same shall descend to the said Richard J. Booth, or be conveyed or devised to him by the said Junius B. Booth in full of all claims which he may have on the estate of said Junius B. Booth. In case the said Mary and Richard should both die, before the said Junius' death, the said 50£ stg. annuity is to revert to the latter, provided the said Richard should die without issue: it being understood that the said Mary and Richard take said 50£ stg. annuity subject to the Taxes imposed on the same in England. In Witness whereof the said Junius B. Booth, Marie C. A. Booth, and Richard J. Booth have hereunto set their hands and seals this seventh day of May 1847. In presence of J. Pennington," signed by "J. B. Booth," "M. Booth," and "R. J. Booth." The second and shorter document is appended. "Know all men by these presents that I, Richard Junius Booth, son of Junius B. Booth and Mary C. A. Booth, having this day received from my said father a conveyance or assignment of an annuity of 50£ stg., charged on the residue of the real and personal estate of Elizabeth Booth, late of London, deceased, by her last Will and Testament, or a power of attorney to receive said annuity from the person or persons bound to pay the same, and being a party to an agreement made between my said father and mother for the assignment of said annuity to my said mother for life: do hereby declare and admit that my said mother is entitled to receive from me the said annuity of 50£ stg. as the same is paid to me: And I do hereby promise and bind myself to pay the same to her as soon as I do receive it from the person or persons bound to pay it to me under the conveyance or Power of Attorney aforesaid. In Witness whereof I have hereunto set my hand and seal this seventh day of May 1847. In presence of J. Pennington," signed, "R. J. Booth."

10. Little is known about John Wilkes Booth of London, although his very name establishes another link with John Wilkes, the Clerkenwell ancestor of Elizabeth Booth. The Menken Collection contains a letter from the nineteenth-century John Wilkes, however, revealing the family trait of exact accounting.

Oct 29 1842

Victoria Grove
Stoke
Newington
Middsx England

Sir

I hereby send you a Letter of Credit for £12.0.0 which with 10/ for postage & stamps as under—makes the Quarter due—you sent me the two last receipts both to Lady day last. so that you will please to make this one right—you state in your letter of Aug 30-[18]42 you would rather not sell—as you may visit England. Should you come I should be glad to see you—as regards the House in Taylor's Row, I should say it belongs to you now—I have been [?] they pay no rent—I would have sent before but rents are bad things to collect & I have been very much a loser by some of them & also the repairs—please to acknowledge this as soon as convenient.

Yours
respectfully
JW Booth

5 letters sent to you
4 answers received
9 cost me 1/ ea——9.0
2 stamps 1.0
S10.0

Taylor's Row was about a half mile from Clerkenwell. Kraentzler, "John Wilkes Booth," maintained that John and Elizabeth Booth had three children, among them Mary Ann, born 10 September 1745, Jane born 17 July 1748, and Richard (the father of Junius Brutus Booth), born 14 December 1755, plus another unrecorded son, Wilkes Booth, christened at St. Giles Cripplegate. Boyd's Index of Christenings, examined at the Guildhall Library, lists a John Wilkes Booth christened 10 February 1788, Holborn, St. Andrews, to Wilkes and Hanna Booth.

11. May manuscript, "History of the Theatre in Baltimore," Maryland Historical Society, Reel 521.

12. Baltimore Court House, records supplied by James O. Hall.

13. Asia Booth Clarke, *Personal Recollections,* 15–25.

14. Edwin Booth, "Edmund Kean and Junius Brutus Booth," *Papers on Acting,* edited by Brander Matthews (New York: Hill and Wang, 1958), 246–59. As Edwin recalled, "On our way to rehearsal one day, he was accosted by almost everyone we met. To my frequent inquiries, 'Father, who is that?' he replied, 'Don't know,' until, wearied by my importunities, he exclaimed impatiently: 'My child, I do not know these people! But everybody knows "Tom-fool!"' "

15. Quoted in Skinner and Skinner, *One Man in His Time,* 55.

16. This story has been attributed to many of the actors of this period, especially to Forrest.

17. *New Orleans Picayune,* 14 Jan. 1848.

18. *Vicksburg Whig,* 1 Feb. 1848.

19. *Spirit of the Times,* 4 Mar. 1848.

20. *New York Herald,* 7 Mar. 1848.

21. Booth letter to a Mr. Carr and Henry Warren, 3 March 1848, Chicago Historical Society Library.

22. Phelps, *Players of a Century,* 253.

23. *Philadelphia Times,* 7 June 1893.

24. John Malone, "An Actor's Memory of Edwin Booth," *Forum,* 15 (July 1893), 600–602.

25. Ellsler, *Stage Memories,* 71–72.

26. *Albany Argus,* 18 Aug. 1848.

27. Letters and notes in the Missouri Historical Society, St. Louis.

28. *St. Louis Weekly Reveille,* 3 Dec. 1848.

29. Alfred Bunn, *Old England and New England, in a Series of Views Taken on the Spot* (London: Richard Bentley, 1853), vol. 2, 47n.

30. *Boston Transcript,* 21 Aug. 1849.

31. William Winter, *Vagrant Memories: Being Further Recollections of Other Days* (New York: George H. Doran Co., 1915), 160.

32. Edwin's first stage appearances have stimulated considerable debate. Part of the story comes from McCann, "The Booth Family," 404–10, in which he said Edwin and his cronies, being fonder of theatricals than sports, fitted up an arbor or shed in the North Exeter Street residence's back yard. Local juveniles made up most of the audience, paying one cent for admission. Such parents as attended were charged two cents. The young actors cut all female roles, condensed all scripts, from *Hamlet* to a pantomime, and offered three or four plays as an afternoon's performance. McCann suggested the elder Booth attended a few of these productions. Later, according to McCann, when Edwin was "pretty well grown," he began to appear at the old Mud Theatre, at the corner of North and Saratoga Streets in Baltimore.

This commercial house opened 9 December 1822 as the Adelphi but soon earned its nickname from being located in a low, muddy part of the city known as "The Meadows." By 1842 it was known as the National Theatre, falling on bad times. It was destroyed by fire on 22 June 1876. The elder Booth, Edmund Kean, and Macready had all appeared there, and the Mud Theatre was the site of the Anderson riot of 1833. By the time Edwin appeared at the Mud, he and his friends had formed a Thespian Club, of which he was the leader. Edwin felt his future lay in comedy, whereas his friend John Sleeper Clarke, who would marry Asia Booth, aspired to tragedy. Clarke was a stage name; John Sleeper had been a boyhood friend of the family; his father, a Mr. Sleeper, kept an old-fashioned inn in Baltimore, near the Booth town house, according to Adam Badeau's "Boyhood of Edwin Booth."

33. Henry Clay Barnabee, *Reminiscences Being an Attempt to Account for his Life, with Some Excuses for His Professional Career* (Boston: Chapple Publishing Co., 1913), 80–81.

34. *New York Recorder*, 6 July 1893.

35. Barton Hill, "Personal Recollections of Edwin Booth," *New York Dramatic Mirror*, Special Edition, Christmas, 1896, 2–3.

36. Malone, "An Actor's Memory," 601–2.

37. Harvard Theatre Collection.

38. Kimmel, *The Mad Booths*, 74.

39. Boston Athenaeum, Booth-Kimball correspondence.

40. *Spirit of the Times*, 28 Sept. 1850.

41. Skinner and Skinner, *One Man in His Time*, 92.

42. Joseph Jefferson III, *The Autobiography of Joseph Jefferson* (New York: Century Co., 1890), 129–30. Jefferson became one of America's finest actors, winning international fame as Rip Van Winkle. He succeeded his close friend Edwin Booth as president of the Players.

43. *Spirit of the Times*, 25 Jan. 1851, reprinted from the *Boston Post*. Miss Crouse was no doubt the same attraction advertised in the *Baltimore Sun*, 25 Apr. 1850, as "the AMERICAN MAMMOTH GIRL, 15 years old, weighs 430 lbs., 5 feet 5½ inches in height, and measures 5 feet 3½ inches around the shoulders and 2 feet around the arm." In the Boston Museum advertisements, Miss Crouse was described as sixteen years old, weighing 456 pounds.

44. Folger Shakespeare Library.

45. The full text of the bill (supplied by James O. Hall) reads: "To the Honorable Judges of the Baltimore County Court, sitting as a Court of Equity: Humbly complaining, showeth unto your Honors, your oratrix, Mary Christine Adelaide Booth, of the city of Baltimore, that on the eighth day of May, 1815, your oratrix was lawfully married in the city of London, in the kingdom of Great Britain, to Junius Brutus Booth, then a citizen and subject of said kingdom of Great Britain, but who has since become, and is

now, and for many years past has been a resident of the City of Baltimore, and that your oratrix is now and for more than two years past has been a resident of the city of Baltimore, in the state of Maryland. Your oratrix further shows to your Honors that the said Junius Brutus Booth and your oratrix lived together as husband and wife for several years in the city of London, during which time she bore to said husband a daughter, who died in her infancy, and a son, now living, who is named Richard J. Booth; that in or about the month of January in the year Eighteen Hundred and Twenty-one, the said Junius Brutus Booth, without any intimation whatsoever to your oratrix of his intention or any justifiable cause whatsoever abandoned your oratrix and came to the United States, where he has since remained, and that said abandonment has continued uninterruptedly from the month of January in the year Eighteen Hundred and Twenty-one to this date, being for more than twenty-nine years; and your oratrix alleges that said abandonment is deliberate and final, and that the separation of said Junius Brutus Booth and your oratrix is beyond any reasonable expectation of reconciliation. Your oratrix further shows to your honors that the said Junius Brutus Booth left the kingdom of Great Britain and came to the United States in company with a woman, with whom he had been in the habit of adulterous intercourse from that time to the present, and that he has lived for many years past in the city of Baltimore with said woman in the constant habit of adulterous intercourse with her and that he has for said many years past and now does treat and recognize said woman as his wife, and that he has had by her a large family of children; and your oratrix asks leave to state that in charging this fact she is impelled alone by the necessity for the vindication of her own rights [four lines crossed out] and not by any desire to add infamy and disgrace either to her said husband or to the said woman whom he has professed to herself or to the children, the fruits of said adulterous intercourse, and she dismisses the said grossly insulting to herself and painful subject by charging and alleging that the said Junius Brutus Booth has been whilst he has resided in the city of Baltimore guilty of adultery which is one of the causes as she is advised for which she is entitled according to the Act of Assembly in such cases made and provided to the divorced from him a vinculo matrimonii. In tender consideration whereof, and for as much as your oratrix is remediless in the premises save by the aid and interposition of your Honorable court when matters of this sort are properly cognizable and relievable, may it please your Honors to order and decree that your oratrix shall be divorced a vinculo matrimonii from the said husband, Junius Brutus Booth, and may it please your honors to grant to your oratrix a con't of subpoena to be directed to the said Junius Brutus Booth commanding him on a certain day therein to be named to be and appear in your honorable court, then and there to answer the premises and to show cause, if any he has, why a decree should not pass as prayed and to [?] he perform and fulfill such order or decree as your honors may pass in the premises, and to grant to your oratrix such other and farther relief as in Equity she may be submitted to and she will pray to WM. P. MAULSBY, E.G. KILBOURN Solicitors for the complainant. February 27, 1851."

46. Kimmel, *The Mad Booths,* 64–65. Kimmel offers no documentation for this story, and a Booth family Bible is held by the Museum of the City of New York. See also Ruggles, *Prince of Players*, 47.

47. *Spirit of the Times,* 5 Apr. 1851.

48. Supplied by James O. Hall.

49. Asia Booth Clarke, *The Elder Booth*, 127–28.

50. Card No. 1026, Baltimore City, Maryland Hall of Records.

51. Letter from Asia Booth Clarke to Jean Anderson (Mrs. William R. Sherwood), Peale Museum, Baltimore.

52. The only available evidence of the completion date of Tudor Hall is in a letter by John T. Ford, saying it was finished in 1852. Folger Shakespeare Library, W.a. 231, interleaved in William Winter, *Life and Art of Edwin Booth* (New York: Macmillan, 1894). Transcript supplied by Gayle Harris. James J. Gifford was Booth's architect for Tudor Hall. In 1861 Gifford converted a Baptist church in Washington, D.C., into a theatre for an enterprising young manager from Baltimore, John T. Ford. Eventually known as Ford's Theatre, the playhouse enjoyed a few successful seasons until the spring of 1865.

53. Theatre Museum, Boothbay, Maine, copy supplied by Franklyn Lenthall.

54. Asia Booth Clarke, *Booth Memorials,* 48.

55. The trip across the isthmus is described in unpublished material attached to the University of Illinois' copy of Asia Booth Clarke, *The Elder and Younger Booth*, as described above in chapter 6, note 1.

56. The Jenny Lind Theatre (Lind never played California, but the manager-owner, Tom Maguire admired her) was the third building to bear that name. The first burned on 4 May 1851, and Maguire promptly built another, which just as promptly burned down nine days after it opened on June 13. Maguire, undaunted, built yet a third Jenny Lind, a sandstone structure on Portsmouth Square, seating two thousand. By the next spring, Maguire, who had yet to pay his workmen, sold the building to the city for a city hall.

57. J. J. McCloskey, "Edwin Booth in Old California," *Green Book Album*, 6(June 1911), 1322–27. This article cannot be trusted. McCloskey held that the Booths arrived in San Francisco in late 1851 or January 1852; the date was 30 July 1852. He also described Junius, Jr., and Harriet Mace waiting in San Francisco for Booth and Edwin, when in fact they arrived together. Another supposed eyewitness account of the Booths in California, the anonymous "The Four Booths," from *Green Book Magazine,* 14(July 1915), 34–45, is equally detailed and equally mistaken, taking advantage of the elder Booth's eccentricities for dramatic effect.

58. The story of Edwin Booth's first benefit in Sacramento has been

widely cited and variously attributed; this version is from Asia Booth Clarke, *The Elder Booth*, 131.

59. *San Francisco Call*, 14 July 1889.

60. Matthews and Hutton, *Actors and Actresses,* 102.

61. Theatre Museum, Boothbay, Maine, courtesy of Franklyn Lenthall.

62. Ludlow diary, Missouri Historical Society, St. Louis.

63. *New Orleans Picayune,* 14 Nov. 1852.

64. *New Orleans Picayune*, 16 Nov. 1852.

65. Missouri Historical Society, St. Louis.

66. James H. Simpson, a citizen of Salem, New Jersey, sent the letter to the *Philadelphia Public Ledger*. Durang, "The Philadelphia Stage," reprinted the letter and vainly attempted to identify Simpson. Simpson's letter also appeared in the *New York Times*, 1 Aug. 1856. Asia Booth Clarke, *The Elder Booth*, 106, related a somewhat different story: "On reaching Cincinnati the Masonic fraternity had the body embalmed in a metallic coffin and deposited in the Baptist vault. Mrs. Booth was telegraphed for, and arrived in Cincinnati expecting to find her husband very ill,—the second despatch, announcing his decease, not reaching Baltimore until her departure from that city. She returned home as soon as possible, bringing the body with her for interment."

67. Details of the funeral are drawn from Asia Booth Clarke, *Personal Recollections* and *The Elder Booth*, as well as from Baltimore and New York newspapers of the time.

68. Widely reprinted, the original of this letter is held by the Missouri Historical Society, St. Louis.

8. Coda

1. Unidentified newspaper clipping, "Tombs of the Booths," dated 26 July 1891, Harvard Theatre Collection.

2. Moses, *Famous Actor-Families,* 18.

3. Naturalization records in the Baltimore City Criminal Court (Naturalization) 1851–1854 11[MdHR 18, 121], p. 6, Mary C. A. Booth from Belgium, 7 February 1852. Information supplied by John Brennan. Adelaide's naturalization under the name Booth lays to rest confusion caused by a coincidence; on 20 September 1851 a Minister Chandler married Mary Adelaide Booth to one William Rogers in Baltimore. Evidently this M. A. Booth had no relation to any of the actor's family.

4. Enoch Pratt Free Library, Baltimore, Baltimore city directories.

5. Leander Richardson, "Town Crier," *New York Dramatic News,* 33(1 Aug. 1891), 1–3. This is the only known account of Adelaide Delannoy's death. The information about Adelaide's grave, Lot 384, Section S, Grave #6, and date of the transfer was supplied by John Brennan.

6. Richard Junius Booth's death certificate, St. Catherine's House, London.

7. *National Intelligencer,* 26 Apr. 1865.
8. Information supplied by John Brennan.
9. *New York Times,* 16 Dec. 1883.
10. *Baltimore Sun,* 2 June 1888.
11. *New York Herald,* 20 July 1891.
12. The only substantive treatment of the youngest of the elder Booth's children is John Brennan, "John Wilkes Booth's Enigmatic Brother Joseph," *Maryland Historical Magazine,* 78(Spring 1983), 22–34.
13. Unidentified clipping dated 19 Nov. 1902, the Players.
14. *New York Dramatic Mirror,* 25 Dec. 1912, 12; and *Essex Countryside,* June 1978, 32–33.
15. Deed of Assignment, Maryland Historical Society.
16. Mahoney, *Sketches of Tudor Hall,* 5–7.
17. Interview with Howard Fox.
18. John Foster Kirk, "Shakespeare's Tragedies on the Stage," *Lippincott's Magazine of Popular Literature and Science,* 33(May 1884), 501–10; (June 1884), 604–16. Kirk (1824–1904) considered a stage career for a time but took a sort of apprenticeship with the noted historian William H. Prescott. His own work after Prescott died in 1859 won wide acclaim. He was also editor of *Lippincott's Magazine* from 1870 to 1886 and devoted his last years to the preparation of *Lippincott's New Dictionary.*
19. Jefferson, *The Autobiography of Joseph Jefferson,* 43–45.
20. James E. Murdoch, *The Stage: Or Recollections of Actors and Acting from an Experience of Fifty Years: A Series of Dramatic Sketches* (Philadelphia: J. M. Stoddart and Co., 1880. Reprint. New York: Benjamin Blom, 1969), 174–80.
21. Murdoch, *The Stage,* 183.
22. Murdoch, *The Stage,* 189.
23. Edwin Booth, "Some Words about My Father." Typed manuscript from the Folger Shakespeare Library, edited in Edwin Booth's hand.
24. For a discussion of disturbed genius in modern art, see Michiko Kakutani, "Is Genius Nothing but Personal Quirk?" *New York Times,* 14 Mar. 1989, 15–16.
25. Charles Shattuck, "The Romantic Acting of Junius Brutus Booth," *Nineteenth Century Theatre Research,* 5(Spring 1977): 1–2.
26. *New York Times,* 3 Mar. 1981.
27. Copy of letter supplied by Booth Colman.

Works Cited

Books

Ball, Robert Hamilton. *The Amazing Career of Sir Giles Overreach Being the Life and Adventures of a Nefarious Scoundrel. Who for Three Centuries Pursued His Sinister Designs in Almost All the Theatres of the British Isles and America, the Whole Comprising a History of the Stage.* Princeton, New Jersey, and London: Princeton University Press, 1939.

Barnabee, Henry Clay. *Reminiscences: Being an Attempt to Account for His Life, with Some Excuses for His Professional Career.* Boston: Chapple Publishing Co., 1913.

Blake, Charles. *An Historical Account of the Providence Stage: Being a Paper Read before the Rhode Island Historical Society, October 25th, 1860 (With Additions).* Providence, Rhode Island: George H. Whitney, 1868. Reprint. New York: Benjamin Blom, 1971.

Broadbent, R. J. *Annals of the Liverpool Stage.* Liverpool: Edward Howell, 1908. Reprint. New York: Benjamin Blom, 1969.

Brown's General Law List. London: John Browne and J. Butterworth, 1796.

Bunn, Alfred. *Old England and New England, in a Series of Views Taken on the Spot.* 2 vols. London: Richard Bentley, 1853.

Clapp, William W., Jr. *A Record of the Boston Stage.* Boston and Cambridge: James Munroe and Co., 1853. Reprint. New York: Greenwood Press, 1969.

Clarke, Asia Booth. *Booth Memorials: Passages, Incidents, and Anecdotes in the Life of Junius Brutus Booth (the Elder) by His Daughter.* New York: Carleton, 1866.

———. *The Elder and the Younger Booth.* Boston and New York: Houghton, Mifflin and Co., 1881.

———. *Personal Recollections of the Elder Booth.* London: Privately printed, n.d.

———. *The Unlocked Book: A Memoir of John Wilkes Booth by His Sister Asia Booth Clarke.* New York: G.P. Putnam's Sons, 1938. Reprint. New York: Benjamin Blom, 1971.

Clarke, Charles, and Mary Cowden Clarke. *Recollections of Writers.* New York: Charles Scribner's Sons, 1878.

Cordell, Eugene Fauntleroy. *The Medical Annals of Maryland: 1799–1899.* Baltimore: Williams & Wilkins Co., 1903.

Delano, Major Joel Andrew. *The Genealogy, History, and Alliances of the American House of Delano 1621 to 1890.* New York: n.p., 1899.

Drew, Mrs. John. *Autobiographical Sketch of Mrs. John Drew.* New York: Charles Scribner's Sons, 1899.

Ellsler, John A[dams]. *The Stage Memories of John A. Ellsler.* Edited by Effie Ellsler Weston. Cleveland, Ohio: The Rowfant Club, 1950.

[Ford, Thomas.] *The Actor: Or, A Peep behind the Curtain. Being Passages in the Lives of Booth and Some of His Contemporaries.* New York: Wm. H. Graham, 1846.

Forester, Izola. *This One Mad Act . . . The Unknown Story of John Wilkes Booth and His Family.* Boston: Hale, Cushman & Flint, 1937.

Gould, Thomas Ridgeway. *The Tragedian: An Essay on the Histrionic Genius of Junius Brutus Booth.* New York: Hurd and Houghton, 1868. Reprint. New York: Benjamin Blom, 1971.

Grossman, Edwina Booth. *Edwin Booth: Recollections by His Daughter Edwina Booth Grossman and Letters to Her and to His Friends.* New York: The Century Co., 1894.

Harrison, Gabriel. *John Howard Payne, Dramatist, Poet & Actor, and Author of Home, Sweet Home! His Life and Writings.* Philadelphia: Lippincott, 1885. Reprint. New York: Benjamin Blom, 1969.

Hawkins, F. W. *The Life of Edmund Kean from Published and Original Sources.* 2 vols. London: Tinsley Brothers, 1869. Reprint. New York: Benjamin Blom, 1969.

Highfill, Philip H., Jr., Kalman A. Burnim, and Edward A. Langhans. *A Biographical Dictionary of Actors, Actresses, Musicians, Dancers, Managers & Other Stage Personnel in London, 1660–1800.* Vol. 5. Carbondale and Edwardsville: Southern Illinois University Press, 1978.

Hone, Philip. *The Diary of Philip Hone 1828–1851.* Edited by Allan Nevins. New York: Dodd, Mead and Co., 1927.

Hoole, W[illiam] Stanley. *The Ante-Bellum Charleston Stage.* Tuscaloosa: University of Alabama Press, 1946.

Ireland, Joseph Norton. *A Memoir of the Professional Life of Thomas Abthorpe Cooper.* New York: Dunlap Society Publications, 1888.

———. *Mrs. Duff.* Boston and New York: Houghton, Mifflin & Co., 1882.

James, Marquis. *The Raven: A Biography of Sam Houston.* Indianapolis: Bobbs-Merrill Co., 1929.

James, Reese D[avis]. *Old Drury of Philadelphia.* Philadelphia: University of Pennsylvania Press, 1932.

Jefferson, Joseph III. *The Autobiography of Joseph Jefferson.* New York: The Century Co., 1890.

Johnstone's London Commercial Guide, and Street Directory. London: Printed for the Proprietor, 1817, 1820.

Kendall, John. *The Golden Age of the New Orleans Theatre.* Baton Rouge: Louisiana State University Press, 1952.

Kimmel, Stanley. *The Mad Booths of Maryland.* 2d ed. New York: Dover Publications, 1969.

Lockie, John. *Topography of London.* London: G. & W. Nicol, 1810.

Logan, Olive. *Before the Footlights and Behind the Scenes: A Book about "The Show Business" in All Its Branches.* Philadelphia: Parmalee & Co.; San Francisco: H. H. Bancroft & Co., 1870.

Ludlow, Noah. *Dramatic Life as I Found It: A Record of Personal Experience; With an Account of the Rise and Progress of the Drama in the West and South, with Anecdotes and Biographical Sketches of the Principal Actors and Actresses Who Have at Times Appeared upon the Stage in the Mississippi Valley.* St. Louis: G. I. Jones and Co., 1880. Reprint. New York: Benjamin Blom, 1966.

McCain, William D. *"The Story of Jackson": A History of the Capital of Mississippi 1821–1951.* Jackson: J. F. Myer Publishing Co., 1953.

McElroy, Archibald. *Philadelphia Directory.* Philadelphia: A. McElroy, 1840.

McGlinchee, Claire. *The First Decade of the Boston Museum.* Boston: Bruce Humphries, 1940.

Macqueen-Pope, Walter. *Theatre Royal, Drury Lane.* London: W. H. Allen and Co., 1945.

Macready, William Charles. *Macready's Reminiscences, and Selections from His Diaries and Letters.* Edited by Frederick Pollock. New York: Macmillan, 1875.

Mahoney, Ella V. *Sketches of Tudor Hall and the Booth Family.* Bel Air, Maryland: Tudor Hall, 1925.

Mallalieu, H. L. *Dictionary of British Watercolour Artists up to 1920.* Woodbridge, England: Antique Collectors' Club, 1976.

Matthews, Brander, and Laurence Hutton, eds. *Actors and Actresses of Great Britain and the United States from the Days of David Garrick to the Present Time.* 5 vols. New York: Cassell & Co., 1886.

Memoirs of Junius Brutus Booth, From His Birth to the Present Time: With an Appendix, Containing Original Letters, From Persons of Rank and Celeb-

rity; And Copious Extracts from the Journal Kept by Mr. Booth, During His Theatrical Tour on the Continent. London: Chapple, Miller, Rowden, and E. Wilson, 1817.

Memoirs of Mr. Booth, Containing a True Statement of All the Circumstances Attending His Engagement at the Rival Theatres, With a Few Remarks upon His Conduct; By an Old Actor. London: T. Keys, 1817.

Moody, Richard. *Edward Forrest: First Star of the American Stage.* New York: Alfred A. Knopf, 1960.

Moses, Montrose J. *Famous Actor-Families in America.* New York: Thomas D. Crowell & Co., 1906.

Murdoch, James E. *The Stage: Or, Recollections of Actors and Acting from an Experience of Fifty Years.* Philadelphia: J. M. Stoddart and Co., 1880. Reprint. New York: Benjamin Blom, 1969.

Odell, George C. D. *Annals of the New York Stage.* 15 vols. New York: Columbia University Press, 1927–49.

Odell, Mary Theresa. *The Old Theatre, Worthing.* Aylesbury: George W. Jones, 1938.

———. *Some Playbills of the Old Theatre, Worthing.* Worthing: Aldridge Brothers, 1953.

———. *The Theatre Royal. 1814–19: Mr. Trotter of Worthing and the Brighton Theatre.* Worthing: Aldridge Brothers, 1944.

Oxberry, William. *Oxberry's Dramatic Biography and Histrionic Anecdotes.* 7 vols. London: G. Vertue, 1825–27.

Phelps, Henry Pitt. *Players of a Century: A Record of the Albany Stage.* Albany: Joseph McDonought, 1880.

The Post-Office Annual Directory. London: T. Maiden, 1812, 1822, 1823.

Rees, James. *The Dramatic Authors of America.* Philadelphia: G. B. Zieber, 1845.

Reports of Cases Argued and Determined in the Court of King's Bench. Vol. 4. London: J. Butterworth and Son, 1821.

Roberts, Peter. *The Old Vic Story: A Nation's Theatre.* London: W.H. Allen, 1976.

Robinson, J. W. *Theatrical Street Ballads: Some Nineteenth-Century Street Ballads about the Theatre.* London: The Society for Theatre Research, 1971.

Robson's Improved London Directory. London: William Robson, 1820, 1831.

Ruggles, Eleanor. *Prince of Players: Edwin Booth.* New York: W.W. Norton & Co., 1953.

Skinner, Maud, and Otis Skinner. *One Man in His Time: The Adventures of H. Watkins, Strolling Player 1845–1863 from His Journal.* Philadelphia: University of Pennsylvania Press, 1938.

Skinner, Otis. *Mad Folk in the Theatre: Ten Studies in Temperament.* Indianapolis: Bobbs-Merrill, 1928.

Smith, Sol[omon]. *The Theatrical Journey-Work and Anecdotal Recollections of Sol. Smith, Comedian, Attorney at Law, Etc.* Philadelphia: T. B. Peterson, 1854.

———. *Theatrical Management in the West and South for Thirty Years.* New York: Harper & Brothers, 1868.

Todd, William B. *A Directory of Printers and Others in Allied Trades, London and Vicinity, 1800–1840.* London: Printing Historical Society, 1972.

Triennial Directory of London, Westminster, Southwark, and Ten Miles Distant, for the years 1817, 1818, 1819. London: W. Flint, 1819.

Universal British Directory. London: British Directory Office, 1790 and 1793.

Vandenhoff, George. *Dramatic Reminiscences; Or, Actors and Actresses in England and America.* London: Thomas W. Cooper & Co., John Camden Hotten, 1860.

Warren, William. *Life and Memoirs of William Warren, Boston's Favorite Comedian.* Boston: Daly, 1888.

Watermeier, Daniel J., ed. *Between Actor and Critic: Selected Letters of Edwin Booth and William Winter.* Princeton, New Jersey: Princeton University Press, 1971.

Wearing, J. P. *American and British Theatrical Biography: A Directory.* Metuchen, New Jersey: Scarecrow Press, 1979.

Weisert, John Jacob. *The Curtain Rose: A Checklist of Performances at Samuel Drake's City Theatre and Other Theatres at Louisville from the Beginning to 1843.* Louisville: n.p., 1958.

Wemyss, Francis Courtney. *Theatrical Biography: Or, The Life of an Actor and Manager.* Glasgow: R. Griffin & Co., 1840.

———. *Twenty-six Years of the Life of an Actor and Manager.* New York: Burgess, Stringer and Co., 1847.

Willard, George O. *History of the Providence Stage 1762–1891.* Providence: The Rhode Island News Company, 1891.

Winston, James. *Drury Lane Journal: Selections from James Winston's Diaries 1819–1827.* Edited by Alfred L. Nelson and Gilbert B. Cross. London: The Society for Theatre Research, 1974.

Winter, William. *Vagrant Memories: Being Further Recollections of Other Days.* New York: George H. Doran Co., 1915.

Wood, William B. *Personal Recollections of the Stage, Embracing Notices of Actors, Authors, and Auditors, During a Period of Forty Years.* Philadelphia: Henry Carey Baird, 1855.

Unpublished Dissertations and Theses

Benoof, Stephan Michael. "The Jenny Lind Theatre." Master's thesis, University of California, Los Angeles, 1966.

Bergfald, Milburn John. "Productions of Shakespeare in Chicago 1837–1857." Master's thesis, Northwestern University, Evanston, Illinois, 1936.

Dietz, Mary Martha. "A History of the Theatre in Louisville.". Master's thesis, University of Louisville, 1921.

Duggar, Mary Morgan. "The Theatre in Mobile: 1822–1860." Master's thesis, University of Alabama, Tuscaloosa, 1941.

Dunlap, James F. "Queen City Stages: Professional Dramatic Activity in Cincinnati, 1837–1861." Ph.D. dissertation, Ohio State University, Columbus, 1954.

Fenton, Frank. "San Francisco Theatre: 1849–1859." Ph.D. dissertation, Stanford University, 1942.

Fletcher, Edward Garland. "Records and History of Theatrical Activities in Pittsburgh, Pennsylvania, from Their Beginnings to 1861." Ph.D. dissertation, Harvard University, Cambridge, Massachusetts, 1931.

Free, Joseph Miller. "The Theatre of Southwestern Mississippi to 1840." Ph.D. dissertation, University of Iowa, Iowa City, 1941.

Grisvard, Larry Eugene. "The Final Years: The Ludlow and Smith Theatrical Firm in St. Louis, 1845–1851." Ph.D. dissertation, Ohio State University, Columbus, 1966.

Holmes, Susan Carol. "Junius Brutus Booth, Jr.: A Pioneer Actor-Manager of the California Stage." Master's thesis, San Jose State College, 1971.

Hume, Charles Vernard. "The Sacramento Theatre: 1849–1885." Ph.D. dissertation, Stanford University, 1955.

Landau, Penny Maya. "The Career of Mary Ann Duff, the American Siddons: 1810–1839." Master's thesis, University of Texas, Austin, 1942.

Langworthy, Helen. "The Theatre in the Lower Valley of the Ohio, 1797–1860." Master's thesis, University of Iowa, Iowa City, 1926.

Leonard, James Marshall. "The Letters of William Duffy, Albany Theatre Manager, 1830–1835." Ph.D. dissertation, Cornell University, Ithica, New York, 1971.

McKee, Edna H. "History of Theatrical Entertainment in Jackson, Mississippi, from August 1839 to April 1860." Master's thesis, Florida State University, Tallahassee, 1959.

Morrow, Marguerite Hess. "A History of the English Stage in New Orleans from 1817 to 1837." Master's thesis, University of Iowa, Iowa City, 1926.

Roman, Lisbeth Jane. "The Acting Style and Career of Junius Brutus Booth." Ph.D. dissertation, University of Illinois, Urbana, 1968.

Shank, Theodore. "The Bowery Theatre, 1826–1836." Ph.D. dissertation, Stanford University, 1956.

Shockley, Martin Staples. "A History of the Theatre in Richmond, Virginia, 1819–1838." Ph.D. dissertation, University of North Carolina, Chapel Hill, 1938.

Turner, Vivian. "The Stage in New Orleans, Louisiana, after 1837." Master's thesis, University of Iowa, Iowa City, 1929.

Webb, Dorothy Beck. "The Early History of the Arch Street Theatre, 1828–1834." Ph.D. dissertation, Indiana University, Bloomington, 1970.

Wilt, James Napier. "The History of the Two Rice Theatres in Chicago from 1847 to 1857." Ph.D. dissertation, University of Chicago, 1923.

Articles

Albach, Ben. "A Dutch Actor's Experiences with English Theatres in Amsterdam, May–July 1814." In *Western Popular Culture*. London: Methuen & Co., 1977.

Badeau, Adam. "Boyhood of Edwin Booth." Unidentified Chicago newspaper clipping dated 29 Jan. 1893. Howard University, Emma Marble Album, 134, Channing Pollock Collection.

———. "A Night with the Booths." *New York Times.* 7 Aug. 1858.

Barker, Kathleen. "Better than Fiction?" *Theatre Research/Recherches Théâtrales,* 10(1969): 86–88.

Brennan, John. "John Wilkes Booth's Enigmatic Brother Joseph." *Maryland Historical Magazine,* 78(Spring 1983): 22–34.

British Stage and Literary Cabinet (London).

Brother Jonathan.

Burr, Frank A. "Junius Brutus Booth's Wife Adelaide." *New York Press.* 9 Aug. 1891.

Carson, William G. B. "Sol Smith and Theatre Folk 1836–1865." *Glimpses of the Past,* 5(1938): 99–136.

Durang, Charles. "The Philadelphia Stage from the Year 1749 to the Year 1855, Partly Compiled from the Papers of His Father, the Late John Durang." *Philadelphia Sunday Dispatch,* 1854.

"The Four Booths." *Green Book Magazine,* 14(July 1915), 34–35.

Gates, William Bryan. "Performances of Shakespeare in Ante-Bellum Mississippi." *The Journal of Mississippi History,* 5(Jan. 1943): 3–12, 28–37.

"Hamlets on the Stage." *Atlantic Monthly.* Aug. 1869.

Hill, Barton. "Personal Recollections of Edwin Booth." *New York Dramatic Mirror.* Special Edition, Christmas, 1896, 2–3.

Kakutani, Michiko. "Is Genius Nothing but Personal Quirk?" *New York Times.* 14 Mar. 1989, 15–16.

Kirk, John Foster. "Shakespeare's Tragedies on the Stage." *Lippincott's Magazine of Popular Literature and Science,* 33(May 1884): 501–10; (June 1884): 604–16.

Kraentzler, Ernst Friedrich. "John Wilkes Booth—Ancestry and Family." *Genealogical Digest: Genealogy Club of America Magazine,* 8(Aug. 1977): 163–70.

Literary Subaltern (Providence). "Junius Brutus Booth of the Theatre Royal, and Covent Garden," 15 Jan. 1830; "Dramatic Life," 22 Jan. 1830; "Junius Brutus Booth of the Theatres Royal, and Covent Garden," 29 Jan. 1830; and "Junius Brutus Booth of the Theatres Royal, and Covent Garden," 19 Feb. 1830.

McCann, Walter Edgar. "The Booth Family in Maryland." *Our Newsman,* n.d., 404–10.

McCloskey, J. J. "Edwin Booth in Old California." *Green Book Album.* 6(June 1911): 1322–27.

Malone, John. "An Actor's Memory of Edwin Booth." *Forum* 15(July 1893): 600–602.

Mudd, Aloysius L. "The Theatres of Washington from 1835 to 1850." *Records of the Columbia Historical Society,* 5(n.d.): 64–86.

Schrickx, Willem. "A Shakespeare Season on the Continent: Brussels 1814 and Its Prelude in Amsterdam." *Neophilologus,* 61(1977): 619–40.

Shattuck, Charles. "The Romantic Acting of Junius Brutus Booth." *Nineteenth Century Theatre Research,* 5(Spring 1977): 1–26.

Smith, Ophia D. "The Cincinnati Theatre (1817–1830)." *Bulletin of the Historical and Philosophical Society of Ohio,* 14(Oct. 1956): 251–82.

Sorenson, George. "Sam Houston in the Theatre." *Theatre Southwest,* 12(Feb. 1985): 16–19.

Speaight, George. "Il Diavolo Antonio." *Theatre History Studies,* 4(1984): 116–17.

Theatrical Inquisitor, and Monthly Mirror (London).

Newspapers

L'Abeille (New Orleans)

Albany Argus

Albion (New York)

American Beacon (Norfolk)

Baltimore American and Commercial Advertiser

Baltimore American and Commercial Daily Advertiser

Baltimore Sun
Bath Chronicle
Bath and Cheltenham Gazette
Boston Daily Advertiser
Boston Daily Evening Transcript
Boston Evening Transcript
Boston Post
Boston Transcript
Brighton Herald
Bristol Gazette & Mercury
Bristol Gazette & Public Advertiser
Bristol Journal
Bristol Mercury
Bristol Mirror
Bristol Observer
Brooklyn Eagle
Caledonian Mercury
Champion (London)
Charleston Courier
Charleston Mercury
Chicago Daily Journal
Cincinnati Commercial
Cincinnati Daily Inquirer
Cincinnati Enquirer
Cincinnati Gazette
Daily Alta (San Francisco)
Daily National Intelligencer (Washington, D.C.)
Detroit Free Press
Drakard's Stamford News
Dramatic Mirror
Dublin Weekly Register
Edinburgh Evening Courant
Edinburgh Reflector
Exeter Flying Post
Fremman's Journal (Dublin)
Georgetown Metropolitan (Washington, D.C.)
Georgia Constitutionalist (Augusta)
Glasgow Herald
John Bull
London Courier
London Examiner

London Morning Chronicle
London Morning Herald
London Morning Post
London Sun
London Sunday Monitor
London Times
Louisiana Courier
Louisville Daily Herald
Louisville Herald
Lowell American (Massachusetts)
Manchester Courier
Memphis Daily Express
Mirror of the Times
Mississippi Free Trader and Natchez Gazette
Missouri Reporter
Missouri Republican
Mobile Register & Journal
National Advocate (New York)
National Gazette and Literary Register (Philadelphia)
National Intelligencer (Washington, D.C.)
New Orleans Picayune
New York American
New York Clipper
New York Courier and Enquirer
New York Dramatic Mirror
New York Dramatic News
New York Evening Post
New York Herald
New York Mirror
New York Morning News
New York Post
New York Press
New York Times
Pennsylvania Inquirer
Pennsylvanian
Petersburg Express
Philadelphia Daily Chronicle
Philadelphia Daily Inquirer
Philadelphia Daily News
Philadelphia Inquirer
Philadelphia Pennsylvanian

Philadelphia Public Ledger
Philadelphia Sunday Dispatch
Pittsburgh Advocate & Adviser
Pittsburgh Daily Dispatch
Pittsburgh Post
Poulson's American Daily Advertiser (Philadelphia)
Providence Gazette
Providence Journal
Republican Banner (Nashville)
Richmond Daily Mercantile Advertiser
Richmond Enquirer
Richmond Whig
St. John Evening News (New Brunswick)
St. Louis Reporter
St. Louis Weekly Reveille
San Francisco Call
Savannah Daily Republican
Savannah Morning Daily News
Sheffield Mercury
Shrewsbury Chronicle
Spirit of the Times
Sunday Times(London)
Theatrical Censor
United States Gazette (Philadelphia)
Vicksburg Whig
Washington Gazette
Washington Globe

Collections

Art Institute, Chicago
Baltimore, Maryland, Court House
Boston Athenaeum
Boston Public Library, Booth Scrapbook, Rare Book Room
British Library, London
Brussels Municipal Archives
Charlotte Cushman Club, Philadelphia
Chicago Historical Society Library
Columbia University Theatre Collection, New York
Enoch Pratt Free Library, Baltimore
Folger Shakespeare Library, Washington, D.C.

Garrick Club, London
Greater London Record Office
Harford County, Maryland, Court House
Harvard Theatre Collection, Cambridge, Massachusetts
Harvard University Library, Cambridge, Massachusetts
Howard University, Channing Pollock Collection
International Genealogical Index, Church of Jesus Christ of Latter-Day Saints, Columbia, Missouri
International Theatre Institute, Amsterdam
Kimmel Collection, University of Tampa, Florida
Library of Congress, Manuscript Division
London Public Record Office
Maryland Hall of Records
Maryland Historical Society, Baltimore
Menken Collection (private)
Missouri Historical Society, St. Louis
Museum of the City of New York, Theatre Collection
Netherlands Theatre Institute, Amsterdam
New York Historical Society, New York City
New York Public Library, Manuscripts Division
Peale Museum, Baltimore
Pennsylvania Historical Society, Philadelphia
Players, New York
St. Catherine's House, London
State Historical Society of Missouri
Theatre Museum, Boothbay, Maine
University of Amsterdam Library, Rare Book Room
University of Illinois Library, Rare Book Room
University of Pennsylvania Library, Rare Book Room
University of Texas, Harry Ransom Humanities Research Center
Valentine Museum, Richmond, Virginia
Victoria and Albert Museum, London

Index

STEPHEN M. ARCHER is professor of theatre at the University of Missouri-Columbia, where he teaches theatre history and playwriting. He has published *How Theatre Happens* (1977, 1983) and *American Actors and Actresses: A Guide to Information Sources* (1983), as well as numerous articles and reviews. His current research interests focus on the history of acting.